The Selection
and Use of
Instructional Media

The Selection and Use of Instructional Media

For improved classroom teaching and for interactive, individualized instruction

Second Edition

A J Romiszowski

Kogan Page, London/Nichols Publishing, New York

384584

Dedicated to my father, for getting me interested in problem-solving, and my mother, for insisting on thoroughness and rigour.

First published in Great Britain in 1988 by
Kogan Page Ltd,
120 Pentonville Rd, London N1 9JN

British Library Cataloguing in Publication Data

Romiszowski, A. J. (Alexander Joseph), *1939–*
    The selection and use of instructional
    media: for improved classroom teaching
    and interactive, individualized instruction.
    —2nd ed.
    1. Individualised instruction. Teaching
    aids. Design
    I. Title
    371.3'94

    ISBN 1–85091–379–X

First published in the United States in 1988 by
Nichols Publishing,
an imprint of GP Publishing Inc.
PO Box 96, New York 10024

Library of Congress Cataloging-in-Publication Data

Romiszowski, A. J.
    The selection and use of instructional media.

    1. Educational technology.   2. Audi-visual education.
    3. Computer-assisted instruction.   I. Title.
    LB1028.3.R65   1988   371.3'3   87–7962

    ISBN 0–89397–281–9

Typeset by CG Graphic Services, Tring, Herts
Printed and bound in Great Britain by Billing & Sons Ltd, Worcester

Contents

Foreword

The aims of the book

In the mid-1960s the *Selection and Use of Teaching Aids* was first published. It was intended principally for the classroom teacher, or instructor in a training centre, who was confronted with a numerous and ever-growing array of instructional aids, which he or she could select as means of enhancing the teaching presentation. The title clearly illustrated the intended audience – teachers who plan and deliver their own lessons, to groups or learners, in more or less 'conventional' class teaching situations (whatever that means).

In 1974 this book was substantially rewritten and expanded and became *The Selection and Use of Instructional Media*. It reflected the change that had occurred in the role of (at least some) teachers in the years since the publication of the original book. This changed role was ushered in by the programmed instruction movement and then strengthened by such trends as learner-directed-learning, mastery learning, resource-based learning, guided discovery learning and the ever growing use of simulations, games and other experiential learning technologies. The rallying cry of the day was the individualization of instruction, which was to be achieved, at least in part, by the more extensive use of mediated, self-instructional packages. The emphasis was placed on the 'learner learning' rather than the 'teacher teaching'. The new role of the teacher was as a 'manager of learning resources'. The skills of needs diagnosis, selection of appropriate individual learning materials and formative evaluation, were emphasized in the educational literature. The new book, renamed *Selection and Use of Instructional Media*, reflected these trends. The media selection chapters were extended to provide a practical model for the selection of media and materials as an integral part of the lesson design process. Extra chapters were inlcuded on the new, mediated, self-instructional materials and the methods of using them. However, it was realized that not all teachers or trainers had adopted this new role, so the earlier chapters on 'aids for the teacher teaching' were revised and maintained.

Now, in the 1980s, we are seeing a further role-change that is affecting an ever growing proportion of the teaching profession. This change has been ushered in by the microprocessor, in its many disguises, most notably the microcomputer but also in many special purpose communication devices (teletext, facsimile document transmission, multi-image projector control systems, electronic mail, local networks, teleconferencing systems, massive data bases accessible at a distance, interactive videodisc, CD-ROM and CD-I, to name only a few). This 'new information technology', as it has come to be called, holds incredible potential for transforming the nature of educational and training systems. No longer do teacher and learner have to be present in the same place at the same time in order for the instructional process to occur. Many of the restrictions that earlier individualized systems of instruction suffered may now be overcome. Distance education need no longer be an impersonal process with little or no human interaction and long delays in feedback. Furthermore, the costs of this new technology are relatively accessible and rapidly falling, whereas the costs of conventional educational methods are high and rising.

At the same time, we are passing through a phase of expansion in the need for new educational and training provision, at least partly due to the rapid changes in society and the work marketplace, brought about by these same new technologies. The problem is to provide a myriad of educational and retraining opportunities to relatively small, but often geographically scattered, special-interest groups of students. More and more instructors are finding that these trends mean that at least part of their job is becoming technology-based. At the time of writing, in the State of New York alone, there are over one hundred public school boards, universities and adult teaching centres that offer multi-site courses by means of local, two-way link-ups between two or more campuses in order to allow more students to participate in special courses, offered by hard-to-find specialists. In the United Kingdom, the movement for Open Learning is gaining ever more adherents, among formal educational institutions and industrial training organizations alike. These projects are invariably very dependent on both distance education and computer-based self-instructional techniques. In the developing world, an ever growing number of nations have realized that they have no hope of closing the education gap that exists between them and the developed world, or between the rich and the poor in their own countries, if they rely on conventional face-to-face instruction as the mainstay of their systems. Many innovative distance (or mixed distance/small group) educational systems are already operating throughout the world. An ever growing number of teachers, in all parts of the world, are finding that electronic means of communication, data processing and instruction are becoming everyday tools of their trade.

Such changes, however, are gradual in terms of the proportion of teachers involved and the proportion of their working day that is affected. Most teachers still spend most of their time preparing and delivering classroom-based face-to-face lessons. Those who use learning resources intensively and have invested heavily in paper-based instructional modules, slide-tape learning packages or 16mm film, will continue to use these materials for many years to come. Indeed, all the indications are that electronic communication systems and databases will not supplant other existing media but will complement them. One often hears the word 'technological revolution' associated with education and training today. However, at the grass roots, teachers are not experiencing the violent and sudden changes that are characteristic of revolutions. The more accurate term is 'technological evolution' – new species of instructional methods and media develop and, if 'ecologically' successful, gradually permeate the system. But the previously existing species do not die out. Usually they co-exist, sometimes gradually losing ground to the more powerful newcomers, but in other cases they may even gain a new lease of life, by striking up some form of mutually beneficial symbiotic relationship.

Thus, the second edition of this book (and the third on this topic) aims at three distinct teacher roles, which exist in most educational and training systems today:

— the *teacher as a presenter of instruction*, using simple media and materials as aids to the presentation process;
— the *teacher as manager of instructional resources*, which learners use on an individual or small-group basis;
— the teacher *as user (and sometimes actor and even producer) of mediated, computer-assisted, interactive instructional systems*, whether classroom based, or delivered at a distance.

Structure

The book is organized in three parts, but these do not correspond exactly to the three teacher-roles outlined above. The first part of the book is devoted to the theoretical background to media selection and their use in the instructional process. In contrast with earlier editions, which focused on the lesson planning process as the context for the selection of media and materials and the planning of their use, the present edition offers multiple perspectives. The lesson planning model is retained, but a more general, multi-level model of instructional systems

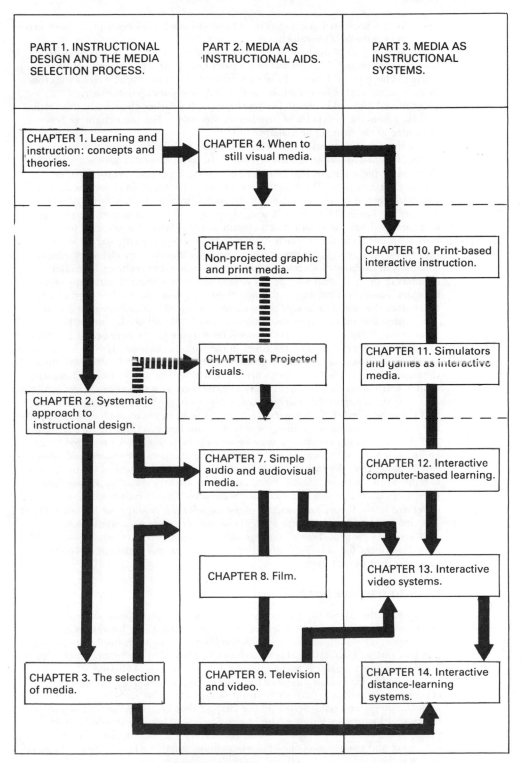

Figure A *Chapter layout in this book.*

design is also presented and this is used to extend media selection procedures to the more general levels of overall course planning.

The second part of the book is devoted to *presentation media* – those which are used to transmit messages *one way only* – from instructor, or instructional system, to learner. This part deals with the most simple of teaching aids as well as with the more sophisticated mass broadcast media and their packaged derivatives (educational films and video). The treatment of the earlier chapters in this section is mainly from the viewpoint of 'teacher as presenter'. The later chapters, however, are aimed at the 'teacher as manager' role.

The third part deals with **interactive media**. This term is used as a handy way of classifying all *two-way communication media*. In some cases, the media are basically the same as those already discussed in Part two (for example print-on-paper learning materials) but the organization or use of the medium is such as to provide a certain amount of two-way interactive communication. It may be debateable whether the topics of Chapters 10 and 11 (programmed instruction, simulations and games) should be included in a classification of media (as opposed to methods), but their discussion at this point in the book is particularly valuable as they throw light onto the methodological benefits that the new electronic media discussed in the later chapters may offer to education and training. The later chapters in this part deal with progressively more sophsiticated additions to the educator's toolbox. Progressing through these chapters, the teacher is gradually taken from the role of 'manager of resources' to that of 'user of integrated systems'.

It is probable that many of the readers of this book will not be currently performing all three of the roles outlined above and will not have access to all the media alternatives which are described in the various chapters. If your intention is to gain an overview of the field, or to study it from an academic viewpoint, then the sequence in which the chapters are presented will be appropriate. Those who wish to learn about specific media may use the book as a reference source, accessing the material that interests them, by use of the list of chapter contents and the subject index. If, however, your aim is to learn about media selection and use in a systematic manner, then some further guidance to the structure of the book and the many ways of reading it may be of some help. Figure A presented here is an attempt to show the way in which the various chapters are related and to give some assistance in the planning of your reading. The three parts of the book, together with the respective chapters, are shown as three columns. By and large, these three main parts can be used independently. Those readers who are interested in the theory and practice of media selection would read Part one. Those who are concerned with the use of media to enhance their presentations, or to package some parts of their lessons, would concentrate on Part two. Those interested in the use of individualized or group interactive instruction, would naturally turn to Part three.

How to use the book

In Figure A the arrows drawn between some of the chapters point out some recommended pre-requisite sequences, which will ensure that the reader does not miss important earlier information which is later used as an example, or starting point for further elaboration. These arrows also show that the first chapter of each of the three parts is related to the other first chapters – all of Chapters 1, 4 and 10 are devoted to the establishment of basic concepts. A learner who wishes to concentrate on only one part, would do well to start at the 'north-west' of the chart with Chapter 1 and read 'across' to the chapter that heads up the part of particular interest. Other arrows indicate where specific earlier chapters should be read as pre-requisites to a later chapter. Where the arrows are broken, the linkages are only weak and readers may only make occasional reference to the earlier chapter if they feel the need.

In order to help you plan your reading, some possible sequences for the three 'roles' of the teacher are suggested in Figure B.

IF YOU ARE IN THE ROLE OF:	THEN A POSSIBLE SEQUENCE FOR READING RELEVANT CHAPTERS IS:
Teacher as presenter of face-to-face instruction – and you are in a hurry . . . – and you have the time . . .	1, 4, 5, 6. 1, 2, (3.1), 4, 5, 6, 7.
Teacher as manager of learning resources – and you are in a hurry . . . – and you have the time . . .	1, 2, 3, 4, 7, 8, 9. 1, 2, 3, 4, 5, 6, 7, 8, 9, 10, 11, 12.
Teacher as producer, user or manager of interactive instruction – and you are in a hurry . . . – and you have the time . . .	1, 2, 3, 10, 11, 12, 13, (7 & 9 in part), 14. 1, 2, 3, 4, 7, 8, 9, 10, 11, 12, 13, 14.

Figure B – *Reading sequences for the three teacher 'roles'.*

If you feel that two (any two) or more of the roles we defined earlier are relevant to your current job situation, or to your future aspirations, then the whole book is probably of interest. However, if you are very specialized in one or other of these roles and already have some considerable experience, then you may find that this book does not go far enough. You may require more detail on the preparation of simple audiovisual materials, or on the management of individualized, resource-based learning systems, on the use of specific computers or courseware or on the availability of materials on a given subject matter area or specific objective. Such information sources are referenced at appropriate points in the body of the text.

The principal aim of this book, I repeat, is to act as a handbook to the general decision-making issues that face a teacher in an educational setting, or an instructor in a business setting, when faced with the task of planning for the effective use of media and materials in the instructional process. Instructional designers and developers will find much of interest also, but will no doubt wish to go much further into the aspects of design that are touched on in the first part of the book. Media producers and material authors will find a useful general framework here, but will find more media-specific information in a variety of specialist literature. Administrators and managers of instructional development projects will gain an understanding of the task that faces their subordinates and how early administrative decisions may often make their subordinates' task more difficult. They may have to turn to other sources, however, to learn how to facilitate the work of their team of specialists.

I hope, however, that anyone interested in education or training and particularly in the question of how instructional media may be used to the best effect, will find something of use in these pages. As is the case with any wide-ranging handbook, the sources of information, expert opinions and practical experience are too many to acknowledge individually. However, the errors and omissions are mine. Any constructive feedback will be gratefully received.

A. Romiszowski, Syracuse, New York, January 1988.

Part 1.
Instructional Design and the Media Selection Process

Introduction

Quite often, media and materials get selected and used not for a clearly thought-out reason but because they are available. Whereas 'because it's there' may be a valid reason for undertaking the task of climbing Mount Everest, it is not acceptable as justification for investment in special, often quite costly educational equipment and materials. The climbing of a mountain may be seen as an end in its own right, or alternatively, as a proven way of developing and strengthening both body and spirit. The selection of a given educational method or of particular media and materials, is never an end in itself, but a means towards some end. Usually, the ends of education are to do with learning and this is particularly true when we consider that part of the educational process which may be termed *instruction*: the activation of a well planned and tested process in order to lead students to the achievement of specific learning objectives.

In this book, the selection and use of instructional media is studied in the context of the design and development of instruction. Other, possibly equally valid, approaches, such as media used for creating impact, for selling products or services (persuasion), or for providing 'extensions of man' (in the sense used by McLuhan) are not dealt with directly. Sometimes I might mention such other media uses in passing, when this helps us to understand their instructional capabilities. Whereas, there is probably nothing new for the reader in the observations I have just made, the specific approach to instruction and its design that will be used as a backdrop to our discussion, may be new. In particular, some of the basic concepts and principles, as well as some specific procedures of instructional design and development, will often be referred to in later chapters. For this reason, the first part of the book, in addition to dealing in detail with media selection, presents an overview of the theoretical context of instructional design and a specific model for instructional development.

In **Chapter 1**, I shall define some of the basic concepts upon which the rest of my discussion shall rest. I shall also take a rapid, partly historical, tour of the growth of the discipline (or technology) of instructional design over the past thirty or so years, finishing off with a glimpse into the future.

Chapter 2 presents a practical model for the design and development of instructional systems, in which our later discussion of media selection fits. The chapter opens with a review of the 'Systems Approach' as a methodology for problem solving and continues by outlining four levels of decision making that may be involved in instructional system design and development. The chapter closes with a practical example of the application of this approach, which is then used in the next chapter as an example of the media selection process in its various levels.

Finally **Chapter 3** deals with media selection. The first part of this chapter presents a basic and rather simple media selection procedure, which is based on the models used in the earlier editions of this book. Readers who are interested in the selection of media and materials to be incorporated in lessons that they themselves will deliver, may find this to be all that they require. However, the second part outlines several other models and approaches that have been proposed, to enable those especially interested in the topic of media selection to follow up the literature in-depth. Finally, part three presents a multi-level model for media selection, which is compatible with the overall ID model presented at the end of Chapter 2. This may be of especial use to those readers who will be engaged in the planning of curricula or in the design and development of new courses.

1. Learning and instruction

1.1 Basic concepts

1.1.1 Communications and learning

Various theories or models for communication have been put forward. They are of two main types: *psychological models*, which examine the interaction between the learner and his environment (who says what to whom, under what conditions and with what effect); and *engineering models*, which explain the process in such terms as 'input', 'output' and 'message' and use analogies to communication in electronic circuits or servo-mechanisms.

An engineering model of communication

An example of the engineering kind of model is represented diagrammatically in Figure 1.1. This is the Shannon-Weaver model (1949). A message is generated at source and is transmitted by some medium to a receiver at the destination. Any other irrelevant or distracting messages being received are referred to as 'noise' in the communication system. The objective of effective communication is to maintain the maximum 'signal to noise ratio' in the system. So far so good; the question is how to do this. A complex mathematical theory of communication has been developed on the basis of this model and its derivatives. It purports to explain communication in all its forms, human, electrical and so on. It has led to the design and production of machines which learn and machines which teach. The new science of cybernetics is largely concerned with the application of such communication theory to the explanation and simulation of human thought processes. Practical results so far include computers that play chess and learn from their mistakes to play a better game, and complex training devices which adapt the course of training on the basis of the individual learner's error pattern. Apart from such devices, which are in the main still only used experimentally, the average teacher is likely to feel very little direct impact of cybernetics in the classroom for some time yet. However, the simple concept of signal to noise ratio may prove useful in considering the effects of various teaching procedures.

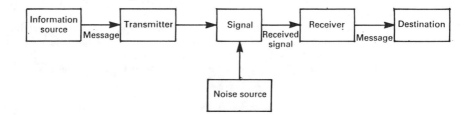

Figure 1.1 *An engineer's model of the communication process. Any distracting or conflicting messages being received at the destination are regarded as 'noise' in the communication channel. Efficient communication aims at reducing 'noise' to a minimum. (From* The Mathematical Theory of Communication, *C E Shannon and W Weaver, University of Illinois Press, 1949.)*

Psychological models of communication

The second class – psychological models of communication – is concerned with the effect of the message as well as its source and destination. The effect we are particularly interested in is the effect at the destination – what happens to the recipient of our communication. Now, we can only tell that the message has had any effect at all if we observe some sort of action or behaviour of the recipient. For example, if we ask someone to close the door we know that if he does this then the message has been received and understood. If we get a flat refusal we are not so sure. He is probably being plain awkward, but he may have misunderstood our message. If we get no response at all, then we do not know whether any message has been received. He may not have heard or he may perhaps be waiting till we say 'please'. We may of course be speaking the wrong language. If our man responds to our message eventually by closing the door, then we may say that he has learnt something, particularly if he persists in this habit of closing the door when we ask him. He may have learnt the meaning of 'close the door' or he may have simply learnt to obey us. We may never know which unless we have more information about the man and his previous background. However, we know for sure that he has learnt something, because his behaviour pattern in a particular situation has changed. Learning can be defined as a change in behaviour or as a capacity for new behaviour.

Communication, learning and feedback

Thus the concept of communication is closely linked to the concept of learning. Our earlier model acknowledged this also. The message is received at the destination and understood. This implies that the meaning was already known or has just been learnt. Now consider our man again, and let us assume he is willing to learn. If we ask him to close the door but he opens the window instead, we would attempt to inform him that this was not the required response. If he does indeed close the door we may congratulate or otherwise reward his efforts. Psychologists refer to this as the *supply of knowledge of results* or *reinforcement*. Communication engineers refer to it as *feedback*. A feedback communication channel is absolutely necessary if a servo-mechanism such as a governor or a thermostat is to function. In the absence of all knowledge of the results learning will not take place. Indeed, performance on a simple task such as drawing lines of a particular length may deteriorate with practice if subjects are blindfolded and are given no indication of their performance.

When we communicate with informed individuals who speak the same language, we simply transmit information or directives. These are understood and are acted upon, if necessary. 'Shut the door, please' will produce a characteristic response. 'My name is John Smith' may produce a snigger or a polite 'hello'. It is unlikely that next year the hotel manager will greet you with a warm 'Hello Mr Smith', though of course it happens sometimes. (This is called one-trial learning.) Most learning tasks of any difficulty require more than one trial. One may have to stay at the hotel on the first of every month for a year before the hotel manager remembers one's name. Generally, he will learn the name faster if there are special circumstances which force him to recall it: 'I seem to be missing an ashtray, Mr Smith'.

When attempting to teach, we must arrange appropriate circumstances for practice and recall. We must then also supply feedback to the learner to inform him of his progress. In Figure 1.2 we see such a process in action: the communication process is constantly being adjusted as feedback is received by one party from the other.

1.1.2 Instruction: a definition

To limit our area of interest, it is necessary to define our use of the term 'instruction'. Not all education or training is necessarily instruction, but instruction is a necessary and an important part of educational and training systems. I shall use the term 'instruction' to mean a goal-directed teaching

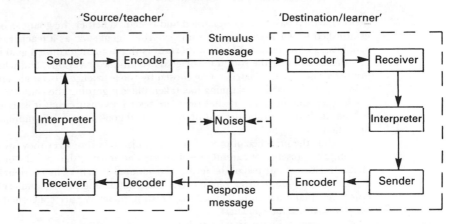

Figure 1.2 *Two-way communication. A model which incorporates both engineering and psychology concepts – Norton Weiner's modification of the Shannon-Weaver model, further modified by the present author. Note that 'noise' may originate from either party or from other external sources.*

Introduction	Generally we think of education as 'what goes on in schools' and training as 'what goes on in industry'. However, because education involves some level of training and training involves some form of education (unplanned learning) it is difficult to use these two terms discriminately. Hence, we as instructional designers shall define the concept of instruction a bit more precisely.
Definition	Instruction is a goal-directed teaching process which is more or less pre-planned.

Diagram			**Specific objectives exist?**	
			Yes	*No*
	Pre-planned study resources exist?	*Yes*	Instruction	Visits to theatre, museum, study tours
		No	Projects Apprenticeships	Incidental learning

Example One	A grade 11 maths teacher's objectives are to teach the basics of trigonometry using the lesson plans as described in the school board's chosen textbook *Introducing Trigonometry — A Step by Step Approach.*
Example Two	Train a new group of tellers in the bank's policy regarding hold-ups using the book and film titled *What to Do in a Hold-Up.*
Non-example	Formal education is not always as structured as instruction. There is usually some kind of goal; however, the route is not as well defined. Consider the examples listed to the right in the diagram above.
Comment	Whether it be education or training, both require 'instruction' — that is, an attempt to impart certain defined skills or knowledge — at times.
Analogy	Education provides a 'map' to the learner and allows him to wander through the 'field' at his own pace and in his own direction. The 'map user', however, requires *instruction* to learn to read the map.

Figure 1.3 *Instruction – a definition.*

process, which has been pre-planned and tested. Whether the goal has been established by the learner, or by some external agent such as a teacher or a syllabus, is immaterial. What is important is that a predetermined goal has been identified. Whether the routes to the goal are unique or various, and whether they are prescribed by the instructor or chosen by the learner, is also immaterial. What is important is that pre-planning has taken place regarding the routes available to the learner and an end route has been pre-tested, to ensure that it is indeed likely to lead the learner to the desired predetermined goal. Figure 1.3 summarizes this definition.

It is thus the presence of precise goals or objectives (however they are arrived at), and the presence of careful pre-planning and testing, that are the main characteristics of our use of the term 'instructional system'. Instructional systems design is, therefore, a three-phase process of establishing precise and useful objectives, planning study methods and testing them. We are concerned with *analysis, synthesis* and *evaluation.*

The instructional process The process of instruction itself, is therefore a two-way communication process, in which

(a) the 'teacher' transmits a variety of messages (information to be understood and learnt, information on what to do in order to learn, etc), and then the learner, by performing certain tasks,

(b) communicates to the 'teacher' that learning is progressing (or not progressing) towards the pre-set goals – this information is, in turn, interpreted by the 'teacher', who decides whether any corrective or other action should be taken and this decision is translated into . . .

(c) feedback information to the learner.

We can see in Figure 1.2 how the instructional communication process would recycle one or more times until one specific learning goal is achieved. Then the process would repeat for a further goal and so on.

As, in this book, we shall be concerned with instructional media, our 'teacher' may or may not be a real-life classroom instructor. Most commonly, the use of media in a classroom setting results in a cooperative effort between the instructor and the media/materials that he or she uses; we can refer to this combination as an *instructional system.* In such a system, the media used for communicating basic knowledge may be, for example, an audiovisual, whereas the corrective feedback would be given by the instructor.

It may therefore be clearer to represent the instructional process as in Figure 1.4 – an instructional system which is in communication with the learner by means of at least *three* channels, which are capable of transmitting, respectively,

(a) the information to be learnt and used by the learner,

(b) information about the progress of learning, and

(c) corrective, congratulatory or guidance feedback.

1.1.3 Methods, materials, media and messages: definitions

On a recent session in a course, I asked a group of teachers to 'brainstorm' all the 'instructional media' that they knew of. The group, about twenty strong, went to it and in about ten minutes had generated the wall display illustrated in Figure 1.5. The ground rules of brainstorming are that, first, the group participates in an 'ideas generation' phase, during which no one is allowed to criticize the contributions made. But the next phase – 'ideas organization' – is when all contribute with suggestions on how to clean up the original outpouring of ideas,

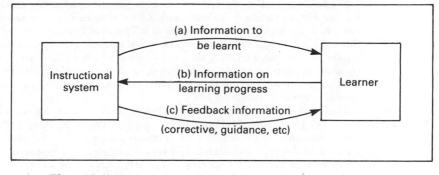

Figure 1.4 *The instructional process – three essential types of communication.*

tape	television	drama
demonstration	radio	records
film	books	games
videodisc	film strips	computers
radio	textbooks	teleconference
film strips	brochures	overhead projector
teacher	episcope	newspaper
crayons	groups	slides
role play	interactive video	white board
oral presentation	teletext	magnetic board
dance	bulletin boards	blackboard
discussion	audiotutorial	models
graphics	TV programmes	photographs
lecture	humour	pamphlets
song	dance	transparencies

Figure 1.5 *First phase of a brainstorm exercise which aimed to define the concept of instructional media.*

what structure to impose on it, etc. The result of this second phase is shown in Figure 1.6. This phase took all of two hours to complete and even at the end of that time, one or two of the teachers were not quite happy with the classification of some of the items. Which just goes to show how varied and often woolly are the concepts we hold. So let's try to fix on some basic definitions which we shall use systematically, at least in this book.

What are media?

To some people instructional media refer only to complex items of equipment such as television or film. An alternative point of view, expressed by Marshall McLuhan in *Understanding Media*, is that media are any extensions of man which allow them to affect other people who are not in face-to-face contact with him. Thus to McLuhan, communication media include letters, television, film and telephone, and even roads and railways as these are extensions by which one man can communicate with another (McLuhan 1964).

However, we shall take a middle course between these two extremes, defining 'media' narrowly to include only those media which can effectively be used for the process of planned instruction, but sufficiently broadly to include not only complex electronic communication media but also simpler devices such as slides, photographs, teacher-made diagrams and charts.

We define 'media' as *the carriers of messages, from some transmitting source* (which may be a human being or an inanimate object) *to the receiver of the message* (which in our case is the learner). These carriers of information interact with the learner through his senses. The learner may be called upon to use any of his senses to receive information, including the often overlooked kinaesthetic sense, which is the sense of muscular coordination (of 'feeling' that one is doing a job correctly). Quite often messages are received by a combination of senses in order to render the desired communication complete.

What are messages?
Having said that, we had better be quite clear about what we mean by the term 'message'. Here again, McLuhan in his writings (1964) helped to confuse the issue somewhat, when he argued that 'the medium *is* the message'. Of course, he was referring to observed sociological effects of the large-scale adoption of new media (that, for example, TV has an effect on society, how it lives and perhaps even how it thinks, irrespective of the exact content which the TV programmes transmit). Be that as it may, the content does have its own specific effects and, in the context of education or training, we have ample evidence that it is the content and how it is treated that is the key factor in the communication/learning process.

The message is nothing else than the information which is being transmitted, in our case from instructional system to learner. This message may be quite complex and may involve very careful design in order to communicate the exact intent of its author. We shall come back to this later.

'METHODS'	'MEDIA' TRANSMITTERS (HARDWARE)/MATERIALS (SOFTWARE)		NOT SURE
group activities		photos, etc	
discovery learning		charts, etc	
discussion		books, etc	
demonstration		brochures	
experiment		newspapers	
lecture · — — — —	(teacher)?	models, etc	
audiotutorial — —	tape recorder — — — — — — — —	audio tapes	
distance education	television — — — — — — — — — —	TV programme	drama
		teletext	
	radio — — — — — — — — — — —	phone-in	humour
	gramophone } — — disc — — — — — — — — — — — —		— song
	compact player }		
computer-based instruction — — —	computer — — — — — — — — — —	courseware	
interactive video —	videoplayer and	videodisc and	
	computer — — — — — — — — — —	software	
instructional game	— — — — — — — — — — — — — —	board/cards	
management game	— — — — — — — — — — — — — —	case study	
role-playing — — —	(video recorder) — — — — — — —	role/setting	
	(for feedback)		
simulation — — — —	simulator — — — — — — — — — —	software	
teleconference — —	telephone		
	film projector — — — — — — — —	film	dance
	slide projector — — — — — — — —	slides	
	film strip projector — — — — — —	film strip	
classroom instruction {	overhead projector	transparencies	
	episcope		
	magnetic board		
	flip-chart		
	chalk board		

Figure 1.6 *Second phase after critical analysis of the original list of contributions.*

What are materials?

The restructuring that was done in Figure 1.6 illustrates quite clearly the meaning we ascribed to the term 'instructional materials'. We weeded out such items as 'crayons, chalk' and avoided the inclusion of consumable materials such as 'paper', thus limiting our list to materials which are used to store and/or transmit information (messages). We considered that instructional materials are commonly referred to as 'media' (as for example in the library science usage – non-print media) but we wished to distinguish them from the transmission media which, on analysis, just did not match the attributes of our definition of 'media'. messages. We can best cope with this by thinking of the 'hardware' and 'software' components of media systems – the projector is 'hard' and the slide containing the message is 'soft'. Of course there are special cases, notably the book, which seem to fulfil both these functions, but I think our concept is elastic enough to accommodate this (indeed, we do tend to talk, in this electronic age, of books as the *hard*copy version of a text, which presumably whilst in the wordprocessor's memory is still softcopy – it makes sense).

Our brainstormers also initially included a number of items in their media list which, on analysis, just did not match the attributes of our definition of 'media'.

What are methods?

By far the largest group of these we agreed to classify as *methods*. The group they generated has some attributes in common, but there are marked differences between some of the members. For instance, 'discovery learning' or 'group activities' are very general statements implying nothing about what media will be used, whereas 'distance education' conjures up the vision of remote students interacting through the 'mass media' with a teacher and perhaps with each other. But it is still fairly general, as compared to 'teleconference' or 'simulation'.

However, what all these have in common is that they define the characteristics of a specific instructional process – each one conjures up a general image of how information gets from teacher to learner, how learners use it and interact and how they receive guidance and feedback. Referring back to Figure 1.4, 'methods' defines (more or less precisely and completely) how the whole process of instruction is expected to occur. Even the familiar 'lecture' method conjures up the image of one teacher/many learners, largely one-way transmission of information, and limited opportunity for interaction and feedback. The term 'interactive video' of course first brings to mind the media involved (videodisc and computer), but any explanation will really dwell on the interactivity that this media combination allows, emphasizing the variety of ways in which each of the three types of teacher–learner communication (essential to instruction) may occur. So *methods* describes instructional processes, whilst *media* are system-components that may be used as part of these processes.

However, it will be useful to sub-classify methods (our suggestion is shown in Figure 1.7). We will discuss this in detail in chapter 2.

What about song and dance?

The right hand column of Figure 1.6 contains a few 'strays' which defied all efforts at unanimous classification. These strays were dance (as used for the transmission of cultural tradition and history in many societies), song (as for example the role of protest songs in disseminating the anti-nuclear movement's message), and humour (as used systematically by cartoonists to achieve political or social aims). They appeared initially in our brainstormed list of 'media', probably because it is quite common to hear such colloquial phrases as 'the medium of dance' (as indeed song, drama, art, music, analogy, parable). But they don't sit comfortably in the company of 'overhead projector, tape recorder and computer'. Nor do they seem to classify with 'slide, record and picture' (although a slide is excellent for transmitting a work of art, a record is ideal for music and a picture is the preferred transmissor for certain types of humorous messages – cartoons). Nor are they good bedfellows with 'discovery learning, lecture, demonstration and role play' (although drama may be used in a simulated conflict that leads to discovery learning, or to demonstrate a particular interactive skill).

Some of the brainstormers resisted all efforts to remove this group from the 'media' class. Others wanted to invent a separate class. And some of these noted that those who speak of the medium of dance also use, as a near-synonym, the

INSTRUCTIONAL METHODS may be usefully subclassified into three levels of generality or specificity.	**GENERAL STRATEGIES** (the overall way in which the process of instruction is organized and executed)	EXPOSITIVE PRESENTATION EXPERIENTIAL/DISCOVERY FACE-TO-FACE TEACHING DISTANCE-TEACHING LARGE-GROUP INSTRUCTION SMALL-GROUP 'DYNAMICS' INDIVIDUALIZED INSTRUCTION
	TECHNIQUES (METHODS) (well-known procedures that have a more or less defined set of steps/phases and tend to promote certain overall strategies)	LECTURE, SEMINAR, PANEL BRAINSTORM, LABORATORY TUTORIAL, WORKSHOP, CORRESPONDENCE, TELECONFERENCE KELLER PLAN, TEAM-TEACHING PHILLIPS 66, INTEGRATED PANEL AUDIOTUTORIAL, INTERACTIVE VIDEO
	SPECIFIC TACTICS (the detailed events of instruction that are planned in order to achieve a specific instructional goal)	Some are dictated by the principles of instructional design (SEQUENCE, NUMBER OF EXAMPLES, AMOUNT OF PRACTICE). Others are dictated by content and clientele (EXACT EXAMPLES TO USE, LANGUAGE TO USE, TYPE OF EXAMPLES FOR PRACTICE, ETC)

Figure 1.7 *Instructional methods: three meanings of the term.*

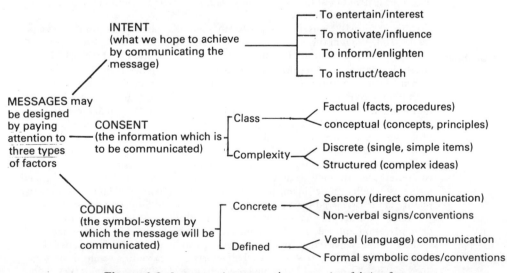

Figure 1.8 *Instructional messages: three categories of design factors.*

expression 'language' of dance. Perhaps that's the clue. Experts in the arts agree that each art form has its peculiar symbolism with which it communicates to the 'initiated'. These symbol-systems, or 'codes' must be used skilfully by the sender and must be known to the receiver of the message, in a way that is analogous to 'speaking a common language'.

Method selection and message design as precursors of media selection and materials development

We may turn back to Figure 1.2 to see a model of the encoding-decoding-interpreting cycle that forms an integral part of the communication process. In the sense in which they entered into our brainstorming session, song, dance and drama are symbolic encoding systems which some groups choose to use for some types of message content and with some types of communication intentions – just as some groups choose to communicate by means of mathematical symbol systems when the content and intent of the message justifies this.

These three factors – intent, content and coding – are critical attributes of any *message*. The balancing of these against the characteristics of the audience is what *message design* is all about. Figure 1.8 shows a more detailed model of the design factors that are involved in instructional message design.

In Figure 1.7 I present my view of what's involved in *method design*. Taking method design and message design together, we have *instructional design*. Finally, somewhere along the line, as outcomes of the instructional design process, we have *media selection* and *materials development*.

The learning of concrete symbol-systems

Learners receive information through the senses, mainly sight and hearing (hence *audio-visual* aids). However, in the training of industrial or craft skills two other senses play almost as important a part: the *sense of touch* and the *kinaesthetic* sense. The latter, the 'sixth' sense, is the one which tells us something is wrong when we try in the dark to climb a stair which is not there. It is the kinaesthetic sense which controls the coordination of physical movements and enables us to reach unerringly for the gear lever or handbrake without the need to look down, or to exert just the right amount of force when tightening a screw. Many of us have learnt to reach for the gear lever; few can tighten a nut to a pre-determined pressure. Both skills have to be learnt by appropriate practice. The use of kinaesthetic sense requires practice. This is also true of the other senses. We all have various levels of skill at judging distances, which can be improved with practice. Some people have an ear for music, for example, while others are tone deaf. Experiments show that this skill can also be trained. Psychologists talk of sensory, motor and sensory-motor skills, depending on whether learning involves the development of a sense, an action pattern or a combination of senses and actions.

Learning defined symbol-systems

The defined coding systems, such as the languages we speak in, mathematical symbols, road signs, are even more dependent on systematic learning. If the receiver of our message has not learnt the particular 'language' to a sufficient level of proficiency, then communication breaks down. Whereas this is relatively easy to diagnose in the case of formal spoken languages, it is not always so easy to identify when other symbol systems are in use. Teachers of languages have a long tradition of measurement of reading-age, vocabulary richness, and so on. They are somewhat more fortunate than the teachers of science and mathematics, who have not traditionally paid the same attention to distinguishing the learning problems of their students that are due to lack of mastery of the concepts and principles, from those that are caused by lack of knowledge of the basic 'language' of mathematics.

Using appropriate symbol systems in communication

Non-verbal communications conventions are yet more open to misinterpretations. Cultural differences abound. What is considered politeness and hospitality in one place is the height of rudeness in another. Artistic and musical criteria in the rock culture are quite different from that of the rocker's parents. All this is learnt and thus can be taught. But as it's not taught, it falls on the message designer to establish what symbol systems are in fact understood and to work within these limitations.

In Figures 1.9 to 1.11 I present a few examples of audiovisual communication, which in fact use quite different symbol systems for part of the communication.

Figure 1.9 *Part of a script for an audiovisual on media selection.*

INTENT: (1) to instruct, and (2) to entertain/interest
CODING: (1) verbal and visual (2) humour through non-verbal analogy
CONTENT: conceptual (a classification of sensory channels) (from Romiszowski 1975)

VISUAL	AUDIO
(An earlier part of the slide set, showing the role of communication to instruction.)	(An earlier section of script, about as long as the part reproduced here.)
	Now, how about the SENSORY CHANNELS used for communicating our messages? Our message may use any one, or a combination of the senses, to reach its destination. For example, the girl here is receiving the boy's message by the AUDIO channel.
	But what about the girl's message to the boy? (pause — 4 seconds) The hankie she has dropped is a VISUAL 'come on' message to the boy . . . and a pretty old fashioned one at that!
	The boy however is a bit more up to date. He knows not only WHAT message content will be effective but also that sending it by both AUDIO and VISUAL channels, simultaneously, will be more efficient! (pause — 4 seconds)
	As our tale unfolds, the other sensory channels come into play . . . taste, smell and the tactile, or touch senses . . . . . . How many sensory channels do we use in communication anyway? (pause — 4 seconds)

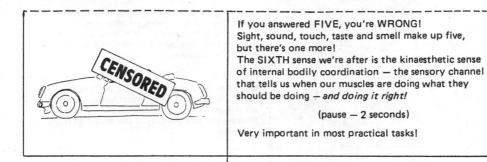

If you answered FIVE, you're WRONG!
Sight, sound, touch, taste and smell make up five,
but there's one more!
The SIXTH sense we're after is the kinaesthetic sense
of internal bodily coordination — the sensory channel
that tells us when our muscles are doing what they
should be doing — *and doing it right!*

(pause — 2 seconds)

Very important in most practical tasks!

Figure 1.10 *Part of a script for a slide-tape-workbook on Industrial Safety (Pressed Steel Co, 1964).*

INTENT: (1) to instruct, and (2) to motivate/influence
CODING: (1) mainly visual stimuli and verbal feedback
(2) motivation through verbal slogans
CONTENT: conceptual (classification of good/bad practice and habits)

VISUAL	AUDIO
Fred	In this module, we will study the basic principles of industrial safety. Remember: SAFETY BEGINS AT HOME, when you PREPARE YOURSELF to come to work. Fred, here, is about to strangle himself with his own scarf. He should never have entered a workshop, full of fast moving machinery, dressed like that!
Bill	What about Bill? He's just arriving to work. Look at his appearance! What's wrong with the way he's turned out? Switch off the tape for a moment and turn to page 1 of the workbook. Read the rules listed there and answer the questions about Bill. (pause with music, as signal for switching off) You should have written down three criticisms of Bill's turnout: — his untied shoelaces. — his loose, oversize jacket. — his long hair — Yes! Many people get scalped every year by getting hair caught in machinery.
OIL RAGS	Now here's Fred again — without his scarf. But he's behaving in a potentially dangerous manner again! Oily rags seem harmless enough, but if the oil gets on the shop floor, someone may have a nasty spill. Remember: THINK AHEAD — PREVENT ACCIDENTS BEFORE THEY OCCUR!

Figure 1.11 *Part of an introduction to a typist recycling course installed by the author in Brazil (CENDRO/CEPED, 1976).*

INTENT: (1) to motivate/influence, and (2) to entertain/interest
CODING: (1) verbal story appealing to (non-verbal) organization codes of behaviour and reward of behaviour (2) visual support to story, using non-verbal allusions to well known situations and people in the organization

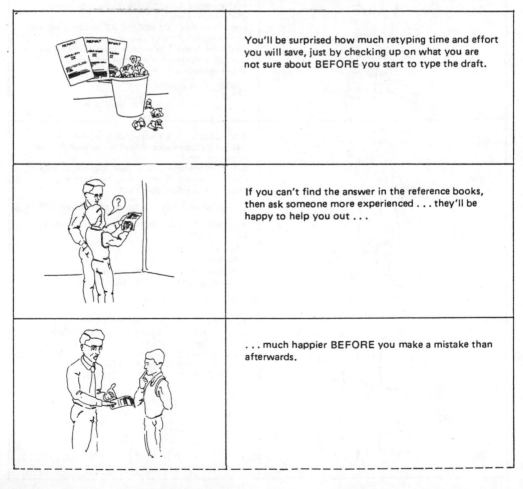

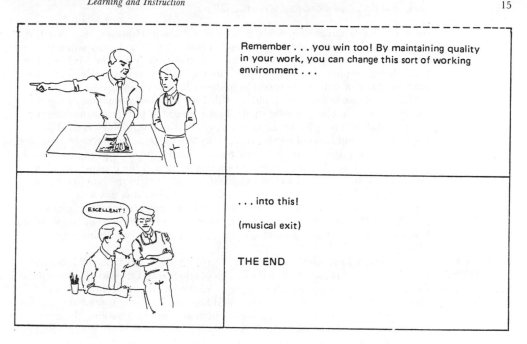

1.2 The theories of instruction and their use in method/media selection

1.2.1 Emergence of an educational technology

Technology as a process of invention

A commonly accepted definition of 'technology' is the systematic application of knowledge (usually scientific knowledge) to achieve a particular practical purpose. Thus construction technology applies what we know about structures, properties of materials, local climatic conditions, social habits and so on, to the systematic design and construction of bridges, buildings, airports, etc. Notice that we may draw upon more than one area of knowledge. Notice also that one aspect of a technology (which distinguishes it from an art or a craft) is that as knowledge is applied systematically, we can check back and improve our design as a result of problems which occur in the finished product. For example, for some time now we have had a fairly well-developed knowledge of structures, which enabled us to build bridges which could be guaranteed to carry a certain loading. This

The medieval builder: a craftsman

differentiated us from the craftsmen of a few centuries ago who were never quite sure whether their stone-arch bridge would stay up when they removed the wooden supports from under the arch. The bridges usually stayed up because, by trial and error over centuries, a set of techniques had been built up which generally produced bridges so solid that they could carry several times the loading required of them. It is amazing how many medieval bridges still withstand the pounding of heavy commercial traffic today. None of the medieval bridge builders could accurately predict the maximum safe loading for their structures. Now we can do this with great precision.

However, our own technology is not always perfect. Between the wars, the suspension bridge over the Tacoma Narrows in the USA blew down due to a relatively mild cross wind (about 40 miles per hour), soon after it was built. The designers knew how to allow for the expected vertical loading, but not for the

Modern bridge-building: a technology

horizontal loading.

Now we have learnt to build suspension bridges that are well-ventilated, giving the minimum of resistance to cross winds. By trial and error, a series of rules for the improved design of suspension bridges was devised. However, the present state of development of our technology in respect of the problem of cross winds is probably closer to the state of development of arch-building in the Middle Ages. Nevertheless, we have learnt from previous applications very quickly, and it is unlikely that a brand-new suspension bridge will blow down again.

This digression into bridge building will, I hope, throw some light on the concept of a 'technology of education'. This current 'in' phrase means different things to different people. At one extreme, educational technology is used to describe the application of hardware, such as film strip projectors, videotape recorders, or computers, to education. Such a 'hardware' concept of educational technology is rather limited. It implies the application of the products of other technologies (notably electronics) to education, rather than the 'application of knowledge to the systematic design of education'. Surely it is this latter connotation which is in line with the general definition of 'technology' given earlier. It is this definition of educational technology which we shall adopt. If you like, we are referring to a technology *of* education, rather than technology *in* education.

Is there a technology of education?
Do we really have such a technology? Certainly there are areas of knowledge which are, or can be, applied to the design of education. Obvious examples include educational psychology, sociology, comparative education and the history of education. Not so obvious examples would be economics, management sciences and the physical sciences, yet it is these which are currently making themselves felt in proposals for educational reform (eg concepts such as the cost/effectiveness or cost/benefit of a course, or the teacher as a 'manager of resources', or 'individualized, automated instruction' have only recently crept into the jargon of educationalists).

How systematically is our knowledge applied to the design of educational systems? We must assert that in general our level of technological development in education is akin to the medieval bridge builders. The main aim of this chapter is to outline some of the efforts being made to upgrade the level of our technology in just one area of the educational enterprise – the process of instruction. Work such as that of Skinner, Gilbert, and other early work such as that of Pressey and Bloom, laid a foundation upon which a more systematic technology of *instructional* design is being built.

Skinner's model
Behaviourists tend to describe their models in terms of *stimulus* and *response* (S–R). Learning has occurred when a specific response is elicited by a specific situation or stimulus with a high degree of probability. The more likely and predictable the response, the more efficient the learning has been. Learning of complex behaviour is regarded as the building up of chains of simple S–R bonds. Professor B F Skinner (1961) described the building up of such chains in animals. His techniques of 'shaping' behaviour were then applied (some would say mis-applied) to human learning in the form of the now familiar linear teaching programmes. These attempt to shape human behaviour by presenting a gradual progression of small units of information and related tasks to the learner. At each stage the learner must actively participate by performing the set task. He is then immediately supplied with feedback in the form of the correct answer. In addition, as even pigeons do not learn effectively if allowed to practise incorrect responses, Skinner ensures that the human learner is almost always correct in his responses by the process of reducing the difficulty and supplying extra practice at any points where errors are habitually committed.

Many feel that Skinner's model of human learning is incorrect, or at least incomplete. People do learn from their mistakes if the error of their ways is explained to them. Sometimes they jump a step or two yet come up with what appears to be full understanding. In particular, it is difficult to explain all learning tasks in terms of a chain of S–R bonds built up or 'shaped' one after the other.

Gilbert's mathetics
One of the first people to use the term 'technology of education' in the sense defined above, was Tom Gilbert, a disciple of the Skinnerian school. In 1961 he re-organized many of the ideas put forward by other behaviourists and presented

A classification of basic patterns of behaviour	A behaviourally oriented approach to the classification of the outcomes of learning would focus on characteristic patterns of stimulus-response connections that may be formed during the learning process. Thomas Gilbert, for example, presented a model of three basic patterns of behaviour, suggesting that complex behaviours are formed by the combination of the three basic patterns.

	Behaviour pattern	*Diagram*	*Examples*
	1. *Behaviour chain* A step-by-step procedure, in which the outcome of one step acts as the stimulus for the next response.	$S_1 \to R_1.S_2 \to R_2.S_3$ $R_3.S_4 \to R_4$ (etc)	Tying a shoelace. Dividing two numbers. Operating a photocopy machine.
	2. *Multiple discriminations* A simple decision-making procedure, involving a choice between two or more responses, depending on the stimulus.	$S_1 - R_1$ $S_2 - R_2$ $S_3 - R_3$	Reading a symbolic message like Morse Code, or indeed our alphabet (discriminating between b and d).
	3. *Generalization* A simple classification procedure, in which several possible stimulus situations are seen to have something in common.	S_1 S_2 $S_3 — R$ S_4 S_5	Classifying red objects correctly. Identifying the extroverts in a group. Identifying all situations in which it is unsafe to park a car.

Some combinations	1. What is commonly referred to as 'having a concept' involves the performance of a combination of generalization and discrimination behaviour — classifying correctly any example or instance of the concept and not including any non-examples, however similar they may be. Example: Having a 'well-formed concept' of honesty involves the identification of honest and dishonest practices in a given case — all possible honest reactions should be correctly identified and no dishonest reactions admitted into one's classification.
	2. Most complex procedures are combinations of chains of activity and discriminations at decision points. Sometimes, the decisions are unique, matter-of-fact choices between predetermined alternatives (plain multiple discriminations). At other times the decisions involve the application of a concept (generalizations and discriminations). Examples: The first case is illustrated by the procedure of following a set of instructions like a travel itinerary or a recipe. The second one is illustrated by procedures for mathematical problem-solving, etc.
Reading guide	For detailed accounts of this approach, see: Gilbert, T F (1961); Mechner, F (1965); Romiszowski, A J (1981) (Chapter 10).

Figure 1.12 *Gilbert's (and Skinner's) model of behaviour categories.*

them as a set of procedures for the design of instruction. He outlined these in a near-incomprehensible treatise which he entitled *Mathetics* and sub-titled *The Technology of Education* (Gilbert 1961). In this he lays down a set of rules for the analysis of learning tasks, and the construction of appropriate training exercises. His rules are somewhat strict and were originally based more on reasoning than on experimental evidence. Some of his suggestions do however seem to be borne out by subsequent experimentation. In particular his three-class classification of learning tasks into chains, discriminations and generalizations has been of value to trainers.

Gilbert suggests an analysis of the performance required in terms of stimulus and response, to identify whether the performance is made up of chains, discriminations or generalizations. This 'prescription of the mastery performance' then undergoes several further analyses, in which it is compared with the performance of typical trainees, the most common errors they perform, other behaviours they have previously mastered which are similar and may therefore help or hinder the acquisition of the new performance, and so on.

Many writers of instructional materials have found Gilbert's work stimulating. Although few use his techniques in their totality, many have adopted S–R notation as a technique of analysis, and the 'Demonstrate, Prompt, Release' model as a basis for exercise design. Some have found they can adapt these techniques to deal with almost any instructional task, while others find that the three main behaviour constructs of chain, discrimination and generalization are insufficient to deal with all forms of learning tasks. Creative behaviour in particular does not seem to be very well described by stimulus-response techniques. Readers who feel this way may find the classification suggested by Robert Gagné more attractive.

Gagne's categories of learning
Robert Gagné (1965) suggested a hierarchical list of eight categories of learning. The list is hierarchical in the sense that it proceeds from very simple conditioning-type learning, up to complex learning, such as is involved in problem solving.

1. Signal learning
This may be equated with the Pavlovian conditioned response. The subject learns that a given event is the signal for another event, as the dinner bell was the signal for Pavlov's dogs' dinner.

2. Stimulus-response learning
This is differentiated from signal learning in that the response is not a generalized emotional one, but a very precise act.

3. Chaining
Chaining is the type of learning we have already described when discussing Gilbert's work.

4. Verbal chaining
Gagné says 'verbal association might well be classified as only a subvariety of chaining . . . But because these chains are verbal and because they explain the remarkable versatility of human processes, verbal association has some unique characteristics'.

5. Discrimination learning
This is the same category as Gilbert's multiple discriminations.

6. Concept learning
This may be compared to the 'generalization' of mathetics. In this form of learning a stimulus is *classified* in terms of its abstract properties, as shape, position, number, etc.

7. Rule learning
In a formal sense, a rule is a chain of two or more concepts. The simplest type of rule may be 'If A, then B' – eg 'If a (German) feminine noun (concept A) then the feminine article (concept B)'.

8. Problem-solving
Once a human being has acquired some rules he can combine these rules into a great variety of higher order rules. In doing this he can use what he already knows to *solve problems* which are new to him (though they may or may not be so to other people).

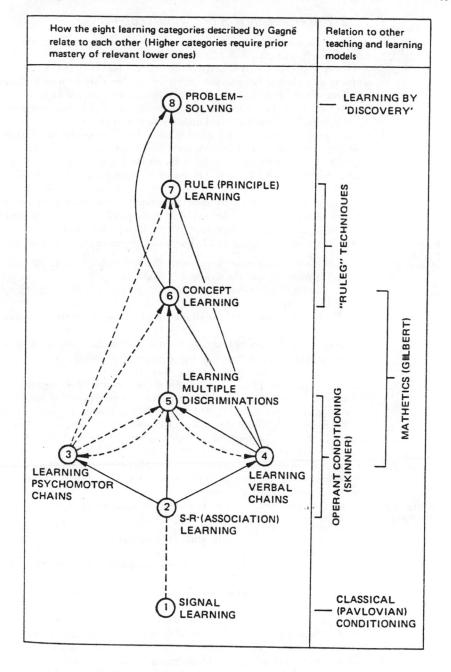

Figure 1.13 *Gagné's hierarchy of learning categories.*

1.2.2 The emergence of behavioural objectives

At about the same time that Gilbert was working on his treatise, another American psychologist, Bob Mager (1962), was writing a book in praise of behavioural objectives. It is based on the simple inference that if one defines learning as a change in behaviour, then the teacher may be wise to define the aims or objectives of his lesson in terms of the behaviour patterns he wishes to establish. This is useful, because it implies a student-orientated, learning-orientated approach, rather than one based on subject matter coverage. It is also useful because once an objective is defined in behavioural terms (ie the student should be able to perform tasks A, B and C), then it is simplicity itself to design an appropriate test situation to evaluate the method of teaching: we simply get the student to attempt A, B and C. Of course, the crunch is to have the objectives defined in behavioural terms. It is not as easy as it sounds, especially in traditional schoolroom subjects which are sometimes taught more through tradition, than for any practical end purpose. The problem perhaps is not so much in stating an objective as in stating the right one. We shall come back to this later on.

Mager's 3-part objective

The essential ingredients in a behavioural objective, according to Mager, are:

1. A statement of what the student should be able to *do* at the end of the learning session (the terminal behaviour).
2. The *conditions* under which he should be able to exhibit the terminal behaviour.
3. The *standard* to which he should be able to perform (the criteria).

For example: 'The student (1) should be able to find the square root of any number, (2) using tables of square roots or logarithm tables, and (3) getting the answer correct to 3 significant figures 9 times out of 10.'

Mager popularized the precise statement of objectives for programmed instruction. Later his approach became more widely applied to the design of any form of instructional material. After all, as Mager put it, 'if you don't know where you're heading you'll probably end up someplace else'. However, the concept of objectives stated in performance terms is of a much earlier date. The term has of course always been used in the context of education, but often in a general sense, such as 'to provide equal opportunities for all' or 'to create an environment for self-development'. Gradually it became usual to discriminate between such general *aims* and more detailed *objectives*.

Domains of learning

It also became usual to think of three categories of objectives:

1. *Cognitive objectives*   what the student should know or be able to do.
2. *Affective objectives*   what the student should feel and should be prepared to do.
3. *Psychomotor objectives*   physical skills that the student should develop.

One person who used these three categories and then developed sub-divisions was B S Bloom. Bloom's taxonomy of the cognitive objectives of education published in 1956 became (and still is) a standard handbook for many concerned with curriculum planning and instructional design. Much later (in 1964), the second volume, giving a suggested classification of affective objectives, was published. Psychomotor objectives have not yet been dealt with so thoroughly. The table in Figure 1.14 describes the categories of objectives in the cognitive and affective domains, suggested by Bloom *et al.* (1956) and Krathwohl *et al.* (1964).

Bloom's and Krathwohl's taxonomies of objectives

Notice again that these are arranged as a hierarchy in which the lower levels are prerequisites to the higher levels. To this extent the categories of Bloom's taxonomy are similar to Gagné's categories of learning tasks. Indeed, as far as the cognitive domain is concerned, the similarity is very pronounced, as can be seen by examining a few examples of the application of Bloom's taxonomy.

Introduction	Many authors have proposed models, or schemes, for the classification of different types of learning. Usually, these models present definitions of learning outcomes, or objectives. Occasionally they also list learning process (eg 'learning to learn') or the content or inputs to be learned (eg 'verbal information').
A basic classification into 'domains' of learning	The most traditional approach to the classification of learning uses broad categories such as knowledge, skills, attitudes, values, etc. Perhaps the best-known model, popularized by the writings of Benjamin Bloom and his collaborators is the three domains of educational objectives.

Domain	Short definition
Cognitive domain	Learning of knowledge; its application, thinking, etc.
Psychomotor domain	Learning practical tasks, that require perception, decision and action.
Affective domain	Learning of feelings, preferences, value systems, etc.

Each of these domains may be further subdivided into specific categories of learning outcomes, or objectives.

Sub-classifications in the cognitive domain	Category name	Brief description
	Knowledge	The remembering of previously learned material. The lowest level of learning outcomes in the cognitive domain.
	Comprehension	Ability to grasp the meaning of material. Interpreting, paraphrasing, explaining.
	Application	Ability to use learned material in new and concrete situations. Applies, demonstrates.
	Analysis	Ability to break down material into its component parts, so that its organizational structure may be understood.
	Synthesis	Ability to put ideas together to form a new whole. Proposes, integrates, designs.
	Evaluation	The ability to judge the value of material for a given purpose.

Sub-classifications in the affective domain	Category name	Brief description
	Receiving	The student's willingness to attend to particular phenomena or stimuli.
	Responding	Active participation. The learner not only attends but also reacts favourably.
	Valuing	Demonstration of a preference, belief, or commitment with respect to certain behaviours/phenomena.
	Organization	Bringing together different values into a consistent and coherent value-system.
	Characterization	The total adoption of a value-system, so that it becomes a personal life-style.

The psychomotor domain	Bloom and Krathwohl did not get round to sub-classifying the domain of psychomotor objectives. Several other authors have tried to do this, but there is no generally accepted taxonomy.
Reading guide	For detailed accounts of this approach, see Bloom, B S *et al* (1956); Krathwohl, D R *et al* (1964); Romiszowski, A J (1981) (Chapters 3 and 11); Simpson, E J (1967).

Figure 1.14 *Bloom and Krathwohl's taxonomies of educational objectives.*

1. Knowledge
This is considered the lowest level of cognitive objective. To demonstrate the attainment of objectives at this level, students would be expected to do such tasks as: *name* the parts of an object; *point out* a certain object; *state* a definition; *recognize* a phenomenon when he sees it. (Gagné would classify most of these as examples of stimulus-response learning or as learning of verbal chains.)

2. Comprehension
Bloom identifies this level by signs of 'understanding' on the part of the student – such signs as: *selecting* an example of a particular phenomenon; *giving reasons for* a phenomenon; *classifying* an object into a category; *contrasting* two objects/phenomena. (These seem to be examples of multiple discrimination and simple concept learning in Gagné's terms.)

3. Application
This level is characterized by the student's ability to apply theoretical statements and generalizations to real situations, for example: *calculate* a mathematical result; *perform* a task; *use* a particular set of rules and procedures; *predict* the result of a proposed course of action. (There seems to be much in common here with what Gagné terms 'rule-following'.)

4. Analysis
Being able to *compare* and *contrast* alternatives; *justify* the adoption of certain procedures; *break down* a problem into its components.

5. Synthesis
Being able to *select* among alternative courses of action; *organize* the components of a problem; *derive* a solution to a problem. (Analysis and synthesis are both involved in Gagné's description of problem-solving activity.)

6. Evaluation
This is, according to Bloom, the highest level of cognitive objective. It is characterized by such activity as being able to *judge* the value of a particular block of knowledge; *argue* for or against a proposal; *defend* or *criticize* a particular viewpoint. (Although some evaluation is involved in problem-solving, Bloom's concept of evaluation seems to go further into the realms of intellectual activity than does Gagné's classification of learning categories.)

Bloom and Gagné contrasted

There are, however, some important differences between Bloom's and Gagné's classifications:

(a) If you look at Figure 1.14 it is quite obvious that Bloom is suggesting a continuum in the development of a set of objectives from the simple and concrete to the complex and abstract (note the parallel here with well-used instructional clichés). The six levels are like milestones on the way to perfect accomplishment, rather than watertight categories. Gagné's hierarchy on the other hand has specific and exclusive characteristics defined for each category of learning, particularly at the lower levels.

(b) Bloom's taxonomy merely sets out to classify objectives, and, by stating them in terms of observable student behaviour, to indicate appropriate types of test questions. It does not attempt to formulate general rules about how one should teach in order to achieve particular objectives. Gagné's hierarchy, on the other hand, was constructed with this latter aim in mind. Each learning category is not only associated with particular conditions for testing but also with conditions for learning (both external – how the teacher should plan the instructional event – and internal – the state of readiness of the learner).

There have been several other early attempts to build up a comprehensive model for preparing objectives, eg Miller (1962), and for the classification of types of learning, eg Merrill (1971), Tennyson and Merrill (1971).

1.2.3 The cognitive/developmental viewpoint

The influence of Jerome Bruner on teaching (particularly elementary school mathematics in the USA) has been immense. He is probably the foremost proponent of the discovery approach in mathematical education. However, he is not by any means the inventor of the discovery approach. This concept was well known in mathematics education at the beginning of the century (Young, 1906). Bruner's approach (1966) to discovery learning is characterized by three stages, which he calls enactive, iconic and symbolic. These stages are firmly based on the developmental psychology of Jean Piaget. Piaget was perhaps the most prolific researcher in developmental psychology. His interests have centred on the study and definition of the stages of cognitive development of the child. I shall not reiterate here the Piagetian stages of cognitive development. This is available in many other works (Piaget, 1957, 1965). I shall concentrate on the characteristics of Piaget's view of the growth of intelligence as they may relate to the process of instruction.

Piaget's view of learning and development
Piaget views the development of intelligence as part of the more general process of biological development. Gallagher (1964) has suggested five major themes running through Piaget's work.

1. Continuous and progressive changes take place in the structures of behaviour and thought in the developing child.
2. Successive structures make their appearance in a fixed order.
3. The nature of accommodation (adaptive change to outer circumstances) suggests that the rate of development is, to a considerable degree, a function of the child's encounters with his environment.
4. Thought processes are conceived to originate through a process of internalizing actions. Intelligence increases as thought processes are loosened from their basis in perception and action and thereby become reversible, transitive, associative, and so on.
5. A close relationship exists between thought processes and properties of formal logic.

Piaget observes that only in man can intelligence develop to the point where the domain of ideas and symbols can serve as the environmental source of disequilibrium. That is, we can construct intellectual universes, for example, 'transintuitive spaces, which can stimulate our own cognitive growth as surely as the confrontation by a baby with the problem of reaching his pacifier can lead to new insights of equilibria on his part' (Shulman and Keislar, 1966).

Piaget has written little specifically directed at problems of education. He has repeatedly disavowed any expertise in the pedagogical domain. Yet, either directly or through such interpreters as Bruner, his influence has been strongly felt.

Piaget's emphasis upon action as a prerequisite of the internalization of cognitive operations has stimulated the focus upon direct manipulation of concrete materials in the early grades. His description of cognitive development occurring through autoregulation has reinforced tendencies to emphasize pupil-initiated, problem-solving activities. Much of the work of such practical innovators as Z P Dienes (1960, 1964) and such theoreticians as Bruner is directly based on Piaget.

Bruner's theory of instruction
The general learning process described by Bruner (1966) occurs in the following manner. First, the child finds in his manipulation of the materials regularities that correspond with intuitive regularities he has already come to understand. Notice that what the child does, according to Bruner, is to find some sort of match between what he is doing in the outside world and some models or templates that he has already grasped intellectually. For Bruner, it is rarely something outside the learner that is discovered. Instead, the discovery involves an internal reorganization of previously known ideas in order to establish a better fit between those ideas and the regularities of an encounter to which the learner has had to accommodate.

Bruner almost always begins with a focus on the production and manipulation of materials. He describes the child as moving through three levels of representation as he learns. The first level is the enactive level, where the child manipulates materials directly. He then progresses to the iconic level, where he deals with mental images of objects but does not manipulate them directly. Finally he moves to the symbolic level, where he is strictly manipulating symbols and no longer mental images of objects. This sequence is based on Bruner's interpretation of Piaget's developmental theory. The combination of these concepts of manipulation of actual materials as part of a developmental model and the Socratic notion of learning as internal reorganization into a learning by discovery approach is the unique contribution of Bruner.

Bruner, in describing the process of mathematics learning, identified three stages in the learning of a new mathematical concept: enactive, iconic and symbolic. Optimum learning should pass through these three stages. These stages are identifiable in most of the practical procedures for working in the mathematics laboratory mode.

Ausubel's approach

David Ausubel (1968) has been a powerful (though perhaps now a waning) influence on instructional thinking. He stands in opposition to the discovery movement, claiming that much of the apparent superiority of discovery over exposition is due to research generally comparing discovery techniques with rote learning approaches. Ausubel argues that much instruction, particularly at higher levels of education, is (and has always been) successfully performed by the process of exposition leading to *meaningful reception learning*.

Meaningful reception learning

He states (1968):

'In reception learning (rote *or* meaningful) the entire content of what is to be learned is presented to the learner in final form. The learning task does not involve any independent discovery on his part. He is required only to internalize or incorporate the material . . .

The essential feature of discovery learning . . . is that the principal content of what is to be learned is not given but must be discovered by the learner before he can incorporate it meaningfully into his cognitive structure. The distinctive and prior learning task, in other words, is to discover something . . .

It is evident, therefore, that reception and discovery learning are two quite different kinds of processes, and . . . that most classroom instruction is organized along the lines of reception learning. Verbal reception learning is not necessarily rote in character. Much ideational material (concepts, generalizations) can be internalized and retained meaningfully without prior problem-solving experience, and at no stage of development does the learner have to discover principles independently in order to be able to understand and use them meaningfully.'

1.2.4 The expanded model of Gagné and Briggs

Gagné's approach to the design of instruction

We have already seen that the Bloom model has nothing to say about instructional methods, but Gilbert's model and Gagné's model had much to contribute. The best part of Gagné's books was devoted to the 'conditions for learning' for each of his learning categories. These conditions were:

(a) The internal conditions – readiness to learn. What has to be learned prior to the new learning taking place.
(b) The external conditions – the particular instructional tactics to be employed.

Limitations of Gagné's early model

What we notice about Gagné's model is:

(a) It is rather woolly about the conditions (particularly the external conditions) for learning problem-solving. One thing Gagné does say is that whereas at the lower levels (including concept learning) the 'discovery approach' does not pay off particularly (except perhaps in terms of motivation), at the higher levels there are benefits in terms of long-term retention and the ability to transfer the skill to a greater variety of problems.

(b) Many writers have commented that problem-solving is a learning category (perhaps several categories) worthy of more attention. Even Bloom's model identifies three types of mental processes involved just in problem-solving: analysis, synthesis and evaluation. Polya (1945), Landa (1976) and many other writers draw a distinction between algorithmic and heuristic problem-solving (Landa even subdivides these). It is not all that clear to which type of problem-solving Gagné is referring and which are missing from his scheme.

(c) Other writers (Bruner, 1966) commented that creativity and such capabilities as 'learning to learn' are overlooked. Others (Merrill and Wood, 1974) suggest essentially very similar categories but with some differences in definitions and nomenclature.

Gagné's revised model   Thus in the 1970s Gagné drastically modified his thinking of the 1960s, or rather, he attempted to modify and enlarge his model to take into consideration the indicated shortcomings, to placate the humanists, the 'mental process' fans, the 'information processing theory' fans and cyberneticians. At the same time, he played down the behaviourist roots of many of his earlier concepts, whilst attempting to keep most of them in his model (See Figure 1.15).

Capability	Verb	Example
Intellectual Skill Discrimination	Discriminates	Discriminates, by matching, the French sounds of 'u' and 'ou'.
Concrete concept	Identifies	Identifies, by naming, the root, leaf, and stem of representative plants.
Defined concept	Classifies	Classifies, by using a definition, the concept 'family'.
Rule	Demonstrates	Demonstrates by solving verbally stated examples, the addition of positive and negative numbers.
Higher-order rule (Problem-solving)	Generates	Generates, by synthesizing applicable rules, a paragraph describing a person's actions in a situation of fear.
Cognitive Strategy	Originates	Originates a solution to the reduction of air pollution, by applying model of gaseous diffusion.
Information	States	States orally the major issues in the presidential campaign of 1932.
Motor Skill	Executes	Executes backing a car into driveway.
Attitude	Chooses	Chooses playing golf as a leisure activity.

Figure 1.15 *Gagné and Briggs' model of learning outcomes.*

Type of Learning Outcome	Essential Prerequisites	Supportive Prerequisites
Intellectual skill	Simpler component intellectual skills (rules, concepts, discriminations)	Attitudes Cognitive strategies Verbal information
Verbal information	Meaningfully organized sets of information	Language skills Cognitive strategies Att`tudes
Cognitive strategies	Specific intellectual skills	Intellectual skills Verbal information Attitudes
Attitudes	Intellectual skills (sometimes) Verbal information (sometimes)	Other attitudes Verbal information
Motor skills	Park skills (sometimes) Procedural rules (sometimes)	Attitudes

Figure 1.16 *Essential and supportive prerequisites for five kinds of learning outcomes.*

An important consideration in sequencing instruction is to ensure that the learner has mastered the necessary prerequisites. There are two types. *Essential prerequisites* are those subordinate skills that must have been previously learned to enable the learner to reach the objective. Also these prerequisites become an integral part of what is subsequently learned. *Supporting prerequisites* are those that are useful to facilitate learning but are not absolutely essential for the learning to occur (see Figure 1.16).

The various skills identified as prerequisites must be selected as enabling objectives (and hence as part of the content) for the course, unit, or lesson, unless the learners have already mastered those prerequisite skills. The essential prerequisites also help prevent the designer from including non-essential objectives for a given instructional sequence.

In the domain of intellectual skills, Gagné has shown that essential prerequisites and their relationship to one another can be diagrammed in the form of a *learning hierarchy*, in which the terminal skill is at the top and below it are all the essential prerequisites.

Another use of a learning hierarchy is to designate a level at the lower part of the hierarchy as the *entry level* for given learners. This means that all the competencies below that level have to have been mastered before the learner can begin a particular instructional sequence that teaches the competencies above the entry level. For example, the learning hierarchy for solving algebraic equations with two unknowns would show, low in the hierarchy, that the student must have mastered basic maths facts and operations. Such competencies would be considered as entry-level behaviours for instruction in algebra.

In addition to offering guidelines for selecting objectives and prescribing sequences for learning the objectives, Gagné and Briggs offer useful information for prescribing the details of instruction through the application of instructional events. These are classes of events that occur in a learning situation. Each event functions to provide the external conditions of learning described previously. Therefore, one designs instruction in part by ensuring that the events used in instruction are planned to satisfy the necessary conditions of learning. The events, in the order in which they usually occur, are listed in Figure. 1.17.

Instructional Event	Type of Capability		
	Cognitive Strategy	Information	Attitude
1. Gaining attention	Introduce stimulus change; variations in sensory mode		
2. Informing learner of objective	Clarify the general nature of the solution expected	Indicate the kind of verbal question to be answered	Provide example of the kind of action choice aimed for
3. Stimulating recall of prerequisites	Stimulate recall of task strategies and associated intellectual skills	Stimulate recall of context of organized information	Stimulate recall of relevant information, skills and human model identification
4. Presenting the stimulus material	Present novel problems	Present information in propositional form	Present human model, demonstrating choice of personal action
5. Providing learning guidance	Provide prompts and hints to novel solution	Provide verbal links to a larger meaningful context	Provide for observation of model's choice of action, and of reinforcement received by model
6. Eliciting the performance	Ask for problem solution	Ask for information in paraphrase, or in learner's own words	Ask learner to indicate choices of action in real or simulated situations
7. Providing feedback	Confirm originality of problem solution	Confirm correctness of statement of information	Provide direct or vicarious reinforcement of action choice
8. Assessing performance	Learner originates a novel solution	Learner restates information in paraphrased form	Learner makes desired choice of personal action in real or simulated situation
9. Enhancing and retention and transfer	Provide occasions for a variety of novel problem solutions	Provide verbal links to additional complexes of information	Provide additional varied situations for selected choice of action

Figure 1.17 *Gagné and Briggs' suggestions for lesson planning (adapted from* Principles of Instructional Design, *2e, R Gagné and L Briggs. Copyright 1974, 1979).*

1.2.5 Other approaches to the design of instruction

The work of Gagné and Briggs has been very influential on the practice of instructional design over the last 20 years or so. There have, of course, been other approaches. Some of these are extensions or refinements of the Gagné/Briggs methodology, while others are based on quite different assumptions about the learning process. A notable extension is **Component Display Theory**, which has refined the general heuristics offered by Gagné and Briggs into a set of specific and detailed procedures for exercise design (Merrill, 1983). Another refinement is **Elaboration Theory**, which considers how to knit together into an overall instructional design the single-objective exercises developed by the Gagné/Briggs approach (Reigeluth, 1973). Other, substantially different approaches include Scandura's **Structural Learning Model**, Gropper's extension and refinement of the behavioural analysis (and Mathetics) approach, Landa's methodology based on the design of learning algorithms and heuristics and many others which lack of space precludes mentioning. A very useful and thorough analysis of many of these approaches can be found in Reigeluth's (editor 1983) '*Theories of Instruction*' which is recommended as further reading, especially for those who are interested in learning in the cognitive domain.

The other domains identified by Bloom and Krathwohl – *affective* and *psychomotor* – have been relatively neglected in comparison. Few of the theoretical models reviewed in Reigeluth (1983) go into any depth with regard to the development of attitudes or physical skills. To set this right, I developed a more all-embracing framework, which I called **Knowledge/Skills Analysis Schemata** (Romiszowski, 1981). In addition to bringing together in one model many of the ideas which have stood the test of time in other models, this approach gives equal prominence to the three learning domains outlined earlier and introduces a fourth one – the *interactive skills learning domain*. One advantage of this model is that it may be used both at the 'macro' level for the design of general instructional strategies during curriculum development, and at the 'micro' level for the design of specific instructional exercises and materials. (Interested readers will find more detail on the 'macro' approach in Romiszowski (1981) and on the 'micro' approach in Romiszowski (1984) and (1986).)

In spite of their detailed differences, all the approaches mentioned have one aspect in common – the definition of precise learning goals or objectives, and later, the analysis and classification of these into some form of schema, as a starting point for decisions on how to teach. There is another group of theoretical approaches that use a different starting point – the definition of a body of knowledge to be communicated and the analysis of this into some form of schema (a knowledge structure). These approaches, at their simplest, are topic analysis and concept mapping procedures, useful for the 'macro' planning of a course content outline and an overall sequence of instruction. Examples include the preparation of topic networks or maps (Rowntree, 1974), curriculum matrices (Gilbert, 1969 a and b), the original RUL-EG approach (Glaser *et al.*, 1963 – see also Romiszowski, 1986).

At a more sophisticated and detailed level, such approaches become methods for the design of knowledge-bases that may be used for reference or learning, for a variety of objectives, largely under learner control. Examples include: Information Mapping (TM) procedures for structured writing (Horn, 1973, 1974 – see also Romiszowski, 1986); Conversation Theory and the CASTE methodology for conversational tutorials (Pask, 1976, 1984); Structural Communication (Hodgson, 1972, 1974 – see also Romiszowski, 1986) and the many techniques currently being developed by computer scientists under the banner of 'knowledge engineering'. The knowledge-based approaches in general are currently growing in practical importance, as the use of expert systems, massive knowledge-reference systems and other computer-based techniques of knowledge dissemination become more widespread.

I shall not go any deeper into the theoretical aspects of the design of instruction, space limitations make it impossible to do the topic justice in one chapter. The overview given in this chapter should be sufficient to establish the general context within which we shall consider the selection and use of media for instruction and, possibly, might whet the appetite of some readers to follow up the references in order to get a more complete picture of the field. In later chapters, I shall return occasionally to one or other aspect of instructional theory, to explain specific questions of media selection and use.

2. A systematic approach to instructional design

2.1 The emergence of the systems approach

What happens when you put the theoretical ideas just discussed into practice? Very soon, two questions assume great importance:

1. How do we know we have the right objectives specified?
2. How do we measure the success of our course?

1 Valid objectives

Taking the first question and re-phrasing it, we might ask – where do course objectives come from? Several answers are possible:

(a) A need for certain knowledge or skills is dictated by the trainee's future job.
(b) Certain knowledge or skills are held to be desirable by the society in which the trainee lives.
(c) The trainee himself is interested in attaining certain knowledge or skills.
(d) The teacher has personal interests or preferences which he intends to transmit if at all possible.

The first two summarize the vocational and non-vocational objectives of a course, the third to a large extent governs whether students will partake in the course and what they will gain from it. The last is the inevitable 'noise' in the communication channel, generally held to be of supreme value in non-vocational instruction (education??) and often a problem in vocational instruction (training??).

Discrepancies between any of these categories of objectives and those set up (or discernible in retrospect) for your course are going to lead to inefficiency (high cost), ineffectiveness (high dropout), lack of relevance (student revolt) and so on. Similarly there may be conflicts of objectives within or between categories which must be resolved.

We are implying the need therefore for a very thorough analysis of the whole system in which the course, the trainees and the teachers operate – a systems analysis.

2 Course evaluation

Monitor success in achieving objectives (Effectiveness)

The success of a course is similarly judged by various criteria. As before:

(a) Can students do the job for which they have been trained? (are cognitive and psychomotor objectives met?)
(b) Do students fit into the society and can they operate in it? (cognitive, psychomotor and affective)
(c) Are students satisfied with the course? (affective)
(d) Are teachers satisfied with the course? (a reflection, one hopes, of the above three sets of objectives being met).

Monitor the efficiency of the process

But there are many other criteria. Just a few of these are:

(e) Is the cost of the course acceptable?
(f) Is the course structure in line with our philosophical or political viewpoint?
(g) How does this course compare with other alternative courses?

(h) Does the course use all resources efficiently (teachers, time, media, buildings, environment as well as money)?

(i) What are the organizational problems associated with this course structure?

and in general terms:

(j) What can we learn which will enable us to *improve this course?*

(k) What can we learn which will enable us to *improve our general course-design procedures?*

These last two avenues of evaluation summarize the *development* and the *research* aspects of evaluation. They imply that there is feedback from course evaluation to course design, and maybe even to the objectives of our course. They imply that defects in original analysis and course design will be identified and corrected.

This concept of self-regulation is one of the key concepts in the educational technologist's approach to course design – an approach now commonly named 'the systems approach'. Although its techniques may only bear a slight resemblance to those used in engineering system design, and the scientific basis of educational systems may be much less developed than in the case of natural systems such as animal nervous systems, the systems approach to education involves the following basic types of activity common to all systems approaches:

1. **Analysis**
   - of system needs (job and task analysis, society's needs, students' aims)
   - of system resources (manpower, space, time, materials, money, students' existing abilities)
   - leading to a statement of the problem (usually in terms of overall objectives)

2. **Design**
   - identification of whether the problem is entirely a training problem (other strategies may involve job redesign, redesign of society, change in selection procedures, etc)
   - if a training problem, identification of precise course objectives
   - deriving instructional strategies and tactics (use may be made here of models such as Gilbert's, Bloom's or Gagné's)

3. **Development**
   - planning of available resources (*this involves selection of presentation media*)
   - preparation of materials, organizational structure, etc

4. **Implementation/evaluation**
   - small-scale try-out concentrating on the instructional effectiveness of materials, efficiency of organization, etc (this is variously called developmental testing, validation, or more recently *formative* evaluation, as it helps to establish the form of the system's components)
   - large-scale try-out which, in addition to following up the above factors in the wider context, concerns itself with the value of the course to the organization, the community and the individual. (As this is in a way the summing-up of an existing implemented system, it is sometimes referred to as *summative* evaluation. However, this distinction between formative and summative evaluation refers mainly to the use made of the information gathered – ie does it lead to changes in the system? – rather than to the stage at which the information is gathered.)

Systems approach - definition	An overall approach which involves tackling problems in a disciplined manner keeping priorities in mind. The sub-system making up the overall system can be designed, fitted, checked and operated so as to achieve the overall objective efficiently (Rowntree, 1974).
Properties of the systems approach	Inputs, outputs and process are defined in relation to each other. A change in one part will affect all other parts. Each decision is justified in terms of pre-planned objectives. Systems models are used which show how each phase fits into the next and feedback loops facilitate revision and review. Environmental constraints which impinge on the school or teaching centre are considered. Systematic consideration of the suitability of solutions to problems as compared to their alternatives is carried out.
Description	The systems approach is a problem-solving method which helps to: 1. Define the problem as clearly as possible. 2. Analyse the problem and identify alternative solutions. 3. Select from the alternatives and develop the most viable solution mix. 4. Implement and test the solution. 5. Evaluate the effectiveness and worth of the solution.
Comment	The systems approach is not necessarily a step-by-step process. Analysis, synthesis and evaluation are recurring stages repeated throughout the process and not necessarily in the traditional format of beginning, middle and end. Therefore heuristic problem-solving techniques are often better suited than algorithmic procedures. The heuristic process features the creative use of general principles rather than the employment of specific rules. Although it does not lead necessarily to a solution at all times, it does increase the possibility of arriving at a viable solution.
Example	Polya's approach to mathematical problem solving is an example of the systems approach in practice (see Polya (1945) *How To Solve It*). 1. You must first understand the problem. 2. You must find the connection between data and the unknown and obtain a plan of the solution. 3. Carry out the plan. 4. Examine the solution obtained.

Figure 2.1 *The systems approach.*

Representa-
tion of the
systems
approach by
means of
flow charts

These overall stages in the application of a systems approach to course design may be variously broken down into subsidiary procedures. Different people specify different procedures often illustrating the sequence of procedures by some sort of flow diagram. Several such flow charts are illustrated in Figures 2.2, 2.3 and 2.4.

Although extremely helpful in illustrating the author's overall approaches, such flow charts are a trifle misleading in that they imply a fixed sequence of procedures. Although some overall sequence is generally followed the intelligent use of a systems approach involves the user in analysis, synthesis and evaluation at all stages of course design. It is not the sequence of the procedures, or the exact methods by which each procedure is carried out that makes the systems approach work, but the intelligence and experience of the course designer (or more commonly the course design team) in performing the procedures and drawing the correct conclusions.

Some
examples
of ID
models

The pictorial flow chart (Figure 2.2) was used as a general guideline by the National Special Media Institutes, which included the Universities of Michigan State, US International, Syracuse and Southern California. It illustrates the overall concept very well but does not spell out the procedures to be carried out. It does, however, hint at different levels of activity, such as the project management level (steps 3 and 9), the design level (steps 1, 2, 4 and 5), and the development level (steps 6, 7 and 8).

The flow chart in Figure 2.3 is the 'Dick and Carey' (1985) model for instructional materials development. The flow chart is much more detailed, but concentrates on one level of the instructional design/development process. This model is close to the reality of many teachers, who cannot step far out of the bounds of the content and objectives as specified by some already existing curriculum and will not face the tasks of large-scale dissemination and implementation of their materials on several sites.

Macro and
micro levels
of ID

The third example (Figure 2.4) is Robert Diamond's model for instructional development in a university setting. This model quite clearly identifies two levels, or phases, which we might call the *macro* and *micro* design phases. The first phase is concerned with curriculum and even organizational change. The second is not unlike the Dick and Carey model.

The
implication
for the media
selection
process

In order to clarify these different levels of operation, in the next section I present an expanded 4-level model of the total instructional design and development process. Within this model we will identify how and why media selection decisions are taken. We will see how the rationale and the procedures used for media selection are quite different in each of three levels.

2.2 The four levels of instructional design/development

2.2.1 The four levels of analysis

We can define four levels of analysis. These can be summarized as follows (Romiszowski 1981):

Level 1. Defines the overall instructional objectives for our system, as well as certain other non-instructional actions that should be taken to ensure success in resolving the initially defined problems.
Level 2. Defines:
(a) the detailed intermediate objectives that have to be achieved to enable us to achieve the overall objectives (hence the term 'enabling objectives');
(b) the interrelationship between these objectives (in terms of prerequisites); and
(c) the level of entry, or the knowledge and skills which will not be taught but which the learner must have mastered before entering the instructional system we are developing.
Level 3. Classifies the detailed objectives according to some system or taxonomy of types of learning and assigns specific instructional tactics to each objective or group of similar objectives. Thus, typically, one might find that

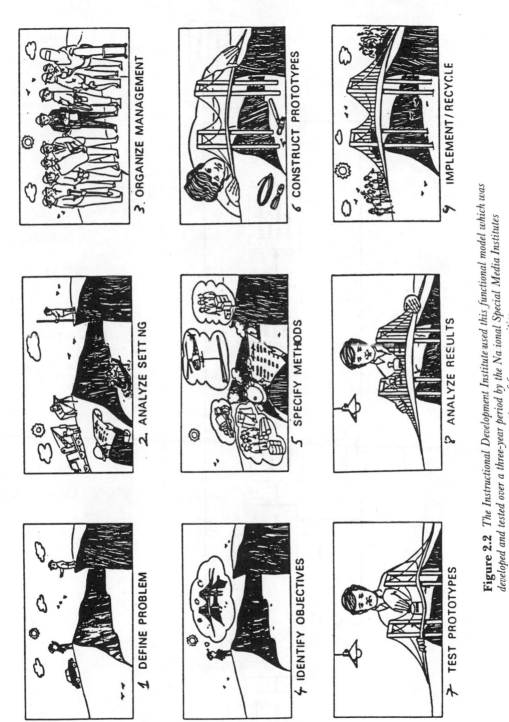

Figure 2.2 *The Instructional Development Institute used this functional model which was developed and tested over a three-year period by the National Special Media Institutes consortium of four universities.*

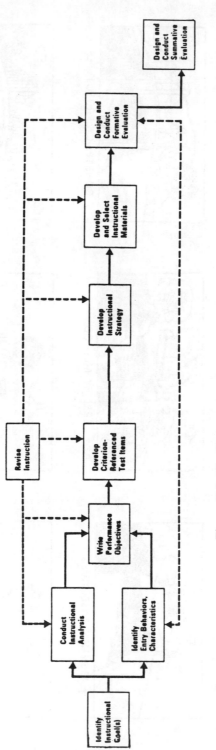

Figure 2.3 *The 'Dick and Carey' model for instructional development.*

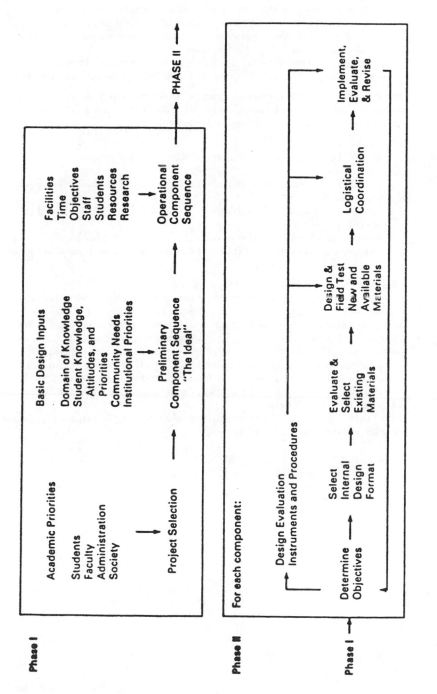

Figure 2.4 *An instructional development model for a university. (From R Diamond, 'The Syracuse University model for course design, implementation and evaluation', Journal of Instructional Development, 4, no 2 (1980)- 21. Reprinted with permission.)*

the objectives of one lesson were all the same category or type (say, 'verbal information'), so one would dip into one's bag of tactics, pull out a set labelled 'for teaching verbal information' and use it in the lesson.

Level 4. Does not take the objective 'as found' from Level 2, but

(a) analyses it further in order to discover exactly what is entailed in achieving this objective (in terms of basic motions for physical skills, in terms of basic behaviour patterns or in terms of basic mental operations for other skills and for knowledge); and

(b) matches instructional tactics at this micro level, generally in order to develop and produce special-purpose instructional materials or exercises.

These four levels are in a sense arbitrary, but they do help to define four levels of instructional design which correspond more or less to the four levels of system with which the instructional designer has to deal.

The four system levels are:

Each level or analysis is related to a level of design

Level 1. The project level – final objectives, principal measures and constraints.

Level 2. The curriculum or course units level – detailed objectives, sequence and content.

Level 3. The lesson plan level – the 'instructional events' that should take place at each stage in a lesson.

Level 4. The learning step or individual exercise level. This implies that a given lesson is planned in detail and written out in some form of script or self-instructional material.

This structure is summarized in Maps 2.1–2.8.

Each level of design leads to a greater level of 'transparency'

At Level 1 we treat the course more or less as a black box, concentrating on the specification of the outputs, inputs and control mechanisms for the course as a whole. At Level 2, the course structure will become apparent in terms of the sequence and interrelationship of the lessons that will make up the course and each lesson will be specified in terms of its outputs, inputs and control mechanisms. However, the lessons themselves – their internal structure and sequence and the detailed events which take place during each lesson – will remain to a large extent black boxes. At Level 3, the structure of each lesson becomes apparent in its overall detail.

At Level 4, the instructional events themselves become 'transparent', allowing us to see exactly how they will take place.

Map 2.1 *The four levels in greater detail.*

Level 1: Purpose	In order to identify the worth of a subject/job, Level 1 analysis: — defines the subject/job system — analyses subject/job structure — selects key topics/tasks — decides what needs to be taught.
Products	This analysis results in: — main topics/job description — topic network/task listing — key topics/tasks — course/training objectives.
Level 2: Purpose	Level 2 further analyses by: — examining structure and content — establishing a hierarchy of topics/objectives/tasks — listing what is necessary in the mastery of a topic/task — identifying where problems may arise — assessing target population.
Products	Level 2 analysis results in: — entry prerequisites and standards — possible learning/teaching sequence — general plans (methods, media) — the 'curriculum' — tests — intermediate and enabling objectives.
Analysing worth	Before Level 2 analysis and after, an analysis of worth must be done to determine whether further analysis should go on or indeed if the project should continue. This analysis is done on the following bases: — value — cost — potential development problems — potential implementation problems.
Level 3: Purpose	Objectives from Level 2 are matched with instructional tactics (classification methods, taxonomies of learning, etc).
Models	Gagnés categories and conditions of learning (Gagné and Briggs, 1974) Mager and Beach's performance-type approach (1967) The author's model (Romiszowski, 1981, 1984, 1986)
Products	Lesson plans Storyboards Group exercises.
Level 4: Purpose	Level 4 analysis is performed: — only if complexity of problem warrants it — only if such data is needed — only if it can be afforded. Objectives from Level 2 are broken down into behaviour or skill elements. This allows for more precise details of instruction (used most frequently for learning difficulties).
Models	Seymour's skills analysis (Seymour 1966, 1968) Gilbert's mathetics approach (Gilbert, 1961) Landa's mental operations approach (Landa, 1976) Merrill's component display theory (Merrill, 1983)
Products	Instructional materials Scripts.

Map 2.2 *Level 1 instructional design: an overview.*

Purpose of Level 1 analysis	*Level 1:* Defines the overall instructional objectives for our system, as well as certain other non-instructional actions that should be taken to ensure success in overcoming the initially defined problems.
Two stages of Level 1 analysis	**Stage 1**　Is there a problem? What is the problem? Is the problem worth solving?
	Stage 2　What causes the problem? Can instruction contribute to the solution? How exactly?
Stage 1: Define the problem to be solved	'Real' problems are those that generate enough dissatisfaction to justify that something should be done to reduce them. Someone is sufficiently dissatisfied with 'what is' in order to pay the cost of achieving 'what should be'. This cost may be simply the inconvenience caused by a simple change, or it may be a complex of real costs: time, money, and other resources required to develop and implement a solution. The amount one is prepared to pay is a measure of the 'worth' of a successful solution. One may sometimes be able to calculate this worth objectively, from the value of changing the 'what is' into 'what should be'. In industry and commerce, productivity increase, reduction in waste or overtime or turnover can all be quantified to establish the worth of a successful solution (perhaps training is the solution). In general education, it is somewhat more difficult to establish the worth of an innovation, but this is no excuse for not trying.
Procedure

First, identify the system which best defines the problem in input/output terms. Second, define the problem as a *discrepancy* between the *current* state of the system and the *desired* state. Do this in *input/output* terms only. If you find difficulty in doing this you are probably looking at the wrong system. |
Stage 2: Analysis of causes and solutions	2.1　Is the problem caused by a human performance deficiency? 　　－ If NO:　Analyse the other causes (material, procedural, etc) 　　－ If YES:　Proceed to 2.2. 2.2　Is the human performance deficiency caused by lack of knowledge or skill? 　　－ If NO:　Analyse the other causes (supervision, motivation, feedback, consequences, etc) 　　－ If YES:　Proceed to the analysis of the objectives and content of instruction.
Tools	Job analysis/Occupational analysis/Job synthesis Performance problem analysis (front-end analysis) Clientele (target population) analysis Future (development) needs analysis Human resources (supply and demand) analysis Subject matter (content) analysis.
Products of Level 1 instructional design	*A project proposal* － Objectives (long term) － Overall resources allocation － Overall implementation plan － Overall evaluation plan.

Map 2.3 *Level 2 instructional design: an overview.*

Purposes of Level 2 1D	Thus the purposes of a deeper, Level 2 analysis are to have a closer look at the tasks/topics deemed to be worth teaching at Level 1, in order to: ☐ Examine their structure and content ☐ Identify what is involved in their mastery ☐ Identify which parts give the learners most problems ☐ Generate ways of helping them to overcome these problems.
Products of Level 2 ID	The chief products of Level 2 analysis are: ☐ The final test instruments and exercises ☐ The entry or prerequisite tests and standards ☐ The learning/teaching sequence (or alternatives) ☐ Curriculum plans (with some idea of the methods/media) ☐ Lesson tests (for on-line evaluation during the course).
The tools	Task analysis Topic analysis Target population analysis Knowledge and skill analysis
Stage 1	The preparation of a formal, but not too detailed project proposal, which specifies the overall objectives, specific intermediate objectives and their sequence or interrelationship, any overall method or media decisions which are forced on the project by general constraints or previous Level 1 decisions/policy.
Stage 2	The preparation of an overall instructional plan, or curriculum document, defining: — objectives and their sequence/sequence alternatives; — content (knowledge and skills to be mastered); — methods/techniques to be used for each objective; — specific media/materials required for each objective; — estimates of resources, time, etc.

Worksheet	Objectives	Tests	Content	Methods	Media	Time
	1. . . . . . 2. . . . . . 3. . . . . . etc.					

Map 2.4 *Levels 1 and 2 of the ID process: a summary.*

The table below has been prepared to compare and to contrast the practical procedures that we have mentioned in this chapter to date.

Note that there are alternative procedures commonly used in education and training.

Note also that the distinction between education and training gradually blurs, the last stages of each procedure being more or less equivalent.

Questions in the analyst's mind (the heuristics)	Analysis techniques and procedures	
	Education context	**Training context**
AT LEVEL 1	Subject	Job
What is the system of interest? What is its boundary?	definition of the subject area/aims, definition of a notional job	definition of the job's duties and responsibilities and objectives
	Chief topics **or** Master performer	Job description
What are its components? What is its structure?	analysis of structure of subject	analysis of the job's structure
	Topic network or model **or** Topic matrix or map	Task listing or mapping
What is worth teaching/learning?	Selection of 'key' or useful topics from expert's view	Selection of key, difficult and frequently practised tasks
What needs to be taught?	Assess usefulness from learner's view. Target population analysis (existing knowledge/skill)	Specify job aids or practice as required. Target population analysis (existing related performance)
	Syllabus (course content) **or** Course objectives ⟷	Training objectives
AT LEVEL 2		
How is each task/ topic done or structured?	Analyse topic into information elements Analyse objectives into sub-objectives	Analyse task into steps or operations
	Teaching points **or** Objectives hierarchy **or**	Task structure or list of steps
What is involved in mastering the topic/task?	Apply a taxonomy (eg Bloom) Look for prerequisite skills or knowledge essential for satisfactory performance	
	Intermediate test items ⟷ Intermediate/enabling objectives and test items	
What will the learners bring to the learning situation?	Target population analysis of an in-depth nature, to assess suitability of sequence, pace, specific examples, methods, media, and entry levels	
What shall we do about it all?	Entry test + Learning sequence + Lesson outline + Lesson tests + Final test	
	(The overall instructional plan)	
TO LEVEL 3	Continue detailed lesson planning	

Map 2.5 *Level 3 of the ID process: an overview.*

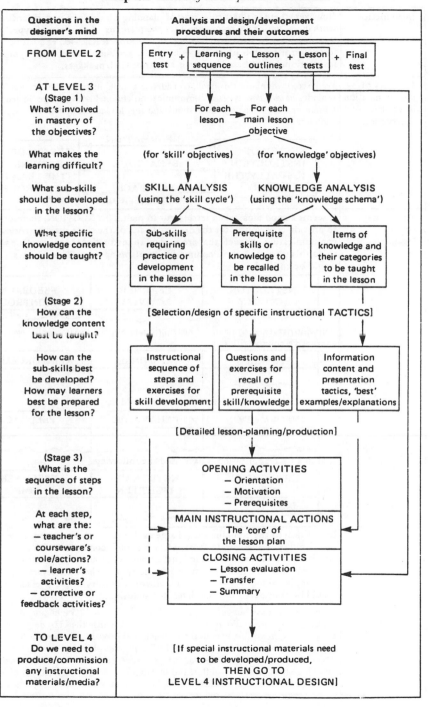

Map 2.6 *A procedure for detailed lesson planning.*

Introduction	However, there is a particular way of planning a lesson — a particular form of worksheet, which we recommend for the planning of a variety of types of lesson. It may be used for planning conventional teacher-led expositive instruction, group-learning activities, games and simulations, some types of self-instructional print-based materials and some CAL packages.
The lines of communication in a system of 'instruction'	We have, throughout this book, considered a 'true' instructional process as one that provides *at least three* types of communication channel between the 'instructor' (whether human or a self-instructional system) and the 'learner'. The following diagram is well known.

INFORMATION →

SYSTEM OF INSTRUCTION (USUALLY THE TEACHER)

← BEHAVIOUR

FEEDBACK AND CONTROL →

SYSTEM OF LEARNING (THE LEARNER OR A GROUP)

The three-column lesson-plan	It seems a good idea, when setting out to plan INSTRUCTION, therefore, to provide consciously for the design of each of the three main activities/communication channels that are part of an instructional process. One way to do this is to use a three-column lesson-planning sheet. The columns would be entitled:

INSTRUCTOR ACTIVITY	LEARNER ACTIVITY	FEEDBACK/ CONTROL

Behaviourists (and some other instructional designers) may like to use the alternative column titles:

STIMULUS	RESPONSE	REINFORCEMENT

Yet another near-equivalent set of titles would be:

INFORMATION	BEHAVIOUR	FEEDBACK

And in a CAL application, I have used the following:

CRT SCREEN INFO.	KEYBOARD/ LIGHT PEN	FEEDBACK/ CMI

The three stages of a lesson	In addition to the communication aspects, however, there are sequence aspects to the planning of a lesson. In short, a lesson should commence with some opening activities, then the main instructional activities should be performed, and finally, the lesson should end with some closing activities. There are several possible activities in each of these stages. Not all are obligatory in every lesson, but they should be considered as 'candidates' for inclusion.
The activities	Many writers have suggested typical 'steps', or 'events' (Gagné and Briggs, 1974) or 'tasks' or 'activities'. We prefer the latter term because the plan describes the activities of the sub-systems involved in the instructional process. The term 'events' conjures up the idea of 'points in time' (as in the PERT project planning/control technique) or also 'objectives achieved' (targets reached). However, the list of activities used in the planning sheet is strongly influenced by Gagné's (1975) suggested list of 'instructional events', as well as the views of many other writers on the subject of lesson planning.

Map 2.6 – *continued*

The lesson planning form: structure and activities		INFORMATION	BEHAVIOUR	FEEDBACK
	OPENING ACTIVITIES 1. Attention and motivation	'Now hear this!' 'Have you ever . . . ?' 'A funny thing . . .	'?????'	
	2. Statement of objectives	'This is where we are going . . .' 'This is why it's useful to . . .'	'Aha!'	
	3. Recall/ revision of prerequisites	'Do you remember . . .?' 'Can you still do . . . ?'	'@@@@'	'Well, not quite; it's like this . . .'
	MAIN INSTRUC-TIONAL ACTIVITIES (for each lesson task or objective in sequence) 4. Instructional activity 5. Learning activity 6. Feedback activity	(This part of the lesson may loop around several times, depending on the number of specific objectives and the 'parts' into which a given instructional sequence has been divided) 'Here is the news . . .' 'And this is what you should do . . .'	'Busy, busy, busy'	'Oops . . . let's try it again . . .'
	CLOSING ACTIVITIES 7. Transfer of learning	'And now for something completely different . . .'	'More busy, busy'	'Can you see the relation between this and last week's?'
	8. Evaluation of the lesson	'So let's see where we have got to . . .'	'Do the post-test'	Results and comments.
	9. Summary and guide to further study	'Here's where we can go now — if we so wish.'		
Observation	The short comments placed here are just a light way of indicating how the lesson planning sheet is completed. The examples which follow in map 2.7 is more indicative of the level of detail that may be registered.			

Map 2.7 *Lesson planning: an example.*

The example lesson plan shown here first appeared in *Producing Instructional Systems*, together with many others. This one has been chosen for reproduction here for a number of reasons:

- it is a pretty complete and detailed plan for a fairly well understood topic and uses a well known instructional method (brainstorming)
- it loops several times through the steps of the instructional activities, for successive lesson 'parts'
- it has multiple and varied objectives (output and process)
- the main strategy is experiential rather than expositive
- it involves small group learning activities

Readers are invited to compare this plan, if possible, with others using the same planning methodology, which are expositive, teacher-led, mediated, computer-based. Such examples can be found in *Producing Instructional Systems* and in *Developing Auto-Instructional Materials* (Romiszowski, 1986).

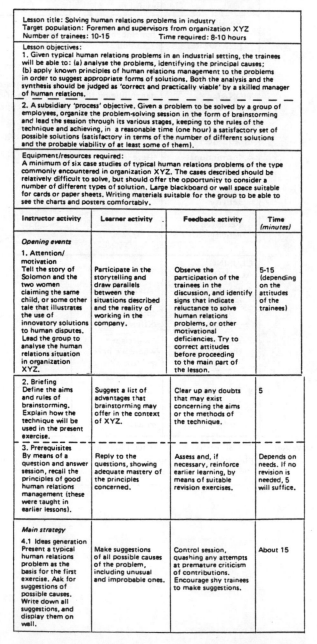

Lesson title: Solving human relations problems in industry
Target population: Foremen and supervisors from organization XYZ
Number of trainees: 10-15   Time required: 8-10 hours

Lesson objectives:
1. Given typical human relations problems in an industrial setting, the trainees will be able to: (a) analyse the problems, identifying the principal causes; (b) apply known principles of human relations management to the problems in order to suggest appropriate forms of solutions. Both the analysis and the synthesis should be judged as 'correct and practically viable' by a skilled manager of human relations.

2. A subsidiary 'process' objective. Given a problem to be solved by a group of employees, organize the problem-solving session in the form of brainstorming and lead the session through its various stages, keeping to the rules of the technique and achieving, in a reasonable time (one hour) a satisfactory set of possible solutions (satisfactory in terms of the number of different solutions and the probable viability of at least some of them).

Equipment/resources required:
A minimum of six case studies of typical human relations problems of the type commonly encountered in organization XYZ. The cases described should be relatively difficult to solve, but should offer the opportunity to consider a number of different types of solution. Large blackboard or wall space suitable for cards or paper sheets. Writing materials suitable for the group to be able to see the charts and posters comfortably.

Instructor activity	Learner activity	Feedback activity	Time (minutes)
Opening events			
1. Attention/ motivation Tell the story of Solomon and the two women claiming the same child, or some other tale that illustrates the use of innovatory solutions to human disputes. Lead the group to analyse the human relations situation in organization XYZ.	Participate in the storytelling and draw parallels between the situations described and the reality of working in the company.	Observe the participation of the trainees in the discussion, and identify signs that indicate reluctance to solve human relations problems, or other motivational deficiencies. Try to correct attitudes before proceeding to the main part of the lesson.	5-15 (depending on the attitudes of the trainees)
2. Briefing Define the aims and rules of brainstorming. Explain how the technique will be used in the present exercise.	Suggest a list of advantages that brainstorming may offer in the context of XYZ.	Clear up any doubts that may exist concerning the aims or the methods of the technique.	5
3. Prerequisites By means of a question and answer session, recall the principles of good human relations management (these were taught in earlier lessons).	Reply to the questions, showing adequate mastery of the principles concerned.	Assess and, if necessary, reinforce earlier learning, by means of suitable revision exercises.	Depends on needs. If no revision is needed, 5 will suffice.
Main strategy			
4.1 Ideas generation Present a typical human relations problem as the basis for the first exercise. Ask for suggestions of possible causes. Write down all suggestions, and display them on wall.	Make suggestions of all possible causes of the problem, including unusual and improbable ones.	Control session, quashing any attempts at premature criticism of contributions. Encourage shy trainees to make suggestions.	About 15

Map 2.7 – *continued* 45

Instructor activity	Learner activity	Feedback activity	Time (minutes)
4.2 Ideas organization Ask trainees to classify, improve or eliminate items in the list of causes. Identify the most likely causes.	Trainees may now comment and criticize earlier suggestions, as long as they are constructive.	Control any tendency to purely destructive criticism.	5-10
5.1 Generation – phase 2 Now ask for suggestions of possible solutions. Write down and display all the suggestions on the wall or blackboard.	Trainees should make as many and as varied suggestions as they can in the time available.	Control and encourage, as in step 4.1.	10-15
5.2 Organization – phase 2 Ask trainees to classify, improve or eliminate items in the list of possible solutions. Identify the most plausible solutions.	See step 4.2	See step 4.2	5-10
5.3 Ideas evaluation Lead trainees to the evaluation of the alternative plausible solutions and to selection of a solution to be implemented.	Trainees should discuss the pros and cons of each plausible solution previously identified. They should reach a consensus on the most viable one.	Evaluate the process of discussion and critical evaluation performed by the trainees. Evaluate the choice of solution.	15-20
6. More practice Repeat steps 4 and 5, using the other five cases of human relations problems. In each case, appoint a different trainee, or a team of two or three trainees, to organize and coordinate the session.	Each trainee has the opportunity of leading a brainstorming session, as well as ample extra practice in the analysis and solution of human relations problems.	The feedback activities that are listed in steps 4 and 5 above are now executed by the appointed trainees. The instructor observes the session as a whole and the performance of the leaders, in order to redirect them if necessary.	About 1 hour for each of the exercises (total 5 hours)
Closing events **7. Debriefing** Start a discussion on the solutions chosen. Question the theoretical bases for each solution. Question the practical viability. Invite analysis of the way in which the solutions were selected. Question the overall usefulness of brainstorming. Question the value of this particular exercise.	Trainees should demonstrate, by their arguments and comments, that they have formed sufficiently powerful and general problem-solving strategies and associated schemata of the principles involved. They should also describe how to implement the proposed solutions in the real-life situation of XYZ.	Evaluate the strategies and schemata of the trainees. Take decisions on whether more practice exercises are required to ensure transfer of the new skills to the job situation. Extend and/or replan the training sessions if necessary.	About 45
8. Transfer of learning Arrange for regular small group discussions, similar to the debriefing session described above, to analyse the real life decisions taken, after training, and to resolve problems occurring on the job.	Trainees should describe to the group how they came to make their decisions. The group analyses the decisions and predicts or comments on the end results.	As in item 7, the instructor attempts to evaluate the structures and strategies that are developing in the trainee's mind, in order to offer useful advice.	No prediction of the time needed

Map 2.8 *Level 4 instructional design: an overview.*

The flow chart presented here, starts with the 'detailed lesson plan' of Level 4 and illustrates where we go from there, as we descend to the level of development of purpose-designed, objectives-based, individualized, instructional materials.

Questions and activities of design team	Analysis and design/development procedures and their outcomes

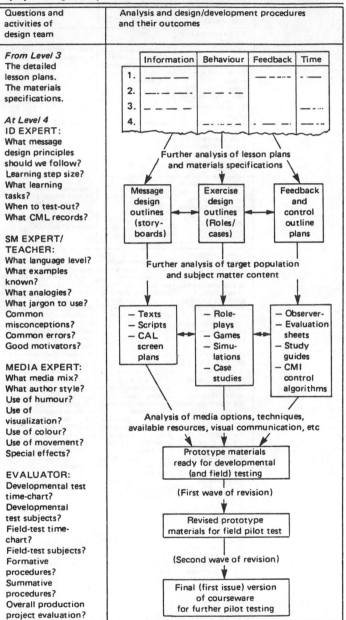

From Level 3
The detailed
lesson plans.
The materials
specifications.

At Level 4
ID EXPERT:
What message
design principles
should we follow?
Learning step size?
What learning
tasks?
When to test-out?
What CML records?

SM EXPERT/
TEACHER:
What language level?
What examples
known?
What analogies?
What jargon to use?
Common
misconceptions?
Common errors?
Good motivators?

MEDIA EXPERT:
What media mix?
What author style?
Use of humour?
Use of
visualization?
Use of colour?
Use of movement?
Special effects?

EVALUATOR:
Developmental test
time-chart?
Developmental
test subjects?
Field-test time-
chart?
Field-test subjects?
Formative
procedures?
Summative
procedures?
Overall production
project evaluation?

2.3. A practical example

2.3.1 Level I decisions in a training context

The following example is taken from a real consultancy project, carried out a few years ago, which involved the training of personnel for a real-estate chain.

The secretaries/receptionists who are the target population for our training are the first link between the company and its clients, so their performance is of vital importance. A job description reveals that secretaries/receptionists divide their time between attending to clients, in the office or on the phone, and acting as general secretaries to their bosses. They receive clients and make them comfortable, often attend to their requests for information directly, and at other times take them to see the appropriate person or make an appointment at a suitable time. They keep their boss's appointments diary up to date, exercise tact and courtesy, both personally and on the phone, and, in general, make themselves indispensable. They also do the typing and filing.

Specification of training objectives and sequence

On the basis of a task analysis, we were able to prepare the training objectives. These are listed in the first column of the overall instructional plan presented in Figure 2.5. Seven terminal objectives are identified. These are expressed in behavioural terms, complete with given conditions and expected criteria. They are listed in the intended order of mastery. As there are many possible sequences for teaching these objectives, we shall explain how the order was determined. A close study of the seven objectives reveals very little sequential interdependence. Objective 1 is, indeed, the only one that is a prerequisite for any of the others. Almost all the objectives depend on the trainee's knowledge of the company, its structure and the work that is performed. It seems most apt to put the objective that directly uses this knowledge at the beginning of the training programme.

Thereafter, there seem to be many alternatives. For example, objectives 2 and 3 could be taught in the reverse order. Also, objectives 4, 5, 6 and 7 could be taught at any point after objective 1. To select an appropriate teaching sequence, we therefore applied another criterion – the usefulness of the trainee to the company. We were planning to shorten the introductory training so that it could be given more often than twice a year. The ideal would be training in small groups whenever new staff were admitted. We did not choose wholly individualized self-instruction, as some of the skills to be mastered are social skills and must be practised in a group. One other important factor taken into account was that the critical tasks, where most damage can be done by poorly trained staff, are those concerned with the reception of clients, when social skills and knowledge of the company count most. Objectives 1, 2 and 3 are taught during the initial small group training session. If a person joins the company at a time when no training session is available, he or she may master objective 1 by individualized self-instruction while waiting for the training course.

Overall selection of methods and media

The remaining objectives are to be treated mainly through on-the-job training, under the supervision of the trainee's boss, but organized largely in the form of self-instruction, from manuals and other specially prepared materials. The objectives can be mastered in any order, or indeed in parallel.

Figure 2.5 *A 'Level II' course design.*

Objectives	
Specific instructional objectives (in the sequence of instruction)	*Proposed system of measurement and evaluation of learning*
1. Given requests from clients concerning the rental or purchase of property, and all the lists of property duly updated and manuals/tables of reference that are normally used on the job, the trainees should be able to: ☐ give the addresses and characteristics of all properties still available; ☐ give the costs of rental or purchase and any special conditions that may apply in a specific case; ☐ prepare all necessary documentation in order to process the rental/sale. The information given and documents prepared should be 100 per cent correct.	One should present a series of typical cases of requests for information, covering all the types of situations normally encountered in the working environment. These cases may be evaluated 'live' when used as the basis of group discussion in the classroom, or may be used as the basis for written tests, as a form of final examination. Both models will be employed – the observation of group discussion exercises as a means of formative evaluation and a final written test for summative evaluation.
2. Given any form of contact with a potential client (visits to the office or telephone calls etc) that involve personal contact and verbal exchange, the trainees should be able to: give information, explain procedures, resolve clients' doubts or complaints, always maintaining a pleasant tone of voice, a sense of respect, tact and politeness, patience, etc.	This type of objective can only be evaluated through the observation of the trainees' behaviour in real or simulated contacts with the company's clients, the analysis of this behaviour followed by feedback, more practice if required, until a satisfactory level of performance is demonstrated, even in trying circumstances.
3. Given any incoming telephone call, the trainees should be able to use the firm's switchboard and connect the call to the person/department best able to deal with the query. Trainees should connect 80 per cent of calls correctly at the first try.	One should prepare simulation exercises of the principal types of requests and other messages normally received by telephone. The set of exercises should be sufficiently representative of the real work to *guarantee at least 80 per cent correct performance* on the job.
4. Given instructions on the content of a letter, verbally, by one's boss, the trainees should be able to compose an appropriate form of letter or other missive, obeying the company standards for official correspondence, and produce a grammatically correct and well-constructed text.	Present a variety of typical letter-planning exercises. Analyse the resultant letters and feedback corrections or suggest extra practice if necessary. Practice the company standards to 'perfection' and the letter style and structure to a 'reasonable' standard as judged by secondary school teachers.
5. Given a normal office workload, the trainees should be able to plan, distribute and organize the work of the office staff, establishing realistic deadlines and using the skills of junior staff to the best advantage.	Evaluate the planning and distribution of work by analysing written plans to be prepared by trainees. Evaluate the execution of the plans by later observation of on-the-job performance.
6. Given a normal workload and a typical flow of requests for meetings, the trainees should be able to plan the boss's daily schedule and keep his diary up to date allowing an adequate time for each type of meeting arranged, taking into account the current work priorities, etc.	Final evaluation must be performed in-service as the constraints to be taken into account are different in each department and for each boss. One may use some simulated planning exercises during initial training stages (an opportunity for formative evaluation).
7. Given a normal workload and a typical flow of correspondence, reports, lets and sales, new properties, new building projects, etc, the trainees should be able to plan, organize and keep updated an adequate filing system, which is easy to maintain and capable of allowing any document to be located by any person with the minimum of training.	During initial training, the principles of filing systems may be tested by verbal questions and simple filing exercises. Final evaluation should take place in the real job situation by means of job performance evaluation techniques, as each department's filing requirements are somewhat different.

Figure 2.5 – *continued*

Content	
Skills content	*Knowledge content*
The skills of analysing a request for information, to identify the exact data to be given to a client: this is a relatively standardized, reproductive, intellectual skill. Skill in the use of tables and charts such as interest tables, to extract the correct information from the table: this is a reproductive, intellectual skill, based on the practice of reading a variety of tables.	A schema of concepts used for classifying requests into categories that require different information, different documents, etc. Knowledge of the procedures to be followed when completing specific documents or using specific tables or reference manuals.
Personal and interpersonal skills of tact, self-control and polite behaviour: these skills fall into the reactive and interactive categories and are, in general, reproductive in the case of this objective. The receptionist is not a creative problem-solver of client complaints; she must merely follow the rules of normal, polite behaviour.	Knowledge of the procedures of polite treatment of clients, including any special procedures laid down by the company. Also requires the above mentioned schema of concepts for classifying requests, in order to avoid upsetting the client through incompetent interpretation of his request and inappropriate action or information.
Skills of handling and operating telephone switch board equipment: *reproductive, psychomotor* skills. Skills of classifying/interpreting the incoming calls according to types of request/types of action to be taken: *reproductive, intellectual* skills.	Knowledge of the procedures for operating the specific telephone equipment installed in the office. A schema of concepts relating to the way the company operates, how it is organized and which department does what. Also the names (facts) of key people in the office.
Skills of authorship and composition of written communications that really say what they mean: productive, intellectual skills. Skills of writing/typing grammatically correct communications: reproductive, intellectual skills – we regard the typing skills as prerequisites.	Cognitive schemata composed of the concepts and principles of creative, persuasive and clear writing. Knowledge of the rules of grammar and punctuation. Knowledge of special norms for business letters, or special company standards/rules.
Skills of planning and organizing work: productive, intellectual skills. Skills of control and motivation of the work of subordinate staff: productive, interactive skills.	Knowledge of the skills and capacity for work of each staff member (job-specific facts). Knowledge of procedures of work planning (time charts, PERT, etc). Concepts of human relations, motivation, principles and strategies for motivation and control of fellow workers.
Skills of evaluating the priority of a given meeting in relation to the boss's current work deadlines/priorities: productive, intellectual skills. Skills of dealing with requests politely: reproductive, interpersonal skills. Skills of time estimating/planning: productive, intellectual skills.	The boss's work schedule and priorities (job-specific facts). Identification of work/project that a given meeting is concerned with (conceptual schema of work in progress). Proceedings for diary updating. Principles of time planning, of human relations, of negotiating with superiors.
Skill in planning and organizing filing systems: productive, intellectual skills. Skills of self-discipline required always to file documents at the earliest opportunity – on arrival or as soon as reference to them has been made: reproductive, reactive skills.	The types of work performed in the department (facts and concepts). The principles of filing systems. Knowledge of the problems that might arise for the company if filing/data systems are out of date or poorly organized (knowledge and conceptual understanding).

Figure 2.5 – *continued*

	Methods	
	General strategies to be implemented	*Specific techniques/methods to be used*
	Part expositive, part experiential: definition of basic concepts, followed by skills practice on simulated cases.	Case studies (written). Orientation by *instructor*. Work in *small groups*. Final discussion/*debriefing*.
	Expositive strategies for the use of tables, etc: demonstration followed by drill and practice exercises, until error-free performance is achieved by all trainees on all the job aids used in the office.	Study of a self-instructional manual which presents worked examples of the use of all job aids and then supplies practice exercises and feedback for self-correction by the trainee. (Could be in the form of information mapping.)
	Expositive strategy at first; demonstration of the required procedures. Experiential strategy later; simulation of the client/receptionist interaction.	Demonstration of models of good receptionist behaviour. Explanation of procedures. Role-playing: simulation of problems between client and receptionist and how to handle them.
	Expositive strategies for the operation of equipment. Expositive strategy for the explanation of company structure/organization, followed by experiential strategy for the matching of requests to actions taken.	Practical demonstration and individual practice, guided by the operator's manual. Classroom exposition with visuals/charts, followed by group analysis of taped incoming telephone calls.
	Experiential strategy for writing skills; composition and analysis of letters on simulated work topics. Expositive strategy for the company rules. (We hope we do not need to teach the rules of grammar.)	Practical exercises of composition of letters from given short notes. Analysis of the letters produced. Self-instruction from a manual of company rules and examples of their use.
	Expositive strategies for the procedures and the principles of work planning. Experiential strategies for the skills of planning, motivating, delegating, etc.	Classroom instruction on the procedures and principles of planning/organizing. On-the-job training for the development of skills, specific to the work actually done.
	Expositive strategies for the facts, concepts and procedures that are to be learned. Experiential strategies to develop skill in dealing with actual job situations.	On-the-job training for all aspects of this objective. The boss must explain his work, priorities and must keep this knowledge updated as work changes. He must set appropriate tasks and monitor trainee progress.
	Expositive strategies for the facts, concepts, procedures and basic principles to be learned. Experiential strategies to develop the skills and attitudes required.	On-the-job training for most of this objective. General principles and procedures of filing may be given in introductory classroom instruction. Department-specific knowledge and skill development under the boss's control.

Figure 2.5 – *continued*

Methods	Resources	
Group size and structure and methods of working	*Instructional/materials*	*Equipment/tools/job aids/media*
Large group (12 trainees) subdivided into small groups of three or four for the case study analysis.	10–15 case studies each one prepared on separate sheet of paper – to be selected from real examples of company work.	Classroom organized for small group discussion.
Individual study in the class or at home, aided by the instructor when difficulties arise (trainee seeks help from the instructor only when the feedback supplied in the self-instructional text proves to be inadequate).	Self-instructional text (70 pages estimate) – to be specially written to accompany a typical set of tables and manuals as used on the job. The text presents the problems and refers the trainee to the job aids.	Comprehensive set of the tables, manuals and other job aids actually used in the office.
Demonstrations to the whole group of 12.

Role-playing in pairs, or in some cases threes or fours (to complicate the problem situations). Rest of group act as observers and evaluators, until their turn comes to act. | A set of demonstration videotapes, showing good and bad examples of client treatment. It is also possible to record on videotape the performances of the actors in the role-play exercises. The roles of these actors must be printed and available beforehand. About eight sets of roles. | Videotape, or cassette, recorder/player and television. Compatible video camera, if recorded video feedback is to be used in the role-play debriefings. A set reminiscent of the office may be necessary, if training in a classroom setting. |
| Demonstration to pairs, then practice in pairs (one practicing on the equipment; one evaluating his partner's performance).

Whole group initially, followed by three groups of four trainees. | Programmed introduction on the use of the telephone switchboard equipment used by the company. (To be written – 10 pages.) 30 simulated telephone calls, recorded on audiotape, based on a frequency analysis of the most common types of requests. | Operator's manual (supplied by manufacturer). Access to the switchboard (or a simulator) for practical training. Three tape recorders. |
| Work on groups of four. Each member prepares a version of the letter and then four are compared. Individual study of the manual. Feedback by analysis of written work. | 12 different boss's notes, giving three exercises for each member of a group of four trainees. Programmed text of questions and exercises on company standards and business norms in letter writing. (To be produced – 80 pages approximately.) | Classroom arranged for small group work. Writing materials, or typewriters, as preferred. Printed copy of the company norms and standards (already exists) for reference. |
| Whole group of 12. Possibly some small group work.

Individual training under one's immediate boss. | Overhead projector transparencies to accompany the classroom instruction (12 sets artwork). Printed training plan/checklist for controlling on-the-job training (for the boss). | Overhead projector. Classroom arranged for flexibility – small/large group.

Standard forms or charts used on the job for the planning and control of office work. |
| Individual learning, adapted to the real job content and controlled by trainee's immediate superior. | Self-study and reference materials on procedures for office meetings, etc (these already exist, but should be updated). Checklist for controlling the trainee's learning on the job (to be used by boss). | The boss's diary and a similar dummy one for practice exercises. |
| Initial classroom study in whole group of 12 and some small group filing exercises. Later on-the-job training as individually adapted to the department's needs controlled by boss. | Learning and reference material to be used in class and on the job, on the principles/procedures of file organization. Checklist for controlling the trainee's learning on the job, to be used by the boss and then returned to training department. | Empty files, file cards, labels and all other materials needed to organize a filing system of the type used by the company. Adequate variety of real job filing requirements to give necessary practice to trainees. |

2.3.2. Level II decisions and the overall training plan

The decisions outlined so far all form part of what we have called Level I instructional design. These are the macro decisions taken on the basis of the initial analysis of the problem. We now proceed to Level 2 design. This involves more detailed analysis of the tasks that comprise the job, the planning of suitable methods for the evaluation of training results, the deeper analysis of the knowledge and skill content of each objective in turn and the classification of this content as an aid to the later selection of appropriate methods and media. The decisions taken are documented in the second, third and fourth columns of Figure 2.5.

Detailed specification of methods: strategies, techniques, groups

The planning of methods has been divided into three stages: (i) the selection of the intended general strategy; (ii) the specific techniques to be used for each objective; and (iii) the group size and structure to be employed. It is possible to use other ways of mapping and descriptions of the decisions taken, but the chosen one is the most apt for the present case. We have specified the strategies, techniques and group structures in some detail. This was done because the map was used to communicate the details of the instructional plan to people who were not involved in its preparation. It must therefore be sufficiently complete to make sense.

Detailed specification of resources: media, equipment, time

Finally, we come to the last main section of our map – the specification of resources. Once more, we have opted to subdivide this section into two columns: (i) instructional media/materials (the 'software' that must be obtained in order to put our plan into operation); (ii) equipment/tools/job aids (that is, everything else that must be provided to make the training system work).

The totals of the resources columns can be transformed into costs, which can then be compared with available budgets. The totals of the group and technique columns give an idea of the variety of teaching methods to be employed and these can be compared against available teaching expertise. The totals of the skills and knowledge columns give an idea of the quantity and type of information that will have to be included and these can be matched against available subject matter expertise.

Checking for coherence and viability

The variety of content, techniques, media and materials, and the sequence in which they occur in the plan, give a clear picture of the amount of variety or repetition that is built into the plan. Steps, at this stage, can be taken to enrich or to simplify the plan.

As well as looking for structure and 'vertical' coherence in this way, we may also use the map to assess 'horizontal' coherence. Are the proposed evaluation systems and instruments compatible with our objectives? Are the skills and knowledge identified compatible with the objectives? Can they be adequately evaluated, in sufficient detail, by the tests proposed? Are the general strategies selected compatible with the category of the objectives aimed for? Are the techniques selected capable of implementing the preferred strategies? Is the group size and structure well chosen, in view of the type of objectives to be achieved and the techniques to be adopted? Are the media and materials well chosen, in relation to the objectives and strategies? We can ask similar questions of every entry on the map in relation to every other entry.

2.3.3. Level III: lesson planning

The three-column lesson plan: an example

To begin the study of this general lesson planning system, we present an example (Figure 2.6) of a lesson plan prepared for a course that aims to train supervisors in a given organization to evaluate the performance of their subordinates.

The division of the lesson content into three stages is an attempt to apply the principle of progress in small steps.

The three steps deal, respectively, with:

☐ Basic knowledge concerning job evaluation in general and the system used in this organization in particular.

☐ The basic skill of applying a five-point evaluation scale.

☐ The practical skill of operating the job performance evaluation system of the company.

In the structure of this lesson plan, we can see a certain amount of care exercised to ensure that the instructional actions really do lead to the achievement of the planned objectives. There are, however, several additional activities that are added to make the lesson more effective, more motivational, better integrated into the course as a whole, or better able to promote the transfer of what has been learned to a wide variety of real-life situations.

Opening actions, instructional actions and closing actions

To plan the extra activities proposed above, it is useful to follow, as a guide, a general model for lesson planning which, in addition to the main steps of the instructional strategy adopted, contains provision for certain 'opening' and 'closing' actions. The opening actions should motivate the learners to participate fully in the learning activities that follow, by making the lesson's objectives clear and establishing their importance to the learner. It is also important to ensure, at this stage, that the learners are ready to study the content of the lesson: for example, do they have all the prerequisite knowledge and skills? The closing events should evaluate the results of the lesson, but they should also ensure that the learning will be of real future use. We present an outline of our model below.

Opening actions

'Now hear this'

1. *Attention and motivation.* We should begin the lesson with some form of statement, quick presentation or initial activity, which will grab the attention of the learners and make them receptive to the lesson and ready to participate in the activities to follow. This may be a short story, a joke, a captivating visual, or some form of question to which the learners relate, but to which they have no immediate answer. This opener should leave the learners with the feeling that 'something worth learning' is about to be introduced.

'This is where we are going'

2. *Statement of the objectives.* Once the learners' interest has been awakened, it is usually a good idea to define more precisely what they are going to learn. The learners deserve to receive the lesson's objectives, clearly stated, right at the beginning of the session. They may then use these objectives to self-evaluate their learning progress during the stages that follow. They will probably ask more relevant questions, tackle the learning exercises more intelligently and avoid too many digressions into other topics.

'Do you remember?'

3. *Recall and revision of prerequisites.* A lesson often requires the use of certain knowledge or skills that the learners should have acquired in earlier stages. These prerequisites are identified during the analysis of the lesson's objectives and may include recent learning included in earlier lessons, or some basic skills which should have been developed at much earlier stages of the learner's development. In both these cases, it will be necessary to include some exploratory questions or diagnostic activities to verify that the prerequisites really have been mastered by all the learners. This is of vital importance when a sequentially structured topic is being taught, as in the case of any principle learning, which depends on the previous learning of the component concepts.

When these diagnostic questions reveal incomplete mastery, it is necessary to revise and reinforce this previous learning before going on. The lesson plan should make provision for the revision of prerequisites, when necessary, indicating how this revision may be carried out, how much time may be required and what the effects will be on the execution of the later stages of the lesson. If such revision is carried out regularly, there is less chance of the creation of large gaps in students' learning.

Instructional actions

'Here comes the message'

4. *The instruction activities.* These are the activities carried out by the instructor, or by some other component of the instructional system, with the intention of transmitting new information to the learner, orienting him in his studies or setting up a problem or situation for the learner to experience. In the case of expositive strategies, these activities are mainly explanations, or demonstrations of what is to be learned. In the case of experiential strategies, they may take the form of data

Figure 2.6 *A detailed lesson plan illustrating the use of an expositive strategy.*

Lesson title: Job performance evaluation.
Target population: Foremen and supervisors at XYZ company.
Number of trainees: Maximum 20.
Time: 1½ hours.

Lesson objectives: The trainees should be able to use standard company procedures and documentation in order to evaluate the job performance of their immediate subordinates, being judged as competent by an experienced evaluator who compares their evaluations of certain workers with his own evaluations of the same workers.

Equipment/resources required:
☐ Documentation used for evaluating job performance (20 sets).
☐ Handout, describing 10 performance case histories to be used in group training exercises (20 copies).
☐ Flipcharts, showing the structure of the documentation used and other summary information, to be used as visual aids.
☐ Chalkboard or overhead projector for other classroom work.

Information (stimulus)	Behaviour (response)	Feedback (reinforcement)	Time
Opening actions			
1. Attention Hold a short discussion of the use and limitations of job performance evaluation, in the departments of XYZ company.	Trainees should demonstrate their attitudes, both positive and negative, to the use of job performance evaluation.	Observe the attitudes and attempt to form uniformly positive ones, by illustrating the possible uses of evaluation as a management tool.	10 minutes
2. Objectives Explain the lesson objectives, as stated above. Invite questions.	Trainees should clarify any doubts they may have.	All trainees should understand the objectives before continuing.	5 minutes
3. Prerequisites Explain importance of specific criteria for each job in the department. Set a criterion definition task.	Each trainee should define the criteria for each job performed in his department.	Trainees may compare notes, or seek help from colleagues in their department. The criteria must be realistic.	20 minutes
Instructional actions			
4. Knowledge Explain the principles of the system of performance evaluation adopted by the company. Distribute copies of the forms that will be used.	Study the forms to identify the way that each one should be used. Ask for explanations of any aspects that are not quite clear.	Correct and explain any difficulty of comprehension of the principles and procedures on which the company's job evaluation system is based.	10 minutes
5. The scale Distribute 10 descriptions of job performance. Demonstrate the use of a five-point scale for the classification of four of the 10 described cases.	In groups of three, study the other six cases and try to agree on the classifications of the performance described. Then each group should compare and discuss its results with the others.	Observe the work of the groups, helping them to classify the examples correctly. Distribute a checklist to assist the groups in the self-evaluation of their work.	20 minutes

Figure 2.6 – *continued*

Information (stimulus)	Behaviour (response)	Feedback (reinforcement)	Time
6. The forms Demonstrate how to complete the job evaluation forms for the four cases that were used as demonstrations previously.	Each trainee should complete one or two forms evaluating some of the other six cases and should then compare his evaluations with those of other participants.	Observe the individual exercise and assist anyone with difficulties. After 10 minutes, distribute a completed form as a model to be used for self-evaluation.	20 minutes
Closing actions **7. Evaluation** Organize a practical exercise to be performed by each supervisor at his place of work. Explain that he should evaluate three of his immediate subordinates. Supply the necessary forms.	Each trainee, on returning to his job, should evaluate three of his staff, each on different jobs. He should then send the forms to training department, within one week of the course ending.	Compare the evaluations made by the trainees with other evaluations of the same employees that were made as part of the routine job evaluations in the company. Feed back comments and corrections to the trainees.	This is to be done after the lesson.
8. Summary and further study Distribute checklist of procedure to be followed in evaluating staff. Indicate a reading list that may be used to learn more about performance evaluation and how to use the results.	–	–	5 minutes

presented as a case study, the rules of a simulation or game that the learners will participate in, or the arrangement of particular real-life experiences for the learners.

'And this is what you should do'
5. *The learning activities.* These are the activities that should be performed by the learners, both to learn the content being presented in the lesson and to show what they have learned. In the case of expositive strategies, these activities are mainly composed of answers to questions posed by the instructor, or the performance of tasks previously demonstrated by the instructor. In the case of experiential strategies, the learning activities may take many forms, such as participation in group discussions, brainstorming sessions, games, role-play exercises, simulations and projects.

'Oops . . . let's try again'
6. *The feedback activities.* These are the activities of online formative evaluation – observation of the effects of each step in the lesson and reinforcement of any weak aspects. Usually these activities are performed by the instructor, even when the basic transmission of information is effected by means of other media, such as videocassettes. However, in truly self-instructional systems, these activities must be performed by the learner himself through his interaction with the material. This can be achieved up to a point in printed materials, by means of various questioning techniques as in programmed instruction. A much more powerful and varied approach is possible through the imaginative use of computer-assisted instruction.

In the case of expositive strategies, the feedback activities generally take the form of formal tests or informal questioning and observation of the learners by the instructor, followed by corrective actions, reorientation, new explanations, extra practice exercises and so on, until all the learners exhibit an adequate mastery of the specific objectives of the lesson. In the case of experiential strategies, the feedback activities take the form of analytical discussions with the learners, debriefing sessions, individual discussions, or presentation of the results of actions or decisions taken in simulation sessions, etc.

Closing actions

'And now for something completely different - or is it?'

7. *The transfer of learning.* In many lessons, especially those which attempt to teach general principles or problem-solving strategies, it is necessary to provide ample opportunities for varied practice to ensure that the learners are capable of transferring what they have learned in certain specific situations (used as examples during the lesson) to other quite different situations, where the same principles or strategies still apply. Often, transfer may be promoted during the lesson, by deeper analytical questioning or by the presentation of a wide variety of problems for solution by the students. Sometimes, however, transfer may best be promoted after the lesson, through real-life situations, either on the job or at home. Another way is through homework or individual projects to be completed after the lesson. In all these cases, however, the planning of these transfer activities forms part of the process of planning the lesson. They should, therefore, appear in the lesson planning document.

'So let's see where we have got to'

8. *Evaluation of the lesson.* Although the formative evaluation of learning progress is a continuous activity, forming part of all the lesson steps (especially 4, 5, 6 and 7), it is nevertheless usually necessary to arrange a final end-of-lesson evaluation of the results of learning. This evaluation may be used for summative purposes, as in the grading of students on a continuous basis, or formative purposes, enabling the instructor to plan the next lessons of the sequence better, or to replan the current lesson to improve its effectiveness on the next occasion he has to give it. Generally, the final evaluation of the lesson takes the form of a test of the lesson's objectives, by means of written or oral questions or practical exercises. Often, an attempt is also made to evaluate the learners' reactions to the lesson and its content by means of open discussion or a formal attitude questionnaire. This does not have to be done at the end of all lessons, but should occur with reasonable regularity. Sometimes, however, the final evaluation can only be performed after the lesson, by observation of on-the-job performance standards of certain tasks, or the behaviour of the learners over a period of time after instruction. Affective objectives, for example, must generally be evaluated by measuring the changes in the learners' attitudes and general behaviour after completion of learning. In such cases, follow-up activity must be performed. The plan of this follow-up should appear in the lesson planning document.

'And where can we go from here?'

9. *Summary and further study.* The last step in the lesson is a summary of what has been achieved, and an indication of where the learners might proceed next. At this point, there is the opportunity for the distribution of reference notes, enrichment materials, extra, optional exercises, reading lists and suggestions on how interested learners might extend their study of the lesson's topics beyond the objectives that were pre-set for the lesson.

We are not suggesting that all nine steps must necessarily appear in every lesson plan. Some of the steps are of particular importance only in lessons dealing with certain types of objectives. The list should be used as a general model for lesson planning and should be adapted to the special characteristic of each particular lesson. It may also be of interest to compare this lesson, which employs an overall expositive strategy, with the earlier example of a lesson plan employing an experiential, or discovery-learning strategy (Map 2.7 earlier in this chapter).

3. The selection of media

3.1 A basic media selection model

3.1.1 Factors affecting media choice

Let us first consider briefly the factors which might affect decisions about the choice of particular media. Some of these are illustrated in Figure 3.1. Firstly, a choice of a particular instructional *method* will often dictate, or at least limit, our choice of presentation media. For example, if it is necessary to use a method involving group discussion and the sharing of experiences, then obviously a one-direction medium of presentation such as a tape recorder or television would not be suitable, as it limits the opportunity for feedback and exchange of ideas. Secondly, the type of *learning task* facing the student will also eventually influence the media choice, because it dictates or limits the choice of suitable methods of instruction. For example, the training of some supervisory and personnel management skills is often achieved by group discussion, where individual managers share experiences with others. This may be built round a standard case study which is filmed. However, the necessary group discussion element in this type of training will influence the methods chosen and therefore dictate the appropriate media. Thirdly, the *special characteristics of some students* will directly influence the media to be chosen. For example, it would be unrealistic to attempt

Instructional method

Learning task

Learner characteristics

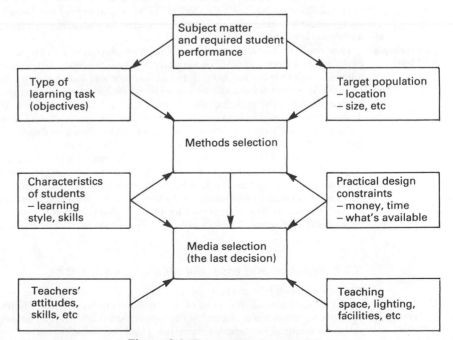

Figure 3.1 *Factors influencing media selection.*

Practical constraints

to instruct a group of slow readers using printed material, as you would be introducing other problems into the learning process. And finally, we should not overlook the *practical constraints*, both administrative and economic, which may limit the choice of methods and media. It appears reasonable, therefore, that before we make any decision about appropriate media we should first of all make appropriate decisions about the instructional methods to be employed; and to make these decisions we should consider the students, the type of learning concerned and any practical constraints which happen to exist.

Human factors

Perhaps we should add one further factor to our list – the teacher. You may like using an overhead projector or you may hate it. If you do happen to have a particular aversion to or phobia of a certain medium of instruction, then you are unlikely to use it well. Whatever the theoretical benefits of the device, they are likely to be wiped out if the skills to use the device are lacking. And it is not only a question of skills. Attitudes count too. In most of the long-term evaluation studies of the use of such 'automated' media as programmed instruction or broadcast television, it has been found that the way the medium is integrated into the course and the feelings of the teaching staff have been among the most important factors affecting the success of the experiment. Thus, while we hope that the teacher has an open mind towards the use of alternative media, we also hope that when faced with equally appropriate alternatives, he will follow his instinct and 'do his own thing'. Blatant disregard for important characteristics of the learning situation (whether task factors, learner characteristics or practical constraints) will inevitably lead to poor course design. But it is no good having a perfect design if you are unable or unwilling to implement it.

Is this book an appropriate medium for its message?

Teachers' skills and attitudes are probably outside the scope of this book, but let's follow them up as an example of media selection. One indirect objective of this book is certainly that the reader should form favourable attitudes towards the systematic use of media (ie should attempt to apply the principles outlined and seek out more information about them). However, we must be realistic. Books impart information but information by itself is seldom sufficient to change attitudes (consider traffic infringements, industrial accidents, wars). However, the print medium, though not the best for achieving *affective* objectives, is often very good at achieving *cognitive* objectives. Thus we might expect this book to be more successful at teaching already interested readers to plan and implement lessons in a systematic manner.

How can we find out?

How could we test the attainment of such an objective? By comparing teacher performance before and after on standardized lesson-preparation exercises. What follows in this chapter has been tested in this way and found to work quite well. How could we test for the affective objectives? By following up the performance of readers for a lengthy period of time both before and after exposure to the book. This is quite impractical, so one relies on snippets of feedback such as the comments of one's own students, readers' letters, etc. Such feedback, though imperfect, is still useful, and is always welcome. Please write!

The structure of the rest of this chapter will be made up in part of algorithms, check lists and decision tables, which are designed to serve as job aids for the systematic selection of media. It is hoped that these will be useful to the reader in the practical lesson-design situation for long after the book has been read. Readers are encouraged to choose their own lesson topic and try the job aids out on that as they read this chapter. A fairly practical topic should be chosen initially.

3.1.2 *Optional and essential media characteristics*

Classifying media:

Before we launch into the body of this chapter, we should consider the range of media at our disposal, and some of their general characteristics. Figure 3.2 presents a classification of some of the media. Although a large number are shown, this is by no means a comprehensive list. However, sufficient are included to illustrate the general characteristics that may be used to classify them.

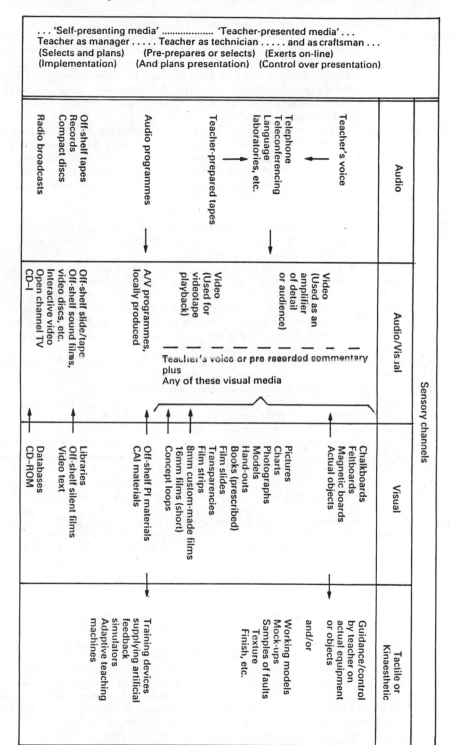

Figure 3.2 *A classification of presentation media.*

Two important points emerge from this classification:

– by sensory channel

1. The 'sensory channel' classification is fairly precise. Most people would agree where to place a given medium in this classification. The 'teacher control' classification is much less precise. Certain films, for example, being short and in clearly defined sections, are more under the teacher's control than others (in the sense that the teacher may think of many ways of showing the film, altering the sequence of parts, stopping for a discussion, etc).

– by teacher control

2. The 'teacher control' factor is but one of a large number of similar factors that one might have used for classifying the media. Examples of other factors which are particularly important to consider are: large groups, small groups or individual study; fixed or variable rates of presentation; suitability for stable subject matter or for subject matter which often changes; learner-control etc.

– by many other possible factors

This classification is not therefore particularly useful as it stands. One would require a multi-dimensional classification and even if one could devise such a comprehensive classification, different people would no doubt wish to place particular media in different positions.

The sole purpose of presenting Figure 3.2 here is to illustrate that the choice of media is a complex decision, influenced by a variety of factors, and therefore no quick and easy all-embracing rule is likely to be developed. Also it illustrates that the search for a classification or taxonomy of media is a counter-productive exercise, if approached in terms of the normal 'labels' attached to media (ie film, TV, concept loop). If we need further evidence of this, we need only look at the results of half a century of media research.

What does the research say to help us?

Whenever media are compared we usually get 'no significant difference' results. Peggie Campeau (1972) suggests that this may well be due to the 'blanket' nature of the research. One medium favours the achievement of some of the course objectives while the other favours the achievement of others. Thus existing differences cancel out in the overall experiment. Another reason may be that the subject matter chosen for experiments may pre-judge the result. Naturally you compare two media on a topic where both have a reasonable chance of success. No one would set up a comparison of a printed book and a tape recording for a course on bird-song recognition: one medium is obviously inappropriate. So you choose an experimental topic which does not seem to favour either medium particularly, and are then surprised when no significant differences are found in the experimental results.

The message, not the medium, is what teaches

The 'mythology' of media must be stripped away. A particular medium, be it reality, book or BBC broadcast, is no more than a particular form of 'packaging' for a set of instructional stimuli. The quality of the packaging should not be neglected (ask any ad-man), but what really matters is the functional aspect of the package. Can the package hold the contents – is the medium capable of presenting the instructional stimuli required for learning? Can it arrange for the students to engage in the required learning activity? Very often, no one medium is capable of presenting *all* the required stimuli, so we are led to prescribe a 'multi-media package'. However, the only scientific justification for a multi-media approach is that one medium either is not capable of presenting all the required learning stimuli, or is not capable of eliciting all the required student responses.

The thoery that presenting the same information in several media enhances the learning process, though widely held, is little supported by experimental results. Similarly, experiments on the quality of a presentation (eg should we use colour or black and white TV) give inconclusive results when performed under controlled conditions. The trend of media research so far appears to lead to the conclusion that (as far as cognitive objectives are concerned) learning is influenced by the quality of the presentation only to the extent that the quality influences the clarity of the message.

We shall go more deeply into specific research findings related to specific media in relevant later chapters. We will see that most of the findings that seem to be reasonably conclusive relate to specific aspects of the medium concerned (what can be done with it) or to questions of the efficiency with which specific media can be used to perform specific instructional tasks. In this chapter, we shall consider the general research on media as promoters of more effective learning. We shall see that, as our purpose is merely to summarize the useful findings, we shall not take up much space at this point.

Inconclu-siveness of early research

Since Peggie Campeau, many other researchers have devoted themselves to reviewing and summarizing the thousands of research studies that the media effectiveness question has spawned over the last 70 years or so. Early reviews tended to perform a sort of 'head count' of all reported studies, weed out those that were obviously too unreliable in terms of their experimental design and then classify the others into three categories – medium *A* more effective, medium *B* (usually the mythical 'traditional instruction') more effective, and thirdly 'no significant difference'. After several such studies consistently gave between 70% and 80% in the 'nsd' category with the remainder divided pretty close to equally between the other two categories, researchers stopped to think.

Insigni-ficance of the findings of meta-analyses

What they came up with was the 'meta-analysis', which involves the statistical combination of the results from various studies into one, more thorough analysis – if one solitary study shows little then perhaps a hundred similar studies, combined, will indicate a significant trend. In this field, perhaps the most prolific meta-analyst has been James Kulik, who, together with his collaborators, has meta-analysed just about every significant media/technology trend of the last decade, including the Keller Plan (1979), the Audiotutorial (1979), programmed instruction (1980), computer-based college teaching (1980), visual-based instruction (Cohen, Ebling and Kulik, 1981), computer-based education in secondary schools (1983), ditto in elementary schools (1985), and adult education (1980). Unfortunately, despite all this effort and statistical sophistication, the conclusions persist – the majority of studies individually show no significant differences and when 'pooled', yield, at best, only slight advantages for the innovative technologies. For example, the study on visual-based instruction analysed 320 research studies on all manner of audiovisual-versus-teacher comparisons, selected 72 that were soundly designed and comparable, and found that 74% of these showed the dreaded 'nsd' result. On the other hand, 75% of the remainder registered significant differences in favour of the mediated instruction. But hang on, that is only 19% of the total. And *how* significant is significant? Kulik reports that the size of these 'statistically significant' gains is of the order of 1.5 percentage points on a final exam. There is a world of difference between statistical and practical significance!

Media as 'mere vehicles'

The upshot of such studies is that researchers at last agree that they have been asking the wrong questions all these years. But they do not yet agree on what are the right questions. For some it is the study of visual literacy, or semiotics. For others (eg Salomon, 1979) it is the pursuit of media 'attributes' defined by the symbol systems they operate with. Yet others, for example Richard Clarke (1983, 1985), have come to the conclusion that no media, in their own right, have any influence on learning effectiveness, but are mere 'vehicles' for more, or less, well designed instruction.

But vehicles vary in the pleasure they provide . . .

Having said that, however, who would deny that they get more pleasure (and perhaps spend more time) watching colour TV than black and white TV? The completely unexpected speed with which colour television became established cannot be simply explained as 'keeping up with the Joneses'. Pressures built up which caused the BBC to go for colour in their schools broadcasting several years earlier than planned. Furthermore, who would deny that a multi-media presentation, if well put together, is more enjoyable than a presentation using only one medium throughout? It would seem therefore that design factors which

. . . and in their efficiency

influence the quality of the 'package' may have a very important role in helping to ensure that learners participate in the presentation, and thus may help to achieve the course objectives in the open, non-experimental, situation.

It seems appropriate therefore to think in terms of two classes of media characterics:

1. *Essential media characteristics.* These are the ones which control the *clarity* of the message. For example, the demonstration of a high-speed manual skill demands a moving visual presentation for clarity (it may even demand a slow-motion movie presentation). Learning a foreign vocabulary requires print (to recognize the words) and audio media (to pronounce them).
2. *Optional media characteristics.* These are the characteristics which will improve the *quality* of the presentation. There are several considerations which might influence one's choice, for example:
    (a) Choosing media which are attractive to the learner (eg use of colour, dramatization, animation, cartoons, illustration, etc).
    (b) Choosing media which fit the learner's study habits (it appears that some learn better from print, others from the spoken word). As we know so little about learner preferences, this may best be arranged by incorporating alternatives and giving the learner a choice.
    (c) Choosing media which fit the teacher's teaching habits, skills and preferences.
    (d) Choosing media for a particular application where there is some evidence from previous research that marginal improvements in learning efficiency will result.

3.1.3 Media selection as part of lesson design

Given the overwhelming evidence from the research that in the field of instruction it is the design of the message and the teacher-learner interactions, rather than media factors, which really make the difference, it seems logical that media selection should be part of an overall procedure for the design of instruction. This is a gratifying conclusion to reach in the 1980s, as it coincides with the approach I adopted when first called upon to develop a media selection procedure back in the 1960s.

This procedure was developed in 1966/67, initially for the training of technical instructors, but then used more widely and first published in *Selection and Use of Teaching Aids* (1968). This early book was rewritten and expanded in the 1970s (*Selection and Use of Instructional Media*, 1974), at which time the model was somewhat enlarged, but not modified substantially. Now the book is undergoing a rewrite in the 1980s and the chapter which requires the least amount of updating is the one which presents the basic model. The context of the model has changed out of all recognition, however. New media, from computers to videodiscs, have appeared. Many other media selection models have been developed and, not least, the mushrooming growth of distance education systems has added a new dimension to the selection of media: the process is no longer the sole prerogative of the teacher or 'micro' instructional designer, but is ever more often the responsibility of some central group of 'macro' planners.

For this reason, the present chapter has been much enlarged. In the first part, the original lesson-design-based model is presented, much in its original form. In the second part, other models are presented, analysed and contrasted. Finally, in the last part we look at the different levels of planning in which media selection decisions may be taken and analyse the factors which should be taken into account at each of these levels.

We shall in the last section also come back to the lesson planning model presented here, and update it in certain respects. In particular, we shall develop some improved tools and instruments for the practical implementation of the model. These include 'conceptual schemata' as tools to think with more creatively, and improved, more detailed lesson planning instruments as tools to document our thoughts more completely.

Procedure for lesson design

The overall procedure suggested is shown schematically in Figure 3.3. It is based on an application of the systems approach, and has been drawn to concentrate on the stages of media selection. The initial task analysis stages which lead up to the statement of behavioural objectives have been omitted (they were described in the previous chapters) and the implementation and evaluation stages (stages 9 and 10) have been merely hinted at. Let us now look more closely at each stage in the procedure.

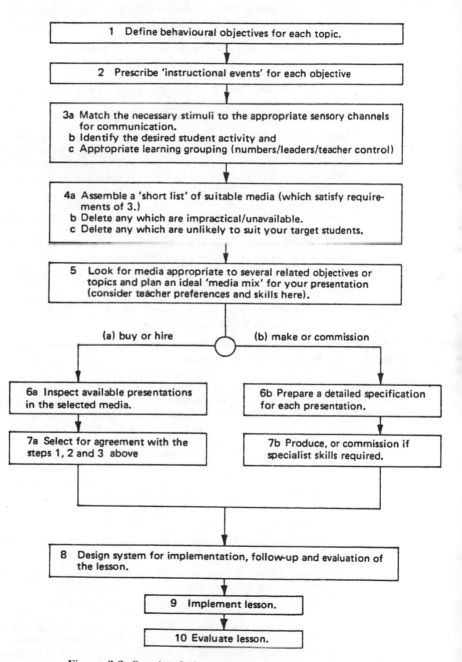

Figure 3.3 *Procedure for lesson design (emphasis on media selection).*

– objectives   1. *Define behavioural objectives for each topic*
We select media for each objective in turn. A one-hour lesson may contain one, five, ten or perhaps twenty quite distinct behavioural objectives. It is highly probable that different objectives will require different instructional methods, which in turn will demand different media characteristics.

– instruc-   2. *Prescribe the 'instructional events' for each objective*
tional   The term 'instructional event' is used here rather than 'teaching method' because
events   it illustrates the 'micro' level at which we are operating. Teaching methods are made up of instructional events. For example, a classroom demonstration of how a particular mechanism works might involve:

(a) showing the mechanism (presenting the stimulus);
(b) directing attention to the relevant parts;
(c) explaining their function;
(d) encouraging students to apply previously learnt general principles;
(e) questioning students;
(f) providing feedback to students, and so on.

This particular example calls for both visual and verbal media (whether the verbal should be written or spoken is not clear from our analysis so far, and may well be optional). Gagné suggested that different media may not be equally good at performing different instructional functions. Some of his suggestions are summarized in Figure 3.4. This figure is presented only as a general outline. It is not to be used as a job aid, since it is not precise enough for this purpose. For example, if we examine his first instructional function 'presenting the stimulus', then surely we will agree that still pictures are good at presenting certain visual stimuli, moving pictures may be equivalent and in some cases better, but neither will communicate an audio stimulus if this is necessary.

The left-hand column of Figure 3.4 lists a sequence of instructional 'events' which Gagné recommended in 1965 as a basic outline for lesson design. Since 1965, Gagné has somewhat modified this list of events, adding one important event – the transfer of learning to new situations – which we also shall introduce in our planning instrument, later in this chapter.

– essential   3. *Identify essential media characteristics*
charac-   This is how we fix the *essential* media characteristics:
tereristics

(a) The type of responses required of the students (ie discriminating, manipulating, identifying, deducing, etc) suggest certain practice exercises which in turn dictate certain media characteristics.
(b) The type of stimuli required to communicate the message clearly are identified, and dictate the sensory channels which our presentation uses.
(c) The student group size and geographical scatter may be fixed factors, or may be variable in certain situations. Certain instructional events may demand large or small groups for efficiency. Others may suggest individual study. Nevertheless, once the audience group size and their geographical scatter is fixed (whether by the course designer or by external constraints) certain essential media characteristics are also fixed.

As jobs aids for fixing the essential media characteristics, a series of algorithms have been prepared:

● Figure 3.5 aids the matching of the type of responses required by the learning task to appropriate media characteristics.
● Figures 3.6 and 3.8 aid the matching of visual and audio requirements of the stimuli to appropriate media characteristics.
● A further flow chart (Figure 3.7) matches group size and type of learning task to appropriate media. This differs from the other three in that it is not really an algorithm. The relation between the learning task and group size is not precise.

Functions	Media						
	Objects; Demonstration	Oral Communication	Printed Media	Still Pictures	Moving Pictures	Sound Movies	Teaching Machines
Presenting the stimulus	Yes	Limited	Limited	Yes	Yes	Yes	Yes
Directing attention and other activity	No	Yes	Yes	No	No	Yes	Yes
Providing a model of expected performance	Limited	Yes	Yes	Limited	Limited	Yes	Yes
Furnishing external prompts	Limited	Yes	Yes	Limited	Limited	Yes	Yes
Guiding thinking	No	Yes	Yes	No	No	Yes	Yes
Inducing transfer	Limited	Yes	Limited	Limited	Limited	Limited	Limited
Assessing attainments	No	Yes	Yes	No	No	Yes	Yes
Providing feedback	Limited	Yes	Yes	No	Limited	Yes	Yes

Figure 3.4 *Instructional functions of various media as suggested by Gagné (1965).*

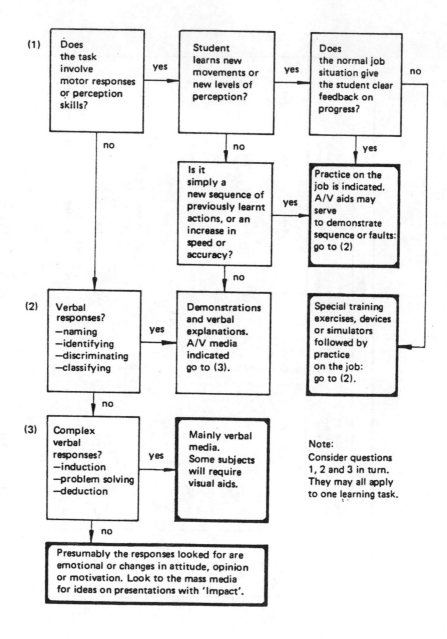

Figure 3.5 *Decisions for the matching of learning task to media characteristics.*

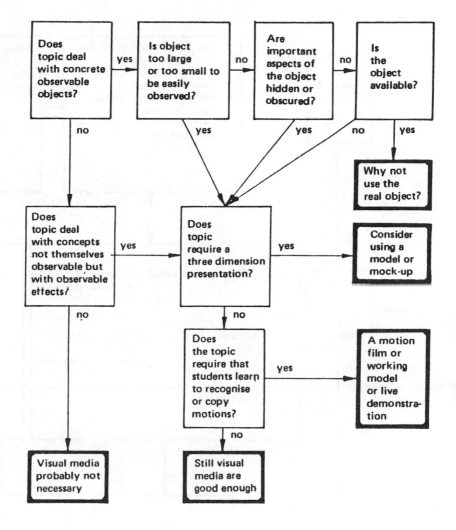

Figure 3.6 *Decisions for selecting visual media.*

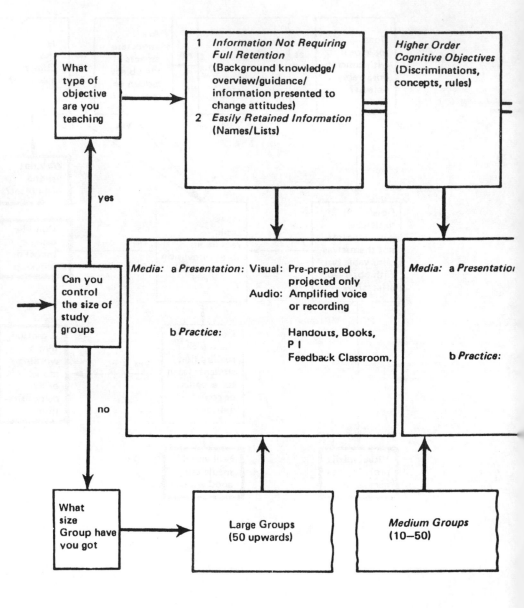

Figure 3.7 *Decisions for matching group size to media characteristics.*

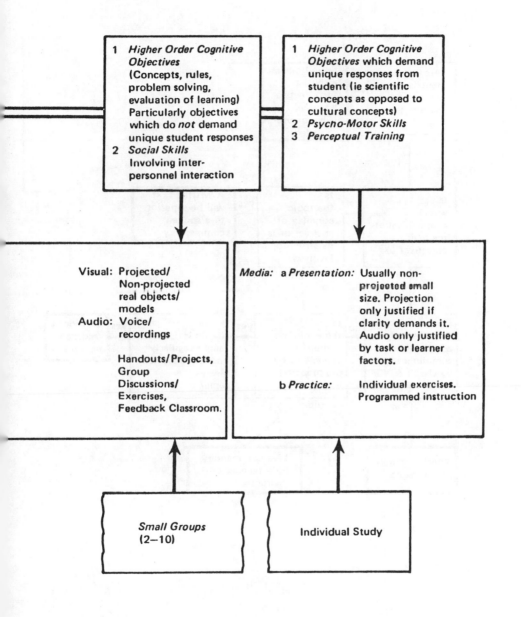

1 *Higher Order Cognitive Objectives* (Concepts, rules, problem solving, evaluation of learning) Particularly objectives which do *not* demand unique student responses
2 *Social Skills* Involving inter-personnel interaction

1 *Higher Order Cognitive Objectives* which demand unique responses from student (ie scientific concepts as opposed to cultural concepts)
2 *Psycho-Motor Skills*
3 *Perceptual Training*

Visual: Projected/ Non-projected real objects/ models
Audio: Voice/ recordings

Handouts/Projects, Group Discussions/ Exercises, Feedback Classroom.

Media: a *Presentation:* Usually non-projected small size. Projection only justified if clarity demands it. Audio only justified by task or learner factors.

b *Practice:* Individual exercises. Programmed instruction

Small Groups (2–10)

Individual Study

70   *Instructional Design and the Media Selection Process*

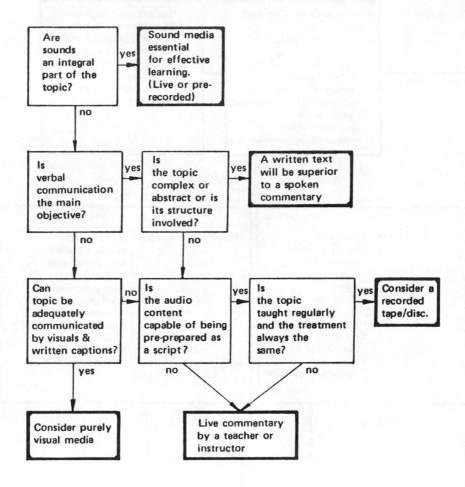

Figure 3.8 *Decisions for selecting verbal and sound media.*

– media short-list

4. *Assemble 'short-list' of suitable media*

It is at this stage that one 'exercises one's options'.

(a) The first short-list includes all the media which satisfy the essential media characteristics identified in stage 3.

(b) Delete any which are impractical or unobtainable, or otherwise unsuitable due to environmental constraints. Figure 3.9 may be used as a job aid at this stage.

(c) Delete any which are unlikely to suit your students, whether due to their learning habits, past experiences or psychological characteristics. This is probably the most difficult to do. We often know so little about our students. Sometimes, however, we know with a fair level of confidence that, for example, our students are happier studying individually at home or in the library, than in formal groups, or we may know that a previous teacher used so much TV (and used it badly) that the group is heartily sick of it. Psychological characteristics are more difficult still, for not only must we know what the research findings are (precious few valid studies exist anyway), but also we must be able to recognize these characteristics in our students. There are some indications from research that 'realism' pays off more with low IQ groups than with high IQ groups; that being able to touch and manipulate objects is more important for students with poor mechanical ability, and so on. However, these differences (although they have led to statistically significant results in experiments) are not usually very large, and not always easy to identify in our student group. Furthermore, any group is likely to have a spread of IQ, of mechanical abilities, spatial abilities, reading ages or what have you. Unless we develop individualized course materials, with alternative sets of materials (using alternative media and having alternative contents) we cannot hope to deal effectively with individual differences. Although we may well subscribe to this ideal of individualized instruction, in practice we often have to compromise, developing one set of materials which will suit most of our students reasonably, but few of them perfectly.

To illustrate the variety of interrelated factors which might influence our decisions, let us consider just one decision which might be called for in a hypothetical course. Suppose we wished to teach the working of a mechanism (perhaps the internal combustion engine). Suppose we have identified that visual stimuli are essential. Suppose furthermore that we may practicably make available a set of still diagrams (overhead projector transparencies) or a movie film, or a working (but simplified) model. As the cost increases considerably for each of these options, we wish to assess whether we will get away with the still pictures, or whether the more expensive options are worth considering. Figure 3.10 presents a set of considerations which should be weighed up in making our decision. The first ten considerations are concerned with the learning task, the next ten are concerned with student factors.

Try for yourself the internal combustion engine example.

– select from the list

5. *Plan final 'media mix'*

At this stage our choice of media for each lesson objective should be relatively small. A final choice should now be made in the light of the following two factors:

(a) Certain groups of objectives, to be taught together, may well be taught by means of the same media, for convenience. Look for media common to several related objectives.

(b) The personal preferences of the teachers who will be involved in the course should be considered. If you are planning a course which you will teach, your personal preferences may already be partly mirrored by the weight you attach to various practical constraints and optional media characteristics. If, however, you are planning a course for other teachers (and you know who these will be) you would do well to investigate their

When more than one media option seems appropriate the alternatives should be considered in the light of the following questions, and the most practicable chosen.

Any option which gives one or more 'No' answers, should be avoided. If no options seem appropriate, consider how you could modify either the media or the environment to eliminate the objections.

Negative considerations

		Yes	No
1	Can it be obtained or made at an economical price, relative to the importance of the topic being taught?		
2	Is there enough space to use it effectively?		
3	Will it operate in the conditions of the training area (temperature, humidity, power sources, transportability)?		
4	Is it student-proof (withstands careless handling, not prone to vanish)?		
5	Is it capable of being maintained, and repaired by the user?		
6	Will it have a reasonable working life (bearing in mind the cost), before it is rendered obsolete by changes in the subject?		

Figure 3.9 *Practical and environmental constraints.*

Keep a score of the letters A, B, and C for those questions where you answer YES. Select the high scoring medium.
A . . .Model; B . . .Still Visual; C . . .Movie Film.
Note Questions 1 — 7 relate to real objects only. They may be skipped if you are attempting to visually explain an abstract concept etc.

1 Complex shape or inside details which should be studied?	A: C.
2 Many inter-related parts, the relative position being of importance to the learner?	A: B.
3 Are the functions of the parts to be studied?	A: C.
4 Are the relative sizes important to learner?	A: B.
5 Is it so complex that detailed breakdown and analysis is required to fully understand it?	A: B.
6 Is the motion of the object or its parts to be studied?	A: C.
7 Is the sequence of opération to be studied?	A: B.
8 Is the purpose to demonstrate the performance of a manipulative or motor skill?	C.
9 Will student apply what he learns in an identical situation?	A: C.
10 Will student apply what he learns as general principles in a number of similar situations?	B.
11 Are students of above average IQ?	B.
12 Average or below average IQ?	A: C.
13 Do students need motivation?	C.
14 Are they already well motivated?	B.
15 Do they already have experience of the topic?	B.
16 Do they lack relevant experience?	C.
17 Do your students learn well from verbal or from visual material?	B: C.
18 Do they need to handle or operate equipment to ensure efficient learning?	A.
19 Do they have good mechanical ability?	B: C.
20 Do they have poor mechanical ability?	A.

Figure 3.10 *Optional media characteristics: model, still visual or film – check-list.*

instructional methods and preferences, and also the present level of their skills with respect to the media you are selecting.

6 and 7. *Make or buy*

– make or buy what is necessary

These steps are self-evident from the flow chart of our procedure (Figure 3.3). Whether you decide to use existing materials (usually the more economical solution) or to produce tailor-made materials, the important point to remember is that the statements of objectives for the course, the detailed prescriptions of instructional events and the identified essential media characteristics (ie steps 1, 2 and 3 of the procedure) should be used as controls over the materials to check their suitability for the course being planned.

8. *Design system of implementation and evaluation*

This stage involves:

– put it all together

(a) Designing appropriate tests for the lesson's cognitive and psychomotor objectives. This is therefore very closely linked with stage 1. As soon as the lesson objectives are specified in behavioural terms, one can derive appropriate test situations directly from them. Indeed we suggest that tests for the cognitive or psychomotor objectives of a lesson should be developed at stage 1, so that the conditions and standard implied by the objective are mirrored in the test. Otherwise, there is a danger that tests may not reflect the objectives exactly.

– planning for follow-up

(b) Designing appropriate ways in which the long-term effects of the lesson, and in particular the affective objectives, may be assessed. Very often these cannot be directly measured, but can only be sensed from the general atmosphere of the class, or deduced indirectly from subsequent activities (eg increased popularity of certain library books). Long-term retention of cognitive objectives can of course be measured by re-testing at a later date. Alternatively, indicators such as sustained improved job performance may be used. Affective objectives may also sometimes be deduced from later performance. For example, a greater adherence to basic safety precautions in a factory is generally a sign of a change in attitude rather than knowledge. Similarly, attendance figures at a series of lectures are often a significant measure of whether the lecturer is achieving his affective objectives. A thorough and very entertaining discussion of how to measure the attainment of affective objectives has been written by Bob Mager (1968). In this he stresses the value of observing 'avoidance' and 'approach' behaviour on the part of students.

– collecting the right data

When planning the evaluation of a lesson, or a course, it is well worth considering carefully just which of the many characteristics of the lesson you really want to evaluate, and what indicators are available for these characteristics. All too often data is collected which cannot later be used for any purpose. Sometimes essential data necessary for course improvement is overlooked.

Some further questions for consideration:

(a) If we set a test of cognitive objectives (with a view to improving the course) do we wish to know which students make mistakes, or what mistakes are made (and why)? Surely for course evaluation we need lots of 'mini-questions' (at least one per objective) rather than 'global' questions which test whole areas of knowledge? Furthermore, we need to be able to diagnose a particular weakness in the lesson from a particular error pattern. Tests which do not allow us to do this are useless for course-evaluation purposes.

– and using it correctly

(b) When do we want to compare students against each other? Certainly not when we are designing instruction. Nor when we are honestly engaged in instruction. In both these cases we really wish to compare students' performance against the desired learning objectives. Only if we are selecting students for some purpose do we need to compare their performances. Most educational systems are extremely

Subjects were asked to prepare a lesson plan for given objectives, making full use of any media they thought fit. These lesson plans were judged by a team of educational technologists and experts in teaching method. The lesson plans were classed as ideal, acceptable and poor.

The given objectives were:

At the end of the lesson, students should be able to:

1 State when, how and why a new (decimal) currency system is to be adopted by the UK.
2 Identify the new coins.
3 State their equivalents in the old currency.
4 Carry out simple cash transactions in new and mixed old/new coinage.

The lesson plans were classified as follows:-

Experienced Teachers Without Job-Aids (N = 52)

Objective No.	Ideal Plan	Acceptable Plan	Poor Plan
1	19	23	5
2	19	31	2
3	17	20	11
4	15	15	10
total	70	89	28

Inexperienced Trainee Teachers With Job-Aids (N = 58)

Objective No	Ideal Plan	Acceptable Plan	Poor Plan
1	56	2	0
2	37	21	0
3	41	15	2
4	32	26	0
total	166	64	2

N.B. The figures for each objective (reading across) in the 'Experienced Teachers' table do not all add up to (N = 5) as not all teachers addressed all 4 objectives in their lesson plans. This effect is not observed in the 'Trainee Teachers' group, as the Job-aids ensured that all 4 objectives were addressed separately.

Figure 3.11 *Summary of a study into the value of the algorithms and check-lists (Romiszowski, 1970).*

selection-orientated in their final examinations, and unfortunately this tendency to 'grade' students percolates down into the daily routine in the classroom. Students are given 'marks' which relate to how they have performed in relation to their group (eg the 'ten best essays' are rewarded with an A grade).

Does this media selection model work?

We have dealt in this chapter with our early (1967–74) procedures for lesson design, concentrating particularly on the selection of presentation media. The procedure attempts to be systematic, and in the attempt, may be accused of being a trifle long-winded. Readers can, however, take heart in the knowledge that lengthier procedures have also been suggested. Briggs (1970) outlines a procedure, which together with exercises for practice, fills a book of over two hundred pages. His handbook on instructional design is intended for study a few hours per week over a year or so by teachers in training. And who could argue that this is time mis-spent, on what is after all one of the basic skills of teaching?

Furthermore, although our procedure does appear lengthy, its use, with practice, does not take too much time. Many of the stages become intuitive. One 'telescopes' the procedure, performing several stages at one time. Certain types of objectives immediately trigger off certain approaches, because you have 'been here before'.

We do not claim to have here a procedure which should be followed in every respect, every time. Rather, it is offered as a framework, based on a particular view of the instruction process, which should enable the teacher to set about designing lesson plans which have a fair chance of being successful.

Does the procedure work? It certainly seems to. A small study using a prototype version of the job aids in this chapter was tested on groups of trainee teachers. Groups of experienced teachers were also asked to prepare lesson plans for the same instructional objectives. The results of the study were reported in full at an APLET conference in 1969 (Romiszowski, 1970). Figure 3.11 summarizing this report speaks for itself.

Of course, like any procedure, it works better for some than for others. Many past students have commented on or criticized certain aspects, and this has led to modifications.

We have found, for instance, that the method works better with (and is more readily accepted by) technical training instructors than school teachers. The modified approach presented later is more acceptable to the latter group. No great claims are made for these findings, based as they are on real-time reactions and individual results, rather than some programme of formal research.

The small research study was, however, encouraging and is still, according to Reiser and Gagné (1983), one of the few studies that have tested the effectiveness of a media selection procedure in practice. This point should be borne in mind when analysing the other models presented in the next part of this chapter.

3.2 Other media selection models and approaches

3.2.1 A proliferation of models

Media selection models: similarities and differences

For some reason, the 1970s was the decade for media selection. Only one or two models, apart from our own, originated in the 1960s and only one or two substantially new ones have appeared in the 1980s, but some twenty or more were developed in between. In reality, the similarities between all these models far outweigh the differences. As Ely (1980) points out, 'there are many media selection procedures and each one suggests similar steps'.

There are, of course detailed differences, but these tend to be confined to:

(a) differences in the level of detail, or the methodology of task analysis used, to define the instructional objectives of the lesson;
(b) differences in the instrumentation and type of job-aids used in the selection process.

Models that use a matrix

We shall use this latter aspect to impose some form of classification on the models to be discussed. The most common form of instrumentation used is some form of *matrix*, which crosses specific media (or media attributes) with specific instructional functions (events) or practical benefits (eg cost, flexibility). An early example of this approach was presented in Figure 3.4 (Gagné, 1965). Other models include those of Allen (1967, 1974), Branson *et al* (1975), Briggs (1970), McConnell (1974) and Tiffin and Combes (1980).

Models that use work-sheets

Another approach is to use some form of *worksheet* which guides the selection process as a check-list and documents the designer's decisions in a standard form. Examples include Durham *et al* (1974) and Locatis and Atkinson (1984).

Models that use flow charts

The third approach is of course the use of flow charts, or algorithms, to guide the selection process. This form of job-aid, born in the 1960s, had its heyday in the 1970s and many media selection flow charts of varied complexity were developed. In addition to my own modest effort (Romiszowski, 1968, 1974), notable examples include Bretz (1971), Kemp (1971, 1980), Anderson (1976), and, the most recent addition, Reiser and Gagné (1983). This last model, incidentally, uses a worksheet as well as a set of flow charts, and the worksheet is organized in the form of a matrix – the best of all worlds?

The common elements

Reiser and Gagné (1983), in presenting their model, also presented an analysis of a selection of previous attempts showing that, as Ely (1980) commented, most of them are indeed very similar in their basic premises (see Figure 3.12 and compare it with Figure 3.1 as well).

Factors	Models								
	Anderson	Branson *et al*	Bretz	Briggs and Wager	Gagné and Briggs	Gropper	Kemp	Romiszowski	Tosti and Ball
Learner, Setting, and Task Characteristics:									
Instructional Setting	X	X	X	X	X		X	X	
Learner Characteristics		X	X	X	X	X		X	
Categories of Learning Outcomes	X	X		X	X			X	X
Events of Instruction		X	X	X	X	X		X	X
Physical Attributes	X	X	X	X	X	X	X	X	X
Practical Factors	X	X	X	X	X	X	X	X	X

Note. An 'X' indicates that the factor was prominent in a model. A blank space indicates that a model and its accompanying description either did not mention the factor or gave it little attention.

Figure 3.12 *Factors prominent in various media selection models. (Adapted from Reiser and Gagné, 1983.)*

Having established a basic structure for classifying the models, let us examine some examples a bit more closely.

3.2.2 Matrix-based models

Ely (1980) states:

> 'Media selection often occurs on the basis of *availability, cost* and *personal preference*. Anyone who has used a particular medium and enjoyed success, is likely to use the same medium again. If an instructor knows that there is an overhead projector in the room where the class meets, it is likely that overhead transparencies will be selected. . . . Users of media do not necessarily have to deny the factors of access and preference but should take a moment to consider a basic rule for media selection:
>> A medium of instruction must be selected on the basis of its potential for implementing a stated objective (Gerlach and Ely, 1971).'

Allen's model   An early media selection model was developed by William Allen at the University of Southern California. In his model, the instructional designer must determine the general classification of an objective and then maximize the ability of the instructional media to accommodate that type of objective (see Figure 3.13 – Allen, 1967).

Allen's matrix is based on his review of hundreds of research studies. After discarding those not meeting rudimentary research criteria, he examined the effectiveness of the medium for the type of learning measured. From these results he created his matrix, which classifies media according to high, medium, or low achievement in that type of learning.

McConnell's model   The matrix drawn up by McConnell appears similar but is in fact quite different. It crosses media with media capabilities such as 'edit-ability' – a tool developed with the media developer in mind, not very helpful to the lesson designer (Figure 3.14).

	Learning Objectives					
Instructional Media Type	Learning Factual Information	Learning Visual Identifications	Learning Principles, Concepts, and Rules	Learning Procedures	Performing Skilled Perceptual-Motor Acts	Developing Desirable Attitudes, Opinions, and Motivations
Still pictures	Medium	HIGH	Medium	Medium	low	low
Motion pictures	Medium	HIGH	HIGH	HIGH	Medium	Medium
Television	Medium	Medium	HIGH	Medium	low	Medium
3-D objects	low	HIGH	low	low	low	low
Audio recordings	Medium	low	low	Medium	low	Medium
Programmed instruction	Medium	Medium	Medium	HIGH	low	Medium
Demonstration	low	Medium	low	HIGH	Medium	Medium
Printed textbooks	Medium	low	Medium	Medium	low	Medium
Oral presentation	Medium	low	Medium	Medium	low	Medium

Source: "Media Stimuli and Types of Learning." *Audiovisual Instruction.* Reprinted by permission of Association for Educational Communications and Technology. Copyright 1967.

Figure 3.13 *Allen media-selection model. (From 'Media stimuli and types of learning' in* Audiovisual Instruction. *Reprinted by permission of Association for Educational Communications and Technology. Copyright 1967.)*

Medium	Flexibility	Visual	Colour	Student control over pace of learning	Motion	'Edit-ability'
videotape reel	No, TV monitors are usually confined to a library or a classroom	Yes	Yes and no, it depends on the type of TV monitor and TV production equipment	No	Yes	No, editing requires much effort
videotape cassette	No, TV monitors and cassette players are usually confined to a library or classroom	Yes	Yes and no, it depends on the type of TV monitor and production equipment	Yes, the student can stop, rewind or fast forward the cassette; but learning pace is no faster than the speed of the cassette	Yes	No, editing requires much effort
non-illustrated workbook	Yes, it needs no electricity and can be taken almost anywhere	No	Yes and no, it depends on the production equipment	Yes, the student can read it as quickly or slowly as he likes	No	No, editing requires much effort
Illustrated workbook	Yes, it needs no electricity and can be taken almost anywhere	Yes	Yes and no, it is possible, but very expensive	Yes, the student can read it as quickly or slowly as he likes	No	No, editing require much effort
16mm film	No, 16 mm projectors are too heavy for a student to take home	Yes	Yes	No, unless the student is skilled at running a 16 mm projector	Yes	No, editing requires much effort
slides with script (audiotape optional)	Yes, a slide projector can be taken anywhere where electric current is available	Yes	Yes	Yes, the student can go through the slide script as quickly or slowly as he likes	No, but a series of slides can break a physical activity into its sequential steps; this is sometimes better than motion for study purposes	Yes and no, a series of slides can easily be altered in sequence, added to, or subtracted from; it is more difficult to edit the adjoining tape or workbook
audiotape	Yes, an audio cassette player can be taken almost anywhere but you will need a set of batteries	No	No	Yes, the student can stop, rewind or fast forward the tape but can learn only as fast as the tape runs	No	No, editing requires much effort

Figure 3.14 *A matrix relating key media characteristics to selected media (McConnell, 1973).*

Briggs' approach is yet different, crossing a list of media categories with a set of 26 factors which may or may not be important in a given instructional situation. This matrix is used as back-up to take secondary media decisions, after a short-list of media that satisfy essential instructional factors, has been drawn up (Figure 3.15).

Of course, the number of media has grown over the years and the number of selection factors to consider may also vary. Many other similar matrix models have been developed. One that I have used with success is much more detailed, listing a total of 43 different media, crossed with 23 selection factors. This was developed by Tiffin and Combes (1980), with the design of distance-education systems in mind.

3.2.3 Worksheet-based models

In his *Guidelines for Media Production,* Ely (1980) says:

Durham, Gerheart and Austin's model

'One media selection procedure which incorporates the elements of most models as well as practical factors was developed in 1974 by Durham, Gerheart, and Austin for EPA: *Selecting Instructional Media and Instructional Systems.* The steps developed for that publication are reproduced here with some minor modifications. The table, which helps to determine cost and content suitability for each medium, is an essential part of the selection process. These two selection tools can be used with a high degree of assurance that the "right" medium is being selected if all factors are considered in making the decision.' [See table in Figure 3.16.]

The procedure is as follows:

1. State the new behaviour (activity, performance) the student is to exhibit after the presentation.
2. Classify this new behaviour: (a) cognitive (having to do with factual information), (b) affective (dealing with feelings, emotions), (c) psychomotor (body movement). (If the new behaviour involves combinations of these types of behaviour, rank them in order of importance.)
3. Referrring to Figure 3.16, select the media which indicate greatest suitability (good to excellent) for this type of learning. List them in order of production costs with lowest cost first.
4. State which of the senses the student uses to exhibit this new behaviour. (If more than one sense is involved, rank them in order of importance.)
5. Indicate the media in step 3 which are lowest in cost and, where possible, which present information through the same senses the student will use when exhibiting the new behaviour.
6. Select the medium from those listed in step 5 which you can use most easily with your presentation facilities.
7. Is this medium suited for the kind(s) of presentation mode(s) for which this learning is designed? If not, select the next medium which meets this requirement, is lowest in cost, and is most easily available.

A worksheet which incorporates these steps is reproduced in Figure 3.17.

Locatis and Atkinson's model

A quite different form of worksheet approach uses a detailed check-list of questions. All have to be answered if at all possible and a final decision is reached by summing the positive and negative responses (see Figures 3.9 and 3.10). Other approaches may weight the responses or draw a profile to be compared to an 'ideal'. The example shown in Figure 3.18 is adapted from a model developed by Locatis and Atkinson (1984).

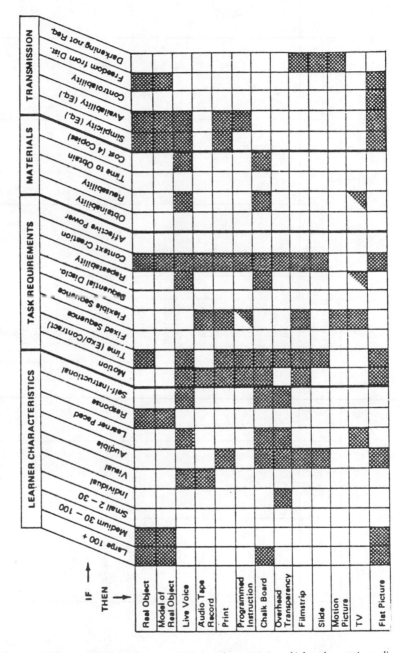

Figure 3.15 *An 'If–Then' chart summarizing characteristics which make certain media unsuitable or partly suitable for instruction. Produced by J G Wilshusen and R Stowe (from L J Briggs,* Handbook of Procedures for the Design of Structures, *1970).*

MEDIA	PRODUCTION COSTS	DUPLICATION COSTS	TYPE OF AUDIENCE	SUITABLE CONTENT			SENSES USED
				Cognitive	Affective	Psychomotor	
Printed materials	very low	very low	individual	Excellent	Fair	Good	Sight
Lecture	low	high	group	Fair	Good	Poor	Sight–Hearing
Audio-tape	low	low	group or individual	Poor	Fair	Poor	Hearing
Slides	low	low	group or individual	Good	Good	Good	Sight
Overhead transparency	mod. low	low	group	Good	Fair	Fair	Sight–Hearing
Slides/tapes	mod. low	low	group or individual	Good	Good	Excellent	Sight–Hearing
Television	high	mod. low	group or individual	Fair	Excellent	Excellent	Sight–Hearing
Motion pictures	very high	mod. low	group or individual	Fair	Excellent	Excellent	Sight–Hearing
Simulation	very high	very high	individual	Good	Good	Excellent	Sight–Hearing Smell–Touch Body movement

Figure 3.16 *Media costs and content suitabilities.*

(Adapted from Durham, Gerheart and Austin 1974. Reprinted in Ely 1980).
This table is used in conjunction with the worksheet alongside (Figure 3.17).

1. New behaviour:

2. Classification of new behaviour: (If more than one type of learning is involved, rank them in order of importance.)

    Cognitive (factual information) _____

    Affective (values, feelings, emotions) _____

    Psychomotor (body movement) _____

3. Media suitable for this type of learning (from Figure 3.16):

4. Sense used to exhibit new behaviour: (if more than one sense is involved, rank them in order of importance.)

    Sight _____

    Hearing _____

    Smell _____

    Touch _____

    Body movement _____

5. Cost of medium (Figure 3.16): Presentation through same sense as exhibited behaviour, in No. 4

6. Medium most easily produced and used locally:

7. Recommended medium for:

    Group presentation

    Individual use

Figure 3.17 *Worksheet for selecting media.*
(Adapted from Durham, Gerheart and Austin, 1974. Reprinted in Ely, 1980).

	Yes	No	?
I. Content			
A. Accurate and consistent?	___	___	___
B. Appropriate level of difficulty for audience?	___	___	___
C. Concise and easily understood?	___	___	___
D. Appropriate sequence?	___	___	___
E. Appropriate pacing?	___	___	___
F. Free of stereotyping, sexism, and racism?	___	___	___
Additional considerations:			
G.	___	___	___
H.	___	___	___
II. Instructional Design Features			
A. Objectives clearly stated?	___	___	___
B. Media format and instructional strategies appropriate for the audience, objectives, and content?	___	___	___
C. Learners required to make responses appropriate to the objective?	___	___	___
D. Learners provided with feedback regarding required responses?	___	___	___
E. Directions for learner and instructor clearly stated?	___	___	___
F. Suggestions provided to evaluate learning outcomes?	___	___	___
G. Are evaluation reports from previous users provided?	___	___	___
Additional considerations:			
H.	___	___	___
I.	___	___	___
III. Technical Aspects			
A. All media appropriate for the audience, objectives, and content?	___	___	___
B. Easy to see, hear, or read?	___	___	___
C. Available in a format that is compatible with existing equipment?	___	___	___
D. Can be used in existing teaching/learning facilities?	___	___	___
E. Do learners and/or instructors possess skills to use required equipment or are they willing to acquire these skills?	___	___	___
F. Time required for the media compatible with teaching/learning time available?	___	___	___
Additional considerations:			
G.	___	___	___
H.	___	___	___
IV. Packaging Qualities			
A. Packaging facilitates identification, storage, and handling?	___		___
B. Packaging durable enough for the use to which it will be put?	___		___
C. Is descriptive information adequate to expedite processing and retrieval?	___		___
D. If appropriate, can individual components be replaced (ie, if one cassette out of a set of six becomes damaged)?	___		___
Additional considerations:			
E.	___	___	___
F.	___	___	___
V. Cost			
A. Is the media affordable, and is the cost reasonable in light of its potential benefits?	___	___	___
B. Is the cost reasonable when compared to other methods of accomplishing the same objectives?	___	___	___
VI. Additional Considerations			
A.	___	___	___
B.	___	___	___

Figure 3.18 *Media selection check-list.*

3.2.4 Flowchart-based models

Perhaps the best known, and certainly one of the more complex flowchart-based models is that developed by Anderson (1976). There are 7 charts in all, of which we reproduce but one (chart 4) in Figure 3.19. The model is very thorough, dealing in chart 1 with non instructional (informational and motivational) uses of media. The model was used extensively when first developed, but I know of nobody who uses it regularly. Perhaps the complexity defeats its purpose.

This complexity could be reduced, as it was in my own 1968–1974 flowcharts, by:

(a) designing the charts to deal separately with major media categories (audio in one chart and vision in another)

(b) listing the outcomes in terms of basic media characteristics (eg still visual) rather than a litany of more or less equivalent specific media (apart from simplifying the chart it protects the model against rapid obsolescence).

Whilst we are making comparisons, one should note a basic difficulty that exists in most of the models being discussed. In order to use them, the user must learn to understand the technical terms (eg rules, principles, concepts. . . .) in the same way as the author of the model understands them. This is often the hardest part of mastering the model.

Another general criticism which may be made of all flowchart-based models is that they are over-rigid, in attempting to reduce to an algorithmic procedure, something which in reality is in large part a heuristic, creative process, of weighing up a host of interacting factors. It is probably for this reason that the model presented at the beginning of this chapter was less well accepted by school and university teachers than by instructors in industry – the former groups could see the limitations of the model, if slavishly followed and were more accustomed to heuristic problem-solving procedures in their day-to-day work. In order to cater for these groups, I developed alternative job-aids, in the form of a schema of factors to be considered in media selection and how they relate to each other. These schemata, together with a worksheet to keep track, have proved more acceptable and every bit as effective as the original flow-charts – indeed they prove effective across a much wider range of subject matters and types of objectives. We shall analyse these schematic job-aids later on in this chapter.

The problems associated with complex, difficult to use flow-charts, were attacked in an interesting manner in the last of the models presented here (Reiser and Gagné 1983). This approach uses a well laid out worksheet (Figure 3.20) and supports this with a flow-chart which is planned on two levels of decision-making. I have telescoped parts of this flow-chart in Figure 3.21. Along the top, we see a flow of relatively 'macro' decisions that set the overall 'scene' for the instruction:

- on-the-job or simulator training,
- distance education/training,
- self instruction (readers or non-readers)
- instructor-delivered training (readers or non-readers).

These lead to one of six relatively simple flow charts that operate at the individual objective lesson planning level. Only one of these subsidiary charts is shown in Figure 3.21.

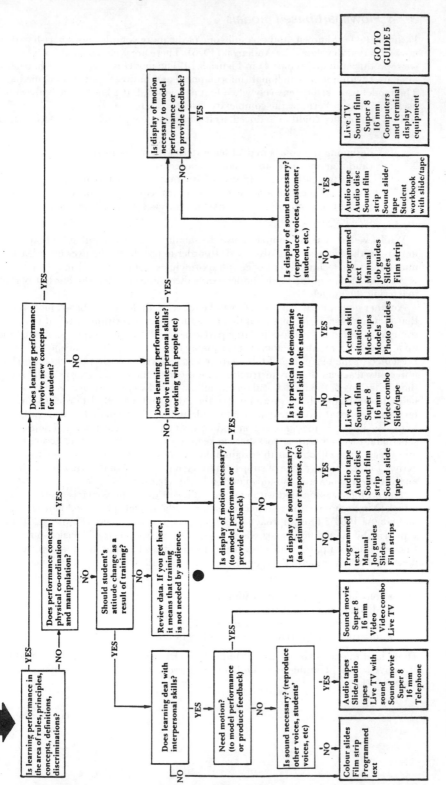

Figure 3.19 *Adapted from Selecting and Developing Media for Instruction by R H Anderson, co-published 1976 by American Society for Training and Development and Van Nostrand Reinhold Co, New York. Copyright 1976 by the American Society for Training and Development. Produced with permission of copyright owner.*

This approach goes a long way towards simplifying a complex decision flow chart to manageable proportions. Furthermore, the worksheet is laid out in a matrix from which encourages the user to see an overall form and structure in his decisions.

How to proceed

1. List each objective or set of objectives on the media selection worksheet.

2. Proceed through the media selection flowchart with each objective or set of objectives.

3. Begin at chart A by entering the diagram at the left and proceeding in the general directions right and down.

4. Diamonds with numbers ⟨1⟩ contain questions indicating that a *decision* is to be made.

5. Rectangular boxes ⬜ indicate *actions* to be taken on the basis of previous decisions.

6. When you reach a box on the bottom line of the flow chart, turn to the media selection worksheet and place a check mark by each of the media listed in the box.

Making a final selection

After you have used the flow chart to identify the appropriate media for each objective in the lesson or course, and have filled in the media selection worksheet, make a final selection using the procedure below. Either a single medium or a combination of media may be chosen when making a final selection decision.

1. *Eliminate media* by crossing off media which are not feasible in the situation for which instruction is being designed. The following questions are relevant:
   - Can the medium be produced by the time needed?
   - Can the costs of production, maintenance, and operation be afforded?
   - Can the medium be approved as compatible with existing policies and programmes?
   - Is the medium practical for use in its intended environment?

2. *Make a final choice of media.* Consider the following questions:
   - Is more than one medium necessary to enable students to acquire all of the objectives?
   - What are the comparative costs of the final candidate media and media combinations?
   - Can each medium meet your estimated requirements for change and updating?

3.3 A multi-level model of media selection

The four levels of decision making

3.3.1 *The realities of media decisions*

The decisions concerning effective communication may be taken early or late in the instructional design process, and may be made in greater or lesser depths of detail.

It is useful, once again, to conceptualize the instructional design process as occurring at four levels of detail, which we have called levels 1, 2, 3 and 4.

1. List objective(s).

2. Check appropriate media for each (from bottom line boxes in flow chart).

3. Make final choice of media using criteria on last page of flow chart.

4. Circle your final selection choices.

OBJECTIVES

Audio											
Chart											
Computer											
Film strip											
Instructor											
Interactive TV											
Large Equipment											
Motion Picture											
Overhead Projection											
Portable Equipment											
Printed Text											
Programmed Text											
Radio Broadcast											
Simulator											
Slides											
Slide/Tape											
Training Aid											
Training Device											
TV Broadcast											
TV Cassette											

Figure 3.20 *Media selection worksheet. (Reproduced from Reiser and Gagné, 1983.)*

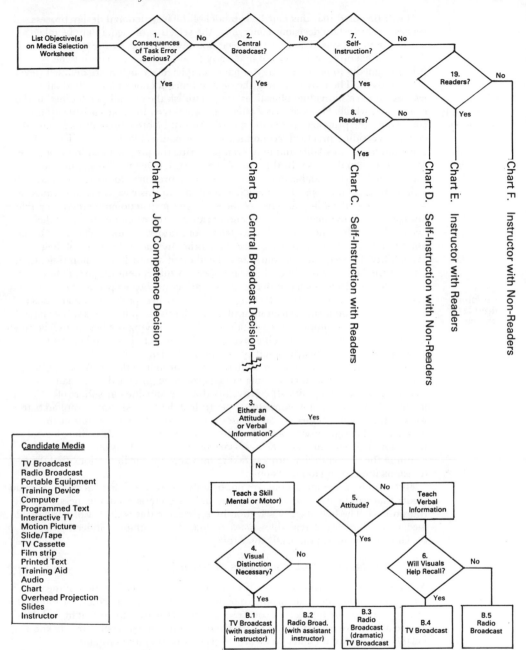

Candidate Media

TV Broadcast
Radio Broadcast
Portable Equipment
Training Device
Computer
Programmed Text
Interactive TV
Motion Picture
Slide/Tape
TV Cassette
Film strip
Printed Text
Training Aid
Audio
Chart
Overhead Projection
Slides
Instructor

Explanation of Questions – Chart B

2. Central Broadcast? Is the instructional system designed to serve students who are dispersed over a wide geographic area and who are able to receive centrally broadcast instruction at scheduled times?
3. Either an Attitude or Verbal Information? Is the aim either to influence the student's values (attitudes) or to have the student learn to 'state' (rather than 'do') something?

4. Visual Distinction Necessary? Is the visual presentation of task features necessary or will it aid in learning the task?
5. Attitude? Does instruction aim to influence the student's values or opinions?
6. Will Visuals Help Recall? Is it likely that the use of visuals will help the student establish images that will aid recall of verbal information?

Figure 3.21 *The overall structure of the Reiser and Gagné model.*

It will be noted that this four-level model of the instructional design process suggests that certain decisions concerning the selection of media may be taken at any of the four levels. The decisions need not always be taken at each level of detail. For example, you may not make any final decisions concerning the principal media to be used until you have completed a much more detailed (level 2 or 3) analysis. Then, by summing the detailed media choices for individual lessons, or even individual objectives, you establish the overall 'media mix' in the course as a whole. However, very often, you are forced to make early decisions concerning the principal media to be used. Almost before any analysis is started, certain overriding practical, economic, social or political factors will dictate the principal media available and may even prescribe the proportional 'mix' of these media in the final course. In the case of the Open University, for example, only certain media are available and there are various pressures to use these in fairly well-defined proportions. The 'principal medium' in this case is print, because of its availability, flexibility in terms of the variety of instructional methods possible, low cost and individualized nature, and because of the economic limits of the availability of the other media (radio, television, tutors, summer schools). On the other hand, there are pressures to use these other media to the limits of their availability. Consequently a course may be allotted so much television time, to be filled in the best way possible (this will appear in subsequent deeper analysis).

Such 'early' decisions naturally limit the variety of choice open to the instructional designer in the later stages. It is, therefore, probably a good idea to delay decisions on media selection until a sufficiently deep level of analysis has been performed to supply all the data needed for achieving the best match between the media to be used and the objectives, learner characteristics and content characteristics of the instructional system under design.

However, in practice, you can seldom go very deep into the detail of instructional design without coming across economic, practical or human (including social and political) constraints that are 'outside our sphere of influence'. As you cannot eliminate or neutralize these constraints, you had better work within their confines. In such cases it is a waste of time to continue the instructional design process as if the constraints did not exist. It is more logical (and more efficient) to make the necessary overall media decisions and then to continue the deeper design process taking into account the limitations that these decisions impose on later decisions.

Fortunately, these limitations are not usually too severe. There are usually many media that can be used to satisfy the essential characteristics of the message being transmitted. The first stage of selection by rejection reduces the list of all available media to a short list of available *suitable* media. We are unlucky indeed if none of the suitable media is practically available.

3.3.2 Media selection decisions at level 1

Analysis at level 1 involves, in the training context, the identification of the tasks that make up the job of the people to be trained, or, in the educational context, the identification of the topics that compose the subject matter to be taught and their interrelation with each other and with what the intended learners already know. Further analysis of the intended learners (the target population) and the job/subject in the wider context helps to identify the tasks or the topics that *need* to be taught (instruction required), those that are too easy to need teaching (information required), those that are too rarely practised or used to justify teaching (reference materials required) and those that are already well known by the target population (prerequisites).

Analysis at this depth gives little insight as yet into *how* to teach. We are primarily concerned with *what* to 'teach' and what to package as 'information'. Thus one valid decision which can be made is whether we require *instructional* media or *informational* media. The difference is important and is quite simple. Information may be disseminated by undirectional (one-way) media. Instruction requires two-way communication between the transmitter and the receiver.

Margin notes:
Reality forces early decisions

Early decisions limit later choice

Effectiveness

Instruction or information?

This entails the use of two-way communication media, or a combination of one-way media that effectively provides the necessary two-way communication. Note that the feedback channel may not be in use all the time, but only at key stages in the process. Hence one-way media, such as television, may be used for instruction, if supported by the necessary feedback media (eg letters in distance education systems, or discussions in normal schools or practical applications exercises in vocational training).

Quantitative aspects

The gross analysis of 'level 1' also tells us quite a lot about the *quantitative* aspects of the target population (eg how many people are to be taught, with what frequency, in what size of groups, how dispersed geographically, etc). This leads to the identification of many constraints and also of certain factors related to effective communication. Our choice of media must be able to reach the learners (and at reasonable cost). We are naturally led to consider the gross alternatives of distance education (mass media are the principal media) and face-to-face education (teachers are the principal media, supported by teaching aids). This distinction was nicely put by Wilbur Schramm when he referred to 'big media' and 'little media', (Schramm 1967).

Types of objectives

Finally, at level 1, we form an overall view of the final (terminal) objectives of the course we are about to design. These objectives may be 'obligatory', in the sense that all learners should achieve mastery of all objectives (this is the case in most vocational training and also in educational courses that apply the mastery learning model), or they may be optional, in the sense that there is room for individual students to choose which objectives they wish to master and to what level of proficiency they wish to master them. This is the case with many non-vocational educational courses, necessary in courses based on the 'cyclic learning' model of the curriculum favoured by Bruner, and is used by proponents of 'open classroom' and resource-based discovery learning fans etc). Thus, we may at this level be led to decide (for practical or philosophical reasons) between media that are capable of presenting a fixed message (thus controlling the uniformity of the message) and media that are capable of presenting information in such a way that it is easy for teachers or learners to modify the content or the sequence of the message (thus allowing freedom of choice and a measure of 'individualization').

Thus to summarize, effective communication, at the overall level, would lead us to consider:

Learner factors: big or little media?
Content factors: one-way or two-way media?
Objectives: fixed or flexible?

A scheme for initial media decisions

The way in which these interact is shown in Figure 3.22. The upper half of the wheel lists, in the outer ring, some 'big' or mass media, together with necessary additions to render the system instructional (which requires feedback), or flexible in use (which requires alternatives and a guide). The lower half of the wheel lists, in the outer rim, some 'little media' combinations.

The outer rim has intentionally been left open at the edge, to indicate that the examples given are not a complete and exhaustive listing, but only examples of a category.

The choices within a category would be influenced very much by the economic, practical and other constraints that exist in the organization or society that is sponsoring the design of the course. Such constraints would render some choices more attractive, and others simply impossible. Thus we may be forced to make definite choices from the examples in these categories, or we may be able to leave the options open a little longer, while indicating preferences.

Cost-effectiveness

Initial cost estimates are approximate

Costs enter as an important consideration at the very beginning of any project. It is, therefore, quite legitimate, and even necessary, to eliminate from the media shortlist any that are quite impossible for reasons of cost. The important concepts to apply at this stage are presented in Figure 3.23.

Applying the concepts of cost-effectiveness, of cost over time and of break-even points enables a more balanced judgement to be made of the economic factors at

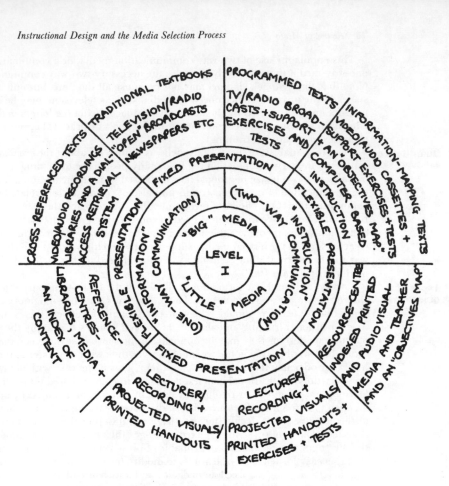

Figure 3.22 *Schema for initial media selection decisions.*

play in media selection. We may only, at this early stage, have a 'hunch' regarding the relative effectiveness of alternative media choices. We have not gone deeply enough into the analysis of the problem to formulate clear hypotheses, nor to be certain how to form hypotheses concerning effectiveness. There may not be sufficient experience nor sufficient reliable empirical data to be able to predict with any certainty the probable effectiveness of a proposed course structure. In this respect, the accumulated research on media comparisons for total courses is singularly unhelpful (Briggs, Campeau and Gagné, 1966).

In such cases it is advisable to postpone final decisions to a later stage of the instructional design process, either until later stages of deeper analysis have given reliable indicators as to probable effectiveness or, if this fails, until we can collect our own empirical data during the pilot project stages of course validation (this would imply the testing out of alternatives on a small scale before making final decisions).

3.3.3 Media selection decisions at level 2

General considera-tions

Unless, at level 1, the constraints were such as to completely define the medium (or media) of presentation, we now have the opportunity to select our media with more precision (or to allocate different learning objectives among the media selected according to their suitability).

Effectiveness of a presentation	Are the objectives achieved? Is the message communicated and understood? Either the presentation achieves its objectives or it does not.
Efficiency of a presentation	How well are the objectives achieved? This is a relative measure. Two presentations may both be effective, but one may be more efficient, in that it used less resources to achieve the objectives. These resources may be: ☐ Time required to achieve the objectives ☐ Quantity of human resources (teachers, etc) needed ☐ Quantity of other resources (materials, support services, etc).
Cost-effectiveness	As most resources can be expressed in terms of their cost, a useful overall concept for media comparison is cost-effectiveness, which may be defined as: 'The relative costs of achieving objectives by alternative media'.
Capital and running costs (definitions)	All costs can be classified as: Capital: development costs, overheads. Running: costs incurred during use.
(Implications)	1. Therefore, the cost per student of a presentation diminishes as the number of students using it increases. 2. And sometimes, media with high development costs, but lower running costs may in the long time be more cost-effective.

Figure 3.23 *Important concepts to apply at level 1.*

The products of level 2 analysis

Analysis at level 2 involves, in the training context, the analysis of the tasks to be taught into the operations or steps that must be executed, or in the educational context, the analysis of the topics to be taught into the sub-topics or elements of information that must be learned. In each case, the sequence and structure of the tasks/topics is identified, which gives insights into the way they should be taught, the prerequisite knowledge or skills that the learner should possess and the intermediate objectives that must be attained during the course as stepping stones to the final objectives.

We now also get some insights into *how* to teach, at least to the extent of establishing the content of individual course units and lessons and determining the possible sequence (or alternative sequences) in which the lessons should be learned.

Often, formal analysis goes no further. At this stage, the rest of the task of course design is left to individual teachers, to plan their lessons as they see fit, in the light of the overall course structure (curriculum) that they have been given. Sometimes, however, the planning of the curriculum goes further, suggesting to the teacher the instructional methods, media and content that he should use. The Nuffield projects (Nuffield maths, science, environmental studies, etc) are examples of well-known curriculum projects that have made such a thorough analysis. In these cases, the teacher receives complete, or virtually complete, lesson plans to apply in his teaching.

'Little media' decisions

Note that we are now concerned principally with the 'little media'. If mass media have been chosen, this is usually a level 1 decision and our task now would be to develop instruction that made good use of these media. However, there is no reason why we may not at this stage decide to use some of the 'big media' such as television, in the classroom setting.

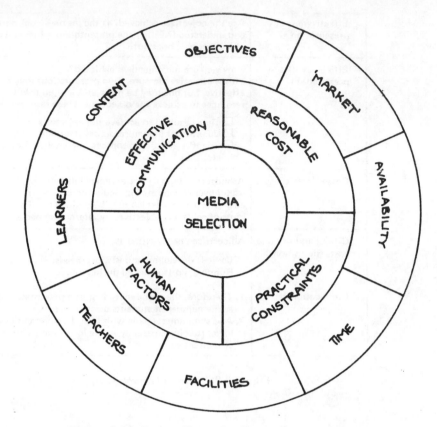

Figure 3.24 *Factors affecting the selection of media for instruction.*

Sensory channels	Sensory channels are the senses through which the learner receives the information. Media use the following channels of communication:	
Types	Vision —	most commonly used, often in combination (audiovisual) for all
	Sound —	types of learning tasks.
	Touch —	less commonly used but important in learning perceptual and
	Kinaesthesis —	psychomotor skills.
	Smell —	rarely used in school learning (only in very specialized skill learning —
	Taste —	eg cookery)
Examples of sensory channels used by certain media	Media	Sensory channels used
	Television	Sound and vision
	Book	Vision
	Wine-tasting session	Taste, smell and vision or sound for the verbal label description
	Samples of textiles	Vision and touch (again perhaps sound for the name)
	Pilot trainer (simulator)	Vision, sound, touch, kinaesthesis

Figure 3.25 *Sensory channels used by certain media.*

**Com-
munication
effective-
ness**

Let us now look at the factors indicated in Figure 3.24 at this more detailed level of analysis.

Level 2 analysis establishes the objectives for each lesson at a level of specificity that enables us to match appropriate media with a high degree of confidence. The approach is based on only two general rules, which are given below.

**Rule 1
(objectives)**

If you expect a certain behaviour from the learner after instruction, you should give him opportunities to practise that behaviour during instruction. Thus if the learner is expected to be able to give examples of a certain concept, he should be presented with examples during instruction; if he is expected to *perform* a procedure after training he should *practise performing* the procedure, and not just observe it or hear it described (although these may both be steps to getting him to perform correctly).

**Rule 2
(content)**

Use the most appropriate sensory channels for communicating the information to be learned. Thus, we should attempt to match the sensory channels to the message. Often this is not a significant factor, as the information to be communicated is verbal, and the only choice open to us is between the spoken and the written word. But in other cases, as Figure 3.25 shows, a wider variety of sensory channels may be involved (See also Figure 3.2.)

**Learner
factors to
consider**

There is one further group of factors to consider from the viewpoint of effective communication – *learner factors.* Much lip-service is paid to the importance of individual differences in the planning of instruction, but less is actually done about them. This is partly because we do not really know all that much about how to allow for learner differences. Certainly a deeper level of analysis is required to identify the learner differences that matter in a specific instructional exercise. At level 2 we can only, from our target population analysis, identify a few general types of learner differences which may influence our choice of media at this stage. The chief types of general learner differences (not specific to a particular learning task) are listed in Figure 3.26, which also presents three other types of learner factors which may be identified at this stage.

Individual differences	Research suggests that learners differ in: ☐ Their preference for learning by observing/by listening (visual learners/aural learners) ☐ Their perceptions of a given message; this is mainly a factor of past experience, and often a cultural difference exists (eg perception of perspective) ☐ Their understanding of the conventions used by various media (eg the grammar of language, the 'grammar' of technical drawing, etc).
Attention span	How long a learner can attend to one type of task. Factors affecting this are: ☐ Age: young children seldom attend to one style of presentation for more than a few minutes, whilst adults may attend for hours ☐ Interest, generated either by the content itself or by the style of its presentation ☐ Motivation on the part of the learner to achieve the objectives of the learning task presented.
Number of learners	The group size to be taught renders certain media difficult or impossible to use; others become uneconomical.
Physical disablities of learners	Poor vision, hearing, dyslexia, colour blindness, etc.

Figure 3.26 *Some learner factors.*

For differences in preference for specific media.	Use a multi-media approach, offering both audio and visual options for the same objectives or content.
For differences in perception.	Either avoid the types of presentation that give difficulty, or arrange extra perception training.
For differences in the understanding of symbolic language or conventions.	Either avoid the types of symbolic language that gives problems, or teach it first, to all students.
For groups with a short attention span.	Use a variety of media, in order to change the style of presentation at intervals shorter than the span.
For dealing with groups of different sizes.	Select media that are well suited to the group size you have, or, if this is difficult, modify the group size or structure to suit the media you have.

Figure 3.27 *Selecting media in the light of learner factors at level 2 analysis.*

Possible decisions resulting from the identification of the presence of some of these learner factors are suggested in Figure 3.27.

Flow charts as aids to media selection

As a further aid to selection at this stage the flow charts may be used. One flow chart (see Figure 3.6) is for the analysis of tasks that have a visual stimulus content.

A second flow chart (see Figure 3.8) is of more application to the analysis of topics, in order to decide whether the verbal information to be communicated should be presented live or packaged, and, in the latter case, whether written or recorded audio media should be preferred. Note that this chart also considers when audio is an essential part of the information to be communicated.

A third flow chart (see Figure 3.5) assists the instructional designer to apply the other golden rule, of providing appropriate practice of the behaviours required by the objectives. This chart concentrates on the responses that the learner should make during learning. This leads to certain choices of instructional exercise, which in turn indicate certain essential characteristics that the media should have, in order to provide optimal learning conditions. The identification of these characteristics helps one to select appropriate media from the chart.

However, as mentioned earlier, not all users like flow charts and for some content areas the charts are totally inadequate. In these cases, the circular schemata of chief factors to consider, together with the supporting tables of more detailed considerations, act as adequate job-aids. The reader is encouraged to refer constantly to the schema (Figure 3.24) and the supporting tables, while reading these few pages of explanation. If possible keep a specific course unit in mind and relate the selection factors to this context.

Cost-effective-ness

The cost questions to ask at level 2 are essentially those discussed at level 1. But now we are likely to have more precise data on which to base our cost estimates. We have specified our media, lesson by lesson, objective by objective, so we can now get quite accurate estimates of the proportion of our course that any given medium will present. We could derive a fair estimate of the study hours through television, the study hours in direct contact with the teacher, the study hours on self-instructional materials and so on. Given the 'standard' costs for the preparation of each of the types of media to be used, one can estimate the costs of media production with a fair degree of accuracy.

We should not forget also to question from the cost-effectiveness viewpoint whether a particular presentation should indeed be developed.

Availability Are there suitable materials already available on the market, which can be bought in at a fraction of the production cost and can be incorporated into the course (with or without some adaptation)? This consideration can now be treated at a micro level (eg are there any suitable slides or photos or verbal descriptions in existing materials?) whereas at level 1 it is treated at the macro level (eg are there any complete courses, textbooks, sets of TV programmes that we can adopt/adapt?).

Market How much will the individual media be used? At level 1 this was a consideration of how many students will take the whole course. Now we should consider whether a particular presentation will perhaps be used many times by each student or whether perhaps it is optional and will be chosen and used by only a small proportion of all students.

Objectives Can the presentation be obtained or made at an economical price, in relation to the importance of the objectives? We are attempting here to make a worth/cost analysis for each individual media presentation, before deciding finally whether to select that option or to go for a more economical solution.

Once again we note that these three types of cost factors interrelate with each other and also with the effectiveness factors to render media choice a complex task.

Practicality Once again the procedure at level 2 is similar to level 1 in terms of the chief categories of factors to consider, but the decisions can now be taken on better data and at a micro level of detail.

Time We can now estimate production times for each group of lessons, or for each specific presentation. Thus, in the case of time constraints, we might assign priorities, so that the media most important to the effectiveness of the course are produced early and without delay.

Resources These can now be allocated on an item-by-item basis, giving a method for the control of media production. Once again, if resources are scarce, it should be possible to establish priorities (from consideration of effective communication), and prune down our ambitions to the size of our pockets, by opting for less problematic and more easily produced media for the less essential objectives. (This may perhaps only marginally reduce course effectiveness and thus, by definition, increases cost-effectiveness – equal results for less resources.)

We should also ask some *practical usage* questions, such as:

- Will the medium operate in the conditions of the training area (temperature, humidity, power sources, transportation)?
- Is the environment well-adapted to its use (space, layout, black-out facilities, acoustics, annoyance to/from others)?
- Is the medium 'student-proof' (robust, withstands careless handling, not prone to disintegrate, etc)?
- Is it capable of being easily maintained at low cost?
- Will it have a reasonable working life (bearing in mind its development costs) before it is rendered obsolete by changes in the subject or in teaching methods? (See Figure 3.9.)

To assist in formulating and answering questions at this level, it is useful to consider the practical advantages and limitations of individual media or groups of related media. Figure 3.28 lists some characteristics of commonly used types of little media.

Human factors We have already considered human factors under other headings: *learner factors* affecting the effectiveness of a message, and *human resources* for the production of media. Under the present heading we are considering constraints that may make a potentially effective media choice ineffective. Among the human factors to consider now are *teacher factors*.

Teacher factors At level 1, we looked at some of the overall constraints that may be encountered in the system as a whole, in relation to certain types of media used on a large scale. These constraints arise from the educational philosophies, prejudices, habits and fears of the people involved in the system. Naturally these constraints, if they are found to exist, should be taken into account in the selection of media, or should be

Material	Advantages	Limitations
Photographic print series	1. Permit close-up detailed study at individual's own pacing. 2. Are useful as simple self-study materials and for display. 3. Require no equipment for use.	1. Not adaptable for large groups. 2. Require photographic skills, equipment, and darkroom for preparation.
Slide series	1. Require only filming, with processing and mounting by film laboratory. 2. Result in colourful, realistic reproductions of original subjects. 3. Prepared with any 35mm camera for most uses. 4. Easily revised and updated. 5. Easily handled, stored, and rearranged for various uses. 6. Increased usefulness with tray storage and automatic projection. 7. Can be combined with taped narration for greater effectiveness. 8. May be adapted to group or to individual use.	1. Require some skill in photography 2. Require special equipment for close-up photography and copying. 3. Can get out of sequence and be projected incorrectly if slides are handled individually.
Filmstrips	1. Are compact, easily handled, and always in proper sequence. 2. Can be supplemented with captions or recordings. 3. Are inexpensive when quantity reproduction is required. 4. Are useful for group or individual study at projection rate controlled by instructor or user. 5. Are projected with simple lightweight equipment.	1. Are relatively difficult to prepare locally. 2. Require film laboratory service to convert slides to filmstrip form. 3. Are in permanent sequence and cannot be rearranged or revised.
Recordings	1. Easy to prepare with regular tape recorders. 2. Can provide applications in most subject areas. 3. Equipment for use, compact, portable, easy to operate. 4. Flexible and adaptable as either individual elements of instruction or in correlation with programmed materials. 5. Duplication easy and economical.	1. Have a tendency for over-use, as lecture or oral textbook reading. 2. Fixed rate of information flow.
Overhead transparencies	1. Can present information in systematic, developmental sequences. 2. Use simple-to-operate projector with presentation rate controlled by instructor. 3. Require only limited planning. 4. Can be prepared by variety of simple, inexpensive methods. 5. Particularly useful with large groups.	1. Require special equipment, facilities and skills for preparation. 2. Are large and present storage problem.
Videotape/ videocassette	1. Permit selecting the best audiovisual media to serve program needs. 2. Permit normally unavailable resources to be presented. 3. Playback capability of video recording permits analysis of on-the-spot action.	1. Do not exist alone, but are part of total television production. 2. Must fit technical requirements of television.
Multi-media presentations (eg slide/tape)	1. Combine presentation of slides with other media forms for presentations. 2. Use photographs, slides, filmstrips and recordings in combination for independent study. 3. Provide for more effective communications in certain situations than when only a single medium is used.	1. Require additional equipment and careful coordination during planning, preparation, and use.

Figure 3.28 *Practicality factors for little media.*

overcome. To a certain extent, they maybe overcome or even eliminated by effective promotion of the proposed system, and if necessary by training the people who will be involved in running it in the new skills that are required to operate it efficiently.

Consideration of a detailed nature should therefore be given at level 2 to ways of preparing teachers to accept and to use any novel instructional medium that we plan to adopt.

Any media presentations that are not absolutely essential and that demand significant changes in practice, or substantial learning to use, on the part of teachers, might perhaps be avoided.

Particular care should be taken to allay any fears or negative attitudes that specific complex gadgetry sometimes produces, as these attitudes may easily be transferred from the specific case in point to whole classes of methods and media, thus increasing future difficulties for innovation.

Learner factors

In a similar way we should consider any *learner factors* which might produce fears or negative attitudes. This would be particularly important in the planning of individualized or resource-based courses, in which the learners come into direct contact with the hardware, having to load their own projectors, recorders, or videocassettes. If the learners are not prepared adequately, then, apart from possible operational difficulties and consequent rejection, there will be a high and costly breakdown rate, which may totally disrupt course efficiency.

3.3.4 Media selection decisions at level 3

During lesson planning, you may have to . . .

The third level of instructional design/development deals with lesson planning and preparation. Given a detailed overall plan, there seems to be no further media selection to be done. Take the second objective of the example presented in the last chapter (Figure 2.5). We have already specified that videotaped examples of good and bad interaction with clients will be used to demonstrate and explain how trainees should behave in client–contact situations. This will be followed by practice in role-play situations, with videotaping to give instant feedback for evaluation/correction purposes. So now we have to plan the details of this lesson. Just what points do we wish to emphasize as regards client–contact? What common errors do we wish to correct? How many examples will we need to show and what is the content of each?

Select off-the-shelf materials

And where shall we obtain the videotapes? Is there a ready course of such interpersonal skill examples that we may buy or borrow, complete with lesson plans, etc? If so, are we sure that the producers have treated the topic in a manner that is appropriate to our needs? Obviously we will want to view the tapes before making a final decision. Maybe there are several such interpersonal skill training videotapes and we must select the one which best meets our needs.

evaluate and select prototype materials

Alternatively, if we find nothing suitable on the market we may decide to produce our own. But probably *we* will not produce the tapes. We will specify what we want and request the media services or an outside consultant to produce them. But we will still want to assess the finished product before we use it in our training. It may be that some of the vignettes really do not quite match up to our expectations and design specifications. We may select some for screening and reject others.

adapt some existing materials

Consider the third objective of the instructional plan in Figure 2.5. Here we specified the use of taped conversations for practice in the classification of telephone calls into useful categories. The easiest way to produce these is to simply record all incoming calls for a week or so. You are sure to bag lots of excellent examples. But someone is going to have to listen to the 300 taped calls and *select* the 30 best examples for use in training.

Thus at level 3 (when lesson planning) you are *selecting the specific materials*, either from available off-the-shelf alternatives, or from among specially produced 'prototypes'. This selection process depends on two things:

(a) knowing what you want (having a detailed lesson plan)
(b) recognizing it (having specific material evaluation skills, which differ somewhat for each type of material).

We shall return to materials evaluation and selection in each of the subsequent chapters, as it becomes more relevant.

**or perhaps
do
it yourself
(level 4 ID)**

And what if you are on your own and have to actually produce the instructional materials required by the lesson plan? Then of course you are down to level 4 design: in addition to (a) and (b), you will require to (c) know the principles/procedures that lead to what you want and (d) be skilled in applying them. But that's beyond the scope of this book.

3.3.5 Media selection at level 4

It may seem that once we get to the level of materials development (level 4) that we have passed the stage of media selection. We are now designing the message to be transmitted by the previously selected medium and developing the actual materials – the visuals, the script, page layout, the embedded questions, the choice of language and style, etc. All of these are areas of materials design and development that have their own extensive research and bibliography of how-to-do-it tests. The details of designing materials for specific media are beyond the scope of this book.

There is, however, one way in which media *selection* is becoming a concern of the materials developer. This has been brought about by the application of Interactive Video. This medium is a blending of several media – text, graphics, audio, video simulation queries, etc, – under computer control. The instructional designer can select from the available media alternatives at a very 'micro' level. Text and graphics can be overlaid on a slide or a moving image. Depending on step-by-step student interaction, alternative media presentation can be brought into play. The term 'media selection' takes on a new 'micro' meaning. This is the fourth level of our media selection scheme. We shall return to this aspect when we discuss Interactive Video, in Chapter 13.

PART 2.
Media as Instructional Aids:
The use of basic presentation media to promote effective message transmission in conventional instructional settings

Introduction

Instruction, the way we have defined the term, requires a two-way communication process. But many media are basically one-way transmitters, quite incapable of receiving and storing (let alone interpreting) any messages that the learner may transmit. These 'presentation media' have been the mainstay of teachers, until now. In typical face-to-face teaching situations, the teacher is the sole receiver, storer and interpreter of anything the student may say or do. Media are used exclusively to enhance or enrich the teacher's presentation. As educational broadcasting came on the scene, the mass media used in these systems took over a greater part of the role of the teacher, but generally this was still limited to the presentation function. Only in rare applications, do we see the media taking on a more extensive role. One example is the use of radio or video paced programmes, with gaps for student responses, followed by feedback (as in foreign language drills). Some, but not all aspects of the teacher's practice-organization and learning-control roles are delegated to the media. But in practice, such examples are the exception, rather than the rule, until we come to get involved in the design and development of self-instructional, interactive learning systems.

As an overall organization schema, this part of the book will deal with the use of one-way presentation media, used as part of a teacher's overall instructional plan. (Interactive media and multi-media systems will be addressed in Part 3.)

Chapter 4 discusses the use of visual presentations in the instructional process. Both research findings and practical considerations are analysed. This chapter serves as an opener for the more specific media-related chapters that follow.

Chapters 5 and 6 deal with what used to be called 'visual aids'. First, we discuss the use of non-projected media, both pre-prepared (charts and pictures) and for use as on-line presentation aids (chalkboard, magnetic board, etc.). This chapter also examines the use of print-and-paper handouts as teaching aids, from the viewpoint of layout, design and advantages. An important topic dealt with here is the use of flow-charts and other visual communication conventions in print material. Chapter 6 discusses all manner of still projected visuals.

Chapter 7 builds on the previous discussion of visuals, by first assessing the uses of pure sound media to enhance both visual and verbal communication. Then the relative merits of printed and spoken text are examined. The slide-tape presentation is singled out for special study, from both the design and the utilization viewpoints. A schema for the classification, analysis and design of all manner of audio-visual packages is presented, together with a range of representative examples.

Chapter 8 analyses the use of film in education and training. The analysis is partly historical, seeking to understand why film has never played as important a role in teaching as may have been expected. This is of importance to the later discussion of video (Chapter 9). The rest of the chapter is devoted to practical hints on the effective and efficient use of off-the-shelf films.

Finally, *chapter 9* deals with both broadcast television and pre-recorded video. A historical review shows how the TV medium has been used and mis-used, why broadcast ETV was not the success it might have been, how the advent of cheap and portable video recording changed the scene and what the very real practical benefits of video are in today's educational and training systems. The second half of the chapter deals with the practicalities of using video.

4. When to use still visual media

4.1. Why use visual aids at all – why not the Real Thing?

Realia or representations? Why not? Very often teachers bring samples of everyday objects into the classroom or take the class out to view real things in their natural surroundings. We soon come across objects which cannot be readily shown. They are too large, too small, too expensive, too dirty, too dangerous, too delicate, or they only come out at night! This is when the teacher turns to an alternative display – a model or a picture. Sometimes the object is available and could be shown, but the characteristics one wishes to demonstrate are not very obvious (they are inside, for example) so some other means of presentation becomes both more practical and more meaningful to the student.

Finally, the thing may not exist, or at least not in an observable form: you can only demonstrate its presence by its effects. Here again a model or chart may be helpful. Energy, for example, may be demonstrated directly – as when we take a swipe at Jones in the front row but he will learn more about its nature and the way it is converted into other forms of energy by studying a chart or performing an experiment.

So, the three main reasons why models or pictures are used are:

1. It is inconvenient to use the real thing.
2. A model or chart can better explain the principle being taught.
3. The real thing cannot be seen anyway.

If none of these objections applies, then by all means use the real thing, and you put this book down till your next teaching problem arises.

4.2. Models or pictures?

3–D or 2–D? It all depends which shows best the principle being taught. If the third dimension plays an important part in communicating your message, then you can expect better results from a model. If the shape, texture or inside structure is unimportant, or if it can be adequately represented in two dimensions, a diagram or picture will probably be just as good. Indeed, there is evidence that too much realism or detail may hinder the communication of your message. If a picture is sufficient, a model will not improve comprehension, and may indeed hinder it by introducing irrelevant and distracting detail.

Simple or complex? Of course, both models and pictures can be made clearer by the omission of irrelevant detail, so focussing the student's attention on those points which are relevant to the problem in hand. For example, anatomy lessons are simplified by the production of separate charts showing bones, organs, the bloodstream, the nervous system, the musculature, and so on. To show all these details on one chart would be very messy and unclear. At a later stage, however, a model which can be dismantled is most helpful in showing how the various sub-systems fit and act

Figure 4.1 *Dürer. Draftsman drawing a reclining nude. This is a simplification of reality, forced on the artist by the nature of woodcuts, but all essential detail is reproduced. Note also that the picture illustrates a practical method for producing simplified drawings which requires only a modicum of drafting skill.*

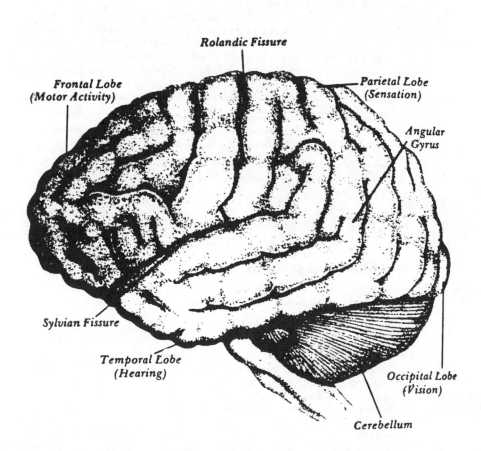

Figure 4.2 *Would you rather learn about the structure of the brain from a picture, a model or a cross-section diagram? It depends on what you have to learn.*

together to give a real working human being. At a still later stage, when beginning to learn 'maintenance and repair' procedures, the real thing becomes necessary.

Static models or simulators?

Occasionally, the transition from 2- and 3-dimensional representations to the real thing can be eased by the use of working models, or simulators. Our budding surgeons are at a disadvantage here, as no one has yet produced a complete simulator of a human being. In the main they have to rely on the traditional training technique of first 'sitting by Nellie', and then having a bash.

In many technical fields, however – as in fighter pilot training – complex simulators are used to train operators in the use of dangerous or expensive machinery. Similarly, models and simulators are often designed specifically to guard human safety and comfort – as in the testing of safety harnesses. And of course, barbers have for centuries learnt to wield a cut-throat by laboriously shaving a wooden head, graduating progressively to softer and softer woods.

Such models and simulators are the subject of a later chapter. Here we are concerned with the visual presentation of objects, phenomena or ideas. The use of models is indicated when:

1. The shape of the object is complex and must be shown.

2. The inside detail must be observed and cannot be better shown by a cross-section diagram.

3. There is so much detail, all relevant, that pictures or diagrams are unclear or misleading (eg crystal or molecular structure; pipework installations in refineries; complex 3-D mechanisms).

In general, models should therefore be employed when the use of the third dimension aids communication. Only details relevant to the message being communicated should be included. Too much unnecessary realism may reduce effective communication.

Information or motiva-tion?

If you can picture the object, concept or phenomenon adequately in two dimensions, there is little to be gained in terms of learning efficiency by using a model. This does not rule out, however, the motivational value of the model, or the 'real thing'. Being able to play with objects is recognized by infant teachers as a valuable educational experience. This is no less true of adults. Many a motor mechanic enters his trade as a result of a love of 'mucking about' with cars. He would soon leave his apprenticeship if given no chance to play with a real engine. But his play will be all the more valuable if he understands, for example, the Otto cycle or the principle of the S U Carburettor. These can be learnt more efficiently from simplified diagrams or models which illustrate the processes.

Instruction or Job-aid?

Our man on the assembly line, however, may assemble the engine quite efficiently with very little knowledge of the principles on which it works. He will be trained on the real thing. However, his training may also be speeded by supplying visual aids, such as a series of photographs of stages in the assembly, or by means of a job-aid: for example, a wall chart of instructions in chronological order.

So again we see the need for precise objectives. Only when we have specified the performance required of the learner and analysed the knowledge and skills required to perform, can we set about the systematic and intelligent design of visual display.

Concrete or symbolic?

There are three main types of visual display materials (Figure 4.3):

1. Pictures – including photographs, line drawings and paintings aiming at a true and lifelike representation of a real object.
2. Diagrams – including engineering drawings, cross-sections, schematic diagrams, flow diagrams, aiming at a clear representation of an object, or specific characteristics of an object, or a process, concept or phenomenon.
3. Graphic presentations – including graphs and charts, aiming to present a trend, or an interrelation, or a set of figures.

These sub-divisions are more points on a continuous scale than watertight compartments. There is an increasing level of abstraction and increasing use of symbolic conventions as you proceed along this scale. Consequently, the further a visual lies along the scale, the more a student must learn 'how to read' the conventions before the visual will communicate the intended message. This is a point often overlooked by users of visual aids.

4.3. Reading of visual material

Visual literacy

We learn to 'read' visual material partly by experience and partly by being taught. Even the understanding of quite simple pictures must be learnt. The appreciation of perspective, for example, is not inborn. Painters only mastered its use during the Renaissance. We now use it unthinkingly, by rule-of-thumb, to produce drawings. Children, however, have to learn to read such drawings by a process of experience – of comparing pictorial representations with the real things around them. Luckily for the users of visual aids, most of our students soon learn to comprehend perspective – at least this is true of Western Europe.

Cultural differences

Experiments in other cultures show that different experiences lead to different perception of visual material. A perspective drawing of a long room with several cut-out windows (Figure 4.4) was shown to Europeans and Africans. An identical head was made to appear at each window. Europeans, used to perspective drawings and long rooms, judged the heads at the smaller (apparently farther) windows to be larger. Africans, not used to conventions and living in round houses, made no allowance for perspective and judged all the heads to be equal.

Unexpected effects

Such aspects of a drawing as facial expression, attitude, or irrelevant detail content may be sufficient to alter or distort the message being communicated. Young children in particular tend to react emotionally to visual material, and the general atmosphere of the picture may register much more strongly than the factual content – 'I don't want to go to Heaven because God looks so strict'. We have also the recent example of a road safety campaign that went wrong. The sight of the badly mangled cars prominently displayed at accident black-spots was meant to communicate 'drive carefully'. What was in fact communicated was anxiety, and the accident rate went up. For similar reasons, one must control the content of a picture to ensure that the viewer's attention focuses on those aspects which are of significance for the lesson in progress. A photo of a nuclear reactor set in parkland with cows grazing may attempt to make the point that the locality is safe and free from pollution. A Hindu might only notice the cows.

4.4. Research on the comprehension of visuals

As we progress to more abstract visual presentation, there is an increasing possibility that the target audience for our visual masterpiece will not be equipped with the skills necessary to read our meaning. We may be better off without the visual aid. Extensive research by Vernon (1952) on the use of graphs to present numerical data and statistics showed that:

Text vs graphs

1. Intelligent and well-educated people could cope with graphical information, but less fortunate individuals needed written explanations of supporting textual material.

PICTURE

CEILING TOO LOW

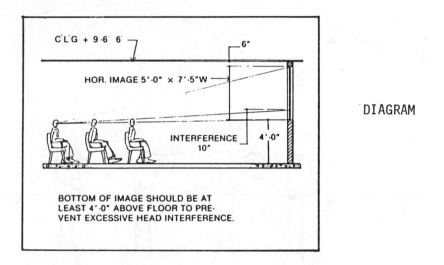

DIAGRAM

C'L'G + 9·6 6'

6"

HOR. IMAGE 5'·0" × 7'·5"W

INTERFERENCE 10"

4'·0"

BOTTOM OF IMAGE SHOULD BE AT LEAST 4'·0" ABOVE FLOOR TO PRE-VENT EXCESSIVE HEAD INTERFERENCE.

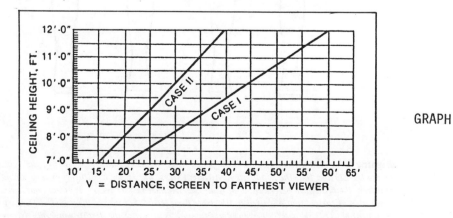

GRAPH

CEILING HEIGHT, FT.

12'·0"
11'·0"
10'·0"
9'·0"
8'·0"
7'·0"

CASE II

CASE I

10' 15' 20' 25' 30' 35' 40' 45' 50' 55' 60' 65'

V = DISTANCE, SCREEN TO FARTHEST VIEWER

Figure 4.3 *Three visuals on the same topic – but three completely different aspects are communicated.*

(a)

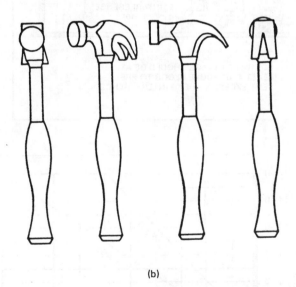

(b)

Figure 4.4 *Visual literacy – some unspoken rules. (a) The convergent lines of the 'wall' create the illusion that the heads are of different sizes, but in some cultures, or with young children, the heads are perceived as of equal size (which in fact is so – it is only our learned perception of the conventions used to illustrate perspective that makes them look different). (b) Familiar objects are usually perceived as having a constant shape despite markedly different appearing shapes.*

2. There was no difference in the effectiveness of line graphs and numerical charts for the communication of factual data, though graphs were a little better at communicating trends.
3. In no case was there evidence to suggest that graphs or charts would help to teach something that would 'otherwise be beyond the comprehension of the reader'.

Text and pictures

Vernon also investigated the effect of pictorial illustrations on the comprehension of a text (1953). The same text was given to two matched groups of 16–18 year olds, but one group also had illustrations. There was no decisive evidence to suggest that the illustrated version was better understood. The points illustrated were better remembered, but at the cost of less understanding of the general theme of the text. Pictures were inefficient at presenting relations or explanations, but did arouse emotions and strong attitudes. Thus, the illustrated version resulted in a less thorough, less objective grasp of the argument presented in the text.

These, at first sight rather unfavourable, results require some qualification.

First, the choice of topic used for such research is likely to influence the results a great deal. The text referred to above dealt with social problems and presented data on divorces, mortality and so on. This is, no doubt by choice, a subject which can adequately be dealt with by a straightforward verbal presentation. The pictures and graphs used simply underlined or re-stated points which were already made in the text. It is not surprising that they added little to the overall comprehension. However, there are subjects which cannot be adequately expressed in words. In the early stages of learning to speak, the child relies heavily on making associations between the things he observes and the spoken sounds he hears. We cannot start using verbal explanations until he has built up a basic mastery of the language. Modern language teaching methods which involve a minimal use of the native tongue could not be operated without the use of visual material. Much technical material in scientific or industrial training can best be presented visually. Imagine a motor car manual explaining engine dismantling procedures, or the wiring circuits, without the use of diagrams.

Prior learning?

The *second* qualification one might make of Vernon's work relates to the choice of student for the research. We saw that the more intelligent, more educated, could cope more readily with graphs. It is all too easy to conclude that graphs are therefore more difficult to read and comprehend than equivalent written descriptions. Might the reason not be, however, that the more intelligent, more educated, simply had more previous experience in use of graphs, because they are encountered later in one's education? Is it not perhaps a question of the readiness of students to benefit from a particular presentation medium; a question of the amount of prior training they had received in the necessary graph-reading skills?

Cultural effects?

A *third* qualification might be made. We are all steeped in the traditions of a verbal, literate society. As he learns to read and write, a child becomes less receptive to other visual stimuli. He tends, through schooling, to be forced into a routine of expressing everything he sees or feels in terms of words. Communication through action is not encouraged. In fact it is often actively discouraged by our society. Two points arise:

1. Are the less intelligent, less educated students less successful with graphs because they have difficulty in 'translating' what they learn visually into a written answer to a question? Are they more successful with a written text because they simply learn to repeat what they read? Does this necessarily indicate greater comprehension?
2. Are we justified in assuming that everything a student learns from a picture is capable of being measured by verbal questioning? Vernon herself reported changes in emotion and attitude, as a result of illustrating the text. May this not be a valid educational objective in itself? Can it be effectively measured by a written test? There is evidence that information presented visually is better recalled in a visual rather than verbal test (Duncan and Hartley, 1969).

There is a school of thought typified by the writings of Marshall McLuhan (1964) which suggests that we are leaving the age of print (the Gutenberg age). Due to electronic mass media, especially television, Western societies communicate more and more on a direct face-to-face level. Also, instantaneous two-way communication over any distance is possible. As a result, the role of gestures, visual displays and tone increases, and the importance of clear step-by-step logical presentation diminishes. Evidence for these views is mainly gathered from an examination of social and cultural changes in society, trends in the arts, and so on. There is also, however, some evidence in educational research. This will be discussed in Chapter 9.

We should perhaps re-examine the present system in which children, reared from birth in an environment of electronic mass media, gaining more and more of their early education through instant, up-to-date visual presentation, are taught and tested in school predominantly by the written word. Do our children perhaps read the language of pictures better than their parents ever did?

It's not what you do, but the way that you do it ... Research by Hartley (1971) tends to bear out some of these observations. He compared the way students reacted to lecture material supported by slides and by blackboard illustration. Although in general they preferred the slides, they learnt better from the blackboard. A detailed look at this experiment will illustrate once more that it is not so much the medium, as the way it is used and the purpose it is used for, that controls the efficiency of the message's transmission.

A lecture was delivered in a lecture theatre fitted with a projection room, where the experimenter sat out of sight of the lecturer and the students. The lecture was tape recorded through the theatre's amplification system. Points made in the lecture that were illustrated with slides were noted. Points made with the aid of the blackboard were noted and the time of their delivery recorded.

The lecturer tended to leave each slide showing until he was ready to show the next, so both the initial time of display and the display length were noted. Generally speaking, the lecturer continued to talk while directing the students' attention to the slides, but if he remained silent for a period this was also noted.

Ten days later the students were given a short test consisting of 12 questions, 6 of which tested material which had been taught in conjunction with slides, and 6 of which similarly tested material presented with the aid of the blackboard.

The students were asked to answer their questions with the aid of their notes, and to indicate whether they had, or had not, notes on the points in question. In addition, the students were given a questionnaire designed to test their opinion on the use of slides in lectures.

A comparison was made between the number of questions in each group of six to which students reported some reference in their notes. This showed no significant difference between the groups, but that there was a tendency for more notes to have been made from the board than from the slides.

A comparison was made between questions which were answered incorrectly, even when students reported referring to their notes. This showed (again not significantly) a tendency for more mistakes to have occurred from points made with slides. In addition, there were more omissions in the notes for material presented with slides than with the blackboard.

The questionnaire results indicated among other things that 90% of students thought that there were sufficient (or even not enough) slides used. Only 10% felt that fewer slides should have been used. However, 71% stated they would have liked to have had a pause in the lecture, to allow them to absorb the slide. So perhaps their relatively poor performance on the slide material was due at least in part to the way the slides were used – presented and 'talked-over' by the lecturer, as Hartley points out.

The criterion for the use of a slide by the lecturer often seems to be that it is a quick way of showing material that is too complicated to write or draw on the board. Such a criterion ignores the fact that if it is too complicated for the lecturer, then it will also be too complicated for the student.

Lecturers need to take more account of the objectives of their slides, and the difficulties of students when using them. For instance, one slide in this study, used to illustrate the size of a crater, did so without a scale. In answering a question on this point only four students gave the correct answer (¾ mile), whilst the rest gave answers of over 10, and one said 300 miles.

Plan method before media

In conclusion, the results should not be taken as a condemnation of visual materials, but rather as another indication of the need for a systematic approach to visual aid design. A visual aid is not an aid unless it performs a specific function, and performs it well. The points to consider are:

1. The objectives – is the student to remember, to comprehend, to form an attitude?
2. The target audience – are they ready for this method of communication; can they use the language?
3. Alternative methods – can the objective be achieved equally or better by a verbal description?
4. Evaluation – does the visual achieve the desired objectives? How can we validly measure this?

Map 4.1 *Summary of research findings on the effects of illustrationsd in text. (From W H Levie and R Lentz,* ECTJ *Vol 30, no 4, Winter 1982.)*

Irrelevant illustrations do not enhance the learning of relevant content	1. *In normal instructional situations, the addition of pictorial embellishments will not enhance the learning of information in the text.* When a student is assigned to read an instructional text, the presence of embellishments (illustrations that present information that does not overlap the text content) should not be expected to provide a 'generalized motivating effect' or in any other way facilitate learning the text content. On the other hand, when the student has a choice of looking at textual material, the presence of attention-getting pictorial embellishments may have a positive effect – simply because of the increased possibility that the material will be looked at.
Relevant illustrations do enhance the learning of related content	2. *When illustrations provide text-redundant information, learning information in the text that is also shown in pictures will be facilitated.* In 46 experimental comparisons of reading with and without pictures, the presence of relevant illustrations helped the learning of illustrated text information in all but one case.
Illustrations relevant to a part of the content have no influence on the learning of the remaining unconnected content	3. *The presence of text-redundant illustrations will neither help nor hinder the learning of information in the text that is not illustrated.* The speculation that the improvement in the learning of illustrated text information would occur at the sacrifice of the learning of non-illustrated portions of the text received essentially no support.

Map 4.1 – *continued*

Appropriate forms of illustration enhance understanding, recall and transfer of what is being communicated	4. *Illustrations can help learners understand what they read, can help learners remember what they read, and can perform a variety of other instructional functions.* Some research indicates that pictures can function to aid comprehension through mechanisms such as providing a context for organizing information in the text. Support for the claim that illustrations can aid retention is the finding that in research testing both immediate and delayed recall, the average learning gain due to the presence of illustrations was five times greater in delayed recall than in immediate recall.
A picture can sometimes be worth a thousand words	5. *Illustrations can sometimes be used as effective/efficient substitutes for words or as providers of extralinguistic information.* This statement is included here simply to acknowledge this important role for illustrations and to serve as a reminder to those writers who occasionally forget that the way of words is not the solitary road to wisdom. Photographs, drawings, diagrams, maps, and other forms of pictures can encourage 'visual thinking' and can carry some kinds of information more effectively/efficiently than linguistic symbol systems.
Complex illustrations tend to be ignored unless they are really essential and their importance is pointed out and appropriate use of them is promoted/demonstrated	6. *Learners may fail to make effective use of complex illustrations unless they are prompted to do so.* Often learners look at illustrations superficially and without expecting to see useful information. Although some information can be gleaned from some pictures easily and rapidly, other pictures require careful study. Complex diagrams, for example, may not be processed by many learners without considerable encouragement and direction. Even with simple representational pictures, the details of objects shown frequently go unnoticed.
Illustrations are welcomed by readers and can motivate or change attitudes	7. *Illustrations usually enhance learner enjoyment, and they can be used to evoke affective reactions.* People like pictures, and learners rate materials that contain illustrations as more enjoyable. Pictures, like words, can also evoke emotional reactions and contribute to affective objectives such as attitude change.
Poor readers may benefit more from appropriate visual support than do good readers	8. *Illustrations may be somewhat more helpful to poor readers than to good readers.* Although individual studies almost always fail to produce statistically significant interactions between reading ability and the presence/absence of illustrations, overall the data show some support for the notion that illustrations are more beneficial for poor readers. This trend is supported by other research indicating that poor readers make more extensive use of illustrations.

Map 4.1 – *continued*

It's better to supply a well planned illustration than to ask students to invent their own	9. *Learner-generated imaginal adjuncts are generally less helpful than provided illustrations.* The research in which learners are instructed to create mental images or to make their own drawings to help them learn shows intermittent positive effects with complex interactions. A problem is that some learners, particularly young children, are unable to produce aids that are relevant to the learning objectives implicit in the text.

5. Non-projected graphic and print media

There is a range of methods used to present still visual material – from the traditional chalkboard to flannelboards, magnetic boards, wall charts, opaque, slide and strip projectors, down to the modern versatile overhead projector. The various methods have particular advantages for certain types of visual material, so although modern equipment like the overhead projector can effectively present diagrams, photos, models and so on, it would not be fair to say that it has rendered other presentation methods obsolete. In this chapter we will consider the full range of non-projected methods at the teacher's disposal, identifying the advantages and limitations of each. In chapter 6 we will consider projected visuals.

5.1. The chalkboard and its derivatives

Old soldiers never die . . .

This was called the *blackboard* until recently when someone noticed that modern blackboards are seldom black – they are blue, green, brown, and even yellow. Reasons for this are less glare and reflection, and less obvious 'ghosting' (the marks left when chalk is rubbed out). Unfortunately, they sometimes give less contrast to white chalk, and the user might experiment with other colours to get maximum readability.

The chalkboard has for long been the standard teaching aid. It is almost universally available, and nearly every teacher uses it. Paradoxically though, it is one of the more difficult teaching aids to use well. More training and skill is required to make good use of the chalkboard than to screen a film, use a slide projector or a tape recorder.

First, you must learn to control the chalk. It takes practice to learn to write legibly and to form sufficiently large letters. It requires practice, together with a gift for drawing, to produce large, clear, freehand diagrams quickly. Standard manuals on the use of the chalkboard list a range of techniques to make its use easier. The preparation of diagrams can be improved by the use of cut-outs or templates for any shapes which are often drawn. Complicated diagrams from books or slides can be projected onto the chalkboard and the essential details drawn by tracing over the image. Small pictures can be blown-up by use of a pantograph, or by dividing into a grid and copying each square separately. Any lines used regularly, such as coordinates for graph drawing, can be permanently printed on sections of the board.

Most of these techniques require the prior preparation of the diagrams. It seems a pity to spend great effort before a lesson preparing a clear diagram by, say, the 'project-on' method, only to rub it off within a short while. Would it not be better to make a more permanent visual which could be used over and over again? It would be economical to spend more time in preparing a better diagram, as re-drawing time would eventually be saved. There are now so many efficient ways of presenting pre-prepared visuals, that the use of a chalkboard for this purpose is obsolete. It's no use moaning that you have no other visual aids. A roll of wallpaper is sufficient to produce a whole range of clear re-usable visuals, for use as wall charts or flip-charts.

The real use for the chalkboard today is for impromptu material (words or diagrams which have become necessary due to an unexpected turn in the lesson) or for work which is developed through the lesson by contribution from the class (experimental results, ideas, theories, solutions to problems, summaries). Therefore, much of our chalkboard use is likely to be 'off-the-cuff' writing or sketching. Unless we have a pretty good idea what sort of contributions the class will make, we are unlikely to be equipped with appropriate templates or cut-outs. However, general purpose drawing aids such as rules, squares and mathematical instruments are invaluable, and their use should be mastered. In the long run, there is no substitute for practice in the use of the chalkboard, in order to achieve clear writing, fast sketching and tidy layout.

Old wine in new bottles   We should mention here a further development of recent years – the white chalkboard, or white-board. Originally, these were used with soap or wax-based coloured chalks and crayons. Now, it is more common to use felt-tipped markers. There are obvious advantages in this equipment. First, there is no chalk-dust. Modern 'dustless' chalks have, it is true, improved the situation and silicosis is unlikely now to be an occupational disease of teachers. However, the term 'dustless' is only relative. Dust is still produced, irritating the lungs of some and destroying the clothes of all. Secondly, the range and strength of colours that can be used on a white-board is much greater. Traditional chalk is available in a limited range of anaemic pastel shades. Wax-based crayons are obtainable in every standard colour, spirit markers in a range of pastel and strong colours. The white-board is therefore particularly valuable when sharp or true-to-life colours are an advantage (for example in art classes and design) as well as for improving the clarity and definition of almost any diagram.

There is one problem, however: that of cleaning the board. Unless the surface is very smooth and hard, colours penetrate. The problem of 'ghosting' is much more acute. Certain wax-based crayons and spirit markers will not wipe off even with a damp cloth, but require special erasers or solutions. If you intend to use a white-board, it is well to get advice on cleaning methods, and the drawing materials permissible, from the manufacturers; or to first experiment with the available materials.

5.2. Felt-boards (flannel boards) and magnetic boards

Displays which can be changed   The felt-board, or flannel board, is simply a board covered in felt or other suitable cloth. Shapes cut out of felt will stay put if pressed onto the board. Other materials such as paper cut-outs can be fixed by backing them with a piece of felt, or if they are heavy, with a special material incorporating thousands of minute nylon hooks. It is possible to use the felt-board to present a display of pre-prepared shapes or items. The main advantage is that these items can very quickly be added to, removed, or their relative positions altered.

The magnetic board is similar in function, but shapes and objects are attached by means of small magnets fixed to their backs. Any sheet of steel would serve as the board itself. Commercially available magnetic boards are generally prepared for use as a chalkboard or a white-board as well, so that lines may be drawn on the surface as well as separate shapes fixed to it. This makes the magnetic board ideal for the presentation of a range of subjects such as work study, strategy or sport. Any problem which involves the movement of things from place to place, or changes in their relative positions, can be very effectively demonstrated, discussed and built up stage by stage.

Elementary school teachers use flannel boards to establish such concepts as 'above' and 'below', or to demonstrate sentence structure. They are used in secondary schools to illustrate Pythagoras' Theorem. Football coaches use them to discuss new tactics. Industry may demonstrate plant layout modifications, or the company structure.

You can equally well use a flannel or magnetic board as a lesson summary. Headings or major points can be slapped up as they are reached, removed for questioning and follow-up, then replaced, without the delay of writing them up and rubbing them off.

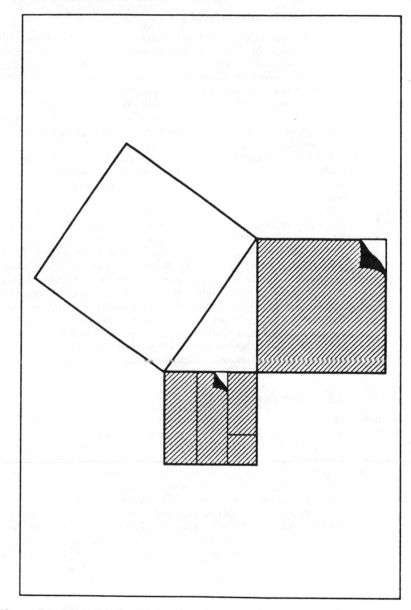

Figure 5.1 *Effective use of flannel or magnetic board. Pre-cut shapes are placed to cover the two small squares. They are then peeled off and replaced on the larger square, demonstrating that Pythagoras' theorem 'really works'.*

Preparation required

It is obvious that both flannel and magnetic boards require the pre-preparation of all materials used. They are therefore a supplement to the chalkboard. Material which is part of the lesson plan would be presented on, say, a magnetic board. Contributions from the students would be developed alongside, on the chalkboard. The chalkboard which is steel-backed, so that it can be used also as a magnetic board, is therefore particularly useful.

However, the special value of flannel and magnetic boards is restricted to display of fairly simple shapes or objects. Complicated pictures or diagrams can be better displayed by projection, or by the use of some form of chart.

5.3. Charts and posters

In this context, charts include all manner of non-projected materials – photographs, maps, diagrams, graphs and cartoons. The particular application of each type of chart or picture – when and how to make best use of its qualities – will be discussed later. From the user's point of view, these materials are all similar, in that they do not need any special equipment to project or display them, and they require preparation in advance. Whereas the chalkboard is used to develop the subject during the classroom session, and magnetic and flannel boards to demonstrate a changing relationship between objects, charts and posters are a permanent, pre-prepared, static display.

It is of course possible to use a sheet of paper and chalk or pen to develop a chart in the classroom, thus using the paper as a substitute for a chalkboard. We will not consider this use here, but confine ourselves to discussing ways of using pre-prepared charts.

Two types of chart

There are two main ways in which charts are used: as permanent displays (wall charts) or as displays which emphasize or summarize certain points in a lesson. The latter will only be shown for a short time, then taken away or replaced by another showing the next stage of development of the subject. The handiest way to store and use such charts is to mount them by the top edge to a horizontal bar, so that one can flip the charts over to reveal any one of them to the class. We will therefore refer to them as flip-charts. Of course, it does not matter in the least whether flip-charts are made to flip, or whether some other system is used, just as it does not matter whether wall charts are actually hung on walls. The essential difference is the amount of control exercised over their use by the teacher. Wall charts are a permanent or semi-permanent display which the student may use in many ways, flip-charts are designed to supply visual support to a specific lesson, and to be used in a specific way.

5.3.1. The use of flip-charts

Controlled presentation of flip-charts

Flip-charts, in use, perform the same function as slide or film strip projectors (to be discussed in chapter 6); they present a visual display for a limited period of time. Each chart has a specific function, some specific message to communicate. A series of charts may, like a film strip, develop a subject being discussed. Like a film strip, the effectiveness of the charts will depend on how well the discussion and the visual are integrated. Flip-charts are seldom designed to stand on their own and communicate the whole message. The exception to this is when they are used as a summary of the main points. Generally, the visual on the chart supplements and illustrates the verbal commentary. To display a chart showing a verbal statement of the point under discussion, and then to read out the statement verbatim discloses either a total unawareness of the function of visuals, or else an awareness that the visual is so bad that the back of the class cannot read it. To re-read a visual presentation is valuable only in reading classes, or perhaps when making a very strong point in summary.

Flip-charts would therefore not normally be overloaded with words, as the reading of the chart interferes with listening to the commentary. Long paragraphs can best be given in hand-outs, but if they are presented as a chart, the teacher should remember to shut up for long enough to let the class read. This technique may be useful when training comprehension, or when introducing a case study.

Active class participation

Both these last examples involve the audience in active participation. Charts are an excellent method of obtaining student participation. The teacher has both the content and the time of presentation under his control. Furthermore, in many subjects the ability to respond to a visual stimulus is more appropriate. How many children do we know who recite their kerb drill faultlessly, yet are quite prepared to step out in front of a moving car? Much industrial training consists of learning appropriate responses to visual stimuli, rather than answers to verbal questions.

There is much experimental evidence that active participation by the class increases the effectiveness of visuals such as charts and film strips. In its simplest

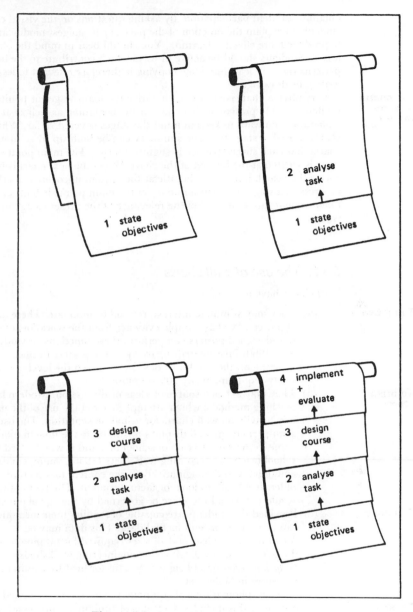

Figure 5.2 *A set of flip-charts for lesson summary.*

and most common form, this participation involves the copying of notes or diagrams from the visual display. This procedure is much favoured, on the grounds that it gives the student notes to refer to, and forces attention to details of diagrams. Others favour free note-making. Another school of thought favours hand-out notes, as they are standard, correct and legible. Still another argues that students seldom, if ever, use notes, and the teacher should plan and carry out systematic revision instead of giving these. There is some truth in all views. Much depends on the level and motivation of the students. However, note copying is probably not very productive in relation to the time it takes, particularly when long paragraphs or complex diagrams are involved. More imaginative ways of obtaining student participation, by asking questions on the visual content, getting students to explain the function of the parts, or to suggest modifications, are liable to produce more effective learning. You should bear in mind the objectives of the lesson. Students should be active in ways which contribute to the behaviour patterns they are learning. Note copying is therefore relevant to lessons in spelling, writing or drawing.

Flip-charts as sum-maries
    Very often a chart is used to summarize the main stages or points in a lesson. It is often useful to present such a chart at the beginning as well as at the end. Sometimes you want to keep in mind the stages covered so far. When a series of charts is used, a stage-by-stage summary can be built up by so mounting the charts that each successive one is slightly shorter. The main point or title of each stage is written at the bottom of the chart. When the next chart is flipped over, it covers the visual, but leaves the title at the bottom uncovered. As the lesson progresses, a stage-by-stage summary of the main points is built up. Thus at any time, students are reminded of the relevance of the present stage to the lesson as a whole.

5.3.2. The use of wall charts

Wall charts have many uses:

To motivate
(a) They may stimulate interest, remind or motivate. These are the functions of posters. We have ample evidence from the world of advertising that well-designed posters can perform these functions. A study by Laner and Sell (1960) investigated the use of safety posters in steel works. In this experiment, the display of posters increased the level of conformity with safety requirements by 20% of more.

To brain-storm
(b) They may act as a source of ideas or discussion. Modern language teaching methods, which attempt to avoid the use of the native tongue, rely heavily on wall charts for visual presentation. The use of semi-permanent wall displays to stimulate the imagination is of special value in the earlier years of school life, and is widely used by primary school teachers. According to Bethers (1956), young children react emotionally and imaginatively to the content of a picture. As they grow older they begin to look for factual content. The types of wall charts we would use would therefore be governed by the age of our students.

To inform
(c) Provided the students are capable of reading their meaning, wall charts can be used to present factual data. This data may be:
Numerical: as the lists of drill sizes required for tapping holes of different diameters (usually displayed in engineering workshops)
Graphical: relation of height to weight for healthy children, steam pressures in boilers, etc
Pictorial: photographs of equipment, with the parts named

To plan
Schematic: this includes diagrams of equipment, processes, structures, engineering drawings, plant layout, flow of materials or cash through a system, the company organization, procedures to be followed, etc

The student may use wall charts in several ways:

To avoid unnecessary learning
(a) he may refer to them at random and gradually familiarize himself with their message – this is the action of posters;
(b) his attention may be directed to them at certain points of a lesson by the teacher, and he may learn or gain inspiration from the content;
(c) he may use the chart systematically as an information store; as a substitute for his memory. The chart becomes a job-aid. This is most commonly the use made of charts loaded with factual details. Memorization of the content would be difficult, if not impossible; the presence of the chart makes it unnecessary.

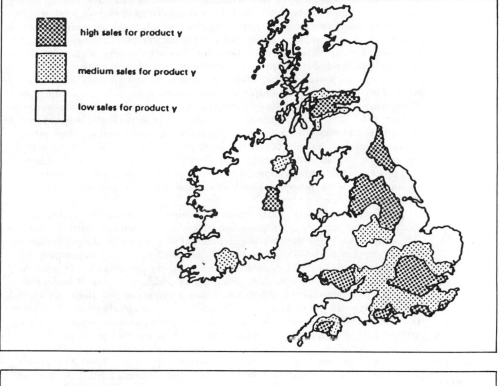

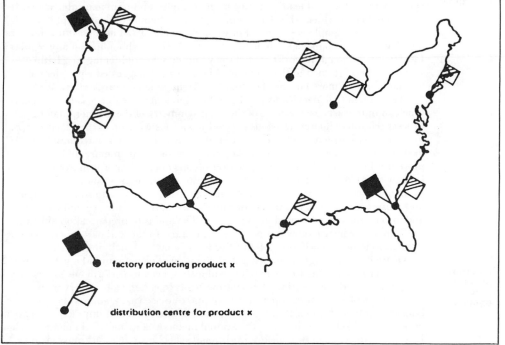

Figure 5.3 *Wall charts used: (a) as a static, permanent reference, and (b) as a dynamic, changeable planning tool.*

The use of charts as job-aids, thus reducing the need for extensive training procedures, should not be overlooked. Unfortunately, at the school level, we are hogtied by examinations which require the memorization of vast quantities of data which can, in practice, be easily looked up. On the job, architects, engineers and chemists all realise that a reference book (or if we need to refer often, a wall chart) is a much more reliable information store than the human memory.

Recently, much work has been done in industry on task analysis, often for work-study purposes. It is a simple step from a task analysis to the production of a chart, listing, step-by-step, the operations a man must perform and the decisions he must take. Such charts, referred to variously as process charts, decision trees or algorithms, can very often act as job-aids, reducing the amount a learner must memorize, and the amount of practice he requires. Charts as job-aids are being increasingly used in business and the professions, from operation on machinery and process plant, through complex office procedures such as tax assessment, to high-level diagnostic procedures such as nuclear reactor fault finding or the diagnosis of disease.

An example of the way charts (particularly those describing procedures or decisions) may simplify communication problems is shown in Figures 5.4 and 5.5. These show two pages from a self-instructional programme on the production of algorithms (Lewis and Wolfenden, 1969). The reader is invited to compare the time taken on the problem in the first page, using the prose as a guide, with the time taken on the second problem, using the algorithm as a guide. Clearly the chart is a more effective job-aid. It saves time, as you read only those parts which are relevant to the job in hand. Also, it illustrates more clearly what outcomes are possible and what decisions must be made to reach a particular outcome. Thus, although the main use of such charts is to 'avoid the need for teaching', they may also be useful as an 'aid to instruction' (Gane, Horabin and Lewis, 1966).

Limitations of algorithms

However, one should not get 'carried away' by algorithms. Even if they are applicable, they are not always the best way of presenting a job aid. A long and complex procedure will lead to a very large, complex and unmanageable chart. It may be better to present the chart in prose form, in numbered paragraphs.

An extreme example is presented in Figures 5.6 and 5.7. The algorithm shown is one developed to enable a student to place the correct verb-ending on any regular Latin verb. Although it works, it is clumsy and may be frightening to a Latin scholar not accustomed to the notation. Figure 5.7 is a suggested equivalent job aid, laid out in a more familiar fashion, less frightening and probably easier to use.

Of course, not all algorithms can be reduced to a manageable, easily read chart. One can in the last case because of the total symmetry of the decision-making process. However if later decisions depend in various ways on earlier decisions, or if earlier decisions have to be re-considered in the light of later outcomes, then feedback loops appear in our algorithm and it becomes much more difficult to present it in any other way. Figure 5.8 represents another algorithm from the book by Lewis and Woolfenden (1969). This diagram, though fairly complicated, is probably as clear a way as any to lay out the procedures for not losing at noughts and crosses. As an exercise, the reader might like to try to improve on this chart and also on the one presented in Figure 5.5. The aim is to prepare a job aid (ie a set of complete instructions but not a learning aid). In the author's experience it is difficult to improve on Figure 5.8 but Figure 5.5 may be much simplified.

The increasing need for good job-aids

We are living through an information explosion. The amount of knowledge we must cover to reach the frontiers of our subject, or even to perform effectively in our jobs, is rapidly increasing. Automation tends to enlarge jobs rather than to fragment them, so even the operative is required to use vast amounts of information to do his job. Rapid obsolescence of jobs renders it impractical, if not impossible, to follow traditional educational methods of memorization and recall. It is only a question of time before traditional school examinations must yield to the pressures of society. First principles are more important than ever before. The necessary factual information can be looked up. Open-book examinations are round the corner. The need is for books which yield their information quickly. Eventually, perhaps, the printed book will be replaced by videotext, capable of

During the first half of 1966, income tax forms were sent to about 20 million people in Great Britain. Accompanying each form was a small yellow leaflet, designed to provide 'general guidance' to the reader concerning the newly introduced Capital Gains Tax. Part of Section F, subsection (i) of the leaflet reads as follows:

(i) If the asset consists of stocks or shares which have values quoted on a stock exchange (see also paragraph G below), or unit trust units whose values are regularly quoted, the gain or loss (subject to expenses) accruing after 6 April 1965, is the difference between the amount you received on disposal and the market value on 6 April 1965, except that in the case of a gain where the actual cost of the asset was higher than the value at 6 April 1965, the chargeable gain is the excess of the amount you received on disposal over the original cost of acquisition price; and in the case of a loss, where the actual cost of the asset was lower than the value at 6 April 1965, the allowable loss is the excess of the original cost or acquisition price over the amount received on disposal.

If the substitution of original cost for the value at 6 April 1965, turns a gain into a loss, or a loss into a gain, there is, for the purposes of tax, no chargeable gain or allowable loss.

Mr Jones bought some shares in 1964 for £2,000
On 6 April 1965 their market value was £2,500
Later in 1965 he sold these shares for £2,300
His expenses came to £50

Problem: What is Mr Jones's Tax Liability?

Answer: _____

Time taken to arrive at answer: _____

Figure 5.4 *This page presents a problem for you to solve. Try to solve it before you turn to Figure 5.5, and note down the time you spent on the problem. (From B N Lewis and P J Woolfenden, Algorithms and Logical Trees, Cambridge Algorithms Press, 1969.)*

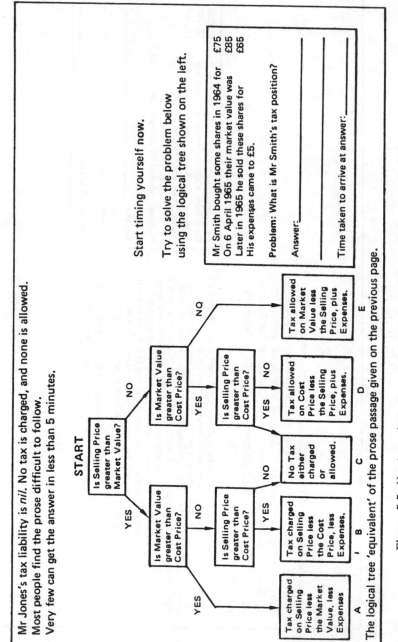

Mr Jones's tax liability is *nil*. No tax is charged, and none is allowed.
Most people find the prose difficult to follow.
Very few can get the answer in less than 5 minutes.

START

Is Selling Price greater than Market Value?

YES ——→ NO

Is Market Value greater than Cost Price?

YES ——→ NO

Is Market Value greater than Cost Price?

NO ——→ YES

Is Selling Price greater than Cost Price?

NO ——→ YES

Is Selling Price greater than Cost Price?

YES ——→ NO

A — Tax charged on Selling Price less the Market Value, less Expenses

B — Tax charged on Selling Price less the Cost Price, less Expenses.

C — No Tax either charged or allowed.

D — Tax allowed on Cost Price less the Selling Price, plus Expenses.

E — Tax allowed on Market Value less the Selling Price, plus Expenses.

The logical tree 'equivalent' of the prose passage given on the previous page.

Start timing yourself now.

Try to solve the problem below using the logical tree shown on the left.

Mr Smith bought some shares in 1964 for   £75
On 6 April 1965 their market value was   £85
Later in 1965 he sold these shares for   £65
His expenses came to £5.

Problem: What is Mr Smith's tax position?

Answer: _____

_____

Time taken to arrive at answer: _____

Figure 5.5 *Here is an alternative presentation of the same content as Figure 5.4 – as a decision tree. Have a go at solving this second problem and compare the time it takes with the previous unstructured version of the text.*

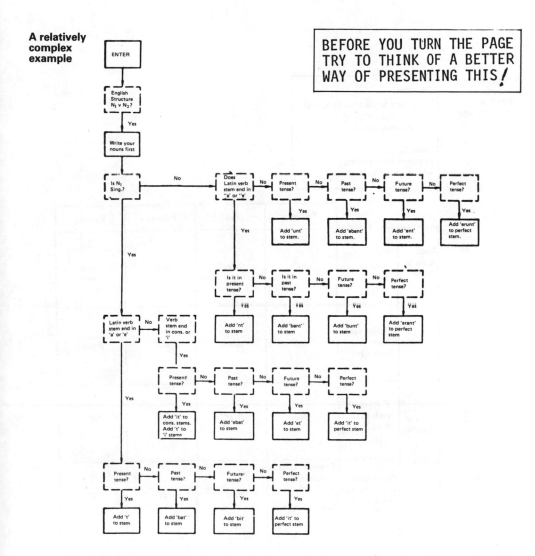

Figure 5.6 *An algorithm for obtaining Latin regular verb endings. (Adapted from J L Evans,* A Potpourri of Programming Technology, *1964.)*

**A simpler
job-aid
with the
same power**

consider:

1   is first noun singular/plural
2   verb stem ending
3   required tense

Read off:
required verb ending
add it to the verb stem

		Present	Past	Future	Perfect
First noun is Plural	Verb stem ends in A or E	'nt'	'bant'	'bunt'	'erant'
	Other verb stem endings	'unt'	'ebant'	'ent'	'erunt'
First noun is Singular	Verb stem ends in A or E	't'	'bat'	'bit'	'it'
	Other verb stem endings ie consonant or 'i'	Stem ends with consonant: Add 'it' Stem ends with 'i' : Add 't'	'ebat'	'et'	'it'

Figure 5.7 *Latin regular verb endings: an alternative chart to the algorithm.*

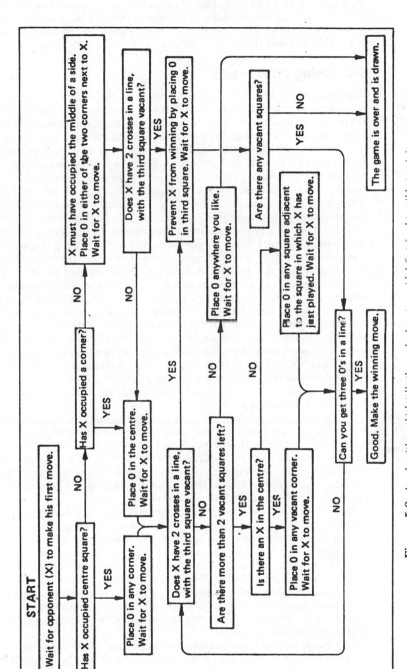

Figure 5.8 *An algorithm which tells the reader how to avoid defeat (and possibly to win) when he is second player in the game of noughts and crosses. (From B N Lewis and P J Woolfenden, Algorithms and Logical Trees* Cambridge Algorithms Press, 1969.)

instant recall on personal receivers through a computerized library system. Experience with computers, however, indicates that small size databases, often used, and used for a limited range of purposes, can be more efficiently stored and recalled by simple files or charts at the place of work. Charts are by no means obsolescent. We can look forward to their increasing use, particularly in the form of job-aids and data stores.

5.4. Using print media

Print and the new information technologies

Printed materials have been, and continue to be, the single most common category of teaching support materials. Indeed, the currently spreading trend towards electronic communication (E-mail systems, electronic encyclopaedias, database networks and so on) has added several new media of transmission for printed messages and is thus contributing to the overall amount of reading that a typical person has to cope with. Just a short while ago, we all had to go out to shop, whatever the commodity we were interested in. In order to interest us, manufacturers would use print (and graphics) in newspaper advertising, brochures through the post, or outdoor posters. Then the telephone and television reduced the amount of printed messages – advertising is in large part filmed, relying on situational, visual and spoken stimuli to communicate its message. Instead of going out or writing a letter, we started to do part of our shopping by telephone. But most recently, the new electronic media of computer networks, videotext systems and centralized databases have once again reversed the trend. The modern shopper does not have to wait for a chance advertising message to alert interest, but may access a database on, say, all the cars for sale in local used-car showrooms and browse through the information as if it were one big catalogue. The database may possibly have pictures of the cars (unlikely though, as this would increase the cost enormously for a very short-life message), but it will certainly contain most of the information as a printed message. As this message is limited to the size of a television screen, it is probable that some standard layout conventions will develop, that will help to put the maximum of information into this display size in a way which will make it easier for users to compare data of one car or one showroom with others.

The future for paper texts in instruction is secure

In other words, the role of print, far from being superseded, is being enhanced by the information revolution. But what about print on paper? Are the days of the book (especially the textbook) numbered? Most futurologists think not. It may be that paper will be less used, but it is unlikely to be superseded. All seem to agree that books which aim to entertain are 'nice to have' – I want to have the leather bound complete works of Shakespeare on my bookshelf, not accessible electronically over a phone line and a modem.

What about books which inform? Sometimes, electronic storage and transmission offers great advantages – cost reduction, storage space reduction, easy updating and revision, etc. But when the information is likely to be required often, over a long period of time, in many locations, or away from the place where I have access to a terminal, then a hard copy version is still preferred. For our purposes here, it makes little difference if that printed version is produced by traditional publishing and printing methods and is distributed through traditional bookshops, or whether a locally laser-printed copy of an electronically stored master is run off when required. We still end up with print on paper, to be used as part of an instructional system.

Printed media and their abuse

So, printed materials will continue to be used and abused in instruction. I say 'abused' because the ease with which these materials may be obtained, reproduced and circulated leads to their often excessive or inappropriate use in the instructional process. The teacher who would never dream of using a half-hour film in a class without first previewing it and carefully selecting the useful parts, planning introductory and follow-up activities, etc, may, when it comes to print, recommend a reading list which would require ten hours to complete, without a clear definition to the student of what to look for in the readings, how to be selective and critical in order to get the required information in a reasonable amount of reading time, what to do with the information in order to organize it for learning or future use, or even what the long-term objective of the reading assignment really is. Sometimes, the teacher has not even read all the assignment material, but recommends it on some other person's recommendation.

The key to effective print media in the instructional process . . .

Just like any other media, print media may be used for any of the four functions of *entertainment, motivation, information* and *instruction*. Often the aim of the message involves a combination of two or more of these (see chapter 1). However, we must deal with them separately here, in order to understand them better. Firstly let us remember the distinction between medium (in the hardware sense) and the message being transmitted (which depends on the structure and planning that has gone into the software). Our selection and use criteria are thus of two types:

. . . and how to plan their effective-ness: message design and . . .

(a) Assuming we wish to achieve certain instructional, or information-dissemination, objectives, is the use of the printed word an essential or desirable component in our system? If so, what is the role of this component, what are the characteristics of the message, its content, when and how in the instructional process will it be used? In short, print materials will be specified in our lesson plans and existing materials will be selected, or adapted, or new materials developed, to satisfy the *message design* criteria specified in the plan.

. . . message delivery and communica-tion

(b) Given all the above and also information about the context in which we will teach, or in which our learners will use the messages, what are the best or most convenient media of presentation, storage and retrieval of the messages? What are the information processing skills of our students – will they cope with the materials we have located or produced? Will they be able to read them? Will they have access to them when necessary? In short, the print materials and the delivery media should be selected to satisfy the existing *message communication* constraints. We must ensure that the message is transmitted and is received just as it was planned.

Reading assign-ments and the lack of teacher-control

All this is applicable to any media/materials selection and use process, but in the case of printed materials it is important to stress it, as it often gets less attention than it deserves. Also, weaknesses in print message design and delivery may often go undetected for longer than is the case with, say, slides or flip-charts. This is because the readers are 'on their own' with paper handouts or library reading assignments, in a way that they are not when a teacher uses a visual display during a classroom presentation. In the class session, it takes only one student to raise a question regarding something that is unclear in the presentation, to alert the teacher to a weakness in the message or in its transmission. The diagram was unclear to one student and all benefit from the revision and clarification that the teacher offers. Some of the group were not even aware that the message they had received was not the one intended, and would have left the classroom blithely misinformed, were it not for one student's question or the systematic questioning and feedback which the teacher built into the lesson. But in the case of a reading assignment, the misconception may go unnoticed until later on it builds on others to create a more serious and more difficult-to-diagnose learning deficiency.

Prog-rammed texts: control of learning built into the medium

One way to avoid this is to build comprehension and learning checks into the material at frequent intervals. This transforms the reading assignment into a controlled learning assignment – the text has been transformed into a programmed-instruction module.

We shall be dealing with programmed instruction later on, but in a separate chapter, as such programmed materials become interactive instructional systems in their own right and, as such, will be better treated in conjunction with other interactive materials and media. In this chapter, we are concerned with text when it is used as a component in an instructional system, but not necessarily in an interactive capacity. In such cases, the function of the message is *informational*, with possible motivational intentions as well (there is nothing against the text being

Purposes	Formats		
	Books	**Periodicals**	**Other formats**
Recreation/Entertainment	• Novels • Anthologies of essays, poems, and short stories • Biographies • Autobiographies • Books on general topics	• Magazines with essays, poems, and short stories • Magazines devoted to hobbies, sports	• Comics • Sheet music
Motivation/Attitude change	• Socially/politically slanted non-fiction • Manifestos	• Religious and similar journals • Mail order catalogue	• Posters • Leaflets
Information	• Encyclopedias and other general reference works • Dictionaries • Thesauri • Indexes and bibliographies to journals, documents, and other materials • Specific reference works	• Newspapers • News magazines • Newsletters/bulletins • Professional journals • Journals devoted to specific topics of general concern (e.g., health, family, business)	• Pamphlets • Brochures • Handbills • Reports • Source lists • Guides • Schedules • Menus • Directories
Instruction	• Textbooks • Books on specific topics used as texts (e.g., treatises of great philosophers) • Programmed instruction information, mapped, or specially formatted texts	• Magazines of the how-to variety (e.g., *Popular Mechanics*) • Serialized study modules (distance/correspondence courses)	• Course handouts • Manuals • Job aids • Written simulations • Workbooks • Algorithms • Study Guide

Figure 5.9 *The range of printed media formats – a selection and rough classification. All may be used occasionally as components in an instructional system, but the lower half of the chart is of more direct relevance. We shall deal with general aspects in this chapter and leave the last, self-instructional or interactive texts to a later chapter.*

entertaining as well, but I don't stress this here, as in the instructional context, entertainment is a subsidiary, albeit ever-useful aim).

5.5 Design of instructional text

Learner-control: selection of relevant content

One great advantage of printed textual material is that it is under the control of the reader, to skip certain parts, read and re-read others, copy or highlight important points, etc. This is not of prime importance in text written for entertainment, or even for motivation – in these situations, the flow of the narrative as the story unfolds is a key element in the overall effectiveness of the text. It is written to be read in a linear sequence. Much of the information which a learner has to receive is not, however, strung together in a unique 'best' sequence. This is an often overlooked fact – witnessed by the way the narrative linear-sequence style continues to be the most common approach to the authoring of informational material. To make my point, I present two versions of a simple informational memo – the type that might be encountered any day in any organizational setting. The reader is invited to compare the linear-narrative version shown in Figure 5.10 with the structured-for-information-retrieval version shown in Figure 5.11.

Structured writing

A manual of structured pages, or 'maps', somewhat resembles an atlas of geography maps. Each map has a definite purpose, clearly defined. Each map attempts to present the 'shape' or 'structure' of the information it contains, and for this purpose it uses certain standardized conventions. Finally, just like in a geography atlas, one will find maps which give the 'global' view ('overview' maps, 'summary' maps, 'structure' maps) and other maps which give more detailed information on certain aspects of the whole topic (individual 'concept' maps, procedure maps, compare/contrast tables, etc).

Cross-referencing

The whole manual is cross-indexed and cross-referenced to facilitate the student's choice of the material he needs to read. Thus the student can apply his own learning strategy to the material, going from the particular to the general, or vice versa, from the simple to the complex, or vice versa, from rules and principles to examples, or vice versa. The student may follow a holist or a serialist learning procedure. Furthermore, as all exercises (feedback questions) are to be found on separate, labelled pages, he may easily 'skip' them, to use the manual as a reference text, or select those he feels he needs to self-evaluate his learning, or read these pages first, to diagnose which sections he needs to review.

He may use the manual as a quick and general overview of the subject, reading only the review and summary maps, or he may look up detailed definitions and examples of specific concepts, or the steps of specific procedures, as and when he needs the information, thus using the manual as a job-aid. He may find what information he needs and at the level of detail he needs, just when he needs it.

Flexibility in use

This flexibility of use adapts it well to the varied needs of learners, coming from different backgrounds, with different levels of prior knowledge.

The emphasis on the presentation of the structure of the topic, and of each manual's contents 'hang together'. This arrangement enables the reader to get a broad view of the subject, if he so wishes, or delve deeper into the parts of the subject which appear new, or particularly interesting, to him. The use of a manual which has been structured in this manner, is thus highly individualized, each reader selecting the content that meets his needs, at the level of detail that he requires in order to understand it. He may act as a first-time learner, or as a 'browser' wishing to gain a general idea.

The structured writing techniques, described here, were developed by Robert E. Horn and his collaborators (Horn *et al*, 1969; Horn, 1973; 1974) under the name of 'Information Mapping' (TM). This term and also the term 'Info-Maps' are now trademarks of Information Resources Inc., of Lexington, Massachusetts, which markets structured writing services under the name of The Information Mapping (TM) Writing Service.

MEMORANDUM

Date: 23 January

From: John Rootes, Managing Director

To: All Departments

As all are well aware, our company has recently taken the decision to diversify from our traditional motor car and engine spares manufacturing, to the manufacture of a range of car accessories. This decision, quite naturally, will necessitate a series of changes in the structure of the company and a number of personnel changes at management, supervision and other levels will take place. This memorandum announces the changes already defined and later communications will define other changes, as soon as the new department managers have had a chance to specify their requirements.

We wish to stress that in planning these changes, we have tried to cause the least possible disruption to existing work groups and have made every effort to relocate existing personnel in preference to the creation of new appointments.

The following changes at department manager level will become effective as from the first of February. Bill White, currently Sales Manager, will effectively continue, but will now be called Motor Spares Sales Manager. He will report to Alan Jones, who leaves the post of Chief of Marketing Policy, to become General Sales Director. John Brown, currently Production Manager, will take over one of our new departments, as New Products Development Manager. His position will be filled by Joe Cole, who will be promoted from Production Supervisor to Production Manager.

We take the opportunity to welcome Clarence Black, who is joining the company to head the new accessory sales department, as Accessory Sales Manager.

The vacancies created — Production Supervisor and Chief of Marketing Policy — will be filled by internal promotions, to be announced by the end of the month, together with a full list of other changes at supervision level. These changes will become effective on February 15th, the day on which all other changes at lower levels will be announced.

We hope, therefore, to be fully operational, with the two new departments — New Products Development and Accessory Sales — fully staffed by the first day of March.

Figure 5.10 *Example of a typical (unstructured) communication.*

The roots of this technique spread into every psychological 'camp'. It draws its principles from the work of such diverse workers as Gagné, Piaget, Lumsdaine, Skinner, Briggs, Ausubel and Glaser. It knits these principles into a set of rules and procedures for the preparation of written materials which may serve the purposes of instruction, of revision or of reference. It may also serve as the basis of organization of material for a computer-based information system.

Other sources of hints on effective text design

The structured writing, or mapping, of information is but one of the techniques that have been developed in recent years for the preparation of more effective textbooks and handouts. It is interesting that this, the oldest and most used of the presentation media, had a very small research literature until a short time ago. Typography aspects were of course well known to the printing and publishing professions, but layout and visual design aspects which might promote comprehension and learning were largely ignored. In the last twenty years or so, the design of text for instructional purposes has promoted ever-increasing interest among researchers and instructional technologists. James Hartley, in the UK, was one of the pioneers of systematic study in this field, and his book, *Designing Instructional Text*, has become a classic 'how-to' reference text (Hartley, 1978, revised and enlarged 1985). Other useful references in this field are Hartley's *The Psychology of Written Communication* (1980) which analyses the research in the field,

---

MEMORANDUM

Date: 23 January
From: John Rootes, Managing Director
To: All Departments

Topic: Impending changes in staffing due to diversification

Motive: The decision to diversify into car accessory production and sales requires a re-structuring of the company which will create two new departments:
           — New Products Development
           — Car Accessory Sales
           This in turn will require certain staffing changes at management, supervision and other levels.

Staffing changes at management level — effective on February 1st		
Name of employee	From (present post)	To (new post)
Alan Jones	Chief — Mrktng. Policy	General Sales Director
Bill White	Sales Manager	Motor Spares Sales Manager
Clarence Black	(new appointment)	Car Accessory Sales Manager
John Brown	Production Manager	New Products Develop. Manager
Joe Cole	Product. Supervisor	Production Manager

Changes at other levels — to be defined as follows		
Level	Date of announcement	Effective as from
Supervision	January 31st	February 15th
Lower levels	February 15th	March 1st

Welcome: We take this opportunity to welcome Clarence Black, who is joining the company to head the new Accessory Sales Department, in the post of Accessory Sales Manager.

Please note: We wish to stress, however, that our policy in planning these changes, has been aimed at causing the least possible disruption to existing working groups and every effort is being made to relocate existing personnel in preference to the creation of new appointments. This applies to the two vacancies created by the announced moves (Production Supervisor and Chief of Marketing Policy) which will be filled by internal promotions.

Figure 5.11 *A 'structured' version of the document shown in its original 'unstructured' form in Figure 5.10.*

and Jonassen's *The Technology of Text* (1982) which is a compendium of text design techniques and tricks. As regards these techniques, we shall not explore them further here, as the aim of this book is restricted to the selection and use of materials. However, as most instructors do get involved in the preparation of written materials for their students, we do recommend a study of the above-mentioned books and the ever-growing list of articles in the educational technology journals devoted to aspects of text design.

Hints on efficient communication through text   The typographical and visual clarity aspects are something that any teacher should verify when assessing existing texts with a view to inclusion in a course. As the literature on this is not always to hand, we close this chapter with two figures that summarize the chief rules that have been found to contribute to the efficiency of communication of printed text and graphic materials.

Map 5.1 *Text design principles.*

Content	• When developing the content for textual materials, consider the audience, the information to be presented, and the way the audience will process the information. • Include all essential content and eliminate extraneous information. • Link new material with what the learners already know.
Writing style	• Use an appropriate reading and vocabulary level. • Short, concise statements with concrete, familiar words will significantly aid your readers. • Use active language and visual and verbal analogies. • Use diagrams or algorithms where appropriate. These will not only add interest, but will greatly assist the reader in learning the material. • Use clear layout and 'blocking' of the information into easy-to-identify parts. Use margin headings or other methods to identify the content of each part. • Be consistent in the layout, highlight, and emphasis conventions used. If italics are used, they should always be used for the same purpose. Let the reader know the conventions that you are using. • When appropriate, try to organize the text so that readers may pick and choose what they need to read and in what order. Do not impose an arbitrary order on material that is not logically sequenced in itself. • Attempt to apply the instructional and message design principles (found elsewhere in this book) to the treatment of the specific type of content and specific objective. Incorporate these principles into your personal style.
Words-print	• Line length should fit a typical group of words. Optimal line length is 39 characters and 25 to 50 is the acceptable range. • 55 lines has been found to be an ideal page length. • Right justification is not necessary; it increases cost and studies show it reduces reading speed. • A variety of page organizations can be used, but within one document a consistent organization should be followed. • All illustrations should be closely related to the text. • When explaining a process, use one illustration per step. • Use a list or outline of the content to help learners in organizing information. • Use bullets, numbers, or white space to separate and focus attention on key items. • The type-size range for good readability is 9 to 12 points. Use the larger sizes if the x height is small. • Even though there is a slight preference for serif typefaces any simple serif or sans serif typeface can be used, but avoid condensed typefaces. • Consider spacing between words and lines. Adequate space between lines increases readability. • Maintain a high contrast between type and the background. However, avoid white or light letters on a dark background.

Map 5.2 *Visual design principles.*

Graphs and diagrams	• Line graphs are particularly useful in showing trends over a period of time and relationships between two or more factors.
	• Bar graphs are effective for comparing magnitude or size.
	• Pie charts (or circle graphs) are good for showing the relationship between a whole and its parts.
	• Simplicity is particularly important in graphs and diagrams for instructional purposes.
	• Numeric scales and data points on graphs should be carefully chosen to avoid confusion, misinformation, or ambiguity.
	• Symbols employed in graphs and diagrams should not be arbitrarily selected and should be familiar to all persons in the audience.
	• When producing graphic materials, consider:
	    the graphic style
	    perspective
	    the technical quality
	• Graphs and diagrams should be located together with text that explains or uses them – if possible, on the same page or on the one facing the text.
	• If complex diagrams are to be used, try to build them up in stages over several figures and if possible guide the reader through the reading and use of the diagram by working through one or two examples. Get the reader to work through an example.
	• Do not include diagrams which have no real function in communicating your message. They do not enhance understanding or motivation.

Pictures	• Carefully choose the elements that are to be included in a picture. Consider their relevance, simplicity, and harmony.
	• When organizing the elements of a picture consider the following aspects:
	    viewpoint
	    visual pattern
	    balance
	    emphasis
	    unity
	    variety
	• When making photographs the treatment of the elements is important. Consider:
	    lighting
	    perspective
	    the instant a picture
	      is taken
	    focus and sharpness
	    value – the lightness or
	      darkness of the picture

Some final rules	• When planning printed materials consider how, where, and by whom they will be used, eg, materials for poor readers must be designed differently than those for good readers. • Consider the type of reproduction. Fine detail can be lost in printing of poor quality.

6. Projected visuals

6.1. Types of still projected visuals

One limitation of graphic display materials, which we mentioned in the previous chapter, is the limitation on the size of group that can conveniently view a poster or a wallchart. As the size of the group increases, so must the size of the visual. The production of very large graphics is a costly and time-consuming business. The alternative is to blow up a small graphic by means of projection onto a screen.

Film strips and slides

This is nowhere more justified than in the use of photographs, particularly colour photos. The cost of very large photographic blow-ups is quite prohibitive for general instructional use, whereas the production of a slide is much cheaper than even the smallest paper photo, if direct reversal film is used, as only one step is involved in the laboratory. Furthermore, the colour fidelity and brightness of a slide projected onto a screen is much better than can normally be achieved in large-size colour prints. Thus, simplicity of production and fidelity of reproduction are two pressing reasons for the popularity of photographically produced slides and film strips.

Opaque projection

Nevertheless, a certain amount of planning and up-front investment of time and money is involved in the use of these types of visuals. What if we have a paper visual in a book or on a small sheet of card? What if its quality is adequate and colour fidelity is not an important characteristic? In today's world of relatively cheap photocopies, we might run off a copy for each student to study and keep. But in earlier days, the opaque projector or episcope was the answer. These were monstrous machines which tended to produce more heat than light, or so it seemed. Yet, no self-respecting school would be without one. Later models, the epidiascopes, doubled as opaque projectors and slide/film strip projectors, being rather imperfect at each task, as is often the case in such design compromises.

Overhead projection

Then came the overhead projector – a breakthrough in many respects, some say the first bit of educational hardware to be designed to cope with the realities of the classroom – daylight projection, no loss of teacher/class contact, simply produced handmade visuals as well as easy ways of copying existing graphic originals. They said that the 'OHP' would replace the opaque projectors overnight and might even threaten the slide and film strip projector market. But in fact, all are cohabiting quite nicely, thank you. Read on to find out why.

6.2. The use of projected visuals

6.2.1 Film strips

These have been with us since the 1920s, but wartime development established their widespread use in education in the 1940s and 1950s. There are extensive libraries of film strips available for hire, for sale, or free, on topics ranging from 'how to read a micrometer' to 'bible stories'.

The quantity of material available unfortunately includes a fair proportion of film strips of rather doubtful quality. Many film strips fall short of the ideal in terms of visual content, arrangement and supporting commentary. Most of them include teacher's notes. Some are even supplied with a recorded commentary on tape or disc to support the visuals. We will discuss the use of such presentations again in the chapter on audio teaching aids. For the moment let us concentrate on the practical use made of film strips and strip projectors.

Common film strip formats

By far the most common film-strip projection equipment takes a 35 mm film. The film may have pictures taken on full-frame, as by any ordinary 35 mm camera, or on half-frame, which gives smaller pictures, but twice as many of them on the same length of film. Commercially produced film strips are most often half-frame, but most projectors can be modified, by means of a shutter arrangement, to screen either half or full-frame film strips. Thus a film taken by a standard 35 mm camera can be screened as a film strip. It is, however, much more common for the amateur to produce his material in the form of slides.

Main advantages and disadvantages of film strips

The film strip medium has distinct advantages and disadvantages as compared to slides. Being in strip form, the sequence of visuals is fixed. This may be a problem, when a teacher wishes to show just one or two pictures which are hidden somewhere in the middle of a long strip of film. Much winding back and forth may be needed and a proportional amount of time is lost. However, when a fixed sequence of presentation is required, the strip offers the advantage of keeping all the visuals in the correct order at all times. Also it is easier to store a film strip than a tray of slides for a slide projector. And if you don't keep each set of slides in its own tray, then all hell is let loose as slides are lost in storage, dropped in the loading, damaged by regular fingering and inevitably put in back to front or upside-down. Whereas this may help to keep the audience awake, it also tends to turn them off – hence the continued preference for film strip presentations among salespersons who use portable audiovisual presentations to 'hook' their clients. Simplicity and reliability of operation is the name of the game. Not to mention the lower cost of producing multiple copies.

These cost and simplicity factors still endear the film strip to commercial producers of educational materials and so schools are still equipped with some form of film strip projection equipment.

6.2.2. Film slides

There are several reasons for the increased use of slides by persons or organizations preparing their own teaching materials:

Advantages of slides

(1) *Ease of filming.* One bad photo on one film would require re-shooting the whole film, or else splicing in an alternative shot. If multiple copies of the finished product are to be prepared, this is no problem. The final strip will be in one piece. If only one copy is required, only the slide which is below standard needs re-shooting and mounting. The same applies to later damage. Only the one damaged slide needs to be replaced.

(b) *Flexibility in use.* As the slides are individually mounted, the teacher has much more control over which visuals he shows, and the order in which he shows them. He may show only part of a sequence to some groups. Any changes in the subject matter which affect some of the slides can be accommodated without re-making the whole sequence. Film strips tend to become obsolescent, particularly when they deal with industrial processes or human problems.

(c) *Durability.* Slides stand up to wear and tear better than film strips. The film surface is protected by glass, or the mount, so that it does not come into physical contact with parts of the projector mechanism.

There is less standardization among slides and slide projectors in the sizes catered for. The most common slide is a cardboard-mounted standard 35 mm film frame. This is the format used by the home-use slide projectors, and the standard mounting supplied by photographic companies. With modern high-class projectors this size of slide gives adequate definition for most educational purposes, except perhaps the largest auditoria, where larger slide sizes may still be used.

Slides vs. film strips

In terms of impact, or the qualities which make them effective, there is no difference between film strips and slides. The main difference in use is the degree of flexibility, already mentioned. Film strips are supported by carefully prepared teacher notes, even scripts. This task is performed by the teacher when using slide

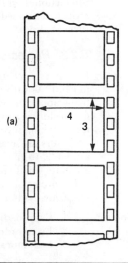

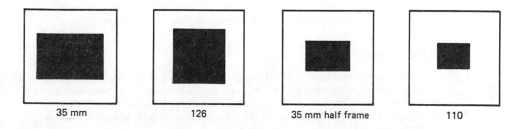

Figure 6.1 *Common film strip projection formats. (a) Half-frame format. This is typical of most commercially distributed film strips. A 'squarer' 3 × 4 image is projected. (b) A standard 35 mm film gives a longer, 2 × 3 picture. Of course, the picture is also larger on the screen.*

35 mm   126   35 mm half frame   110

Figure 6.2 *Different slide sizes. Half-frame cameras use 35 mm film but expose half the film area that 35-mm cameras do. Pictures are smaller and of lesser quality, but twice as many can be taken with a single roll of film. Even though film sizes vary, slides are usually mounted in 2" × 2" mounts and can be projected by standard slide projectors.*

presentations. There is no less need for a well-designed commentary with slides, but the teacher has more scope to use his own ideas. Because of cheap mass production, film strips will continue to be made. For reasons of individual teaching style, teachers will continue to buy them, chop them up, edit them and mount them as slides.

6.2.3. Projectors

Projectors are chosen either for versatility or for special qualities useful to the task in hand. As with most equipment, the versatile machine gives adequate service in many applications, but is perfect in none. The small school or training establishment, possessing only one or two projectors, would settle for a versatile model taking several sizes of slide mounts, and possibly film strips as well. Such projectors are available, and the better ones have a selection of lens units available, to give adequate projection in various sizes of rooms. Modern projectors are quite small and robust, and so are easily transportable.

If a projector is to be used solely for slides, you should consider a magazine-loading machine. The advantages are:

Selecting a slide projector

1. Easy loading of slides.
2. Fixed order of presentation (unless you drop the magazine).
3. Easy storage in correct order.

Of course, deliberate rearrangement of the order of presentation is simplicity itself. Some projectors take a straight magazine, others a circular drum. These have the advantage of automatically showing the first slide after the last one – very useful for continuous presentation at exhibitions. Most magazine-loading projectors have the further advantages of remote-control slide progression. This increases the flexibility enormously. Being able to sit back with the class and watch is the least advantage. A series of slides of stages in an assembly task can be presented at a fixed rate, which can be increased as learning progresses. Slides may be changed by other equipment, such as a tape recorder, by a simple process of synchronization.

Special effects

Synchronized slide and tape presentations, to be discussed later, are a popular and valuable communication method in industry – in training and in sales. Such versatility can be purchased quite cheaply. The Kodak Carousel, for example, is an inexpensive machine with all the extras, and gives excellent results although designed primarily for the holiday slide enthusiast. Educational and industrial models are more robust, but carry the penalty of a higher price-tag. You can also buy zoom-lens models which enable you to 'fill your screen' every time.

If expense is no object, one can purchase random-access facilities, to pick out any slide at will, or even a battery of such projectors, mounted as one, with fade-in, fade-out facilities, capable of presenting the equivalent of a Hollywood epic in still pictures.

Automatic strip projectors are also available, and there are various gadgets on the market that synchronize film strip to recorded discs or tapes.

6.2.4. Screening

Front- or back-projection?

There are two possibilities – direct projection and back-projection. Back-projection requires special equipment in the form of a projection box, or a room with a translucent screen in the wall. Its advantage is a better picture in daylight conditions. Back-projection was all the rage a few years ago. Recent advances in projector design now give excellent results in daylight when projected directly onto a screen. The advantages of daylight projection are very worthwhile (eg class control, note taking), but back-projection is no longer the only way to achieve this. Most portable back-projection set-ups are limited to a small picture size. Thus the attractions of back-projection for occasional use in a general-purpose classroom are lost – there is extra equipment to set up with no special advantages. The method is

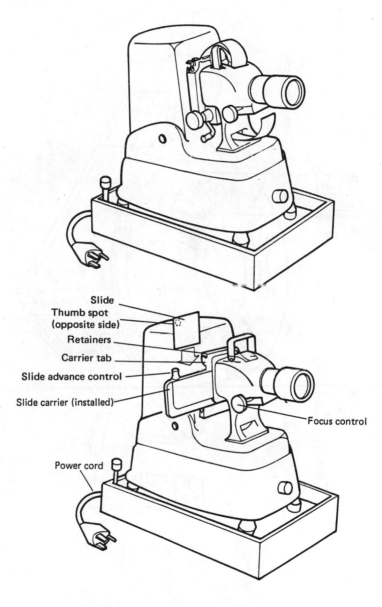

Slide
Thumb spot (opposite side)
Retainers
Carrier tab
Slide advance control
Slide carrier (installed)
Focus control
Power cord

Figure 6.3 *Simple is beautiful. A robust, manually operated film-strip/slide projector. Such models are still made and sold. Note that the film transport and lens assembly may be rotated by 90 degrees to give either a vertical or a horizontal picture. A shutter may be opened in order to screen full-frame film strips. Many of these projectors are convertible to slide projection by interchanging the film transport assembly for a slide transport assembly.*

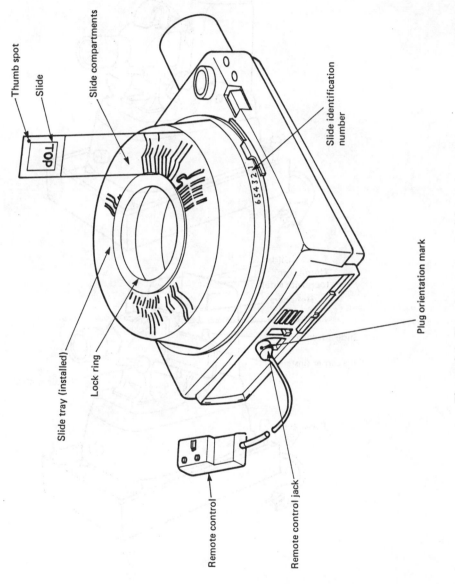

Figure 6.4 *Carousel-type automatic slide projector.*

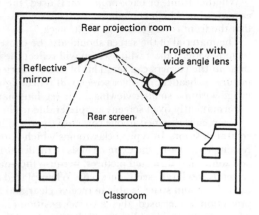

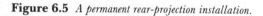

Figure 6.5 *A permanent rear-projection installation.*

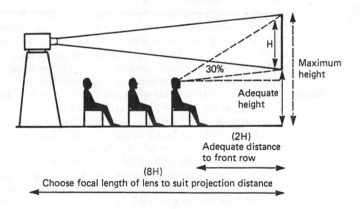

Figure 6.6 *Optimum positioning of projector and screen. Positioning a screen across a corner removes blind spots. A beaded screen could thus be used in a square room.*

still of value in a permanent auditorium, as all equipment is out of sight and out of harm's way.

Position and choice of screen

Whether front- or back-projection is used, the screen should be positioned for easy viewing – high enough for the back rows to see the bottom edge, not so high that the front rows get a crick in the neck.

The material of the screen should also be chosen with the room in mind. If the room is wide, a matt white screen will reflect the light in all directions, so that those in the corners can see. This of course carries the penalty of a less bright picture. A beaded, or silver screen will reflect light more directly, giving a brighter image within a smaller viewing angle (eg long narrow rooms).

Permanently fixed screens are preferable to the portable, wobbly tripod type.

A screen positioned in one corner of the room is preferable to the more common central position. In typical classrooms which approximate to a square-ish rectangle in shape, the extreme ends of the front rows of viewers receive poorly lit and somewhat distorted pictures, because the angle of reflection of light from the screen is too large (see Figure 6.6). When placed across the corner, more of the used classroom space is able to receive clear and bright images. Also, if daylight projection is ever used, then a corner position may be selected in such a way as to minimize the incident light on the screen from the windows. For example, if in Figure 6.6 the classroom were to have windows in the left-hand wall, then the corner screen position shown would be good, but if the windows were in the right-hand wall, then the screen should be in the right-hand corner.

These screen positioning guidelines are of course very general. Each room has its own peculiarities and these should be taken into account when selecting and positioning screens.

6.2.5. Design of slides and film strips

We have already discussed factors which may render subject matter suitable for visual display. Once you have made the decision to use slides or a film strip, there are a few common-sense design considerations.

What affects the clarity of a visual

First, *clarity*. This is affected by the quality of photography, choice of colours or contrast and size of detail, as well as by the quantity of information presented on one slide. Intelligent use of colour may add clarity, but the use of too many colours may add only confusion. Similarly, too much information on one slide will not be taken in during the limited time of display normally allowed. The observations made earlier in the chapter contrasting the use of the flip-charts and wall charts apply here. If your subject cannot be broken down into simple visuals, use a hand-out diagram in preference to a projected image.

What affects its legibility

Secondly, *legibility*. This will again be influenced by how much you cram into your slide, as the more verbal material you present, the smaller the print size. Again, overloading the slide with verbal content is using the medium for something which can better be achieved by a hand-out. A useful guide to the production of verbal content for slides is to work to an absolute limit of 8 lines of print if a slide is used with its larger dimension vertical, or only 6 lines of print if the slide is to be screened horizontally. A good way of planning content is to use a standard typewriter, with cards (or pencil-drawn rectangles) of 2 by 3 inches. If you type your message into this space, laid out as well as possible, you will get a model for a legible transparency. Note that with normal line spacing you could get over twice the recommended maximum number of lines in the space.

How to get it

Incidentally, provided you have a 35 mm camera with the facility for close-up work, so that the 2 in × 3 in card can be photographed to fill the slide, this is an excellent way of preparing artwork. The use of a carbon ribbon on the typewriter gives results every bit as good as the use of Letraset on larger cards, with considerable time and cost savings. The eventual clarity and legibility will of course depend on the distance of the screen from the viewer and on the size of image on the screen.

In the typical classroom (see Figure 6.6) the front row may be about 8 or 10 ft

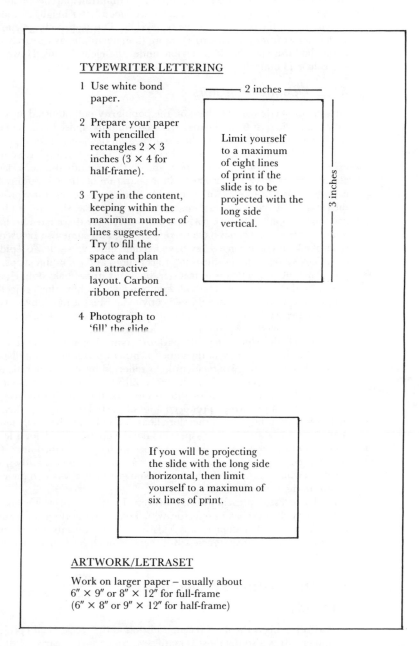

TYPEWRITER LETTERING

1 Use white bond paper.

2 Prepare your paper with pencilled rectangles 2 × 3 inches (3 × 4 for half-frame).

3 Type in the content, keeping within the maximum number of lines suggested. Try to fill the space and plan an attractive layout. Carbon ribbon preferred.

4 Photograph to 'fill' the slide

——— 2 inches ———

Limit yourself to a maximum of eight lines of print if the slide is to be projected with the long side vertical.

3 inches

If you will be projecting the slide with the long side horizontal, then limit yourself to a maximum of six lines of print.

ARTWORK/LETRASET

Work on larger paper – usually about 6″ × 9″ or 8″ × 12″ for full-frame (6″ × 8″ or 9″ × 12″ for half-frame)

Figure 6.7 *Rule-of-thumb for the production of slides of verbal material. To ensure legibility and avoid overloading with information.*

from the screen and the back row about 30 ft. A typical screen size for such a room would be 5 or 6 ft square. If we project a 35 mm transparency made by the above method to 'fill' a 5 ft square screen, we will get a letter height of about 3 or 4 in, depending on the typeface on our typewriter. This is quite large enough to be read with comfort from the back row – more than adequate, as research shows that letters half this size should be legible under these conditions. However, the aim of our rule is to limit the content as well as to ensure legibility.

6.2.6. Opaque Projectors

Opaque projectors are not high on the popularity poll of visual aids. They have suffered in the past from the disadvantages of bulk, noise from the fans needed to cool the powerful lamps, and the need for total blackout in the classroom.

Advantages and uses of opaque projectors

Every school or training institution nevertheless seems to have one. No doubt an excellent case for purchase can be made on the grounds that any visual material already available can be utilized. No preparation of slides is required, illustrations in books, postage stamps, or even small objects can be instantly projected for all the class to see. Nevertheless, opaque projectors, or as they are traditionally called, episcopes, do not get much classroom use. Recently there have been vast technical improvements. Episcopes have become lighter and some can be used in semi-blackout conditions. They have become more versatile. As epidiascopes, an extra lens system enables them to project slides and even film strips. One major use of opaque projectors is to transfer diagrams from books onto chalkboards or charts by the 'project-on' method. Figure 6.8 shows how the 'project-on' method can be used to produce an enlarged copy of an illustration. This may be traced onto a paper wallchart for permanent display, or a sheet of plastic transparency film for later overhead projection.

...and some disadvantages

Figure 6.8 also shows the light path in a typical opaque projector. The light is reflected from the surface of the paper or other opaque material placed on the platen. The percentage of incident light reflected by such materials is quite small and therefore, to get any visible image at all, the incident light must be very powerful. In older models of opaque projectors, this implied the use of very strong incandescent lamps which produced a lot of heat. To cope with this, the projector had to be rather large (and therefore heavy) and had to have efficient, but usually noisy, cooling fans. All these aspects make the opaque projector a less effective projection instrument than the other types we have described here. Its one great advantage is that any available printed material may be instantly projected for group viewing. Many teachers use it to show students' work to the rest of the class for group discussions or evaluations.

For basic lesson presentations, however, the opaque projector has been largely replaced by the overhead projector, which offers many projection advantages and, with access to a photocopier, most existing print materials may be instantly transformed into transparencies. But there is much more than that to the overhead projector.

6.3. The overhead projector

6.3.1. Use

Historically, this is the most recent addition to the range of still projection equipment. It is also the most versatile. It can perform nearly all the functions listed earlier for other still media. Some would claim that the overhead projector will replace all other still media in time. This is unlikely, and undesirable. Some materials can still be better projected on slides, some on charts, and in any case, variety is the spice of life. Over-use of one medium may kill some of the impact of visual presentation. However, if you are limited to only one presentation method, the overhead projector would certainly be the best choice.

Basically, the overhead projector consists of a horizontal table, 10 in × 10 in, on which you place the material to be projected. Light from the bulb below the table

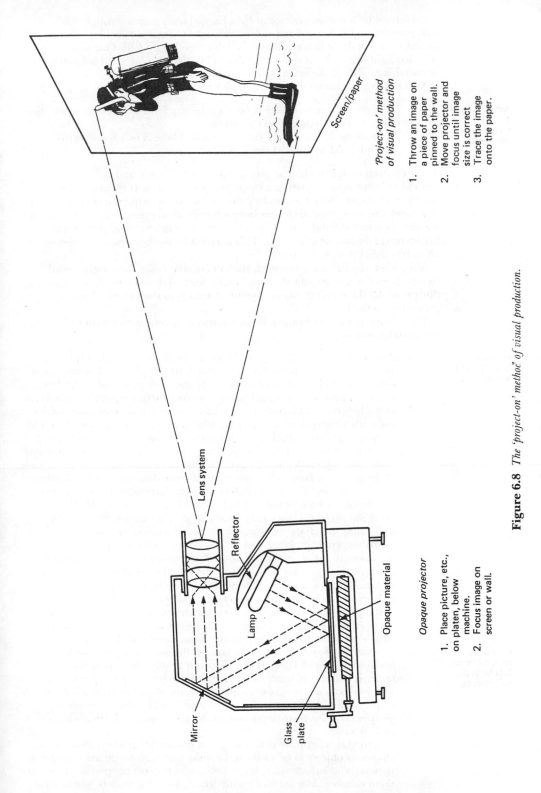

'Project-on' method of visual production

1. Throw an image on a piece of paper pinned to the wall.
2. Move projector and focus until image size is correct
3. Trace the image onto the paper.

Screen/paper

Lens system

Reflector

Lamp

Opaque material

Mirror

Glass plate

Opaque projector

1. Place picture, etc., on platen, below machine.
2. Focus image on screen or wall.

Figure 6.8 *The 'project-on' method of visual production.*

is condensed by a concave mirror or by a Fresnel lens, passes through the transparency and is focused and turned through 90 degrees by a lens system mounted on a stalk or bracket above the table (see Figure 6.9). One model uses reflected light from a bulb above the table. This gives a more compact, table-top or portable model, at slight cost to the brilliance of the image.

Two important characteristics distinguish the 'OHP':

Advantages of the overhead projector

1. Daylight projection. There is no need for any form of blackout unless there is strong direct sunlight on the screen.
2. When using it, the teacher faces the class. There is no need to turn his back; no need to stand at the back of the room.

These characteristics combine to give a much more natural and unobtrusive method of introducing visuals in a classroom presentation. It is easy to show a specific image just when it makes its point in the overall sequence of events. When using slides or film strip, the lesson stops while lights are dimmed, so generally the teacher shows all the slides at one point in time in order to avoid the constant brightening and dimming of lights. This may not be the best use of the slides from an instructional design viewpoint.

Also, when the lights are dimmed, students cannot easily take notes, visual contact between teacher and students breaks down and, sometimes, so does class discipline. All these points, taken together, have led to the success of this projection method.

The advantages in use can best be summarized by contrasting with each of the media so far discussed:

Use as a chalkboard substitute

(a) *As a chalkboard or scribbling pad.* Most overhead projectors (except some portable models) can be equipped with a 10 in wide roll of acetate sheet, on rollers, enabling it to be wound over the projection table. The 10 yards or more of acetate on the roll gives a writing surface equivalent to several of the biggest chalkboards imaginable. The instructor may write on the roll with 'chinagraph' wax pencils, felt-tip pens, or Indian inks. It would seem that we are sounding the death-knell of the venerable chalkboard. There are, however, some disadvantages to the overhead projector. Some materials, especially the wax pencils, tend to be difficult to use in the heat of the projector lamp. Most users find it more difficult to write clearly on the acetate sheet than on a chalkboard. The large lettering necessary on the chalkboard forces the user to form his letters carefully. On the overhead projector one writes small, under difficult conditions, with unfamiliar materials – and any faults are magnified tenfold.

Orthographic problems can be overcome, however. The main argument in the 'save the chalkboard' campaign is that the overhead projector really comes into its own when used to display pre-prepared materials. Using acetate roll, or scribbling on blank drop-on transparencies is both inconvenient and bad presentation. Use of a chalkboard or similar medium for spontaneous work leaves the table of the overhead projector clear for the main-stream visual presentation – switch on, show transparency, make point, switch off. Impact!

Use as a magnetic or felt board substitute

(b) *As a magnetic board.* The stage or table of the overhead projector is horizontal. You can project the silhouette of any object placed on the table. If objects are made of transparent material, such as perspex, you may have colour, or may draw details on the object in Indian ink. Models of inter-connected parts thus may be made up of different coloured perspex, and the relative position of the parts projected, even when the parts overlap.

A further advantage is that to give a reasonably projected image, the shapes or objects to be used can be quite small. Not only are they cheap to make and easy to store, but it becomes a feasible proposition to market them commercially. Sets of plastic letters, working models, geometrical

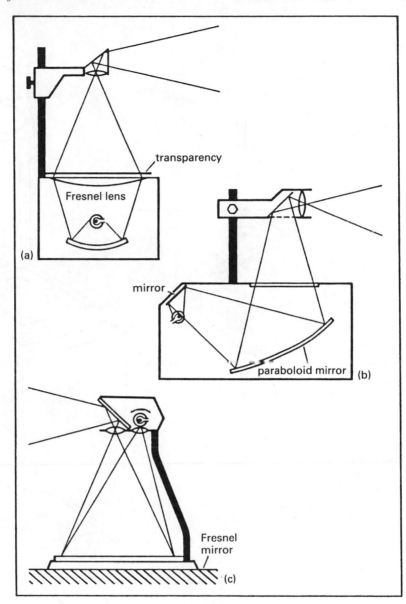

Figure 6.9 *Systems of overhead projection. (a) Fresnel lens system. This type is small, often portable. (b) Condensing mirror system. Large lecture-hall machines. (c) Fresnel mirror system. Table top mounting or collapsible for portability.*

theorems kits, etc, are now available for use with overhead projectors. If you have one, you don't need flannel or magnetic boards.

(c) *As a flip-chart.* Any original of the right size can be used as a master to produce a near-instant, cheap transparency for the overhead projector. Larger or smaller diagrams can be copied photographically. Transparencies are easily handled and stored and are less bulky than charts.

Use to control the presentation

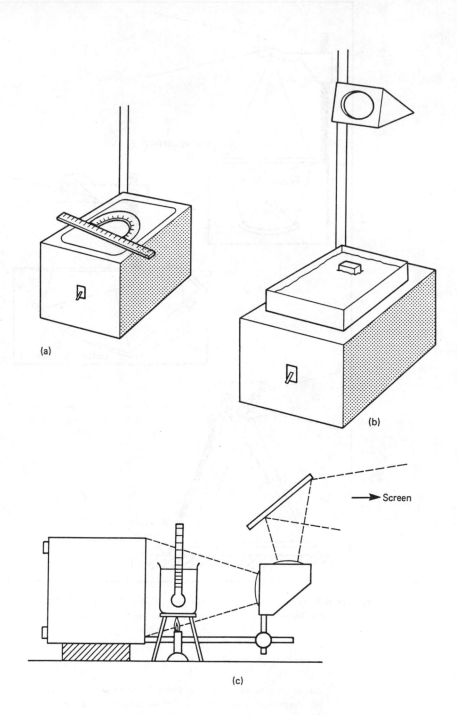

Figure 6.10 *Using the overhead projector with transparent objects and instruments as a 'laboratory demo'. (a) With drawing instruments in geometry and design class. (b) With a flat dish of water (ripple tank) to illustrate the laws of reflection, wave patterns, etc. (c) Projector turned on its side to project a chemistry experiment in action.*

As mentioned earlier, an excellent technique for using the overhead projector is to switch on only when a visual is being viewed, and then to switch off. This gives the same control over presentation as do flip-charts, with much more dramatic impact. Furthermore, with the overhead projector there are techniques possible which are far beyond the capabilities of charts:

1. The 'cover-up' technique. As the visual lies horizontally, it is simplicity itself to cover up parts of it until required, by a sheet of paper, or by cardboard 'windows' fixed to the transparency by sticky tape.
2. The 'overlay' technique. Successive details of a diagram may be superimposed, one on top of the other, by the addition of more transparencies. In our earlier example of an anatomy lesson, our teacher, with only one set of transparencies, could superimpose the musculature, bloodstream, respiratory system, etc, on the outline of a human body one at a time, all at one, or in any required combination.

(d) *As a projector of pictures.* Some of the points under this heading have already been mentioned. To begin, the overhead projector, due to the ease of transparency preparation from originals in books etc, is taking over the role of opaque projectors. Secondly, any materials available in the original, or easily drawn, can be made into transparencies and presented with a degree of control even greater than is possible with charts, film strips or slides.

However, most methods of transparency preparation do not cope very well with half-tone pictures or colour photos. Photographic methods can produce positive transparencies of adequate size, but the processes are long and expensive, particularly if colour is involved.

It is, therefore, far better to use film strips or slides for photographs and detailed pictures. Also, it is uneconomical to use the material in a film strip or an original slide-set for a set of transparencies.

6.3.2. Methods of transparency preparation

Many transparencies are, of course, prepared by hand. The materials used have been mentioned. In addition to coloured wax pencils and transparent inks, one can use transparent stick-on sheet for cut-outs, perspex, or any other material that the ingenuity of the teacher suggests. Suggestions for transparencies in particular subject areas abound in the literature. We will confine ourselves to a very brief look at the relative advantages of the more common automatic transparency production methods.

Use to present all types of visuals

(a) *Photographic methods.* Transparencies can be produced by normal photographic methods, eg from negatives, using an enlarger. The processes are slow, material expensive, and a darkroom and equipment necessary – in other words, it's a specialist job. One way to cut corners is to use a polaroid camera, with a special positive transparency film. This will take colour, but gives only a small transparency – $3\frac{1}{2} \times 2\frac{1}{2}$ in.
(b) *Diffusion transfer processes* (eg A B Dick). These are similar in principle to photographic processes. Production time is not too long, but transparencies must be left to dry. It produces excellent results from black and white and will tackle half-tone. Can be messy and equipment needs periodic cleaning.
(c) *Heat processes* (eg Thermo-Fax). Suitable for most single-colour originals. It does not cope too well with vegetable inks (eg Biro) as they do not absorb heat sufficiently to register on the heat-sensitive copy paper. Extremely fast – the transparency is ready for use in seconds. A clean, dry process.

(d) *Dyeline process*. If you have a map-copying machine, all you need is some Diazo colour foil. The original must be drawn on translucent material (eg tracing paper). It takes longer than heat process and more preparation is necessary.

(e) *Verifax*. Uses liquid developer. It is similar to diffusion transfer in time and work.

(f) *Xerography*. Rank Xerox will take transparency material. It is quick and clean, and will copy any original.

(g) *Spirit duplicator* (eg Banda). Masters will give reasonable impression on acetate sheet.

Preparing overlays

The preparation of effective overlay sets is largely dependent on the creativity and inventiveness of the teacher. It also requires a careful analysis of the content, its complexity and the messages that are to be communicated.

The practical procedures are, on the other hand, quite simple.

The set of overlays shown in Figure 6.12 was produced using existing artwork which was enlarged on a photocopier: several copies were then made. Each overlay was cut out of one copy of the artwork, discarding those parts that were unwanted. Each part of the total picture was then mounted on a separate sheet of paper, with a complete copy of the artwork below, in order to keep everyhing in alignment. Then each of the mounted part-pictures was run through the photocopier to produce a copy on plastic transparency film. The total time taken was not much more than it took to write this description of the process.

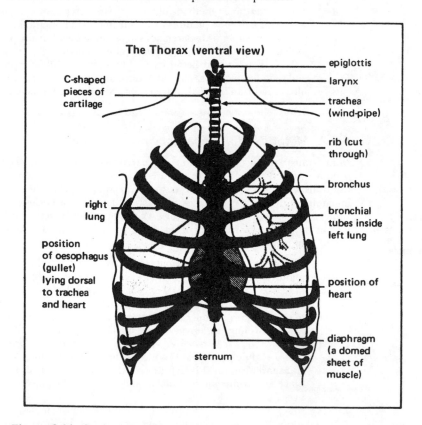

Figure 6.11 *Overhead projector transparency. This is a pre-prepared transparency, one of a series on Human Anatomy and Physiology by Wheeler and Carr. Such a subject is ideal for use of the overlay technique. The rib cage, lungs and the organs may be printed onto separate acetate sheets, and then viewed separately or superimposed.*

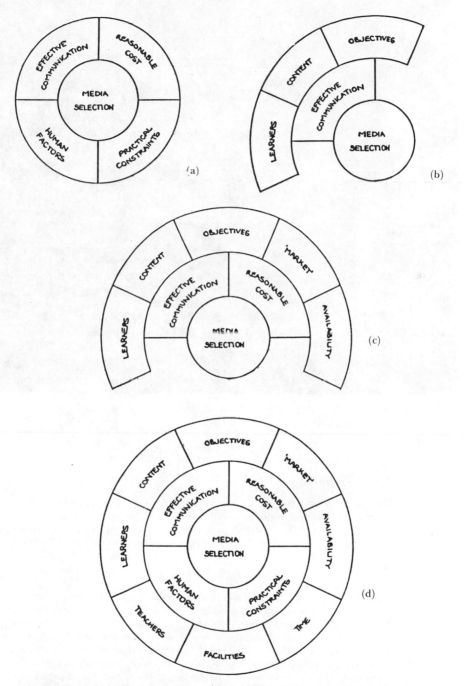

Figure 6.12 *The gradual build-up of our media selection schema during classroom presentation. (a) The four principal goals/considerations are presented and discussed. (b) The four principal considerations are analysed further, one at a time. (c) Slowly, the picture grows, showing interrelations between one consideration and another. (d) Finally, all the overlays together present the complete schema. This complete picture, being relatively complex and of later use as a job-aid, is then also given out to students as a printed handout.*

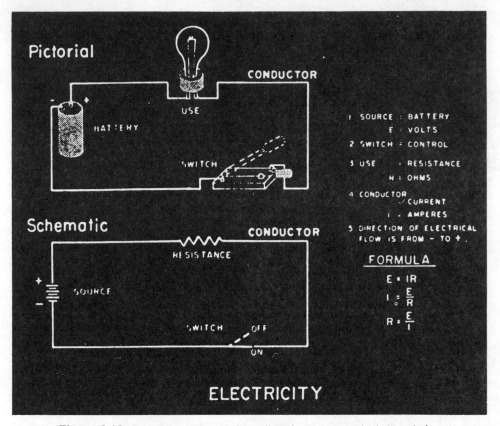

Figure 6.13 *Special materials exist that will produce transparencies in 'negative' white-on-black (or even in other colours). This may improve the projection.*

6.3.3. Screening

The overhead projector will, even in daylight, give a large clear image – much larger than could normally be obtainable from a 'daylight' slide projector. Provided there is room in the classroom to give sufficient 'throw', a screen up to 8 ft square can be used. It is probable that for most classrooms, to get this size of image and yet have the projector near the teacher's desk, a wide-angle lens head should be used. However, a screen of 5–6 ft square is adequate for classrooms up to 40 ft long.

If the screen is mounted high enough for a clear view, you wil probably have to tilt the OHP's head to throw the image upwards. This will cause the familiar 'keystoning' of the image, unless the screen is mounted to compensate. As shown in Figure 6.14 the top edge of the screen should be tilted forward, so as to give a true, rectangular, undistorted image. The seat positions from which the image will be clearly visible will depend on the choice of screen/material, as outlined earlier.

Figure 6.14 also shows one advantage of putting the overhead projector screen in a corner rather than directly in front of a group. There is less obstruction from the lens head of the projector and the teacher's body. The 'straight ahead' position is also left available for projection of films or slides onto another screen, or for a chalkboard, flannel board etc. Other factors such as classroom width-to-length ratio, seating arrangements or the position of windows and direct sunlight will of course influence the possible screen positions for a given room.

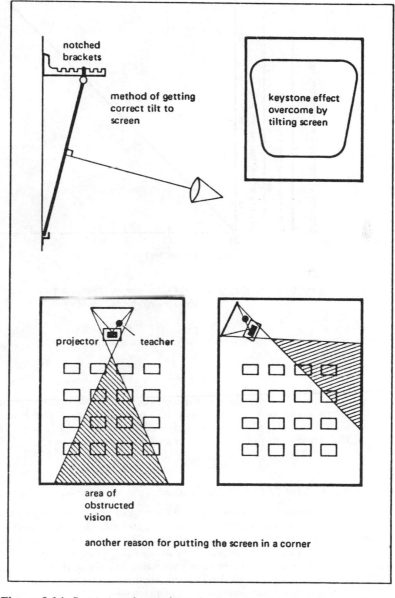

Figure 6.14 *Positioning of screen for overhead projection. Keystone effect may also be a problem with a slide projector fitted with a wide-angle lens.*

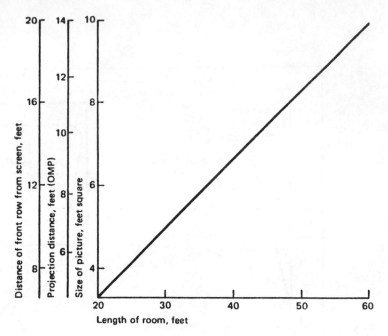

Figure 6.15 *Relation of room and screen size for effective projection (and distance of overhead projector with standard lens).*

Figure 6.15 shows the relationship between ideal screen size and room size, for clarity in the back row. Also, some idea of the distance of projector from screen and comfortable distance from screen for the front row of viewers. The projector distance may be reduced by use of a wide-angle lens system.

6.3.4. Clarity of transparencies

As the majority of transparencies for overhead projectors are prepared by hand, it is important to have some rules for letter size etc. The general rules specified for slides may be taken as a guide, although, due to the greater versatility in use of overhead projector material (eg by overlay or cover-up techniques) it is common for transparencies to carry more material than a single slide should. This is not necessarily bad, though the limits for legibility and good instructional practice would outlaw a fair proportion of the materials we often see at conferences and meetings, even occasionally at conferences on educational technology.

Guidelines do exist, however.

> *Line width.* The main visual parameter controlling the design of a transparency
> is the resolving power of the eye. This varies with the illumination and the
> contrast of the subject, but under good illumination and with moderate
> contrast may be taken as two minutes of arc. This corresponds to a line
> thickness of 0.036 in at 10 ft and 0.108 in at 30 ft viewing distance. The
> thinnest line on the transparency visible at 30 ft, assuming a magnification of
> six, is 0.018 in.

Type height. At a normal reading distance 3 point type is just readable to people with good vision, 6 point type can be read by most people, type for easy continuous reading should ideally be about 12 point. Letters on the screen will have to be 30 times these sizes if they are to be read from the back row. As the magnification of the original transparency is six, we may specify letter sizes on the film as: just readable – 0.1 in letter height; preferred minimum – 0.2 in letter height; preferred for continuous text – 0.4 in letter height.

Another field in which research has been done into readable letter sizes is road signs. The design recommendation here is 1 in letter height for every 50 ft viewing distance. This would lead to a letter height of 0.6 in on the screen under our viewing conditions, or 0.1 in on the film. It is stated that 99% of drivers can read signs drawn to this specification.

These recommendations are in approximate agreement, and it would seem reasonable to take 0.1 in as an absolute minimum for letter height on the film. One might note that 0.1 in is about the size of a normal typewriter typeface, and we all know what results that gives as a transparency. The preferred limit of 0.2–0.4 in is recommended.

Tints and shading. If hatching is used to give a solid or tinted effect (some printing processes use this method) then to appear uniform to all members of the audience, the screen ruling must be finer than 85 per inch. On the other hand if hatching lines or dots in dotted lines are to be visible to all members of the audience, the ruling must be coarser than 28 lines per inch.

Map 6.1 *Principles for the effective use of colour in visuals.*

Colour	• Consider the context in which a colour will be viewed – what colours are to be seen simultaneously or sequentially? • Use the spectral extremes, red and blue, to attract attention. • When acuity is important, employ colours in the middle of the spectrum. • For optimum legibility maintain a high brightness contrast between an image and its background. • Photographing coloured objects demands the use of an appropriate film and judicious lighting to assure good colour rendition. • Saturated cool or warm colours are appropriate for small children. Less saturated cool colours may be more suitable for adults. • Consider the meaning of colours as they relate to your audience. • To attract attention use extremes of value or chroma. • To achieve harmony use familiar colour schemes, organize carefully, and employ colours with similar attributes. • Research shows that colour creates interest and that people prefer colour to black and white. • Easily named colours aid memory more than colours that have complex names. • Use colour to provide structure, to emphasize relevant cues, to differentiate central from peripheral information, and to make distinctions between elements of a visual.

Map 6.2 *Principles for the presentation of projected text.*

Words-projected	<ul><li>Limit the number of points to be made in a visual employing words.</li><li>Use key words, not sentences.</li><li>The number of words in a visual should be no more than 15–20.</li><li>List items in columns.</li><li>For good legibility, lettering should be no smaller than 1/24th the short dimension of the artwork.</li><li>Use a simple serif or sans serif style of lettering.</li><li>Remember, medium weight lettering is generally best.</li><li>When there are several lines of type use a mixture of upper and lower case letters, as appropriate and grammatically correct, to improve legibility.</li><li>Consider the mood of the type face and how it relates to the subject matter.</li><li>Leave adequate space between letters, words, and lines.</li><li>Maintain a moderate to high contrast between the lettering and its background.</li><li>When planning projected materials, consider the ambient light under which these materials will be shown.</li></ul>

7. Simple audio and audio-visual media

7.1 The need for sound media

Review/
overview

In earlier chapters we discussed how both still and moving visual media can seldom stand on their own. We saw the need for spoken or written captions or commentaries in order to focus the student's attention on the important aspects of the visual. We know that pictures or graphs do not necessarily teach better than verbal descriptions, or even clarify the message that the verbal caption communicates – it depends on the type of learner we have and on the type of subject matter we are communicating.

Our theme has been that visual aids should have a precisely defined function, they should be designed to fulfil that function, and they should be evalauted to measure their effectivness.

This chapter deals in the main with sound media – in particular the radio, gramophone and tape recorder, but audio-visual methods employing any of the above, together with supporting diagrams or pictures, are also covered. Such methods, using a recorded commentary and related visual material, are very similar in function to the cine film. The only difference is that the pictures do not move. The audio-visual presentation tells the whole story. For a time, the medium takes over from the teacher. We would therefore expect that audio-visual presentations of this type would be of value in similar teaching situations as films, with the further provision that the actual movements of objects on the screen are of no importance to the learning process.

Audio may
be
an essential
character-
istic

Let us first consider pure audio presentations – radio programmes, records, recorded tapes. These may be used in two ways. First, they may be used by a teacher to bring into the classroom sounds which are of significance to the learning process, for example music, language pronunciation, bird-calls or the noise of a rattling big-end bearing. The sound material is only part of the teacher's presentation. He introduces it for a specific purpose, and demands specific reactions from the class. Students may be required to comment on the sound presentation (as in a music appreciation class), to recognize the sound and discriminate it from others (as in learning musical scales or bird-call recognition) or to discriminate and repeat the sound (as in the language laboratory).

The teacher decides to use a sound presentation on the basis of analysing his subject matter. This analysis pin-points areas of the subject which rely on sound. The teacher then decides whether to use a teaching aid. He may prefer a native Frenchman's presentation to his own (perhaps imperfect) accent. It may be impractical or impossible to demonstrate the sound other than by a recording. We do not have the time to track down birds in the field, or the space in our classrooms for a symphony orchestra.

The Royal Navy have a training course which aims to teach submarine personnel to recognize ships passing overhead by the noises they make. This high-level discrimination skill, when well mastered, enables the seaman to distinguish not only between a ship and a school of whales, but between different types of ships and their countries of origin. As the opportunity to use the skill only occurs in wartime, and then it's usually too late to learn, one naturally turns to recorded sound media for training. The set-up involves a battery of recordings capable of supplying the student with any of 20 characteristic ship noises in any combination. The student must identify each noise as it occurs. If he is wrong, the original noise and his own choice are played together to illustrate the difference. In time he learns to discriminate between more and more similar noises. The structure of the course is based on programmed instruction principles. The choice of presentation medium was dictated from the start by the subject matter. Nothing but sound recording would do.

Audio as an option for verbal information

Sound media may be used as an integral part of a teacher's presentation. Alternatively, they may be used to take over the verbal presentation altogether. The teacher may record his lesson, or he may play a broadcast or recording prepared by someone else. Such a recorded commentary differs little from the classic lecture situation. The message source – lecturer or recording – emits information which is (we hope) received at the message destination – the audience. This is essentially a one-way traffic. No feedback to the message source on the effects being produced at the destination is provided for. Similarly, the slide-tape audio-visual presentations which we will be discussing later are analogous to the lecturer who uses visual aids. This use of a recording to replace the classroom teacher is often quite justified. The broadcast speaker may be a better lecturer, or be better informed. Even if the teacher records his own voice, advantages may result. He has greater opportunity to revise, edit and re-organize what he says. His presentation should be more professional as a result. Furthermore, if a teacher can record his presentation, this may free him for other work which the recording cannot do – individual help, checking progress etc. Indeed all the old arguments as to why teachers should benefit from the use of programmed instruction may be applied in this case, provided of course that broadcast talks are as effective as a live presentation. Experimental research comparing recorded and live lessons has generally yielded inconclusive results.

7.2 Research on sound media

Results depend on the target population

Scupham (1970) summarized Danish research which assessed the comparative effectiveness of matched communications through print, radio, television lecture and a more elaborate televized presentation using film, animation and other visual devices. Of the 500 subjects participating in the study, 120 were soldiers and the rest were students at agricultural colleges. No significant differences were found in the test scores of groups in the various treatment conditions, but there was a significant difference between the average score of the soldiers, whatever the presentation medium, and that of the students.

Audio programmes may in some cases have positive advantages over the equivalent written texts. For one thing, they do not require that the student can read. Where students are used to learning from books, or the subject matter is of an academic nature, there seems to be no clear advantage for either method (Davison *et al.*, 1966).

Where the students are not trained scholars, and the subject matter is mainly composed of simple instructions to be followed, rather than concepts to be understood, a taped presentation often promotes a much better performance. Amswych (1967) found that with apprentices learning to name and operate machine tools, a taped programme may promote better learning and take up to 50% less learning time than the equivalent written programme. This may be explained partly by the type of student, partly by the task (which already employs his hands and eyes – so using the ears for instructions seems more efficient), and partly by the environment: the learner wears earphones which shut out other noises and distractions.

Generally, the differences between media alternatives are negligible

Another experiment attempted to compare the effectiveness of the same lesson when presented by radio, by television and by a live teacher. Students of media would expect the radio presentation to be at a disadvantage in this experiment from the start, as vision is excluded. When tested immediately after the lesson, the 'live' groups were slightly better, but re-testing two months later showed, rather surprisingly, that the television groups remembered least, and there was no difference in the long-term effects of the teacher and the radio programme. As is so often the case with such controlled experiments, however, the differences between the groups were small, and did not point conclusively to the superiority of any one medium. Much greater differences can be expected between the success of different teachers, than on the same teacher using different media.

Effectiveness springs from instructional development effort

It is here that we have the real value of the recorded lesson and radio broadcasts. You can spend more time in preparing the presentation, use the best subject experts and employ the best available teacher. Most important (though seldom done systematically), you can evaluate the presentation before release and eradicate any weaknesses. Such a presentation is sure to communicate more effectively than many a 'live' lecturer, mumbling into his sketchy, jumbled, obsolete notes.

Of course, the good teacher does much more than simply read his notes. He acts not only as a message source, but also as a monitor of the effect of the message. Is it understood? Is further explanation necessary? He then uses this information to plan subsequent messages. Teaching is a dynamic two-way communication process. Normal broadcasts, such as films or large group lectures, are capable only of one-way communication. Like all such methods, they rely for long-term effectiveness on well-designed exercises which involve the student actively. Normally, these take the form of a follow-up session or seminar immediately after the presentation. Occasionally, an element of programming is built in by breaking the sound presentation into short units, with questions or appropriate student activity interspersed.

The practical advantages and disadvantages of recordings

Whichever method is used, sound recordings share with films a permanence and an inflexibility of presentation. In some subjects this is a disadvantage, as opportunities for spontaneous off-the-point but nevertheless useful discussions may be lost. In other subjects, however, this may be a positive advantage, in ensuring an accurate, standard presentation every time:

(a) all understand the terms of reference (in the same way),
(b) all have a mastery of relevant data and information, and
(c) all speak the same language (technical jargon, symbols, conventions).

Every subject has such areas where uniform understanding and practice is essential. It is these areas which may benefit from a fixed, standard presentation. If the information can be effectively communicated without visual aids, then here is an area where one might consider using sound media.

Thus, all decisions on whether to use sound media spring from the task analysis. There are three possible types of applications which may be identified by asking the following questions:

1. Do my students need to have their interest aroused in the subject? If so, are there any broadcasts or recordings which may help to do this?
2. Are there any topics which involve sounds the student should hear that I cannot produce?
3. Are there any topics which must be understood by all in exactly the same way, and which I cover fairly frequently?

7.3 Research on the use of slide-tape presentations

Synchronized slide-tape presentations have become very popular, particularly in industrial and commercial training. The Ford Motor Company, for example, uses the technique in just about every foremanship, supervisory or management course they run (though nowadays they are often transferred onto videotape).

Practical benefits

The practical advantages of such courses are:

1. Instant availability – day or night shifts.
2. Standard presentation – leading to uniform practices.
3. Self-presentation – saving an instructor's time.

But no real instructional improvement

However, Ford's have found in practice that although the courses are professionally prepared and although the visuals are designed to communicate and are produced to the highest technical standards, the greatest value of the slide-tape presentation is to stimulate interest, motivate for further study, and give the general outline of the subject. Long-term retention of detail information was low, a result very much in agreement with studies discussed earlier. In order to ensure retention and enable the foreman to pass a qualifying examination, supplementary texts were required which gave the man practice in applying the information he received from the tape.

Such results do not cast doubt on the value of the slide-tape presentations. Rather, they pin-point the functions each media can perform. The retention figures obtained are every bit as good as one gets from a well-prepared well-delivered lecture. Like the lecture, slide-tape presentations (and traditional training films) give very little opportunity for the learner to participate actively and practise his mastery of the information. They are one-way or open-ended communication channels. They can be made two-way, or closed loop channels, by supplying material for student practice, checking student performance, and if necessary, using this feedback to modify the lesson. This can be done by the methods of programmed instruction, by eliciting appropriate responses at every stage of the presentation.

Townsend (1973) reported some atypical results of research comparing conventional teaching with slide-tape and other audio-visual methods, for topics from school science such as laboratory safety precautions and how to use a bunsen burner, a microscope and a thermometer. This study found a marked superiority of the audio-visual methods over the conventional (although many possibly relevant factors, such as teacher quality or novelty effects, do not appear to have been controlled). Students using the audio-visual materials generally scored 10% better and took between 30% and 60% less learning time.

This study used carefully developed visual materials and taped commentaries. The students were expected to perform relevant procedures during study. The conventional instruction was administered by a teacher who had not been involved in the preparation of these materials, although he no doubt used his own visuals to supplement his own spoken commentary. One wonders to what extent the much improved learning reported above was the result of the 'automation' applied to the audio-visual lesson, or to the extra analysis and care that went into its preparation. How would the author of the packaged course, using the same visuals, compare to the package?

The results of meta-analyses

Generally speaking, the better controlled a comparative study of this type, the less significant have been the findings in favour of one medium or another. In one of his many 'meta-analyses', James Kulik integrated the findings of 74 studies of visual and audiovisual teaching at college level (Cohen, Ebling and Kulik, 1981). These included studies investigating video and film use as well as more simple audiovisual packages. All compared the use of the packages with 'conventional instruction'. The analysis showed that students generally learned slightly more from the packaged versions, typically the difference was of the order of between one and two percentage points in favour of mediated instruction. No other significant effects were noted in respect of course completion, student attitudes, etc. They also noted that the learning differences were smaller in studies where the same instructor taught both classes and negligible in studies where the author of the mediated materials was the instructor in both classes.

Media as 'mere vehicles'

Such results lead some authors, such as Richard Clark, to conclude that instructional media are 'mere vehicles that deliver instruction but do not influence student achievement' (Clark, 1983).

But progress in vehicle technology can change the world

However, this theoretical argument is not of too much relevance to the teacher faced with the practical task of planning effective lessons. If media are only vehicles, they are not 'mere' vehicles, as the delivery of the message to the learner is an aspect of extreme importance. And in many practical situations a given media package may be capable of transmitting a message that the unaided teacher would have great difficulty in transmitting.

Secondly, a media presentation may be prepared on the basis of a much more thorough instructional design effort, an investment which pays off in greater effectiveness and which would be practically impossible for each teacher to make for each and every lesson separately. The economy of scale makes the package much more cost-effective over a period of time.

7.4 The use of simple audio media

7.4.1 Radio

Constraints which limit the use of radio

The use that a teacher can make of radio broadcasts is limited in very much the same way as his use of national television broadcasts. He has no control and sometimes little prior notification of the content and treatment of an impending programme. If the programme is designed specifically for school use, or for further education, then there might be a booklet describing the content and supplying follow-up and preparatory work for the students. In such a case, we can apply our normal criteria of selection. What are the objectives of the course? Do these objectives agree closely enough with our own? If they do, we might wish to use the course. This is where we meet problems of time-tabling and of evaluation. Generally, the course is broadcast at one time only, and this may not be very convenient. Schools broadcasts are put out during normal school hours, but of ccourse it's just sheer luck if the timetabled Physics period coincides with the programme on Heat. Programmes designed for further education or for industrial training are generally put on at the most inconvenient hours – late evening or early Sunday morning are favourite times. Obviously the designers of the programmes really intend them for private study at home, or is it simply pressure on peak listening times by the mass audience?

Even supposing that by some chance we can incorporate a series of programmes into our course, we have the second problem, of evaluation. Having established the course objectives, we structure an appropriate test situation. If, after listening to a radio programme, students do badly on the test, what do we do? If we have time, we may re-teach. We would certainly decide not to use the programme again, as we have no powers to modify it. If, on the other hand, students do well on the test, we would like to use the programme with subsequent groups, but of course it is not going to be repeated.

Recording from radio and the copyright laws

Here we see one valuable use of a tape recorder. Successful programmes may be stored for subsequent use at convenient times. Partly successful programmes may be edited or modified by the teacher in the light of his students' performance.

Having said this, we are immediately up against problems of copyright. Recently, copyright laws have been relaxed in the case of certain educational programmes, such as the schools broadcasts, enabling teachers to record the programmes and use them at will for the length of the school year. Unfortunately, this does not necessarily apply to other broadcasts. While this situation lasts, the use which can be made of radio for instructional purposes will remain limited.

Limited learning from radio alone

Furthermore, the amount of learning which takes place during the broadcast itself is not very large. Research carried out by the BBC on the amount learnt from a short 5 minute discussion revealed some startling figures. The average listener took in only about 28% of the material. Even university graduates (the top 1% in terms of prior training in learning from lectures) only managed to take in 48%. Early school leavers learnt as little as 21% (Belson, 1952).

Now, these figures are for a 5-minute programme, using volunteers as experimental subjects. How much lower are the figures for a 20-minute programme broadcast to a captive, unmotivated audience? The efficiency of the learning depends largely on the effectiveness of the follow-up and preparatory materials.

Radio as a component in a system of instruction

There are two ways in which efficient learning from radio programmes could be achieved. First, the programme authorities could set up their own evaluation studies prior to broadcasting. These would aim at refining the content of the programme, and at designing the most efficient preparatory and follow-up materials. We end up with a sound presentation, prescribed preparatory exercises, prescribed follow-up exercises and standard method of testing the student – a sort of instructional package or kit. Now, the way to get the best out of an instructional package is to ensure that it is used according to its design. Some measure of control over the teacher is required. BBC schools broadcasts suggest that the use of their booklets is beneficial, but they cannot insist on their use. Some developing countries use radio as a backbone of their educational system, in order to reach scattered communities with few teachers. They have found that the effective use of the mass media for this purpose does involve the establishing of control over teaching methods, and the standardization of curricula.

In an educational system such as in Great Britain, relatively well supplied with teachers, and with a history of local autonomy as regards syllabus and teaching methods, the controlled systematic use of the mass media in education is unlikely to succeed. In industry and commerce the training needs of different industries (and different firms within the same industry) are so diverse that systematic use of the mass media is again out of the question.

The second way of utilizing radio for efficient learning is of more value. This is to use it as a source of material. It is left to the individual teacher or instructor, or to a group with similar teaching objectives, to produce an instructional course, or package, based perhaps on a radio programme. The production of such a package involves preparation of student exercises, testing and evaluation – in one phrase, a lot of work. Such a package, if successful, will teach successive groups to the same high standard.

7.4.2 Records

The value of records in instruction

It would seem that records should overcome many of the limitations of 'live' radio broadcasts.

As with radio, records may bring into the classroom the voices of well-known people, music by virtuoso performers and discussions by experts. The resources of the record company, as those of radio, generally ensure high standards of subject-matter expertise, background research and presentation. Unlike radio however, the record may be played over and over to successive groups at any convenient time.

High cost of records

One snag, however, is that records are expensive, and it is this factor which has limited their use in education.

Nevertheless, very extensive use is made of records in the teaching of music, the cost being shared over many schools and institutions – central record libraries charge a moderate hiring fee, or if they are subsidized, no fee at all. Similarly, much material such as historical speeches, animal noises and indeed lectures on certain topics are available on records.

Inflexible presentation

In earlier years, as the need for following-up and integrating student activity had been realised, there was a tendency to produce multi-media presentations and planned instructional kits. Some of the earliest of these took the form of gramophone records linked to a film strip. As the commentary progressed, a recorded bleep would indicate to the instructor, or to a member of the group, to move to the next visual. The advantages of such a presentation are less need for skilled instructional staff, and a standardized, unchanging presentation. One of the first applications of linked record and film strip presentations was in the training of personnel during the last war. Rigidity of the teaching was a positive advantage and the large number of copies required made the recording process economical.

Resultant low usage of records as instructional material

Here we have the reasons for the relatively limited use of the record in education. First, the presentation is rigid, so is suitable only for subjects where uniformity of procedure is an advantage or a necessity. Language learning, and much industrial training at the operative level, fall into this category. Secondly, the subject must be sufficiently studied to make the production of records in quantity economical. We have noted that schools in particular seldom buy records outright. As soon as the cost of individual records drives groups of schools or training establishments to set up libraries, the potential market for a record is reduced drastically, and the whole project becomes uneconomical from the producer's viewpoint.

7.4.3 The tape recorder

The recording revolution
Just as the overhead projector has revolutionized the presentation of still visuals, and the cheap, easy-to-use video camera has made every teacher a potential film director; so the magnetic tape recorder has created a whole range of new teaching methods. Its impact has been most felt in language teaching and related subjects but it is now being applied most effectively to other school subjects and to commercial and industrial training. What makes the tape recorder of especial interest is the control which can be exercised over the recorded content by the teacher or instructor, and the flexibility with which it can be used by the student. Teachers may record their own materials, geared towards their own teaching objectives, and can follow up, evaluate and revise their recordings. Students may stop a recording in order to make notes or solve a problem, record their own comments, and can re-play or re-record as often as they need.

The tape recorder places a number of technical facilities at the teacher's disposal:

No waiting
(a) *Instant playback*. As soon as a recording is made, it is ready for listening; no developing or transcription delays. This is the facility which has made the tape recorder such a powerful medium of language teaching. The student can listen to a phrase, imitate it, then immediately compare his own efforts with the master recording.

No waste
(b) *Instant erasure*. No complicated procedures are required to erase unwanted material from the tape. If a section is badly recorded, you simply re-record a second attempt over the top. The original recording is automatically wiped off. This makes for very simple production of tapes and correction of faults – even by novices.

Multi-track facilities
(c) *Four-track recorders*. These are recorders which can record on four parallel bands of the tape. Two recording heads are fitted. By switching between heads, one can record either on track 1 or track 3 as the tape passes through. By reversing the spools and replaying the tape through the other way, tracks 2 and 4 are available. Four-track recorders get twice as much material onto the same tape. However, they also enable more sophisticated techniques of recording to be used. For example: the language-learning situation described above generally uses a 4-track recorder. The master phrase is on track 1. The student uses track 3. He can play back both tracks simultaneously, to compare his efforts, but can only erase and re-record on track 3. This enables the student to practise a particular phrase as often as he likes, using the same master recording.

Mixing and dubbing
(d) *Mixing or dubbing*. The 4-track recorder also allows you to dub, or to add commentaries to existing recordings. The commentary goes onto track 3 while track 1 plays back. They are then played back together and recorded onto another tape. Another technique may be used which produces a mixed recording on one stage. Some recorders have a number of input jacks. These may be used for several microphones, or one may be used for a microphone, while another records directly from a record, radio or another tape recorder. Both the original message and the teacher's comments appear on one track of the final tape. This technique requires more rehearsal than the former to get good results, as you cannot alter the two inputs separately after recording.

Automatic stop and start

(e) *Automatic stop.* Many tape recorders are equipped with a device which will stop the tape automatically. It is activated by sticking a piece of metallic tape to the recording tape, at the point you want the machine to stop. It is standard practice to have a metallic section near each end of a tape to prevent it running right through the machine and off the spool. The user can, however, arrange for the tape to stop at any point he desires, simply by sticking on some aluminium tape. This enables you to leave recorders unattended, or to present a recording section by section. You can by this means present an 'audio-programme' which stops automatically after each 'frame' of information to allow the student to respond. The student can re-start the tape by pressing the start button which over-rides the metal strip.

Slide-tape synchron-ization

(f) *Automatic slide progression.* The automatic slide projectors discussed earlier operate by an electrical impulse from the remote control. This impulse may be generated by an audio signal of a particular frequency. Some tape recorders are modified to be used in conjunction with an automatic slide projector, to give an automated audio-visual presentation. Recorders which do not have this facility can be modified by an item of equipment designed to supply the impulse. This is simply placed beside the recorder, and the tape is re-threaded to pass through this extra gadget.

Controllable quality, capacity and economy

(g) *Speed variations and recording facilities.* Generally, the faster the tape speed, the higher the quality of reproduction. The most common tape speeds are 7½, 3¾ and 1⅞ inches per second. 15 ips and ¹⁵/₁₆ ips are occasionally found. Other things being equal, the faster the recording speed the better the recording. 3¾ ips has, however, virtually become the standard speed for sound tape recorders. There is very little pre-recorded material that is not available at that speed, and there is much that is available at no other. The next most useful speed to have is probably 7½ ips. Most tape recorders accept 7 in diameter tape reels, corresponding to 1200 ft of standard play tape, 1800 ft of long play, 2400 ft of double play or 3600 ft of triple play. Recording times are, respectively, more than one, one and a half, two or three hours on one track at 3¾ ips.

Conveni-ence of the cassette

(h) *Cassette tape recorders.* Over the last few years these have become especially popular in education and training, being cheap, reliable, robust, extremely portable and easy to handle. Cassette recorders have also been used as the basis for inexpensive, portable language laboratories, often intended as a supplement to the larger installation.

Another common trend is towards integrated A/V presentation systems, such as back-projection slide projectors with built-in fully synchronized cassette player. Such equipment facilitates the production of synchronized slide-sound shows, as well as acting as a portable and convenient way of presenting them to small groups. Similar equipment, often using film strip projection and made as compact as possible, has found application as portable sales presentation equipment, but has also percolated down to the schools.

Multi-image and its use

Yet another development has been the cassette tape-controlled multi-image system, typically a bank of two, three or more carousel projectors, coupled to equipment which fades out one image as another appears. Recorded beeps on one track of the cassette tape keep the recorded commentary and the complex visual presentation in synchronization. Banks of more than four projectors are used for the screening of multi-image 'epics' – these require more sophisticated control equipment, usually a microcomputer. These multi-image shows have become an artform in their own right. They are often used for promotional and motivational campaigns, but their use in everyday instruction is limited, both by the cost and complexity and the unnecessary or even distracting effect of several messages being received at once when the content is to be learnt.

7.5 The functions of AV media in an instructional system

We already have a model for the development of lesson plans: this was introduced in chapter 2. It is characterized by having a three column format, which corresponds to the three forms of intercommunication that occur between teacher and learner in a 'true' instructional process. Figure 7.1 uses this lesson-planning model as a framework on which to organize some of the applications that exist for audiovisual media in instructional systems.

AV media as 'information transmitters'

Perhaps the most obvious, most common and most 'conventional' use of the audiovisual media is in the information transmission role.

Indeed, perhaps the most frequently quoted justification for the use of audiovisual materials in teaching is to bring into the classroom stimulus material which otherwise would require the learner to go out to seek the experience (or, perhaps, could not otherwise be experienced at all). This is the justification for geography films, dramatizations of historical events, descriptions of industrial and other processes, interviews or debates with well known or controversial figures, etc. Such descriptive stimulus material may indeed be built into an instructional design, although the scripting and production of such material may not itself follow strict instructional design principles. For this reason, it is possible to make use of a vast range of existing audiovisual material as components in a purpose-designed instructional plan. Not all materials that you come across are, however, equally effective at communicating their intended message. You should be quite clear firstly about the overall purpose in the mind of the author of the material. Was it to inform? If so, to inform whom about what? Have the characteristics of the target audience and the informational content been adequately taken into account in designing the communication? Was it to influence or to motivate or interest the target audience? If so, to interest or motivate whom, and in what?

Teaching activity (Stimulus)	Learning activity (Response)	Control activity (Feedback)
Pre-instructional or opening activities — AV overview, preview, 'advance organizer' — 'Motivational' AV presentation		
Instruction — Transmission of new information — demo, explanation, etc — Presentation of 'models' of desired performance — Presentation of case material for analysis, etc	— AV as a practice exercise — AV 'job aids' — Use as a guidance or timing device during learning	— AV recording of learner's performance for evaluation — Comparative presentations of correct and incorrect responses
Post-instructional or closing activities — AV summary — AV enrichment		

Figure 7.1 *Possible functions of AV in a lesson.*

AV media as presenters of performance models

Typical examples of the use of audiovisual media as 'models of desired performance' include the 'role-models' presented by means of film or videotape as a first step in an expositive strategy geared at the development of interactive skills. One specific example, often applied, is in the training of office personnel and sales personnel in the procedures of handling customers and clients. Another similar application is the presentation of videotaped 'models' of good examples of specific classroom-teaching skills, as a first step in a 'microteaching' programme of teacher training.

AV media as presenters of cases/ examples

Yet another form of stimulus material is the presentation of good and bad, or appropriate and inappropriate examples, as in the first step in a sequence designed to develop specific discriminations or concepts. In such a case, a series of short snippets of audio, visual, or audiovisual material may be presented as examples for criticism, comment or classification. One application in the training of submarine crews involved the presentation of the sounds of different types of ships, as heard in a submarine below water, to develop the skills of auditory recognition of friendly and enemy ships in situations where the use of sonar equipment is likely to give away the submarine's position. Another application, in medical education, involves the presentation of short excerpts from patients' interviews, as a stimulus to the practice and development of diagnostic skills associated with the interpretation of *what* patients say and also *how* they say it.

AV media as practice
– guides
– aids
– opportunities

Coming to the central, or learner activity (or 'response') column, we note certain highly specific uses for audiovisual media. We may use audiovisual devices as *practice-media* as in the case of the tapes actually recorded by the learner in a language laboratory exercise. We may also supply some forms of 'job-aids' to facilitate practice, by means of audiovisual devices. One example that springs to mind is the use of audiotape as a timing device. This is done in the 'Sight-and-Sound' type of typing training situations, in which the trainee who is looking at an exercise to be typed (presented in the normal way on a sheet of paper) is also listening to an audiotape that is reading the exercise in the appropriate rhythm for typing. Each character to be typed (including spaces and punctuation marks) is read out to the accompaniment of a metronome, set to give a specific typing speed. In time, the typist graduates to progressively faster tapes, thereby being paced to work at more productive levels. A similar timing use was employed in the Swedish 'RITT' system for operative training, which we shall describe later on.

Visual or indeed audiovisual materials may also be used in such an exercise-control function, as in the case of a series of slides that change at a predetermined rate, showing the stages of assembly of a transistor radio on a production line. Such applications, used in the 1960s at the Philips factory in Eindhoven, perform the three functions of partial demonstration (stimulus material), control of the rate of practice (response-control material) and presentation of expected results, by which the trainee can evaluate progress.

AV media as feedback

We have thus come to consider the third, or 'feedback' column of our lesson planning model. The slide sequence just described is characteristic of one type of feedback material, which, in a step-by-step procedure, presents to the learner a visual, audio or audiovisual unit with which to compare his or her own efforts. Such feedback material is especially useful when the learner must identify correct or incorrect procedures or decisions by their results and these results may be identified in reality through the auditory or visual channels. Sometimes, as in the case above, the expected outcome of a task-step is illustrated and the learner is left to compare the actual results achieved with the expected results. In other cases, a recording of the learner's behaviour is presented for self-evaluation, as when videotape is used to show a learner his or her own performance in a microteaching exercise, during an interviewing skills role-play session, during a simulated sales meeting, and so on. In yet other cases, a somewhat more sophisticated feedback approach may be employed, which presents the learner's responses and contrasts them with correct responses. To some extent, the audio-active-comparative methodology of using a language laboratory does just that. In contrast to the simpler audio-active approach, which involves listening to and repeating a series of drills and exercises, the audio-active-comparative approach records the learner's own attempts in the spaces left on the tape presenting the exercise. When the tape is replayed, the learner hears his or her own attempts alongside the models of pronunciation presented in the exercise, thus facilitating the identification of any pronunciation errors.

Is your AV an instructional package, or merely a component?

We have analysed these few examples of the use of audio, visual and audiovisual media in the design of instructional exercises, to illustrate that our general instructional design approach holds good even in this field. We have shown that in some (perhaps only a few) cases, audiovisual media may supply all three of the essential components of communication in an instructional system. More often, however, they are restricted to only some parts of the whole system, most usually to the supply of stimulus material. We thought it useful, however, to illustrate all three possible functions, in order to alert you to the possibilities that exist for the fuller exploitation of certain media in instruction. We meant also to illustrate, yet once more, the value of thinking carefully about the structure of an instructional system, so that we may not fall into the error of expecting too much from a media presentation.

7.5.1 Types of AV packages and components

Now that we have an overall view of the role and the potential of audiovisual media in self-instructional packages or systems, we should have a look at some of the great variety of such packages that can be produced. In the analysis of this variety, which is summarized in Figure 7.2, I have included some categories of both visual and audio components in the packages. In order to give coherence to our classification, I have included '*realia*' (real objects and situations) as a source of principally visual (but also audio, in some cases) information. I have defined a number of horizontal rows for different types of (mainly *verbal*) audio – notably the 'commentary' type of audio component, often in the form of voice-over by a presenter who is never seen, or who only appears infrequently in linking sessions, and the 'conversational' type of audio component, which I take to include two or more people debating or discussing a topic, the dramatized presentation of plays and playlets, attempts to converse with the learners or to involve them in the presentation in ways other than just watching, listening and possibly completing some form of workbook at key moments. This distinction, though not too strict in all cases, is meant to discriminate between media presentations that are purely expositive in nature, and those that might be thought to lead at least in part to experiential learning. Finally, I have also included row 1 and column A, to be able to classify pure 'audio' or 'visual' packages and also, on the visual continuum, a column for 'print' – this last in order to be able to include in our schema such hybrid types of packages as the audio-workbook which is dependent on the interaction of the audiotape and print media. I have not included, however, a listing of examples of purely print-based self-instructional packages, as the variety of these is so great as to overload our schema. In any case, I do not propose to deal with print-based packages in this chapter, as they will be dealt with at some length in chapter 9.

The examples listed in the cells of Figure 7.2 are but a sample of some well known and some lesser known varieties of audiovisual package, selected to give a coverage representative of the possible variety and aimed at stimulating the reader's imagination to invent yet other forms.

I shall now give a short description of some of the examples mentioned in the schema presented in Figure 7.2. These descriptions are quite short, as they are intended to illustrate the conceptual schema which we are presenting in this chapter. Readers interested in learning more about a specific type of package are directed to more complete sources. We shall work horizontally across each row of the schema, commencing with the first one called 'No audio component' (that is, with purely visual materials).

VISUAL COMPONENT

AUDIO COMPONENT	1. No visual component	2. Print	3. Realia	4. Still visuals	5. Moving visuals
A. No audio component	Outside the scope of this chapter		Exercises programmed around the use of real objects – 'fault museum' – on-the-job practical training exercises	Instructional packages using sets of visuals only – radio assembly training at Philips – the game of 'Rust'	Silent moving pictures, as the main instructional component – 'concept-loop' 8mm films
B. Expositive commentary/instructions	Audio-instructional packages/programs – the 'audio-active-comparative' language laboratory tapes – audio-discrimination training – submarine crews, musicians, etc	Audio-workbooks – generally the stimulus material is on tape and practice/feedback in the workbook	Audio-directed practice with real objects/situations – the 'RITT' system – 'Walkman' directed practice/drill	Audiovisual packages – slide/tape – disc/filmstrip – tape/cartoon book which include practice/question and feedback	Video instruction – telephone assembly – on-job, video-based training Instructional television (some) Interactive video (some)
C. Dramatized/conversational (possibly experiential) script	Radio programmes and audio-tapes with stimulus material designed to create experiences – case material – plays (post-listening de-brief required)	Audio-workbooks aiming at attitude change, etc – 'Glaxo' medical programmes – rolemaps – group programmes	Audio directed exploratory discovery – 'Walkman' directed nature walk – audio laboratory experiment guide	Audiovisual systems that attempt to generate group activity – radiovision – narrow band video	Audiovisual/video systems that promote group activity/interaction – teleteure – teleconference – instructional television (some) with group audience participation

'Hybrid' or 'Eclectic' systems
– the 'audio-tutorial' approach developed by Postlethwait
– the 'resource-based' multi-media approach

Figure 7.2 *A schema of audiovisual package types (Romiszowski, 1986).*

Cell A-3: the 'fault museum'

The first cell (the intersection of 'No audio' and 'No visual') is necessarily empty. So is the next ('No audio-Print') cell, for the reasons I gave above, of limiting our schema to the main area of interest of this section of the book. In the third cell, I have included one specific example of a whole range of possible packages which depend on the presentation of a real situation or object, to be 'played with' or 'used as a tool', the result being the achievement of specific instructional objectives. Of course, just about all practical and many simulation exercises could be classified in this category. Also many on-the-job practice exercises can be set up so that just by doing the job, the learner gets feedback of sufficient quality and with sufficient frequency and immediacy to guarantee the achievement of the desired learning objectives. The example mentioned specifically is one often used in the training of quality control skills. Very often, a person must develop specific perceptual skills in order to identify, visually, any deviations from expected standards of quality – surface finish, colour, texture, etc. A 'faults museum' is assembled, of real examples of the product ranging from 'perfect' to quite obviously 'defective' for a particular characteristic (say, shade of colour in a stocking). The range of examples in the 'museum' must include many 'in-between' as well as 'obvious' good and defective examples, so that the learner is exposed to levels of 'fine-grain' discrimination that initially are beyond his or her capabilities to recognize. If several different characteristics are important, the museum should include graded examples for each of the characteristics on its own and in combination with others. Training depends on using the 'museum' as a job-aid. First, a range of standard examples is presented, the trainee attempting to identify and explain each fault. When a modicum of skill is reached, training continues 'on the job'.

Cell A-4: still visual packages

The next column of the first row deals with visual instruction packages, using *still representations* of some form or other. Any form of still visual media could be used: pictures, photos, slides, etc. The two examples are of 'true' instructional systems, in that both use still visual media as the main means of demonstration, practice and feedback. Both have already been mentioned earlier on. The slide-controlled, assembly-task training, as used at the Philips radio factory, breaks the task into such distinct and small steps, that a series of slides are sufficient to show the trainee what to do next, with what components, and how it should look when finished, thus providing both 'up front' information and guidance and then 'end of step' feedback information. In between, the rate of presentation of the slides, which is variable, may be used to control the development of appropriate production speeds. The presentation speed in the case described was under the control of the learner, who would decide when she was ready to progress to a faster rate of production.

The other example mentioned in this cell uses a different form of still media presentation: colour photographs of the leaves of coffee plants in various stages of infection by a disease colloquially called 'rust'. These photographs were used in the form of a card game (based on the game of 'snap'). The game provides stimulus information to the trainees (plantation workers), provides practice exercises and feedback of results. (Thus it is a complete instructional system.)

Cell A-5: the 'concept-loop' film

In the last 'no audio' cell, the 'concept-loop film' is mentioned as an example of highly successful instructional use of silent film, very highly acclaimed in the late 1960s and early 1970s. Its use seems to have gone into decline in recent years, probably as the result of the general displacement of super-eight film by the more versatile, more convenient and, in reality, cheaper videocassette. In its heyday, special loop-film projectors were developed, using cassettes of film that could not be longer than about three minutes and, in most models on the market, without a soundtrack. These apparent limitations, however, proved to be the strengths of the medium, as they forced the designer to plan short video clips that were self-contained and which would use the visual-communication potential of the content to its best advantage. The medium forced the designer to think in terms of specific objectives to be achieved by the visual communication and to make the best use of the short communication time available. Hundreds of effective loop

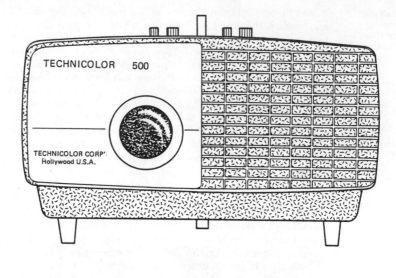

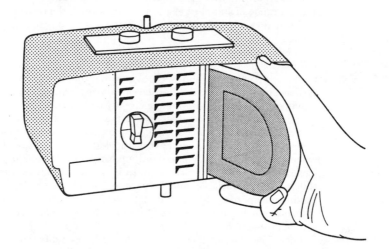

Figure 7.3 *Technicolour 8 mm concept loop projector. Simple cassette loading, daylight projection, stop facilities made this a versatile training tool. Film length limited to just over 4 minutes.*

films were developed in subject areas ranging from physics and biology in the formal 'education' area, to nursing, medical diagnosis, engineering and sports in the 'training' area.

Since the advent of more convenient and cheaper methodologies, the use of single concept super-eight films has waned and production of new films has almost stopped. This has, however, led to many designers forgetting how much could be achieved with the more limited medium, or rather, how many instructional situations may actually benefit from very short self-contained presentations and from a reduction or indeed total elimination of the audio commentary.

Cell B-1:
language
laboratories

This specialist application of the tape recorder is now well established as a language teaching method. It is also being increasingly used as a testing device or to present audio-programmes in many other subjects, so is of more general interest to teachers. Indeed, the Americans are beginning to refer to the equipment by the more general title of 'electronic learning laboratory'.

Essentially, a language laboratory provides facilities for a student to listen to a master recording, and to record his own responses. This is generally achieved by the use of a 4-track tape recorder. When side 1 is being played, track 1 contains the master recording and the student may record, erase and re-record on track 3. This procedure is possible on some sophisticated or modified tape recorders, but the system does not really become a 'laboratory' until a number of such recorders are connected to a central console operated by the teacher. Generally, the teacher may listen in to any one student and can communicate directly to any one or a group of students.

Thus, the student may act as his own judge of his responses, but the teacher may monitor and if necessary supply individual help and guidance. For instance, in learning a language the student may use the language laboratory to listen to words or phrases and then repeat them. He will then compare his pronunciation with the master recording and try again. However, at this stage he is by no means an expert judge of pronunciation. What appears a reasonable attempt to him may jar on the more skilled ear of the teacher. The teacher may then take over, point out the error and eradicate it without disturbing the class. The effective use of a language laboratory for pronunciation training relies heavily on the skill and efforts of the individual teacher.

A later use of the laboratory may involve the practice of sentence construction. The master tape may ask a question, and the student phrases an answer, or the master makes a statement in English and the student translates it. The master then gives the correct response. Here the judgement to be made is much more within the student's capabilities. His effort either agrees with the master or it does not. There is little scope for fine degrees of error as in pronunciation. When used for such a purpose, the teacher's role is much more limited. We have in effect a self-presenting lesson.

It is this technique which is now being applied to 'programme' other subjects. Whether such programmes are effective depends as always on whether the subject is appropriate for such treatment, and on how the programmes themselves are structured. The subject must be one where verbal responses are appropriate, and where the responses are standard and unchanging – subjects which require drill and practice. The rate of progress to more difficult material must be such that at each stage the learner is capable of judging the correctness of his responses, and if necessary identifying his error.

Language laboratory equipment is both expensive and varied. Many systems exist giving progressively greater facilities for student/tape/teacher communication at progressively higher prices. Some have simple tape recorders at the student booths, the master being played from the teacher's console. These have the disadvantage of a lock-step presentation. Others require a 4-track recorder in each booth with an individual tape complete with master recording on track 1. Still others get by with one master tape which can be recorded from the teacher's console onto the student's track for as long as it is required and then replaced with another lesson. This last system is most versatile as it generally allows the use of individual pre-recorded tapes as well.

There are two systems in common use – the audio active comparative (AAC for short) and the audio active (AA). The audio active comparative system, sometimes called listen-respond-compare, requires recording facilities for each student. In the audio active, or listen-respond, system the student hears his voice, as he speaks, by way of his headphones, but it is not recorded. Less equipment is needed, so the system is cheaper than an audio active comparative one. There is much debate about the benefits of the AAC system, and many manufacturers supply both types of laboratory. Some of them offer a 'mixed economy' system, providing a teacher's console with up to half the positions in a class being AAC, the rest being AA.

The teacher's console is usually equipped to transcribe tapes, records or the teacher's voice, onto the student's tapes as shown in Figure 7.4.

Using programme tapes, there are two ways in which the material may be made available to the student. One is to maintain a library containing sets of duplicate recordings. Where a laboratory has to be used by different groups at the same time, this is often a convenient – though expensive – system. The other method is to 'broadcast' a master recording, using the students' recorders to make duplicate copies which will be erased at the end of the lesson. It is not always easy to do this without the students' presence, and it does take time at the beginning of a lesson.

Language laboratories vary considerably in the facilities they provide. It is not always easy, from the sales literature or from a demonstration, to decide whether the presence or absence of some facility will significantly affect the operation of the system. Ask the manufacturer to give you the addresses of some installations that have been in use for at least a year. Visit them, and find out what snags have occurred.

The versatility of the equipment is but one of the potential buyer's considerations. There are further considerations of reliability, student comfort, earphone hygiene, sound-proofing of booths and laboratories, and so on.

Cell B-2: the 'audio-workbook'

This brings us to the consideration of the 'audio-workbook', a combination of an audio recording as the principal stimulus material, with a printed workbook that supplies guidance on use, practical exercises and usually the feedback component. Sometimes, however, the feedback may also be included on the audiotape. Such audio-workbooks, when well designed, are true instructional packages, providing all the system–learner interaction that is necessary to ensure the achievement of the predefined objectives.

Many authors and instructional designers have advocated and implemented the use of audio-workbook systems. They are essentially quick and easy to design and produce and, when appropriately used, are quite effective means of individualizing instruction. Very often, however, due to the limitations of audio as a medium of instruction in certain subjects, the audio-workbook is used in conjunction with other types of exercises. Langdon (1978) mentions three such uses – as a review or revision of course content previously studied in other ways, as an adjunct used in conjunction with other learning materials (for example a book which is referred to as reading assignments at specific points in the audiotape), and as 'update programmes' designed to keep previously trained people up to date on new developments in their job or the subject area related to it. One very widespread application of this type is the provision of audiotapes and audio-workbooks to the medical profession.

Cell B-3: audio-directed drill-and-practice exercises

The next cell presents examples of audio packages involving the use of realia – real objects and situations – to supply the necessary visual stimulus information. An early and 'classic' example is the audio-training RITT system, first developed at the Ericsson company in Sweden, in the early 1960s (Agar, 1962). This method uses an audiotape to describe and to pace the performance of a cyclic industrial task. It was first applied to the training of operatives working with semi-automatic turret lathes and other such-like machines in a ball-bearing factory. This was batch-production work and labour turnover in the factory was high, so that usually, when the time came around to produce another batch of a particular type of product, the previously trained person was no longer available and someone new had to learn the job. The typical learning curve on these jobs was such that full-speed production usually took four weeks or more to be achieved. By then the batch was produced and a slightly different job had to be learned. The RITT system was in essence an audiotape recording that explained the sequence of operations to be carried out. The new trainee would listen to the recording, while a previously trained person, also listening to the tape, would carry out the task as instructed, thus providing a demonstration. Then the two would change places, the new trainee attempting to execute the job while listening to the instructions on

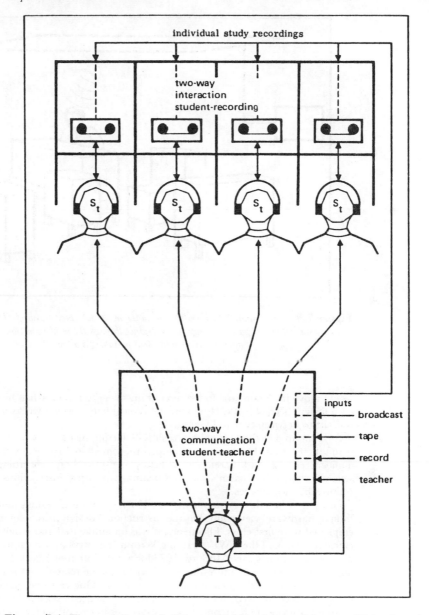

Figure 7.4 *The communication facilities provided by a language laboratory. Obviously, such a communication system may have many other applications: review, drill and practice testing.*

the tape. The experienced worker would watch and, if necessary, correct the novice's actions (physically, by new demonstration, rather than by explanation). Once the novice was managing to complete the tasks to a reasonable (but very slow) standard, the experienced worker would leave. The novice would now work under the control of a series of tapes, each one recorded at progressively faster rates of work. This, of course, meant that more and more of the explanations had to be cut out. Eventually, the trainee would be working to a tape recorded at 100 per cent of EWS (Experienced Worker Standard), which would give only the bare minimum of guidance as to the sequence of actions to be performed. The trainee

Figure 7.5 *The original RITT system for audio on-the-job speed training. The tape recorder beamed an individual paced message to one trainee through the local induction loop. Modern applications would use a portable 'Walkman'.*

would move from one tape to the next at his own discretion, when he felt ready to try a faster speed of work. However, the typical four working weeks to reach EWS was cut to between two and four days.

As compared to the original Swedish RITT equipment, the current 'Walkman' is simplicity itself. The Swedes developed their methodology before the audiocassette age and therefore used heavy, reel-to-reel tape recorders, located in a separate room out of harm's way and beaming the taped instructions to the trainees by radio-waves.

Compared to today's equipment, the RITT system was clumsy and expensive from a 'hardware' viewpoint, but the instructional design principles which it employed were first class. Effectively, it was an automated and much more efficient version of the TWI (Training Within Industry) approach to skills and procedures training (see McCord, 1976 for a description of TWI). It has many applications and some interesting side benefits (some related to drastic cuts in labour turnover on the jobs in which it was used). One very special side benefit reaped by several Swedish firms was related to the use of seasonal labour from Southern Europe, to overcome labour shortages in certain sectors of Swedish industry. (See *Industrial Training International*, September 1966.)

These seasonal workers would stay only a few months in the year and thus created special training problems, especially as most of them did not speak any Swedish on arrival. It was found possible to record tapes with two tracks in parallel presenting a synchronized set of instructions in two languages. This enabled a Swedish worker (who was not a qualified instructor) to supervise the training of an Italian or Spanish trainee (who did not speak a word of Swedish). No words would be exchanged. The audiotapes saw to all communication needs, apart from the visual demonstrations, needed to show the trainee how to work and to show the supervisor that learning had taken place. (See Lundin *et al*, 1968.)

Another example is that of paced typewriting. Variations of this method are used by many commercial schools and secretarial colleges. The method described here is operated by Sight and Sound Ltd, who have a number of installations throughout the UK. Novice students are first trained by means of a simulator. This takes the form of a visual display of the typewriter keyboard on the wall of the class. A tape recorder is synchronized to the display. The voice on the tape slowly reads out a succession of letters. As each letter is spoken, the appropriate key on the visual display lights up. The colour of the light indicates the finger to be used. Students type the letters as they are called out. In successive lessons the rate of presentation increases somewhat, but the main purpose of the first stage of training, with the simulator, is to establish the basic skill of touch-typing without looking at the keys.

Once students have mastered the motor-elements of the skill, and can type accurately (but very slowly) without the aid of the simulator lights, they are transferred to speed training. They now perform standard copy-typing exercises, reading from printed sheets. However, their pace of typing is controlled by tape which reads the exercise, letter by letter, into individual earphones. Students progress to a faster tape once their typing error rate drops below a pre-determined level.

Cell B-4: the 'traditional' audiovisual package

The discussion of 'audiovisuals that don't use visuals' in the more accepted sense, brings us to the category that, to many, is the only meaning of the term 'audiovisual package' – a package composed of an audiotape (or disc) and a set of slides (or a film strip). Many people use the term 'audiovisual' in this restricted sense – you can sometimes come across statements like, 'Should I use an audiovisual or a videocassette for this lesson?'. I prefer the more descriptive terms of 'slide-tape', 'disc-film strip', or whatever, reserving the term 'audiovisual' for the whole field under discussion. I shall not dwell very much here on this category, as we shall return to study examples of slide-tape and similar packages later in the chapter. I should stress here, however, that such packages may, or may not, be 'true' instructional systems. Many (indeed the majority) are not. The teacher must build them into his or her own instructional design. The danger, however, is to use them in isolation, as if they were complete instructional systems, and expect to

Figure 7.6 *An audio-paced typing training system. This could use a language laboratory set-up for initial group-paced practice. Later, individual practice uses personal 'Walkman'-type recorders at the place of work or at home. This system may be adapted to the development of any high speed keyboard skills.*

achieve objectives which actually require the use of further practice exercises, discussions and so on. Many commercially available packages include teacher guidelines on how to build them into an overall design. Some supply supplementary print materials that in effect make the total package into a 'true' instructional system. But most are merely *'information packages'*.

Cell B-5: moving audiovisuals

The last comments are equally valid for the vast majority of audiovisual packages that are based on *moving visual presentations* – film and videotape in particular. The majority of these are also basically informational or motivational materials, which may be used as components in an overall instructional design, but do not by themselves classify as 'true' instructional packages. The problem is that these, as indeed the previously discussed categories, are often labelled 'instructional' and are taken to be such by their users. We shall be careful to distinguish between audiovisual scriptwriting for informational or motivational material and the design of truly instructional sequences.

The South African company, Iconotrain, has developed such video-based operator training systems for many large organizations. Much of the training in the South African gold mines is carried out by means of on-the-job use of short video snippets, similar in style to the RITT system, in that skilled colleagues are used to provide corrective feedback when the trainee applies to the job what was demonstrated in the tape. The skilled employee has a smaller role to play, for all the demonstration is performed by the videotapes but, in the final feedback-giving stages, his role is important. As with the Swedish experience, it has been found quite easy to produce multi-lingual versions of the videotapes and thus overcome previous difficulties of communication with migrant workers from neighbouring countries and territories. Iconotrain claims that whole training centres have been replaced by on-the-job training based on short video segments.

Of course, this operative-training application is not the only type of video that would classify as instructional. In the conceptual learning field, short video sequences followed by questions and discussions can be acceptable instructional designs. Sometimes, the questioning and discussion element is instigated by the video script. Viewers are asked to respond to questions or to solve problems, then to return to the videotape, where a response is given or various approaches to the problem are discussed. Such video-with-questions would not be classed as fully 'interactive video'. It is, however, a step towards the conversion of purely informational material into an instructional package.

Some 'hybrid' or 'eclectic' systems

Finally, we come to the last row on our schema, devoted to packages or systems that employ a more involving, partly experiential, use of the audio medium, allowing some form of involvement or interaction by the viewer/listener. On the 'border' between this and the previous row, I have listed a few difficult-to-classify examples. These are difficult to pin down as they are basically integrated multi-media and multi-method approaches, which could be classified in any combination of the cells on our matrix, depending on the exact way in which they are implemented in a particular case. The 'audio-tutorial' system (Postlethwait *et al.*, 1972) was conceived as a system of learning activities that could take any form and utilize any media combinations, the whole system being controlled by instructions and explanations contained in an audiocassette. The audiocassette may be considered to be a formal commentary, but the learning experiences that it 'knits together' may be both expositive and experiential in nature. The 'audio-tutorial' system developed and spread in the USA from the mid-1960s to the late 1970s and continues to flourish. In Great Britain, during the same period, an approach termed *'resource-based learning'* developed. In essence, there is very little difference between this and the 'audio-tutorial' approach, except that 'resource-based learning' does not necessarily use an audiotape as a study guide. This task may be performed by an audiotape, but is more usually contained in a printed study guide. Once again, however, the resources used may contain both expositive and experiential materials, utilizing a variety of presentation media. Group activities and research projects involving the community may also be included.

Cell C-1: audio programs as experience generators

In the category of experiential audiovisual packages, it is somewhat more difficult to draw the line between what we have called 'true' instructional packages and others (not so 'true'). This is because experiential learning aims to achieve general, attitudinal or cognitive skill objectives, which are not always directly measured by the results of a given exercise, but rather (a) by observing the process by which the results were achieved, and/or (b) by observing the long-term changes that occur after the learning experience, and/or (c) by engaging in a relatively free 'debriefing' discussion that aims to generalize the principles discovered or explore the grounds for the attitudes formed. All this implies that experiential learning exercises are rarely, if ever, composed of just a media-based package. Rather, the media presentations used must be incorporated in an overall instructional design that includes other learning activities.

For this reason, I have been rather more free in my inclusion of examples, on the assumption that they are, or will be, incorporated into a carefully designed instructional lesson plan. I therefore include, in the 'audio only' cell, radio programmes and pre-recorded tapes of dramatized situations, plays, debates and discussions, that are to be used as the stimulus material for specific learning activities on the part of the listeners.

Cell C-2: audio-workbooks aiming at attitude change

Similarly, in the 'audio and print' cell, I mention the form of audio-workbook which is sometimes used in semi-experiential packages dealing with the analysis of dramatized cases of human behaviour. These are sometimes used as parts of management or salesman training programmes, as well as in school study areas such as literature and theatre. One practical example mentioned in the schema concerns some packages developed by the present author for the updating of doctors, as part of a service offered by the Glaxo pharmaceutical company. The content of these packages dealt with controversial issues, on which British doctors held diverging views; one of these was to do with the issue of measles vaccination. Some doctors felt that the official Ministry of Health position in favour of mass vaccination of all children would cause more work and trouble than the 'normal' treatment of measles cases as and when they occurred. The opposite argument hinged on the possible complications (in a small minority of cases) as a result of contracting measles. The package was therefore developed as a dramatized discussion between two doctors, one in favour and one against the mass vaccination programme. This audio-dramatization was accompanied by a booklet, mainly of graphs and other statistical displays reproduced from medical journals, which the doctor in favour would use as visual support for his arguments: 'Now just look at Chart 3; these statistics were quoted in the *Lancet* of May 1968; don't you agree that they prove my case? . . .'.

Cell C-4: audiovisual systems for group activity

In the 'experiential audio and still visual cell' I have included *radiovision* – quite well known, at least to British readers. It is a method quite extensively used by the BBC in its schools broadcasting. The method consists of supplying schools with a package of visual materials, usually slides, in advance of the broadcast of a particular radio programme. The teacher, or some other member of the group, then presents the visuals at appropriate moments, indicated by the programme's presenter. In some applications, the total package differs little from an expositive slide-tape presentation, except that the audio message is being received over broadcast radio – a mere technicality. In other, more creative applications, however, the radio programmes are conversational in style, partially dramatized and the visuals do not only illustrate the audio message, but also guide subsequent group-learning activities in the classroom. This form of radiovision package may indeed have some experiential learning component built into it.

The advantages of radiovision are low cost of production, flexibility in use and the advantages gained by the use of a large, high-quality projected colour picture. Additionally, radiovision uses equipment already available in schools. Tape and film strip may be used by the teacher whenever and wherever needed, as the medium is not limited by broadcast transmission times and the equipment is simple and portable. Repetition and revision are easy. Tape and film strip can be stopped for discussion, or reversed to replay sections which have caused difficulty.

Single frames can be shown. The teacher can use film strip or tape separately, and can 'edit out' or add material as he wishes. Against this, radiovision lacks animation, which makes it unsuitable for some sequences (see Forall, 1972).

Cell C-5: tele-conference or telelecture systems

As we noted earlier, one advantage of radio or television is that it can bring the well-known personality or the acknowledged expert into the classroom. Not only does this guarantee an authoritative presentation, but also students pay greater attention and learn more when they listen to someone known to them, either personally or by repute.

What if there is no suitable radio programme? What if the authority on the subject does not appear on TV? The traditional method of getting information 'straight from the horse's mouth' is to invite the authority to speak. The bulk of management training courses are largely staffed by a 'circus' of visiting lecturers. These are able speakers, well-informed in their subject, who have the time to devote to such activities. People who combine these three qualities are scarce, and so demand fairly hefty lecturing fees. As one proceeds higher up the academic ladder, closer to the frontiers of knowledge, they become scarcer and yet more in demand.

However, to return to the telelecture. Basically this is a lecture delivered over the telephone. A telephone line between your classroom and the lecturer's place of work or private house is hired for an appropriate time. Amplification equipment is installed at each end, so that the lecturer simply speaks while sitting in a chair, or in bed, in a normal voice, and the distant class listens to a loudspeaker installed in the classroom. With two-way communication, it becomes a teleconference. The speaker is able to illustrate his presentation with slides which have been sent by post to be screened at his direction by one of the class. The class can interrupt or ask questions by means of a roving microphone. Thus there is a two-way communication facility over maybe three thousand miles between a class of fifteen and an acknowledged expert on the subject, at about ten per cent of the cost in fees, travel and hotel expenses which would have been incurred by fetching the lecturer to the class. Compared with face-to-face confrontation as in the normal lecture, the telelecture may seem a trifle mechanical. You miss the lecturer's gestures and the lecturer no doubt loses a lot of audience feedback by being unable to observe them. However, these are the disadvantages of any sound broadcast. Against these must be weighed the advantages of two-way communication and the greater accessibility of our rare subject experts.

A teleconference/telelecture system uses standard telephone lines. The exclusive or temporary hire of telephone lines is becoming more and more common, for a range of purposes, such as news reporting or the installation of remote computer terminals. We may look forward to the increasing use of telephones for teaching.

This approach is gaining ever more adepts, especially in the business world. Some national teletraining facilities have been successfully used for years, as for example the TV Executivo service offered in Brazil (Romiszowski, 1986). In the USA, the AT&T telephone company offers a hook-up service to all customers, which is capable of transmitting both audio and some visual information both ways, over the phone lines. One benefit is a possible reduction of travel costs associated with training.

Conclusion

The schema we have just presented has been used to put some order into a very varied and rich field. The examples which have been presented for each cell of the matrix are but a selection of possible real-life cases. Some categories are, of course, more common than others. In part, this is due to the nature and content of what is to be taught but another factor to consider is that possibly those who design and develop audiovisual materials are somewhat 'blinkered' by past practice and fail to observe and seize the opportunities for more creative and relevant audiovisual formats. Another purpose of the matrix is, therefore, to widen one's view of the potential field of applications for audiovisual instruction.

We have limited ourselves here, to applications that *PRESENT* messages to the learner. In Part 3, we shall examine other examples that go further towards becoming instructional systems in the full sense of this term.

Map 7.1 *General design principles for AV packages.*

Structural appeal Clarity	• In order to present information so that it is clear to the learner, use logical organization, divide complex information into small units. • Provide a clear overview, using introductions and summaries, and be sure to show a visual context before focusing in on visual details.
Emphasis	• Use visual and verbal cues plus repetition to emphasize key elements of your presentation.
Pacing	• Use pacing that considers the learner, the subject matter, and the desired response.
Visual/verbal reinforcement	• Be certain the verbal and visual elements are reinforcing each other and are not communicating different messages.
Personal appeal	• Use examples that are familiar to the audience. • Use a learner's viewpoint: this is particularly important in practical 'how-to' materials. • Do not exceed the perceptual capacity of the learner. • Use questions – where appropriate – to keep your audience involved.
Attention Attract	• Use variations in size, colour, brightness, and shape, or employ novel visuals to attract attention.
Hold	• To hold attention, be certain that the material presented is meaningful to the learners. • Consider the complexity of visual materials: very simple or very complex visuals do not hold attention as well as moderately complex visuals.
Span	• Take into consideration the limits of attention span of the audience. Vary the presentation style to extend attention span.
Perception	• Perception is relative, so use size indicators and consider what is seen simultaneously and sequentially. • Perception is selective, so limit the amount of information presented. Use only relevant information, and provide visual and verbal cues to focus attention on key points. • Perception is organized, so arrange material logically in keeping with the subject matter. Use arrows, numbers, or other cues to direct the learner's perceptions. • Perception is influenced by expectations, so use appropriate formats and cues such as headings or instructions to aid the learner in knowing what to expect. High quality graphics and photography can increase the expectation that the material being presented is important.
Memory	• Memory is facilitated when material is meaningful to the learner. • Memory is aided by associating unknown items with known items.

Map 7.1 – *continued*

- Repetition facilitates remembering.
- Memory depends on consequences.
- Using concurrent modes, ie words and pictures, promotes recall.
- Objects and pictures of objects are remembered better than just their names.
- Organizers can provide a structure that aids memory.
- Questions can focus attention and facilitate recall.

Concept learning

- Conceptual learning can be increased by using a variety of examples and non-examples.
- Use realistic pictures to show what things look like. Use simplified pictures to eliminate extraneous information.
- Combine names with pictures to increase conceptual learning.

Attitude change

- Attractive and credible presenters contribute to positive attitude change.
- To promote attitudinal change be sure to organize the message carefully: if the audience has little interest in the topic, present conclusions first. If the audience is interested, but negative, present arguments first, followed by conclusions. Present various points of view.
- Materials should be accurate, carefully designed, and of good quality to promote changes in attitude.

Functions

- Use the audio track to identify or describe visual elements, but avoid excessive redundancy.
- The audio track can add supplementary information that cannot be expressed visually, and it can be employed to reinforce visual messages. Be certain, however, that the two modes (audio and visual) do not convey different meanings.
- Use verbal cues to organize the viewer's visual perceptions.
- The design of the audio track should optimize visual-verbal flow.

Structure

- Maintain a logical organization: use organizers such as 'step 1, step 2, etc', or use preliminary statements that indicate what is to follow.
- Maintain simplicity by breaking complex ideas into simple ones, avoiding extraneous information, unwanted sounds, or misplaced pauses.
- Be certain the narrative style is appropriate to your listeners.
- Start with information that is motivational so the benefits of paying attention will be self-evident.
- Create variety by changing the volume, pace, or voice about every 20 to 30 seconds depending on the audience and the objectives.
- Involve your audience with questions or pauses for discussion.

Map 7.2 *Audio design principles.*

The recording	• Write for listening, not reading. Speak words before finally scripting them. • Avoid complex sentences and use familiar words. • Employ short phrases that will give the listener time to comprehend and synthesize the material. • An informal conversational style is best. Use the direct 'you'. • Avoid any wording that would cause the narrator to falter. • Be sure to choose a credible narrator and one who is appropriate to the audience. • Two or more voices add variety and can increase attention and interest. • The delivery rate must be suitable to the audience and the subject matter (a typical rate of delivery is about 180 words/minute). • Be sure the narrator uses correct pronunciation and emphasis. • Choose suitable music. • Avoid any musical score that might compete with the narration. • Use sound effects to create realism and to add interest and emphasis. Be certain they are realistic and that they are employed judiciously. • Vary the tone of delivery and the style of conversation. • Encourage active listening and participation by posing questions, problems, etc. • Break the recording into short 1–3 minute sections, building in summaries, pauses and occasionally stops for audience participation.

Map 7.3 *Typical structure of audio and simple audio-workbook instructional packages (adapted from Meacham and Butler, 1984).*

Structure of script	Try to include the following in your script: 1. Introduction • aims – motivational and content orientation • overview • context within subject • arousal of interest 2. Clearly stated objectives • student competencies • what students should know/do after listening 3. Logical subdivision • list of contents and sequence • indication of importance 4. Clear explanation of technical terms • define new vocabulary • make meaning clear by context • add glossary of terms 5. Summary of main ideas • revision • repetition 6. Questions and requests for responses • self-help questions • summary questions • checklists
Accompanying printed material	There are many instances where printed material, especially in the form of charts, diagrams, accounts, photographs, formulae, etc, should accompany audio materials. Printed materials usually should include: 1. a synopsis of the topics used in the tape or more detailed statement of content 2. a statement of objectives 3. a statement or model locating the taped material within the total subject or course 4. an annotated list of references .5. self-testing exercises 6. any essential visual material: charts, diagrams, accounts, cartoons, photographs, art prints, formulae, models, statistics, etc.

Map 7.4 *A check-list for evaluating audio and simple audio-visual instructional packages.*

(a) The Structure of the Material	Agree – – – – – Disagree				
1. The educational objectives are clearly stated.	1	2	3	4	5
2. The content of the AV is relatively clearly related to the objectives.	1	2	3	4	5
3. The student's interest is likely to be aroused and interest maintained.	1	2	3	4	5
4. The material encourages critical thinking.	1	2	3	4	5
5. The material requires active learning by including questions, problems, activities, etc.	1	2	3	4	5
6. The main body of content is appropriately introduced and comprehensively summarized	1	2	3	4	5
7. Critical points are clarified and emphasized.	1	2	3	4	5
8. The material unfolds in a structured, logical sequence.	1	2	3	4	5
(b) The Spoken Delivery					
9. The material is communicated in a conversational tone.	1	2	3	4	5
10. The tone of voice is varied, with adequate emphasis where required.	1	2	3	4	5
11. The lecturer speaks cheerfully or dramatically as appropriate.	1	2	3	4	5
12. The lecturer's enunciation is clear, with no distracting speech habits.	1	2	3	4	5
13. Sentences are short and to the point.	1	2	3	4	5
14. Technical terms are spelt out and included in a glossary.	1	2	3	4	5

Map 7.4 *– continued*

(c) *Technical Qualtiy*	Agree – – – – – – Disagree				
15. The volume remains constant, without fade.	1	2	3	4	5
16. There is no extraneous recorded background noise.	1	2	3	4	5
(d) *Accompanying Materials*					
17. The tape is appropriately indexed.	1	2	3	4	5
18. Any visual materials used relate clearly to the tape and its objectives.	1	2	3	4	5
19. All materials needing frequent references is presented visually.	1	2	3	4	5
20. Printed material shows links with the whole course.	1	2	3	4	5
21. Main concepts are summarized in print.	1	2	3	4	5
22. Exercises and activities are presented in print form.	1	2	3	4	5

Map 7.5 *Troubleshooting guide for simple audio/AV equipment.*

		PROBLEM	POSSIBLE CAUSE	REMEDY
1. **Initial start-up problems**	General	Nothing happens when machine is turned 'on'	No power – not plugged in.	Check power plug for snug fit. Try reversing plug.
			No power in the building cicuit.	Try another electrical appliance in the same outlet. Fix, if necessary.
			No power in the machine circuit.	Push the red circuit breaker button (if fitted). Check and change any fuses.
			Faulty cord or wiring in machine.	Try another power cord from a similar machine.
			Safety device on machine.	Close or tighten access cover. Check threading pattern to determine whether clutches or automatic shut-off mechanisms have been tripped.
2. **Visual project ion problems**	Lamps	Motor or fan runs but lamp doesn't light.	Lamp switch 'off'. Bulb improperly installed.	Activate switch.
			Bulb may be burned out.	Replace bulb.
			Faulty switch.	
	Focus	Screen image is fuzzy and not clear.	Lens not focused.	Adjust focus.
			Bulb incorrectly installed.	Correct installation.
	Brightness		Dirty lens.	Clean lens with soft cloth or lens tissue.
			Film not properly positioned in film channel.	Recheck threading.
	Others	Inverted image on the screen.	Slide upside-down.	Invert slide in carrier.
			Film strip improperly threaded.	Rethread film strip.
		Edge of film visible on screen.	Film strip or film not properly positioned in film gate.	Stop projector and rethread.
		Carousel projector tray cannot be removed.	Tray identification number not on 0.	Turn power control on. Remove tray manually.
		Parts of two pictures or frames are seen on screen.	Framer adjustment.	Adjust framing control.

Map 7.5 – *continued*

3. **Audio reprod-uction problems**	**No Sound or Low Volume**	Low volume.	Audio tape not threaded properly.	Check threading.
			Wrong side of tape might be in contact with playback head.	Rewind and re-thread tape.
			Dirty playback head.	Clean head.
			Microphone used for recording was not compatible with the recorder.	Use the proper microphone.
		No sound being produced.	Speaker cord not connected.	Plug speaker in.
			Amplifier not 'on'.	Switch amplifier 'on'.
			Faulty microphone, amplifier or speaker.	Try another microphone or speaker and cord from a similar machine.
	Poor Fidelity	Low-pitched, 'gutteral'.	Machine set at wrong speed.	Adjust speed control (speed up recorder).
		High-pitched, 'chipmunk-like'.	Machine set at wrong speed.	Adjust speed control (slow down playback).
		Audio tape is mushy and indistinct.	Dirty playback head.	Clean head (use cotton swab with alcohol).
		Tempo is slightly off, resulting in distortion of pitch, rate, etc. (See sound system problems section)	Dirty or faulty drive mechanism.	Have the machine cleaned.
			Some object rubbing on record or tape reel.	Remove resistance.

8. Film

8.1 How much is film used in education?

Regular
but not
extensive
use

Cine film has long been established as a teaching medium. Nearly every school or training centre possesses at least one cine-projector, and it is difficult to choose from the large selection of off-the-shelf training films now available.

However, the path to acceptance has been long and not without setbacks. Indeed, it seems that the path has led us in a rather unexpected direction. As long ago as 1900, popular writers, as well as serious educators, were predicting a revolution in education, based on the widespread use of films. This revolution has not yet materialized. Although films are plentiful, the proportion of time spent watching them by the average student is very low. The predictions of higher student motivation and interest, as shown by the 1923 cartoon shown in Figure 8.1 have not materialized either.

Some of
the reasons

Educational films have probably as many failures as successes to their credit. Many of the failures were due to the inappropriate use of film, and the *Chicago Tribune* cartoon illustrates this. Study carefully the second pair of pictures. As an educational technologist, why would you doubt the likelihood of such a transformation in the attitude of the children?

The timetable, *To-day's pictures*, indicates that the cartoonist expected the filmed lesson to do exactly the same job as the teacher – automated chalk-and-talk. But is this not exactly what many educational films do? Think back over the films you have seen. How often did they include lengthy shots of a commentator or teacher talking at the audience or even writing on a chalkboard? True, the film has certain advantages: we can guarantee an accurate, clear exposition, supported by well-produced visual material, which can be reproduced, without change, to successive audiences. But there are disadvantages: the exposition may not be as clear as we hope to all members of the audience; opportunity for questioning and discussion of the visual material may be lost. Such an opportunity can of course be provided by the teacher, during the introduction or follow-up of the film. There is much evidence to suggest that the educational value of a film is dependent on the way it is used.

A quick look at some research in this field will help us to build some principles for the selection of educational films.

8.2 Research on cine film

8.2.1 Are films generally of educational value?

Positive
attitudes
towards
learning
from film

The short answer is yes, based on many large studies carried out throughout Europe and America. These measured the attitudes of teachers and students who had used films. However, these studies tell us little about any precise changes in attitude, knowledge or skill produced by the films. More detailed studies are needed to examine these points. Many of the results are inconclusive.

Figure 8.1 *'The Changing World'. (Mr Edison predicts motion pictures will take the place of books in the schools.) 1923 cartoon from the* Chicago Tribune.

8.2.2 Can films change attitudes or emotions?

Most certainly. For example the US Army has used a film entitled *Why We Fight* in a controlled experimental situation. The film presented the facts behind the case without any emotional treatment. However, the group who had seen the film contained twice as many who were prepared to go to war, as equivalent groups who had not seen the film (Miles and Spain, 1947).

When a film deliberately sets out to change attitudes and emotions, and employs all the actor's and ad-man's tricks, it can indeed be a powerful tool. The teacher should be aware of this power, and be on his guard in case it is abused. For example, films shown to groups of schoolchildren by Furhammar (1963) produced strong anti-German attitudes. Furthermore, the teacher should watch for unexpected or irrelevant attitudes that a given film may produce. We might mention here Belson's study (1956). A series of French language films, aimed at the potential tourist, had the odd effect of teaching efficiently a range of useful words and phrases, but at the same time increasing the general level of apprehension in the group about the difficulties of foreign travel and communication!

8.2.3 Can films increase interest and motivation?

Positive motivational effects

Generally yes. There are innumerable reports on individual films. A wide survey, by Brooker (1946), of instructional films produced by the US Office of Education, showed that the vast majority of users considered that the films 'made the class work more interesting and resulted in less absenteeism'. It should be noted, however, that the interest or motivation produced by a film stems from its content and the treatment the content is given, not from the film medium itself. Gone are the days when seeing a movie was an experience in itself. Today's younger generation accept films as commonplace, and expect surprisingly high standards of production. They 'learn the language' of film almost from birth.

8.2.4 Do students learn more effectively from film?

Little or no improvement in learning over other methods

There is no one answer: the research has often been inconclusive. There is no doubt that you learn from a film, as from any experience. A film may present material which could not otherwise be demonstrated: documentaries from overseas, the interior of furnaces, animated sequences, slow-motion sequences. In such cases, the medium is being used to expand the teacher's normally available resources. It is doubtful, though, whether films *per se* have any advantage over other presentations. Laner (1954) compared two methods of teaching the assembly of a sash-cord window – a sound film, and a set of slides linked to a recording of the same commentary as the film used. No difference in the amount learnt was found. Experiments on tasks which involved the mastery of skilled movements (such as in athletics) do however point to the superiority of moving film. Mackintosh (1947) compared a sound-film presentation on *Water Power*, with a silent presentation of the film supported by a commentary prepared and given by the normal class teacher. He found that, provided the teacher's commentary was well prepared, he could achieve better results than the standard soundtrack, due no doubt to his greater familiarity with the students and their backgrounds.

Psychomotor Domain	*Skill Films* Films which stimulate perception of a task and subsequent performance of the task.
Cognitive Domain	*Record Films* Films made for the purpose of securing data, or of preserving a record of events for commemorative purposes. *Information Films* Films which stimulate learning of facts, processes, verbal development, concepts, principles and so on.
Affective Domain	*Persuasive Films* Films which stimulate viewers to think, feel, or act in certain ways: Propaganda films are films using any of an array of well-known propaganda techniques. Advertising films stimulate and promote good will and the purchase and consumption of products. Documentary films are often one-sided factual films having persuasive themes.
Interactive Skills Domain	*Role-Model Films* Demonstration of desired behaviour – often short. *Case Study Films* Situational dramatization, as stimulus for analysis of interactions, conflicts, etc.

Figure 8.2 *Some uses of film in education and training.*

Experiments in London medical schools (Hughes *et al.*, 1953), compared an 8-minute silent film on *How To Inoculate a Plate* with live practical demonstrations. The carefully prepared film proved no more effective than the run-of-the-mill demonstration. However, the film had greater practical advantages – more people could view at one time, they could view at any time, and as often as they liked.

In case I am accused of quoting only old research, it may be worth stating at this point that there is precious little recent research on the instructional effectiveness of film, or at any rate, precious little worth quoting. Most of the worthwhile research in this field was done before the war. Since then we have had a few experiments repeating and confirming earlier findings and a host of comparative studies so loosely controlled that one cannot in any way generalize from them.

Back in 1924 Freeman reported on the experiments conducted at the University of Chicago in the early 1920s. This consisted of 13 individual experiments, representing the first systematic, experimental investigation of relevant instructional media variables and making the first use of experimentally designed media for this purpose. A few of the major conclusions were:

The main research findings

(a) The relative effectiveness of verbal instruction as contrasted with the various forms of concrete or realistic material in visual media depends on the nature of the instruction to be given and the character of the learner's previous experience with objective materials.

(b) The comparison of film with other visual media (slides, still pictures) as a means of instruction when the medium variable is motion (eg a film showing the motion of a steamboat was compared with a still picture of the same object) indicates that the film is superior within a restricted range and type of content, but that outside this range the other media are as effective or more effective.

(c) The value of a film lies not in its generally stimulating effect, but in its ability to furnish a particular type of experience.

(d) It is inefficient to put into films actions which can be demonstrated readily by the teacher.

(e) In teaching science and how to do or make something, demonstration is superior to the film.

(f) Films should be so designed as to furnish to the teacher otherwise inaccessible raw material for instruction, but should leave the organization of the complete teaching unit largely to the teacher.

Meta-analyses support these findings ...

Since then, little has been added to this list of findings. The results are consolidated by the extensive research during the 1950s sponsored by the US Air Force. A review by Saettler (1968) found no new trends in research to that date and a later review by Peggie Campeau (1972), prepared for the Council of Europe, and covering all media research during the years 1966 to 1971, reported not one study in this field which satisfied her research criteria: carried out recently (1966–71); completeness and availability (fully reported); sample at least 25 subjects per group; study at least one hour in duration; measures of effectiveness taken; statistical analysis carried out. A surprising finding, don't you think, when we consider the number of specialist magazines and journals filled every month with articles about film and its use.

... and suggest that media research was on the wrong track

Campeau argues strongly that, in any case, most research into film and indeed most media (with the possible exception of programmed instruction) is on the wrong track. Investigators are obsessed with comparisons of one medium against another for total courses, when they should be matching media to specific types of educational objectives. However, even this is not all that new. Back in 1930, Weber (1930) was arguing that we already knew all we ever would from comparative studies, and that future research should be conducted to determine optimum length, content and treatment of the subject matter of films.

DO'S	
1 Operator's viewpoint	Showing a skill by placing the camera as near as possible to the performer's point of view – the 'operator's viewpoint' – was considerably more effective than showing the skill from a camera position of 180°, ie, facing the performer.
2 Medium rate of commentary	Commentary spoken as slowly as 71–102 words per minute (slow) and as fast as 155–185 wpm (fast) was used in experimental versions of skill films. But a medium rate, 111–141 wpm, proved to be superior.
3 Direct and simple language	Using direct address, or the second person active mode, eg, 'Now form a loop', was found to be better than the use of the passive mode, eg, 'Now, a loop is formed'.
4 Commentary leads the action	Commentary which leads the action, ie, which begins slightly before the action is shown, is superior to commentary which lags behind the action.
5 Integrate the demonstration and the practice	When the task to be learned is presented slowly enough to permit learner participation, learning is better than that resulting from showing the operation faster, followed by participation.
6 Teach error recognition by showing errors	There was a significant increase in the effectiveness of skill films which showed errors, plainly indicated as such.
7 Repetition	Repetitions of action within a film produced better learning. Repetitions of the entire film one or two times also produced better learning than single showings.
DON'TS	The following experimental variables were found *not* to yield learning increments in skill films:
1 Don't make it too slick and fast	Succinct treatment. A 'slick', fast version of a film, while it did teach, was the least effective of all the fourteen variables compared in one experiment.
2 Don't use unnecessary animation/graphics	Animation showing 'how it works'. At the beginning of one film, a short animated sequence showed the operation of the breechblock during firing. This animated section apparently was irrelevant to skill learning, because it produced no increment in learning.
3 Don't use unnecessary technical jargon	Technical terminology. A version using technical terminology was found not to be more effective than other versions of the same film.

Figure 8.3 *Research-based rules for psychomotor skills training films. (Look for these in films you are evaluating.)*

8.3 The selection of off-the-shelf films

In general, do not select films on the basis of research findings

So the general picture emerges that cine film might enhance the acceptability of almost any presentation, but it only enhances the instructional value significantly if the material to be learnt involves the recognition or mastery of movements which cannot, for various reasons, be otherwise demonstrated. This is not bby any means an argument for a reduction in the use of film in education. Most films are used as a general introduction to or summary of a topic. As such, their prime objective is to stimulate interest, motivate, paint the broad picture and establish certain attitudes – objectives easily achieved by the use of interesting photography and strong personalities.

We might add here that there are limitations to the research described above. Most studies, of necessity, measure the learning that has taken place by some sort of verbal or written test. Perhaps sometimes the apparent lack of learning is really a lack of ability to express verbally what has been learnt. Furthermore, many would argue (and there is evidence to support their argument) that the 'total involvement' produced by a good film might result in learning which is not capable of being tested verbally.

If the film objectives are of a specific training nature however (eg to learn the names of parts or how to operate them), we should first carefully consider whether cine film is the ideal medium for presentation, and, secondly, how the film should be structured to ensure efficient learning.

Better to analyse the structure and content of the film

In many ways, the problems of selecting an appropriate training film off-the-shelf are similar to those of evaluation. One selects a film with the same objectives, aimed at the same type of student, and tests its effectiveness. However, off-the-shelf films are rarely explicit about their target population, and still more rarely have any statement of objectives, let alone one phrased in terms of student behaviour. There is no alternative but to sit down and watch it. Teachers have always done this, but all too often with a view solely to checking the factual accuracy of the material presented. While this is of vital importance, the factors of film structure we have discussed above are equally important in deciding whether a film is worth screening to your students. For example, if the objectives differ widely from your own, or if the commentary assumes vast amounts of pre-knowledge which your students do not have, then it is a waste of time to even attempt to use the film. Greenhill (1956) produced, as part of an extensive study into instructional films, a set of questions the potential film user should attempt to answer when deciding the merits of a film.

The final version of his 'Film Analysis Form' contains 17 questions on the structure of the film, and 10 on the subject matter content. It is shown here in Figure 8.4.

Observations on the use of the film analysis questionnaire

The answers to most of these questions are of course subjective. Individuals will differ in the exact rating given to a specific question. However, Greenhill found that if training was given in the use of the film analysis form, by practising on standard films, a surprisingly consistent and reliable level of rating was achieved. It is suggested that when rating a film, a low score (1 or 2) on any of the questions marked with an asterisk is sufficient to disqualify the film. Those without an asterisk are deemed less important and one or two low scores can be tolerated. The analysis form was originally developed for pinpointing weaknesses in film during production. It has, however, been extensively used for the systematic selection of off-the-shelf films. Finally, we should not ignore the possibility of using only part of a commercially available film. More and more film users are employing the technique of analysing a range of available films, and using only those parts which pass the test.

Each question can be answered as a matter of degree and is rated on a 6-point scale. High scores indicate a strong yes, low scores a strong no. The questions dealing with structure are:

	SCORE
*1 Are the objectives clear?	
*2 Will the *target audience* find the film interesting?	
3 Does the film build on previous knowledge, skills or experience of the target audience?	
*4 Is the subject matter appropriate for the course of training?	
5 Does the content relate directly to the main objectives?	
6 Is the content presented in a well-organized, systematic pattern?	
7 Are the important ideas or procedures clearly emphasized?	
8 Does the film attempt to present too much material for the audience?	
9 Are the new facts, ideas, terminology or procedures introduced at a rate which will permit efficient learning (not too fast nor too slow)?	
10 Does the film provide for adequate repetition of the important content (eg revision, summaries, outlines)?	
11 Is the method of presentation suitable to the subject matter?	
12 Is the difficulty of the *pictorial presentation* appropriate for the target audience?	
13 Are the details of the information or demonstration clearly presented pictorially (camera angle, lighting, close-up etc)?	
14 Is the verbal difficulty of the commentary appropriate?	
15 Does the commentator contribute to the effectiveness of the film (appearance, tone, manner, speed)?	
*16 Is the sound track clearly audible?	
17 Is the information presented in the commentary well integrated with that presented in the pictures?	
Total score (max 102)	

Further questions on subject matter content are:

	SCORE
*1 Is the information *technically* accurate?	
2 What is the relative importance of any inaccuracies?	
3 Is the content up-to-date?	
*4 Is the content specific (precise factual material rather than broad abstract generalizations)?	
*5 Is it highly probable that the information or procedures presented will be confirmed by subsequent experience?	
*6 Is it highly probable that the target population will be able to *use* or *apply* the information or procedures presented?	
*7 Is the subject treated more effectively than it would be through some other medium (lecture, demonstration slide film, text book)?	
8 Is it the most feasible or economic way of teaching the subject?	
9 Does the kind of film used (colour or black and white) effectively show the essential details of the subject matter?	
10 Does the film show common errors (in the performance of a skill), or common misconceptions (in understanding of theory), and how to correct them?	
Total score (max 60)	

Figure 8.4 *A film analysis questionnaire.*

A. SELECTION

1. Where information alone is the objective of a film, a well-organized, straightforward approach, using the most appropriate techniques, such as slow motion, animation, etc, leads to the most efficient kind of informational film.

2. Embellishments such as optical effects, attention-getting devices, plot gimmicks, dramatic structure, humorous treatment, and music, are not needed in informational or instructional films.

3. Films should deal with information as specifically as possible, in short, single idea units.

4. Films can carry a large part of an instructional mission, but must always be integrated into an overall lesson design.

B. USE

5. Users of films can choose from a variety of effective film-use strategies, such as presenting objectives and using pre-testing, study guides, discussion and post-testing, which will increase the effectiveness of informational films.

6. Briefing in order to establish an objective/context for viewing.

7. Debriefing in order to evaluate the film's overall effectiveness, levels of comprehension of key points, attitude changes, etc, and to reinforce/correct if necessary.

8. Stopping the film at intervals, for discussion/practice if not distracting.

9. A second showing of a film is a sure way to achieve increments in learning and should be used when these other suggestions prove impracticable.

Figure 8.5 *Some suggestions for the selection and use of informational films for instruction.*

8.4 Film equipment

Most teachers and instructors are probably aware of the types of equipment available for film presentation. The large 35 mm format is seldom used. Most training films are available in 16 mm stock, but there is a certain amount in 8 mm.

8.4.1 16 mm films

Variations in 16 mm standards

Films have been made in this format for entertainment and for training purposes since the 1930s. Initially, the smaller size of the film limited the maximum size of image, and therefore the audience. Improvements in optics have overcome this limitation, and 16 mm film gives an adequate picture in all but the very largest auditorium. Silent and sound films are available. The sound tracks may be magnetic or optical. In practice this does not matter, as long as the projector you have can handle the type of sound track on your film. It's as well to check beforehand. Many projectors will handle both types of sound track and these are obviously the ones to go for. In addition, it is best to obtain a projector with speeds for silent and sound film. The old silent films run at a slower speed. If run at the speed of the modern sound film, life seems to progress at a Chaplinesque pace and it's all over far too soon: high entertainment value, but doubtful educational merit. It is just as well to invest straight away in a multi-speed projector which will allow one to slow down or speed up certain sequences, or indeed to stop the film at any desired frame. A further facility which increases versatility and the control that the teacher can exercise over the presentation is a socket for a microphone, enabling the standard commentary to be replaced by the teacher's own.

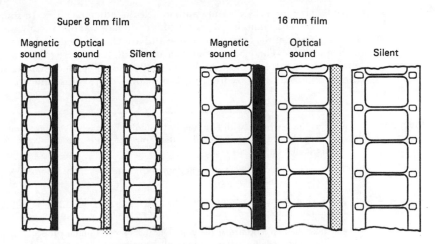

Super 8 mm film   16 mm film

Magnetic sound   Optical sound   Silent   Magnetic sound   Optical sound   Silent

Figure 8.6 *Types of motion picture film.*

8.4.2 8 mm and Super 8

Variations in 8 mm standards

Unlike the 16 mm format, 8 mm films do have a practical limit on the size of image which can be clearly screened. They are not therefore suitable for very large conference and lecture rooms. However, modern projectors have so improved that 8 mm films can now be effectively shown in quite large rooms, and are more than adequate in the typical classroom. Gone are the days when the image was limited to a 30-inch square. We can now project bigger images in full daylight conditions.

The 8 mm format is not that popular in education and training. This is because there is such a lot of material already available in 16 mm, and most establishments are equipped for this film.

Super 8 was introduced in 1965. The major difference is that Super 8 allows about 50% more room for each individual picture, mainly by reducing the size of the sprocket holes which, on Standard 8, are the same size as those used on 16 mm film. The normal speed for Super 8 film is 18 frames per second as against 16 frames per second with Standard 8. Both these differences help to give a rather better picture with Super 8.

8.4.3 Speeds and film capacity

Film speed standards

As I have said, the 'standard' speeds for 16 mm are 16 and 24 frames per second. The standard speeds for Standard 8 were 16 and 24 frames per second, but a number of manufacturers have substituted 18 for 16 frames per second, particularly in dual format projectors. There are even one or two 16 mm projectors

Variable and reverse speeds

on which this has been done. Some projectors provide a variable speed control, so that films can be speeded up or slowed down. The ability to slow down a film, or to project still pictures, is useful in such things as skills analysis. When the film is stopped for the projection of a single frame, a loss of light is experienced because an additional heat filter is brought into use to prevent the frame being burned. Some projectors also allow for reverse projection, useful if you wish to re-examine a section of film. On sound projectors it is often arranged that the sound track is automatically switched off during reverse projection.

Film capacity

Most 8 mm projectors take reels that hold 400 ft of film. This gives a little more than half an hour running time at 16 frames per second, 25 minutes with Super 8 at 18 frames per second. Most 16 mm projectors take 2000 ft reels, giving about an hour's show at sound speed, or an hour and a half at silent speed.

Self-threading   Many cine projectors feature auto or self-threading facilities. In some cases this is a reel to reel section, in others the film is threaded automatically over the most tiresome parts of the threading course and attachment to the take-up reel has to be done manually. There are so many variations that it is wise to ask to use the equipment to see if it suits you. If a partially used film which has become damaged can be removed with ease from a self-threading projector, so much the better.

Procedure	1. Place the feed reel (with film) on feed spindle and take-up reel on take-up spindle. Secure them. Both reels should be the same size (take-up reel must be able to hold all the film on the feed reel).
	2. Open all of the sprocket shoes and open the gate. Never try to force any mechanism on the projector.
	3. Unwind about three feet of film. Place film under the first sprocket wheel, fitting sprocket holes onto the pins. Close the shoe to hold film in place.
	4. Make the first loop before the gate: follow loop diagram for proper size. If this loop is too large, it will chatter; if too small, the claw will tear the sprocket holes.
	5. Place film in the gate, in the path between the runners. Slide it up and down slightly until sprocket holes are engaged by the claw. Check top loop. Close the gate, being sure the film fits flat so you do not crease it.
	6. Leave a second, properly spaced loop below the film gate. This is the loop which determines whether the sound is synchronized with the picture.
	7. Negotiate the rollers and stabilizers and make sure the film fits securely and smoothly round the sound drum; if it doesn't the sound will be mushy, faint or garbled.
	8. Place film around last sprocket wheel and close shoe.
	9. Bring film around the final snubbing roller before it goes up on take-up reel, and attach film to take-up reel.
Diagram	Set top and bottom loops as indicated on your particular machine.

Figure 8.7 *How to thread a film projector.*

8.4.4 Sound systems

Optical sound

16 mm silent films are projected at 16 frames per second, sound films at 24 frames per second. The sound system used on professionally made 16 mm films is an optical one. The sound appears down the side of the film as a pattern of lines. As the film passes through the projector, this pattern is scanned by a photo electric system and turned back into sound. You have to use studio facilities to record optical sound. A number of 16 mm projectors also have a magnetic sound system.

Magnetic sound

Here the sound is recorded on a magnetic stripe along one edge of the film, in the same way as on a tape recorder. Some projectors enable the user to record and replay his own magnetic sound track. Others are designed only to replay a recording made on another machine. Almost all 8 mm sound projectors use only the magnetic system.

8.5 Speaker placement

Speakers differ in their angle of dispersion of high frequencies. You can get an idea about yours through this test: hook up a radio to the system that feeds your speaker, and tune it to the 'hiss' between stations. This is white noise, consisting of high frequencies. Set the speaker up at ear level. Now walk back and forth in front of the speaker and note at which point the sound starts to get 'dull'. Do this at various distances from the speaker, and you'll get an idea of how wide the speaker's dispersion is.

Single-speaker sound systems

Now to the location of single speaker. If you're just doing a screening for a few dozen people in a small room, it won't matter too much; just set the speaker up as high as you can near the screen. In larger rooms for more people, you might see if it's possible to hang the speaker *above* the screen, angling it downwards. Your knowledge of the speaker's dispersion characteristics will tell you how much of an angle to use so that people in the front and back will hear the high frequencies: too steep an angle, and the people at the back won't hear; too shallow, and the sound will pass over the heads of the people in front. The width of dispersion will also tell you how wide you can make the rows of seats, especially in the front.

Two-speaker systems

If you're using a hi-fi or portable PA system, you will probably be using two speakers. There are a number of ways they can be set up, depending on room and audience size, speaker type, and the acoustical problems the room gives you to contend with.

First, make sure the speakers are in phase – meaning that as the speaker cones vibrate, they are moving in and out together, rather than one moving out while the other moves in. If your speaker wire is marked for polarity, connecting both speakers the same way will usually ensure this.

If in doubt, here is a test: connect both speakers and place them right next to each other. If it's a stereo amp, switch it to 'mono'. Play music through the spakers, and listen for the amount of bass. Now reverse the connections on one of the speakers. If there is less bass, the first connection was correct. If more, it's correct now.

8.5.1 Centred placement

If there is room, locate them dirrectly under the screen (assuming they are high enough to shoot over the heads of the people in the front). Angle them slightly *outwards*, away from each other, and slightly downward towards the audience. Use your evaluation of their dispersion characteristics to adjust the angles to cover the whole audience. By locating the speakers next to each other, the sound will appear to emanate from the centre of the screen no matter where the listener is sitting.

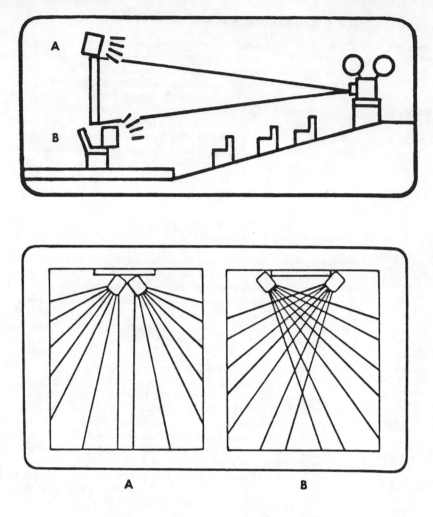

Figure 8.8 *Speaker positions. 1. Single speaker: A. Speaker raised above screen. B. Speaker up off the floor. 2. Two-speaker systems: A. Centred placement. B. Crossfire placement.*

8.5.2 Crossfire placement

If the space beneath the screen is insufficient, raise one speaker as high as you can on each side of the screen. This time, angle them *inwards*, and downwards. When a mono signal is placed through two speakers placed apart, the sound will appear to emanate from a point midway between the two speakers – if the listener is also located between and in front of the speakers. Moving to the side causes the source to move. By angling the speakers inward, the difference in perceived volume between the two speakers will cause the apparent sound source to remain near the centre of the screen, no matter where the listener is. The location of the speakers will also affect the way room acoustics will respond to them. The closer a speaker is to the junction between two room surfaces – say, a wall and the floor – the more bass frequencies will be accentuated.

8.6 The screening of films

**Daylight/
blackout?**

It is not the purpose of this book to teach the operation of particular film projectors. There are, however, some general points. First, do we need blackout? The days of total blackout are over for good. It is generally an advantage to have partial blackout, or at least to avoid direct sunlight onto the screen. However, for many teaching purposes it is an advantage to use the minimum of blackout as it enables the teacher to exercise better class control, and the students to take notes. Some recent films require the audience to write down responses at certain points. Work rating films have used this technique for some time. More recently, 'programmed' films, requiring audience participation, have appeared on a variety of subjects.

**Front/back
projection?**

Modern high-quality projectors, both 16 mm and 8 mm, will give adequate images under daylight conditions, provided the size of the required image is reasonable. The use of a back-projection set-up gives excellent daylight viewing results. As mentioned earlier when discussing slide projection, the quality of the optical systems used has so improved recently, that the previous advantages of back-projection have been much reduced. Now, in a country like England where direct sunlight is a problem seldom encountered and easily overcome, back-projection does little to improve the image. It may of course hide the works and keep the projector noise down. These are both worthwhile advantages in the typical classroom where the projector is set up only occasionally. There is nothing so distracting as a lump of chattering machinery slap in the middle of the audience. Though back-projection helps, a separate projection room is better.

**Screen
choice**

The choice of screen was discussed in the chapter on slide projection. A matt white screen reflects the light in a wide angle. A beaded or silver screen reflects light more directly. It can therefore be viewed from a narrower angle, but gives a brighter image. For most cinema installations, where the front row is at a reasonable distance from the screen, and the room shape tends to be long and narrow, a beaded screen would be the right choice. For occasional use in a squarish classroom, a matt white screen will give better overall results at the cost of some brilliance.

**Screen
position**

Finally, the comfort of the viewer should not be ignored, particularly if a permanent cinema installation is planned or long films are to be used. The screen should not be too high for comfort, or so low that the front row obscures it. Seats should be comfortable, ventilation adequate. I am reminded of the famous research into subliminal advertising. Was the increase in ice cream sales due to the advertising flashes, or to the failure of the air conditioning plant?

Map 8.1 *Data for the planning of 16 mm film screening. (Adapted from Blackby et al., 1980.)*

Room size and seating capacity	Room Ratio/Length:Width							
		1:1		**4:3**		**3:2**		
	Minimum Screen Size	Room Size	Seating Capacity	Room Size	Seating Capacity	Room Size	Seating Capacity	
	40″	20×10′	21	20×15′	16	20×13′	10	
	50″	24×24′	33	24×18′	26	24×16′	23	
	60″	30×30′	57	30×22′	47	30×20′	41	
	70″	35×35′	82	35×26′	69	35×23′	58	
	84″	42×42′	124	42×33′	118	42×28′	90	
	6×8′	48×48′	167	48×36′	141	48×32′	128	
	7×9′	56×56′	234	56×42′	200	56×37′	182	
	8×10′	60×60′	272	60×45′	223	60×40′	208	
	9×12′	72×72′	402	72×54′	347	72×48′	318	

Projector to screen distances in relation to lens size	LENS FOCAL LENGTH	SCREEN WIDTH								
			40″	50″	60″	70″	84″	96″	9′	10′	12′
	12.7 mm–½″		4.5	5.7	6.7	7.8	9.3	10.6	11.9	13.2	15.9
	19 mm–¾″		6.7	8.3	10.0	11.6	13.9	15.9	17.9	19.9	23.8
	25.4 mm–1″	PROJECTION DISTANCE IN FEET	8.9	11.1	13.3	15.5	18.6	21.2	23.9	26.5	31.7
	38.1 mm–1½″		13.4	16.7	20.0	23.3	27.9	31.8	35.8	39.7	47.6
	50.8 mm–2″		17.9	22.3	26.7	31.0	37.2	42.4	47.7	53.0	63.5
	63.5 mm–2½″		22.3	27.8	33.3	38.8	46.5	53.0	59.6	66.2	79.4
	76.2 mm–3″		26.8	33.4	40.0	46.6	55.8	63.7	71.6	79.4	95.2
	88.9 mm–3½″		31.3	39.0	46.6	54.3	65.1	74.3	83.5	92.7	111.1
	101.6 mm–4″		35.8	44.5	53.3	62.1	74.4	84.9	95.4	105.9	127.0

Examples	*Example A:* Your projector has a 2″ lens, and in your space the projection distance is 48′. Thus you will have an image which is about 9′ wide and will need a screen that size. *Example B:* Your room is only 20′ wide. To get a decent size image you will need a projector with a 1½″ lens and a screen which is 60″ wide.

Map 8.2 *Troubleshooting guide.*

No picture	• See if the lamp switch is turned on. • Check and replace the projection lamp if it is burned out.
No sound	• Check sound/silent or optical/magnetic settings on the projector. They should be on sound/optical. • Check to make sure the exciter lamp is on and replace if defective. • Check amplifier and volume switches. • Check the threading around the sound drum. • Check to see if the film indeed has a soundtrack. • Check the connections between the projector and the speaker. Do this at a low volume setting so that you don't blow out the speaker with a loud rush of sound when you make the connection.
Distorted picture	• Adjust focus. • Close the film gate, and make sure the film is flush (between the runners) in the gate. • If the picture is too small for the screen, move the projector back. If it is too large, move the projector closer. • If the frame is split (some of the top at the bottom or vice versa) adjust the framer. • If there is fluttering with a lot of noise, stop and rethread. You have lost your loops, the sprockets and claw are not engaging the sprocket holes properly, and you are tearing the film. • If one side or another is out of focus, realign the projector squarely in relationship to the screen, or realign the screen. Check the position of the film in the gate. • Flickering picture can be caused by running the projector at silent speed. • If the picture is jumping around (unsteady frame line) try rethreading. If this problem is severe, it could mean the projector needs maintenance. • A dim or unevenly illuminated picture indicates either a bulb at the end of its life, or a very dirty lens.
Distorted sound	• Warbling or gargling (the voices sound as though they are underwater) is caused by improper threading around the sound drum. The film must fit snugly over the sound drum, and be held there securely by the stabilizing rollers. • If the sound is not audible, try adjusting the tone controls (treble and bass) until you get understandable sound. A slight adjustment can make a lot of difference. • If the picture is out of sync with the sound track, your bottom loop is either too short or too long. The distance between the gate and the sound lens should be 26 frames for proper synchronization. • Ticks and pops in the sound can be caused by splices in the film or dirt on the film. If a tick, pop or thud is regular, there could be dirt on the sound drum. Remove the film from around the sound drum and clean the drum with a soft cloth or alcohol and q-tip.

9 Television and video

9.1 The variety of educational TV delivery systems

In the 1950s, as soon as television became a practical reality, it was seen to have great educational potential and many attempts were made to set up television-based mass-education systems. In the USA, a notable effort was made to introduce educational television into the public schools, with the aid of some $25 million, supplied by the Ford Foundation. Due to the decentralized nature of North American education, a large number of local 'instructional television broadcast stations' were set up. In the UK, the BBC was not far behind in setting up a regular programme of television for schools. These early broadcasts were 'live' transmissions of classroom lectures, using a certain amount of close-up shots and special camera angles to break up the monotony of the 'talking head' format, so prevalent in the early days.

9.1.1 Live broadcasting

This approach to instruction by television was more or less dictated by the technology available at the time. Video recording was not yet invented, so all programmes had to go out live. Any errors committed during shooting would also be broadcast, so the tendency towards conservative, well tried programme formats and unadventurous camera work was reinforced. An alternative use of the medium at this time followed the entertainment trends. The techniques already developed for the shooting of film were modified to the 'instantaneous' medium of television. Instead of cutting and assembling a final version of the film from a series of separate takes of a number of scenes, the television director was forced to use a number of cameras set up at different vantage points and cut between them on the basis of split-second decisions taken as the programme was acted out and transmitted. This required enormous effort in the prior rehearsal of a programme, as well as great skill on the part of the production team. As the resources, in terms of both time and human skills, available for the early educational programmes were much more limited than was the case for entertainment programming, a very noticeable difference in quality between educational and general television programmes was apparent.

Adaptation of film technique

However, even these early programmes showed how the television medium could enhance the power of education. Two special benefits were noticeable:

Focus of the student's viewpoint

- Control over size and viewpoint, achieved by the camera position and lens characteristics, could present a much clearer and more precise visual image than could normally be achieved by a teacher with a large class of students. All could get the view that only one or two privileged students in the front row would get in conventional classroom situations. Of course, film and even slides or photos (even drawings) may also be used to focus the student's viewpoint, but the television camera did this instantly with little need for preparatory work on the part of the instructional designer, laboratory crew or artist;

Dissemination to large audiences

- Immediate distribution of the programme to a theoretically unlimited audience. One first-class teacher, using one set of exceptionally well produced demonstration materials, could be multiplied. More students could be reached with smaller educational resources, provided, of course, that the necessary technological resources were installed, in working order and switched on.

Limited use for instruction

There were, of course, serious limitations as well. One was the lock-step nature of the 'instant' transmission, which forced all students wishing to study a given topic to study it at one and the same time. School timetabling systems generally had difficulty in synchronizing class sessions with broadcast times. The inability, on the part of the teacher, to preview a live broadcast, made it difficult to build an appropriate overall lesson plan that would take the utmost advantage of the TV programme. One way to overcome this latter weakness was to prepare very detailed lesson outlines and supply printed support materials that the teacher could use with the broadcast. But then the danger was that the teacher would feel that all the teaching tasks had been pre-planned by the TV producers. This often led to the total rejection of the medium by some teachers, and to the delegation of all responsibility for instructional success of the lesson to the programme, by others. In both cases, the long-term result was not very good for the acceptance of televised instruction.

Live, open broadcast television continues to be used in education, but not very extensively. We see its use most frequently in what we may term *educational* television (as opposed to *instructional* television) – in programmes that do not have specific pre-determined instructional objectives, but have educational value either as a source of information on current events (newsreels), opposing points of view (debates), interesting or famous persons (interviews), and so on. It is of course possible to build such programmes into an instructional system, as one form of stimulus component, but the teacher must devise appropriate practice tasks, in which the learners apply what they saw on TV to tasks that lead to the achievement of specific worthwhile instructional objectives.

From the user's viewpoint, the technical aspects of open-broadcast transmission systems, whether of live or recorded programmes, are minimal. It is sufficient to have a TV receiver in working order and an appropriate antenna, in order to receive a clear signal from the transmitting station. Typical link-ups are illustrated in Figure 9.1.

9.1.2 Recorded broadcasts

There are yet other reasons why the early promise of the television medium was not realized. One of these was the natural distrust of the teaching profession of a medium that appeared poised to take over their jobs. Another reason was that television systems and their owners, realizing the extent of resistance on the part of teachers, decided to promote the role of television in teaching, as an 'enrichment' medium that would not be seen as a threat by teachers. In so doing, they avoided intensive and adventurous instructional designs, settling for itsy-bitsy pieces of one-way broadcasting that the teacher had to build into his/her own instructional plan. But teachers were not skilled at doing this, nor were they equipped in terms of basic information about the structure of each programme well in advance of its transmission.

The impact of pre-recording

The situation improved markedly in the 1970s, with the increasing use of video recording. First, the TV stations were able to pre-record their programmes. This offered several advantages and new capabilities:

- Transmission time was no longer the problem it had been as the stations could record programmes at times that were convenient for them, and then broadcast at times that were convenient to the schools;

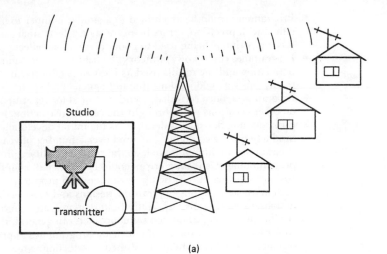

(a)

(b)

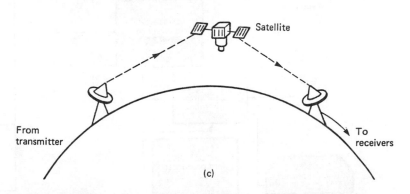

(c)

Figure 9.1 *Types of broadcast television systems. (a) In an open-broadcast system, signals are transmitted over air-waves to receiving antennae. (b) Microwave television involves sending signals point to point. Retransmission is necessary to circumvent barriers. (c) Satellite transmission over long distances.*

- Programmes could be assembled in a similar manner to films, scenes being edited with precision, errors being re-shot, effects such as flash-backs and scene repetitions being used to good instructional effect.
- Programmes could now, in theory, be field-tested on samples of the student population and the results used as indicators of necessary revisions (in reality this was seldom done due to financial and scheduling restrictions).
- Programmes, once recorded, could be stored for repetition to future groups on other occasions – this brought the cost of instructional television programming down considerably, as the initial development and production costs could be recovered over a number of years' use.
- Programme quality improved, as the relative facility with which programming or shooting errors could be corrected, coupled to the lower cost per showing of recorded programmes, led producers to experiment with more adventurous programme designs and more elaborate and well prepared studio props – specially built demonstration and laboratory equipment, colour, animated sequences, etc. In general, the quality of educational and instructional television programmes approached the production quality standards (termed 'production values' in the profession) of general broadcast television.

A typical ETV/ITV studio

Figure 9.2 illustrates the set-up of a studio that should be able to produce near-broadcast quality educational/instructional television programmes. This basic set-up may be enhanced by the addition of more cameras (especially one for transmitting pictures, graphics or captions from printed artwork) a telecine chain (for the incorporation of existing clips of film, slides, etc, into the programme), and a special effects generator which, in this microchip age, can bring the skills of clever fading, split screen, blow-ups, inversions or you-name-it, to the fingertips of any video editor.

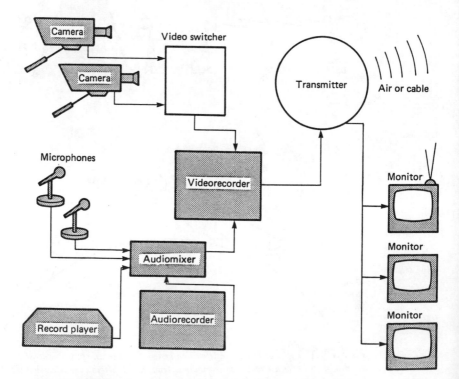

Figure 9.2 *A basic television system, with recording capabilities and mixing of several sources.*

9.1.3 Successes and failures of broadcast TV

As video recording equipment became increasingly available in the schools, a number of further advantages were gained:

1. Time scheduling limitations were further eliminated, as schools could now record broadcast programmes and then replay them to student groups at any locally convenient time, or even several times to different groups at different times (this advantage was also not fully exploited in some cases, due to copyright restrictions which have only recently been relaxed);
2. By recording the programme in advance, the teacher could preview it and thus build other instructional activities around it in a much more systematic manner;
3. The teacher may also select only parts of the programme for a given lesson, may decide to show all or part of it more than once to the same group and, in general, may adapt the programme to the specific course objectives that are to be achieved.

Greater success in non-formal education

Nowadays, most instructional television is pre-recorded and many systems allow a limited amount of local recording and replaying in order to gain the advantages outlined above. However, the impact of broadcast instructional television in schools and other institutions of education is still quite small. It is notable that the majority of recognized 'success stories' lie outside the formal educational establishment. A USA success story is 'Sesame Street', which is possibly so successful exactly because it is aimed at a pre-school audience, watching at home. A success story from the UK, at quite a different level of education, is the Open University, also outside the main stream of established institutions. As an alternative university, designed from the start to rely entirely on mediated instruction and to fill a 'vacuum' – a hidden demand for home-study university-level education – the OU did not encounter the resistance of an established organization of teachers as would be the case if large-scale TV–based instruction were to be proposed for all universities.

... or in Third World countries ...

It is interesting to note, in this context, that most of the successful large-scale projects involving mass media (especially television) as major components of formal educational systems have been in the developing countries, where, once more, the TV-based systems have filled some form of vacuum created by inadequate conventional resources, absence of an established body of teachers, special geographical or demographical problems that render conventional methods inefficient, and so on. Once more, we are led to believe that what has kept television down in education have been the teachers, rather than any limitations of the medium itself.

But also many failures

However, developing nations have not had a clear run of successes either. Over the years, there have been more failures than successes. Often this has been due to inappropriate or unskilful use of the medium by the programme producers or their sponsors. Topics which should not be taught through television (such as colour or pattern recognition, which called for a level of picture quality well beyond what was possible with the TV technology of the time, or topics which require group interactions between course members) led to poor programmes which only served to get the medium a bad name. Administrative or technical inadequacies often led to irregular broadcasts, poor picture quality, or total system breakdown (as in the classic Mexican case study which showed that over 70% of TV classroom hours planned were not being received by the student groups due to signal or receiver breakdowns). This has led to a decline in the number of instructional TV systems 'in business', which is well illustrated by the data presented for Latin America in Figure 9.3 (Tiffin, 1980).

Lest we think, however, that such trends are limited to developing nations, let us remember the $25 million invested by the Ford Foundation into the development of ITV in the USA. Berkman (1976), when commenting this investment, states:

'. . . scant more than a decade later, I defy anybody to show me where this multi-megabuck-backed experiment – by far, still, the largest ever in American education – rates even a footnote in the education texts . . .'

Since Berkman's writing there are signs, however, that in the USA, Instructional TV has started a slow and painful upward trend. It seems that the systems have slowly learnt from their early mistakes and have begun to gain a stronger position in education. This revival has been likened to the 'Phoenix' – it was necessary to burn oneself up in order to be reborn from one's own ashes. Some of the reasons for this slow and painful rebirth will become clear in this and later chapters. But we must not expect such a revival to occur automatically. In Latin America there is as yet no sign of one – and with the current economic crises in the continent. . . . ?

9.1.4 Closed circuit television (CCTV)

What is CCTV ?

Perhaps, all in all, more success has been experienced through the use of the many thousands of Closed Circuit Television (CCTV) systems installed in many modern schools and just about all universities in the developed world (not to mention the many industrial and commercial training centres which are wired up for CCTV). Basically, a CCTV system is a local installation, linking one or more studios to a series of classrooms, usually by means of permanent cables installed in the building. More ambitious systems may link several associated institutions and may allow transmission from any of the classrooms to any or all of the other classrooms or sites 'wired in' to the system. Such systems may transmit 'live' lectures to several rooms, or may be used for the selective distribution of pre-recorded programmes on topics of interest to the owners of the system or certain groups of students. In many cases, the programmes are locally produced, by or with the cooperation of the teachers, so that a strong sense of ownership of the system and its programming can be fostered. Also, the owners of the system, who have invested a considerable sum setting it up, are close enough to the users to be able to monitor and evaluate the use made and the benefits gained by the organization. There is less likelihood of total rejection of the medium by the system, although we do sometimes hear horror stories of expensive CCTV systems that were installed and then hardly used at all.

Availability of pre-recorded programmes

The overall success of this method of employing TV in education and training may be judged by the quantity of locally produced programmes and the growing availability of commercially produced videotapes that find a ready market. In the UK, for example, there has, since the early 1970s, existed an interchange system of videotapes between universities. This was instigated by the then National Council for Educational Technology (NCET, later just CET), through the regular collection of information and publication of a catalogue – *HELPIS*, or Higher Education Learning Programmes Information Service. In its first early 1970s' version, this catalogue contained barely 100 titles of university-produced videotapes. The number slowly increased during the 1970s, reaching somewhat over 300 titles by 1978/9. By 1982, however, the number had shot up to over 3000 titles and has continued to rise so much that the service was taken over by the British Universities Film and Video Council, a body devoted exclusively to the dissemination of information about audiovisual materials that are available for use at university level.

In the USA, the production and commercialization of videotapes for educational and training use had also mushroomed, the amount of material on the market being so large that no single cataloguing organization is handling all the materials, potential users and media librarians being therefore forced to use several catalogues in order to obtain full coverage of what is available. And these numbers do not, of course, include the vast amount of video that is annually produced by business for its own internal training purposes. For the time being, there does not seem to be any slowing down in the production and use of special-purpose instructional videotapes.

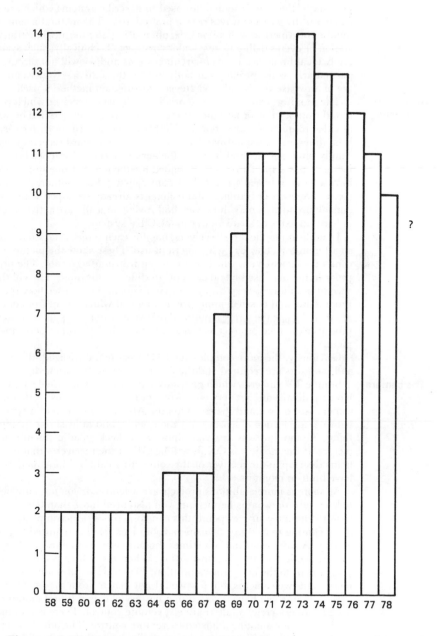

Figure 9.3 *The number of fully operational ETV systems in Latin America (from Tiffin, 1980).*

Closed-circuit television involves basically, camera equipment and viewing or monitor equipment, linked by a cable, to give a 'closed circuit'. In practice nowadays, the term is sometimes used to describe systems which are not linked by cable, but by wireless waves over a limited area. The method is employed by a number of American school boards, often using an intermediate transmission station or even satellite to give wider coverage. Technically, such systems are really local broadcast or open-circuit systems and we will not discuss them further, particularly as the problems at both ends of the system – camera and monitor – are in any case very similar whatever transmission method is used.

The monitor or receiver

The monitor, or viewer, is essentially a television receiver which picks up its signal from a cable or land-line rather than through an aerial. The signal may be at video frequencies, or at normal VHF frequencies. In the latter case, the monitor is no different from a normal TV, and in fact a standard receiver may be used by simply plugging the land-line into the aerial socket. In practice however, it is better to use a special receiver designed for the job. For one thing, it will probably have a 27 inch screen size for classroom viewing. For another, it will give a better picture. Schools or training establishments already equipped with TV receivers for outside broadcasts may, however, find it economically attractive to utilize these as at least an extra or spare viewer in a CCTV system.

In addition to the large receivers, one for each remote classroom, one needs small monitors, one for each camera in use. These show the picture that the camera is focussed on, whether it is being transmitted or not. The producer of the programme may use several cameras in different locations. He will then have several monitors to keep his eye on. He refers to these to see how the programme is progressing and to select appropriate points at which to cut from one camera to another. Hence the name monitor. Further monitors may be used to show the producer the final product as transmitted and to keep other personnel 'in the picture'.

Obviously, the more complex the CCTV system envisaged, the more receivers and monitors are required and the pennies have to be watched.

The camera

Simple TV cameras which give adequate results when used as a visual aid (eg to blow up detail) are not very expensive. For more ambitious work a more versatile camera is required and the cost mounts. Also you do not get far without extra lighting, a selection of lenses (or a zoom lens), and at least one monitor. For one thing, the monitor acts as a view finder and check on adjustment combined. If the picture at the monitor is OK, it will be OK at the receiver – that is as long as no faults develop in the receiver or the connecting cables. Many modern cameras have built-in monitors.

As soon as more ambitious projects are attempted, you not only need monitors to keep tabs on what is happening, you also need more than one camera. If you wish to change your viewpoint, this can sometimes be accomplished by 'panning' or by coming in closer or by using a zoom lens. Skill is required to perform these actions. A safer way, and sometimes the only way, is to move and adjust one camera while the other is transmitting. When everything is under control, then you can cut to the new camera position. Few training presentations would need more than two cameras, but few would not benefit from the use of more than one.

By the time you have invested in a battery of cameras and monitors, you will need a camera crew, or alternatively, remote control. There is nothing about the system which cannot be adjusted by remote control. The only barrier is cost.

The installation

Many small CCTV systems do not really warrant the title of an installation. One or two cameras, three or four receivers, and drums of cable are stored in a locked room and are pulled out when required – probably once a year about Easter time, and again on Open Day.

A successful CCTV installation however, requires permanent land-lines, particularly if the several receivers are very remote from the camera. It also requires careful planning – from where are we likely to transmit, and to where?

Such an installation must be built up around a central studio. Most standard transmission would be screened from the studio, where facilities and equipment

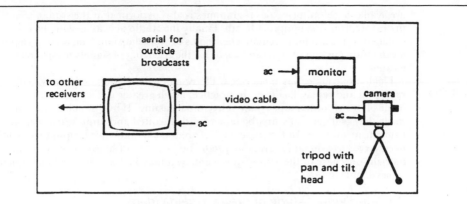

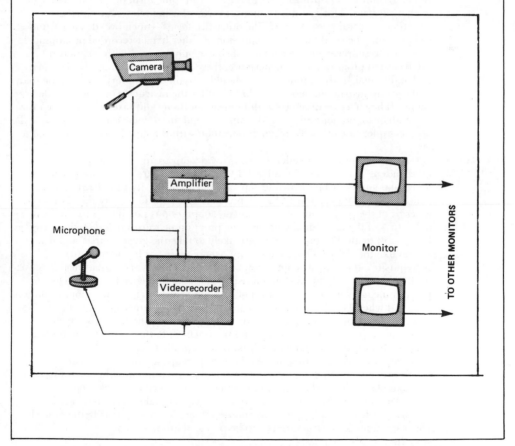

Figure 9.4 *Two basic forms of CCTV system. (a) Basis of a very simple 1-camera CCTV system for live-broadcast only. This system also doubles as an open-broadcast reception system as it employs receiver/monitors in all classrooms. (b) A simple CCTV system capable of both live and recorded broadcasting. Note that the use of video monitors precludes its use for open-broadcast reception (though it could of course be modified by having a central RF tuner feeding a video signal to the amplifier).*

are available. Monitoring of programmes is also performed at the studio, preferably from a soundproof booth. Finally the studio acts as a switchboard. Cable from the studio to remote classrooms or workshops may be used as required for the transmission of programmes or for the receiving of signals from cameras 'on location'.

Video recording

Finally, of course, any modern CCTV system will be equipped with video recording and replay facilities. In practice, much greater use will normally be made of pre-recorded tapes than of live broadcasting. If live broadcasts are to be made they will generally first be tape recorded, edited and improved as necessary before transmission. In that case, tape reproduction and editing equipment will be necessary. Occasional programme production would not however warrant the outright purchase of this extra equipment, as it may be hired by the hour at many professional studios.

9.1.5 Individual study of pre-recorded video

Of course, not all these tapes get used by means of group instruction, through closed circuit TV systems. Many are used on an individual basis, by students in resource centres, non-print media libraries, or in some form of self-directed open learning system. This is a third important way of using television/video in education and training. Whereas the other two forms – open broadcast TV and CCTV – may be used for the transmission of either live or recorded programmes, this third 'resource centre' form may of course only be used with a supply of pre-recorded programmes. Furthermore, these programmes should be designed with individual study in mind. They should contain explanatory information that, in the group instruction mode, would be left for the instructor or course leader to supply. They may be designed with built-in questions and tasks that may require the student to momentarily stop the tape, rewind and review certain sections of the tape, complete a workbook in synchronization with the taped instructions, and so on.

Instructional advantages of individual study of video

If a student may independently study a videotape, can he or she also independently study open broadcast TV? Of course, there is nothing to stop an individual student from watching, say, an Open University broadcast, at home, entirely alone – indeed most Open University students do exactly this. However, in terms of the programme's structure, no adaptation is possible to the needs or difficulties of the individual student. The programme must be designed to cater, as best it can, to all the students that are likely to take the given course, and in a system like the British Open University, where there are few if any entry prerequisites, the student population in one course may vary a great deal in terms of all manner of individual characteristics that may influence learning. The programme is a 'one-to-many' form of communication in its conception. It matters not at all whether it is watched by a group gathered together in front of one TV set in a classroom, or by one lone student at home. During the broadcast, each student receives the same message and treatment in both cases (although what happens before and after the broadcast may be quite different).

When, however, an individual student (or perhaps a pair) watches a pre-recorded videotape, then some form of adaptation to individual learning needs *may* take place. Even when the programme was designed as a lock-step 'one-to-many' communication, the student may stop, take notes, rewind and review, or otherwise adapt the presentation to his/her needs. It is better still when the programme is so structured as to help this adaptation to occur – a 'one-to-one' structure.

It is important to note the meaning I give here to 'one-to-one' programme structure. The essential aspect is that the programme as it were speaks directly to the student and the student may in some way influence the programme. As an analogy, reading a book – any book – is a one-to-one learning situation, in that the reader may stop and start at will, re-read a page, copy a paragraph or work out a problem using the content being read (even if he has to invent the problem for

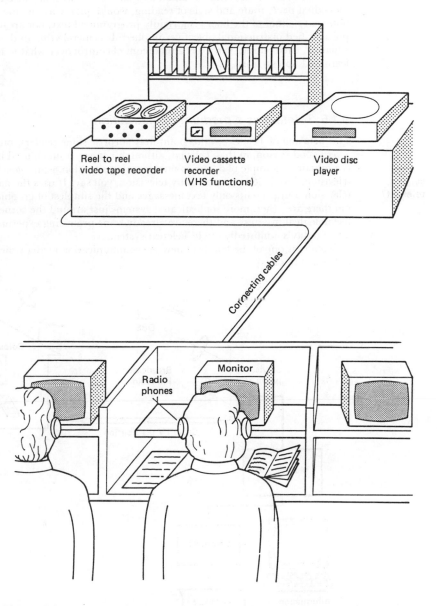

Figure 9.5 *A typical self-study resource centre. Carrells can receive any one of several formats of video recordings, from a central battery of players.*

himself). Of course, a well-structured textbook, with clear paragraph headings, a good indexing system, well chosen and explained examples, and suggested practice problems, will be much more of a one-to-one learning experience. However, neither of these books, read out aloud at a fixed pace, without the opportunity for individual pace, route and style of reading, would qualify as one-to-one. Please note that neither of the books is a rigidly programmed text, nor are unique pre-specified instructional objectives implied. It is merely that in the one-to-one situation, each learner can exert a modicum of control over what to learn, when to learn and how to learn.

9.1.5 Teletext as a medium of instruction

The inclusion of Teletext at this point may surprise some readers, but I do this for a very good reason, in that Teletext, although not as yet much used in education, is a practical example of a 'one-to-one' learning situation, using *open-broadcast*

**What is
teletext?**

television. But Teletext is not really television, you say. It uses the hardware of television, but presents only text messages and the simplest of graphics. Very true, but there are other, more sophisticated systems just around the corner of technological progress and there are already some promising experiments in the use of today's admittedly crude Teletext systems.

Teletext is one of the family of new telecommunication media which Tyler (1979) defines as:

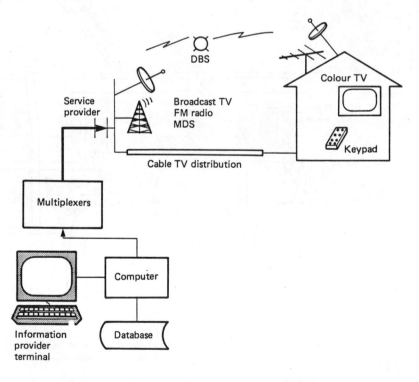

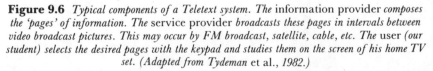

Figure 9.6 *Typical components of a Teletext system. The* information provider *composes the 'pages' of information. The* service provider *broadcasts these pages in intervals between video broadcast pictures. This may occur by FM broadcast, satellite, cable, etc. The* user *(our student) selects the desired pages with the keypad and studies them on the screen of his home TV set. (Adapted from Tydeman et al., 1982.)*

'. . . systems for the widespread dissemination of textual and graphic information by wholly electronic means, for display on low cost terminals (often suitably equipped television receivers) under the selective control of the recipient, and using control procedures easily understood by untrained users . . .'

The 'family' includes such proprietary systems as Prestel and Telidon, which are somewhat more complex, allowing for two-way communication between the user and a distant database. Teletext, on the other hand, is simpler, in that it is a one-way communication medium, but which is, nevertheless under the control of the user. Examples of other proprietary systems include Ceefax and Oracle.

Using teletext

The principle of Teletext is quite simple. A number of screens, or 'pages', of text or graphics are stored in a distant database, just like the pages of a book. They are numbered and indexed, just like a book, to indicate the information that they contain. The indexing system is itself stored on a set of pages as a hierarchically organized set of menus (or any other convenient form). Knowing the number to key in order to get at the index, the user may discover the current content of the system and may select the page numbers of interest.

The process is just like using a well indexed reference book, except that instead of turning to the desired pages, the user keys in their numbers on a numerical key pad. All the pages stored in the database are periodically transmitted, and the desired page is captured by the decoder (a special attachment to the television set) and presented on the TV screen for as long as the user requires. There may be a slight delay in accessing the desired page if very many pages are stored, but the waiting time is usually no longer than the time it takes to find a given page number in a big book. Thus the use of Teletext is just like the use of a reference book (Woolfe, 1987).

There are some important differences between Teletext and a printed book, however. The information in Teletext is updatable at any moment. Current events may be used as real-life case studies in a social science programme, for example. The pages stored in the system may be changed daily or weekly, in step with a series of broadcast ITV programmes – thus the student may watch a half-hour instructional programme and then may access a series of summary pages or practice problem sheets, in order to reinforce and evaluate his understanding of the topic.

The potential applications are many, though not at all sophisticated. The one-way communication capability does not allow full-blown CAL routines, for example, although simple programmed instruction routines of the 'branching text' variety could be implemented. The medium will do nothing that may not be done by means of other, simpler, media, but, in certain applications, it may be more effective, more efficient or more economical. It is presented here to extend somewhat beyond the commonplace the concept of educational television and, principally, to illustrate a possible one-to-one use of open broadcast television. Further educational applications are discussed in Tydeman *et al*. (1982) and Anderson (1987).

9.1.6 A schema of educational TV systems

In the preceding sections, we have examined a number of common (and some not so common) ways of using television in education and training. We have used several terms to distinguish between and classify them:

- Open broadcast/local system or network;
- One-way/two-way transmission of information;
- Live/recorded programmes;
- One-to-many/one-to-one programme structures.

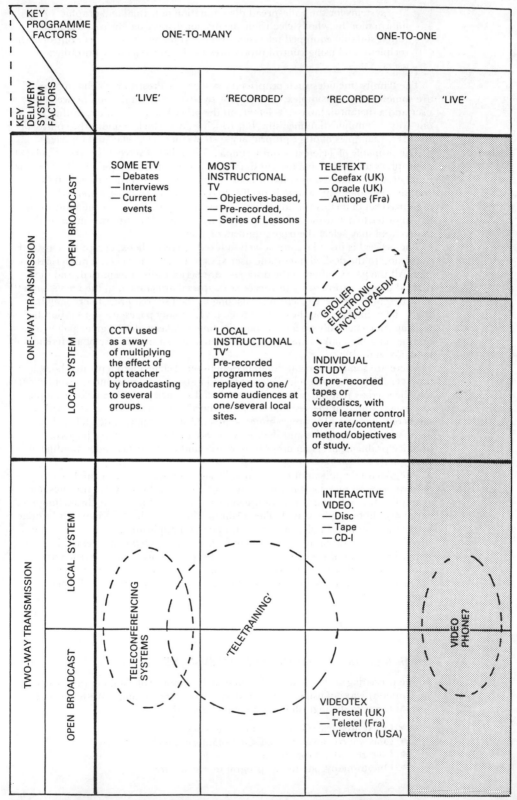

Figure 9.7 *A schema of educational and training applications of TV/video systems.*

How to read the schema

We can bring together all the examples that we have discussed so far into a table or matrix which will better illustrate their similarities and differences (Figure 9.7).

Note that we have only examined one half of this schema so far – the upper half, dealing with one-way transmission systems. We shall leave the other half – two-way transmission systems – to later chapters. These are important new developments in the use of the television medium that put the emphasis on interactivity. I present the whole schema here, however, to establish a context and advantage of this form is the ease of updating information – during the 1986

There is one entry in the top half of our schema which was not discussed earlier. It has been left till now as an 'afterthought', as it were, which illustrates the usefulness and the limitations of the schema we have constructed. The 'Grolier Electronic Encyclopaedia' is a specific case that illustrates the merging of technologies that is currently occurring. A few years back, the Grolier Encyclopaedia (a set of some 20 or more volumes in its text form) was transformed into electronic form and offered as a database to be accessed from a distance. One advantage of this form is the ease of updating of information – during the 1986 World Cup year, for example, a greater amount of detailed information on soccer was included to meet the seasonal demand and was later withdrawn again as demand subsided. More recently, the same encyclopaedia has been made available on a CD-ROM disc. This has of course lost the rapid updating facility, but has gained a sophisticated key-word indexing system that allows rapid searches of the 'small print', right through the complete work, on a personal microcomputer, at zero search fee. The first version is an 'open broadcast, one-to-one' system that is used very much like Telextext (although the technical details are quite different). The second is a local, stand-alone one-to-one system, which has little to do with television as we understand it, except that the information output is presented on a cathode ray tube.

We have also not classified all common uses of video on our schema. For example, the use of video recording of class activities for later evaluation and feedback (as in microteaching systems, interviewing or sales training, etc) has not been mentioned. Here, the video feedback is one component in a more complex, multi-media instructional system. We have restricted ourselves to the analysis of systems in which TV or video are the principal delivery systems. The limitations of our schema are obvious. However, it is a useful way to view the whole field of television and video in education – provided you do not try to interpret the classifications too rigidly.

9.1.7 Current and future growth in video usage

Lest some of the comments made earlier have led you to think that I believe television and video to be underused in education and training, I present here some recent statistics, taken from the 1985 Higher Education Utilization Study (HEUS-85) sponsored in the USA by the Chronicle of Higher Education. According to this report, nearly all US universities (92%) have video distribution facilities and equipment, and seven out of ten have central reception facilities for picking up special education video broadcasts. The two tables presented in Figure 9.8 illustrate the variety and modern sophistication of the delivery systems in use. We might add that some school systems are also big users of the newer distribution technologies – at the time of writing, the State of New York school system has over 100 operating or projected local instructional TV networks using microwave or cable linkups between remote sites. Whereas the early dreams of mass TV-based education did not materialize, today we see a trend toward TV-based variety, individualization and catering for minority interests.

The situation in the UK and Europe is similar, as shown by the variety of video applications in Higher Education which are described in the book edited by Zuber-Skerritt (1984).

Video Facilities Available in US Colleges and Universities	All Institutions
Any central reception facilities	**69%**
Community cable system drop(s)	47
Master TV antenna	33
Rotatable satellite receive-only dish	12
Fixed satellite receive-only dish	11
Other microwave reception equipment	7
ITFS reception equipment	6
Satellite transmission antenna (uplink)	2
Any distribution / exhibition facilities	**92**
Special video or film screening / projection room	63
Campus closed-circuit TV (on-campus origination)	34
Campus buildings wired by community cable TV system ...	34
Community cable TV system educational / access channels .	31
Non-commercial television broadcasting station	11
ITSF transmission equipment	5

(a)

Uses of Video Technologies in US Colleges and Universities	All Institutions
One-way presentation of instruction to students on campus.................	84%
Promotion/recruitment...	64
Counselling	60
Outreach..	54
Staff development..	49
One-way presentation of instruction to students off-campus	35
Pictorial enhancement of programmed instruction using computers...	26
Conferencing or two-way communications between faculty members and off-campus students	8
Conferenceing or two-way communications between faculty members and students in multiple locations on campus...	6
Other	5

(b)

Figure 9.8 *(a) Video facilities available in US colleges and universities. (b) Uses of video technologies in US colleges and universities. (HEUS–85).*

9.2 The benefits of TV and video

9.2.1 Research: TV versus film

TV vs. Film

On the face of it there is little difference, from the audience's point of view, between a television or a cine film presentation. McLuhan (1964) argued that the 'here and now' aspects of a TV image, coupled with qualities such as less precise definition, and presence in your own home, make the TV image a much more acceptable, and hence a much more powerful, medium of communication than the cine film. There is evidence to support this view, particularly from measures of the relative success of advertising on the two media.

However, when both media are removed to the relatively artificial setting of the classroom or workshop, there seems to be very little difference. Munday (1962) compared the effect of television and film presentation of lessons in social studies and geography. He found no difference in the amounts learned through the two media. A similar French study (Bertran, 1962) again found no significant differences in the respective effectiveness of TV and film in general, although those students who knew that the TV presentation was live did respond much more favourably to the presentation. They remembered slightly more and were influenced in their attitudes very much more than students who thought they were watching a filmed recording. This finding tends to suggest that TV is a more powerful medium than the cinema ever was – not because more people watch television, but because people accept its message more readily, get more involved emotionally and are participants rather than observers.

Advantages of CCTV

One major use of instructional television automatically utilizes this 'here and now' quality: the use of a CCTV system to increase the size of the audience, by allowing one teacher to address several classrooms or schools at once. We would normally arrange for someone technically competent and gifted as a communicator to deliver a carefully planned and prepared presentation. In addition however, if the speaker is known to the audience either personally or by repute, their level of involvement will be greater.

This use of CCTV is valuable for economic reasons. It enables one to make the best use of highly skilled or qualified personnel, cuts down the need for duplication of expensive demonstration apparatus and allows a careful presentation to be viewed by many. The imaginative use of the TV camera can also produce a better presentation. For example, the use of close-ups can focus the audience's attention on particular points, or can blow-up the details of a demonstration so that all can see clearly. One can show an operation from the operator's point of view, or cut-in a pre-recorded sequence from a workshop to illustrate the relevance or importance of the task to be learnt. In short, the principles of design of instructional films, outlined earlier, can be applied to produce an altogether better presentation than would be possible in the 'live' teaching situation.

9.2.2 Research: the instructional effects of TV

Inconclusive comparative studies

There has probably been more recently reported research on the use of television in education than on cine films. However, as Peggie Campeau (1972) points out, most of it is subjective and poorly designed. Those studies which are properly controlled generally repeat the pattern of 'no significant difference' found earlier in the bulk of research into film. There are hundreds of reported studies comparing TV with traditional methods, but no conclusive results.

For example, Chu and Schramm (1967) carried out a review of 207 studies involving 421 separate comparisons. At the college and adult level, results of 235 comparisons indicated that 176 found no significant differences between televised and conventional instruction, 29 favoured television over conventional instruction and 30 favoured conventional methods.

Dubin and others (1969) conducted a more rigorous review of studies in which experimental classes taught by television were compared with control classes receiving no televised instruction. They identified 42 studies that could be considered to be comparable on the basis of several criteria, namely, instruction lasted at least one term; identical, written course-content examinations were used for groups being compared; similar methods of instruction were experienced by both groups, etc. First, when teaching methods were matched, face-to-face instruction was superior to *two*-way instructional television, and then only when the lecture method was used by each medium. ('Two-way' television provided students and lecturer with audio facilities for exchanging questions and initiating discussions, thereby approximating to a 'live' instructional situation.) Second, *one*-way instructional television produced the same amount of learning as face-to-face teaching by lecture, by a combination of lecture-discussion-demonstration, or by discussion alone. Third, instruction by either method yielded no significant differences when the studies were grouped by the broad subject-area headings of humanities, social sciences and science/mathematics. In attempting to explain the odd finding that two-way television was definitely inferior to face-to-face teaching, the authors suggested that the need for students and lecturer to use the fairly complicated technical apparatus necessary for two-way communication may have been the cause.

Meta-analyses are also inconclusive In more recent and more rigorous 'meta-analyses' of a group of 74 video-based studies, Cohen, Ebling and Kulik (1981) found very slight benefits for the video mediated instruction as opposed to conventional instruction, but the benefit was of the order of 1 or 2 percentage points only.

The trouble with surveys of this nature, and with comparative studies generally, is that in looking at a mass of evidence concerning the 'total course' we may be masking real differences which exist between media for certain aspects of the learning which is taking place. By lumping together the results of a number of studies, we are aggravating this situation. The greater the sample of studies we take, and the more all-inclusive they are, the more likely we are to cancel out any differences which exist and to end up with 'no significant difference'. As Briggs and others (1966) point out, we should be classifying studies according to the categories of learning taking place. But the 'traditional' categories as used by Dubin – humanities, science, etc – are not precise enough. We ought to be using such categories as procedures, discriminations, or concepts, as outlined in the opening chapters of this book. We ought also to be investigating learning differences between individuals.

Some effects: TV and attitudes Smith (1968) conducted a series of experiments on the effect of television broadcasts on the attainment and attitudes of students taking City & Guilds 'G' courses at technical colleges in England. The largest experiment involved students in 27 technical colleges watching a BBC television series on engineering science. Some students watched the broadcasts. The control group did not. In all, over 800 students were involved in the study, and were carefully matched for ability. There were no significant differences between groups on the attainment test used to assess the instructional effects of the two treatments. On the other hand, large and significant differences both in ability and attainment were found when the scores for individual colleges were analysed separately. The television broadcasts appeared to have a greater impact on students who were above average in ability, and to have more effect on performance in mechanics.

Research of this nature suggests that there may indeed be differences between media which have been obscured in earlier studies. However, more research at this 'micro' level is still needed before a comprehensive picture emerges.

Potential effects of symbolic codes used by certain media Another 'micro' approach has been suggested by Salomon (1976, 1979). He suggests that three groups of factors may make a difference in learning from mediated instruction – technology of transmission; content; and symbolic code of the message. The first is the one most often studied in comparative research and generally has not resulted in very significant differences. The second is not really a media factor except in as much as certain media can transmit the given content and others cannot (see my approach in Chapter three). The third group – symbolic codes – is the one that Salomon considers worthy of further research. He also singles out certain characteristics of TV (eg the ability to show a process in action) as potentially significant in the promotion of appropriate learning through TV. He quotes research (Salomon and Cohen, 1976) which supports his views. However, not all researchers (eg Clark, 1983) agree that this line of research is worth pursuing. Clark believes the only benefits of media are related to costs and efficiency, and practical constraints that may be overcome, not any psychological differences.

9.2.3 Some practical benefits of video

Whether Clark is correct or not on the psychological effects of video instruction being negligible, practical experience, especially in training applications, has often shown enormous benefits of video-based systems. Some examples follow.

Reduced training time

Video is an unusually successful training medium. It saves time, money and resources. It adapts to a wide variety of situations and requirements, and at the same time, it guarantees consistency in repeated viewing.

Even though it usually takes about ten times as long to create a video training programme as it does to prepare and present traditional classroom training, video ultimately saves far more time at the point of delivery and when the material must be repeated. With a well-designed video programme, you save up to 75% of the time it would take to deliver the same message in traditional lecture style. If training time can be reduced by as much as 75%, money and other resources can certainly be saved as well (Marlow, 1981).

In designing traditional media materials like slides and transparencies, you have the advantage of compression. You can cut out unnecessary information and deliver only as much information as is directly related to the objective. This also holds true in video programme design. When you compress information, the student can learn in less time than it would usually take in a classroom setting. The objectives of the training can be attained in much less teaching and learning time (Robson, 1978).

Reduced training costs

By reducing the time spent by staff, management and instructors, video can reduce the cost of training and communications. If it takes less time to communicate corporate messages through the use of video, staff and management time is saved. If it takes less time to train new workers, they become productive that much sooner. If the training process itself takes less time, instructional staffs may be reduced, or their time may be employed more economically. Thus, video effectively creates cost savings throughout the corporation (Dranov *et al.*, 1980).

Time and money are saved when video replaces the travelling instructor. Using a video network (video players placed in field offices), learners in regional or international offices can benefit from on-site training without the instructors having to travel to each location.

Flexible training schedules

Seldom is the viewer ready to receive information at the same time as the trainer is ready to deliver it. Video enables you to bring these two times together and allows the learner to adjust information reception to his or her own schedule. No longer are you locked into prescheduled information delivery. The learner now controls the schedule of viewing.

This is particularly useful for organizations like hospitals, law enforcement agencies, transportation and high technology manufacturing that require workers to be scheduled round the clock.

With well-designed video training, instructors do not have to be present to deliver information. Thus, video can assume the responsibility of training 24 hours a day.

Standard training content

Another significant advantage of using video in training is its ability to deliver information consistently. All viewers receive the same information in the same style of delivery. The videotape records the lecture or programme and preserves its style and meaning exactly as the presenter originally intended them. Individual differences of a number of instructors in the interpretation, style or philosophy is never a problem. All viewers receive the same message every time they view the tape (Dranov *et al.*, 1980; Anderson, 1976).

This is extremely important when it comes to teaching attitudes and philosophy, as in supervisory or management training. The presentation of the organization's policy and philosophy is not left to individual interpretation. Instructors need not feel the pressure of presenting the material over and over again in a consistent, organized manner. All viewers, whether they are impressionable new employees receiving their first exposure to the company or seasoned sales personnel in offices around the country, receive consistent information – information that has been designed, written and controlled by the organization. Video creates a reliable, constant delivery system, readily available, delivering the same corporate message each time.

Multiple modes of communica- tion

Video, like film, has another advantage that contributes to training, and this is motion. Through motion you can provide performance feedback, role modelling, product and safety demonstrations, process examples and motor skill development. Motion helps to deliver the message. If used effectively, it increases the training reception. In some situations, such as skill development, motion is essential for effective learning (Anderson, 1976; Heinich, Molenda and Russell, 1985).

Video is a visual medium, and it has the ability to hold interest through colour, motion and sound. If used properly, video can create interest through visual stimuli. According to some experts, visual images hold interest, and add to retention and recall of information (Kearsley, 1984; Kemp, 1980).

A case study

One case study that I have come across was a project carried out for the Ford Motor Company in South Africa by a small video-training consultancy group. A small team, working with portable video equipment from a van equipped with editing facilities, developed all the operator training required as on-the-job short videoclips to *demonstrate* each step, using previously trained operators as evaluators and guides in a 'TWI' type of overall training system. The in-service, video-based training was so effective that the company closed down two operator training centres that it had previously been supporting.

9.3 Selecting and using TV/video for instruction

9.3.1 Adopt, adapt, repurpose or produce?

Adopt

Let us suppose that your local educational or instructional television system is currently planning to broadcast a programme, or a series, which seems to match the overall objectives of part of a course that you will be teaching. You will be faced with the decision of whether to include the programme or series in your teaching. Assuming that this is the first time this particular offering will be broadcast, you have no past experience on which to base your decision. Also, as this will be a broadcast that is synchronized with the local teaching schedule and (possibly) is protected by copyright so that you cannot, legally, make a preview copy, your decision is limited to whether or not you will *adopt* the programme/series as developed and produced by the network.

Adapt

On the other hand, if you can obtain a preview copy of the tapes or, better still, tape the broadcasts and use the tapes with your group, then your decision is less restricted. You may decide to adopt the programme 'as is', but you may also decide to use only some parts, or to modify the sequence of presentation of certain scenes, or to stop at key points for group discussion. In other words, you may be free to *adapt* the original programmes to better suit the objectives that you wish to pursue, or the learning habits of your particular group of students. In this case you will be acting in much the same way as when you preview and analyse a film before using it in your teaching (see Chapter 8).

In both the above cases, you have come across, or been offered, a video production that was designed for instructional purposes that are similar to yours,

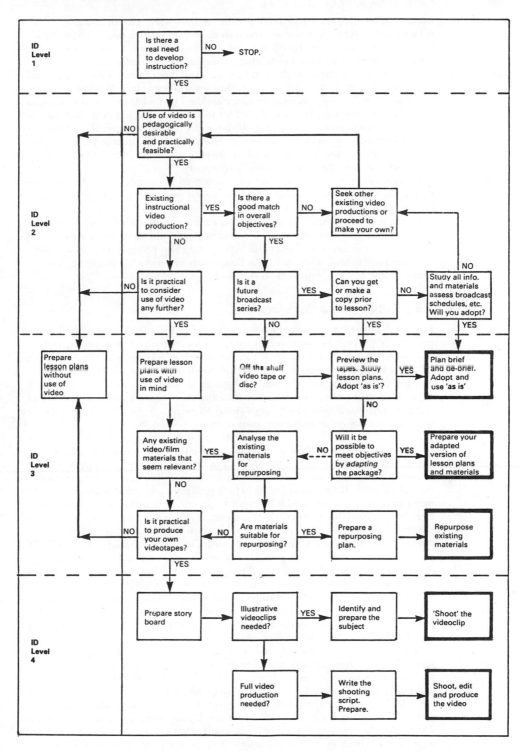

Figure 9.9 *Summary of the procedures for selecting or developing video for instruction. (Note how the procedure flows through the four ID levels.)*

but was in fact designed and developed by someone else. The situation is somewhat different when you set about designing and developing a course or a lesson, decide that some objectives require, or would benefit from, the video medium, and then set about obtaining the necessary video sequences.

Repurpose   You may, for example, wish to show some examples of heated discussions and arguments as material for analysis by a human relations class. If you have access to a video/film library, you may be lucky and find just what you need in some old films that perhaps were never intended for instruction. Having identified the scenes, you mark them in some way for later identification, or get them transferred to a fresh videotape, so that you can conveniently present them at the appropriate moment in the lesson. You are, in effect, inventing new uses for old video – the term which is now often used for this is *repurposing*.

Produce   But suppose that you do not find what you need to complete your lesson design. Either you change your design, abandoning your plans to use video, or you decide to *produce* the sequences that you require.

In this section, we shall be dealing with these four alternative courses of action. We shall, however, only discuss the genral principles involved, as space does not permit the inclusion of a whole video repurposing and production course – this would require a book of its own. The flow charts in Figure 9.9 illustrate in summary the scope of our work in this book.

9.3.2 Initial media decisions

Figure 9.9 illustrates how the four 'levels' of the instructional design/development process are (or may be) involved in your decision-making. This is particularly obvious when we are dealing with a medium such as television as the decisions we take may be influenced by a host of factors, both macro and micro, both pedagogical and practical (logistical, economical, temporal, etc).

We shall assume that initial, 'front end' analysis has indicated that there is a real need for instruction which is not currently being satisfied. We have, therefore, a new course design/development project on our hands. We therefore move on to what I term 'level 2 ID' and start planning the overall course objectives, content, structure, etc. As we do this, we also get involved in considering alternative instructional methods and media for each of the major course objectives (see Chapters 2 and 3). It may be that at this point we decide to consider the use of television/video. If television seems to be a pedagogically suitable medium for the major part of the course, and if it would be practically feasible to use television extensively (available resources, equipment, development time, etc), then we should check whether some existing TV production would be suitable, as, obviously, it will be much cheaper and quicker to adopt (or adapt) an existing TV course than to develop a new one. It may well be quite out of the question to develop a complete video course and only if we find a reasonably suitable existing series of programmes can we consider the intensive use of video in our project.

The procedures for such overall level 2 media selection are outlined in the third section of Chapter 3. Figure 9.10 presents a more detailed, TV-oriented, set of questions which may further assist you to make the overall decision on whether the use of TV is both desirable and feasible.

Of course, in reality, the sequence may be a little different. You may already know of a TV series that you would like to use, or that your local educational authorities are recommending. It may be that the course objectives are not 'crying out' for the use of video. It may be that you could teach the whole course without any television, but here is this interesting series of programmes offered to you 'on a plate'. Too good to resist! But beware! It is still just as important to check that the TV course objectives match those of the course that you propose to give. It is still important to check as closely as possible that the teaching methods, the content and the examples and problems presented are appropriate for your students. So the sequence of the flow chart may, in reality, vary, but its content and spirit remain valid.

	YES	NO
I. PEDAGOGICAL DESIRABILITY		
A. Must both audio and visual information be presented?	____	____
B. Must presentations of audio and visual information be synchronized?	____	____
C. Must motion be shown?	____	____
D. Must information on other media (such as slides, graphics) be shown?	____	____
E. Is extremely fine picture quality and detail unimportant?	____	____
F. Are there ways to get active student response to programme content, either during the programme itself or after the programme is used?	____	____
G. Is it desirable to present information in a fixed sequence? (not applicable to videodisc)	____	____
H. Is it desirable to present information at a fixed pace?	____	____
II. PRACTICAL FEASIBILITY		
A. Is there space available to accommodate television?	____	____
B. Is appropriate (size, format) equipment available for either producing or presenting programmes?	____	____
C. Is television to be used in a way that does not impose undue constraints on teaching time?	____	____
D. Do students and staff have skills to use equipment or are they willing to acquire these skills?	____	____
E. Can the skill levels required for using television be acquired easily?	____	____
F. Is television affordable? Is its cost reasonable in light of its potential benefit?	____	____

Figure 9.10 *A check-list to assist in the assessment of the desirability and feasibility of using television as a principal medium of instruction. (Adapted from Locatis and Atkinson, 1984.)*

If the objectives of the existing TV series are reasonably close to your own, then you should investigate the material further. If at all possible, get copies of all the materials, the printed supporting study material, teachers' notes, and broadcasting schedules as well as tapes of the programmes themselves. In the case of current TV offerings, this may be difficult and you will be forced to make a decision on the incomplete information that you *can* get hold of. You will decide whether to adopt the series or not.

9.3.3 Adopting and adapting existing instructional TV

Planning a lesson around existing video

If you *do* decide to adopt the series, you will possibly receive some outline lesson suggestions in the teachers' notes supplied by the programme producers. But whether you do or not, you should still plan the lesson, paying particular attention to the *briefing* and *de-briefing* of the students. If you have had the opportunity to preview the programme, then you will be able to alert students for specific events or situations that they will witness, and prepare their 'mind set' so that they attend to what is important. You will also be able to develop some follow-up exercises or discussion topics which relate directly to the programme's content. If you were not able to preview, then it is even more important that you plan an introduction and follow-up that address the objectives you wish to achieve. You would do well, also, to prepare some 'contingency plans' in case the programme misfires completely

---

Opening Activities (The Briefing)
- What introductory material has been supplied with the programme? Is it adequate? Must I supplement it?
- Does the programme attract student attention/interest in the topic? How can I enhance this before the broadcast?
- Does the programme explain its objectives? How should I explain *our* objectives in using the programme?
- What prior learning is assumed? What must I do to get students to recall/refresh this before the broadcast?
- What key points or events should students be looking for? How can I get them in the correct 'mind set'?

Adaptations to the Programme (Only if Showing a Video)
- Are anys tops desirable? Where? Why? What activities should be planned for each stop?
- Are any sections worth repeating? Which? Why? At what point in the lesson? How can this be done in practice?
- Are any sections irrelevant? Which? How can I skip them? What about continuity? Will I need to say/do something?
- Would any changes in sequence be beneficial? What are they? How can this be arranged in practice?
- Are any sections weak/unclear/inadequate/incomplete? How can they be improved? Do I have any suitable materials? How can I integrate these with the programme?

Closing Activities (The De-briefing)
- What supplementary materials were supplied with the programme? Are they adequate? How can they be improved?
- How can I encourage transfer of learning? What transfer activities can I include in the de-briefing session?
- How can I evaluate the learning? Are any tests supplied? What other instruments or activities may I use as tests?
- How can I evaluate students' reactions to the programme? Do I have an appropriate instrument? Should I do it 'live'?
- What further remedial/enrichment activities should I have 'up my sleeve' in case the programme 'misfires'?
- What summary should students prepare/receive for later review/study? What further references/homework/projects should I give them to take away?

Figure 9.11 *A check-list to assist in the planning of a lesson around an existing instructional television programme.*

and you have to implement some alternative instructional activities. The final report of the School TV Utilization Study (Dirr *et al.* 1979) reported that, although most teachers (in the USA) who used instructional TV broadcasts in their classroom teaching did spend some time preparing their students and then following up the programmes, the time so spent was very short – less than five minutes on preparation and ten minutes on follow-up. This may, in part, be forced on the teachers by the relation of TV programme duration to overall class duration. However, to get the most out of a TV-based lesson, the briefing and de-briefing times should be much longer – often longer than the programme itself. This should be taken into account when scheduling class times for TV lessons.

Dividing existing video into smaller units

If you do get to preview the programme, it may well happen that certain aspects of it will immediately seem ill adapted to the needs or the capabilities of your particular student group. You may have the chance to plan some adaptations to the original. The most common and simple (and often most essential) adaptation to a 20- or more minute programme is to build in some pauses at key points, allowing discussion or reinforcement of important concepts midway through the presentation. Unless the programme is a dramatization or case study, or is basically descriptive, then it will introduce a new key concept or principle every few minutes and it may be desirable to make several stops in a half-hour video. Procedural 'how to do it' presentations often benefit from progressive application practice step-by-step. There may be a stop every minute or two, each stop lasting longer than the previous video segment. This was the format actually built into the very successful South African operator training programmes, mentioned earlier in this chapter.

Repeating or reinforcing key sequences

Other adaptations that may be made include the repetition of a particularly important or difficult segment, the elimination of any irrelevant segments, presenting the final summary segment first, as an advance organizer, etc. You may also interlace or add on any other existing materials which you think will enrich or clarify the original programme. These will not, of course, be edited into the programme tape, but will be shown during an interval or as part of the briefing or de-briefing process. All of this is, of course, dependent on whether you will be showing a videotaped version of the programme. If you are forced to use the direct broadcast, then you are limited to the design of the 'before' and 'after' activities.

9.3.4 Repurposing existing material

So far we have been assuming that a reasonably well designed instructional video production has been selected as the backbone of our lesson and all we have to do is to build other essential lesson components around it and, possibly, just fine-tune some of the programme's sections for the special needs of our specific student group.

If no suitable programme is located, it is necessary to reassess the feasibility of using video, as the time and cost involved in producing your own programmes may be prohibitive. There is the intermediate possibility of repurposing some existing video or film segments. This is still quite time-consuming, though faster and cheaper than starting from scratch.

Depending on this reassessment of the feasibility of using video, you will now proceed to the lesson planning stage (level 3 ID) with one of two possible mind-sets:

- to plan your lessons on the basis of other media, avoiding the use of video if at all possible, or
- to plan your lessons with the use of video in mind, looking for opportunities to use this medium creatively and to good instructional effect.

Turning non-instructional video into an instructional system

In the latter case, you should once more explore the existence of suitable material. This time, however, you are looking for specific scenes or segments – videoclips – that are required by your own instructional design. You need not limit yourself to video that was originally produced for education, nor even to video – any old film sequences that illustrate what you want to show may also be repurposed. One project for a psychology course required a large number of examples of different styles of behaviour, to illustrate such concepts as introversion, extroversion, and schizophrenia. These were located by searching through several films in a local film library – mostly well known Hollywood movies. The selected scenes – very short segments – were then transferred to one videotape for convenience of presentation. The example set was so designed as to include several illustrations of each behaviour type, obvious and less obvious in ascending order of difficulty. They could be used for initial demonstration, for practice in recognition and as a final test.

This was a commercial project, so copyright permission was sought to reproduce the scenes selected, some interlinking 'talking head' sequences were actually produced to explain the examples, and the segments were edited and assembled professionally. However, it is often possible to produce very effective instruction by simply marking the segments of existing tapes, setting them to the starting points, stacking the cassettes in the order in which the lesson plan calls for them and just loading them into the cassette player as required during the lesson. This avoids all

Detailed Lesson Plan
Follow the general lesson planning procedure outlined in Chapter 2 (maps 2.6 and 2.7). Plan in great detail, so as to specify *when* a video segment is necessary, *why* it is necessary – how it will be used, *what* is the required content, scene, examples, etc.

Consider the value of video for:
   Opening the lesson –
      Gaining attention/stimulating interest.
      Presenting an introduction/overview of the topic.
      Reviewing the prerequisites.
   Implementing the instruction –
      Explaing/defining/demonstrating.
      Providing examples/practice exercises.
      Providing evaluation exercises/feedback.
   Closing the lesson –
      Illustrating generality/promoting transfer.
      Providing enrichment beyond the objectives.
      Providing a summary/wider context.

Analysis of Candidate Audiovisual Segments
 • Does the segment fulfil the purpose for which it is being considered (see the list above)?
 • Is the content appropriate to the purpose, audience? Will they relate to the examples, language, characters?
 • Is the visual imagery and style appropriate, not outmoded, understandable by the target audience?
 • Is the segment clear, free of 'distractors', well filmed, supported by useful and well spoken commentary, etc?
 • Is the length of the segment appropriate?

Analysis of Practical/Logistical Constraints
 • Will copyright clearance have to be obtained?
 • Are all video segments produced in the same standard tape width/line and field-rate standard/colour system/etc?
 • Are there facilities for transfer to one common standard, telecine, editing, assembly, captions, voice-over, etc?

Figure 9.12 *A check-list to assist the process of repurposing of existing video or film material for new objectives.*

the copyright and editing problems, at the cost of some inconvenience in use. It all depends on how often the particular lesson will be taught, how many different source tapes are involved, whether the tapes are of the same video standard (VHS, BETA, etc), whether any cine film sources are involved, and so on.

The key difference between adapting an existing programme and repurposing is that in the latter case, the source material was not developed initially to teach the objectives that you have in mind, indeed it may not have been intended for educational use at all. You design the lesson plan and then seek out the video material that meets your specification. This is often easier said than done. Although you avoid the hassles of video production, you may spend a lot of time in the viewing theatre. Sometimes it turns out to be easier and faster to make your own videoclips.

9.3.5 Producing your own material

When adaptation or repurposing of existing materials is impractical or impossible, you may consider producing your own material. This may be quite easy and cheap, or difficult, time consuming and expensive, depending on the type of video content specified in your lesson plans.

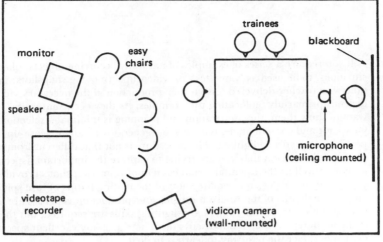

(a)

(b)

Figure 9.13 *Two room layouts prepared for single-camera video recording. (a) The layout used for teacher training at the University of Aberdeen, Scotland. This is set up for self-confrontation in the context of microteaching. (McAleese, 1985.) (b) A set-up suggested for interpersonal skills training. Note the portability of the equipment. This set-up may be used for the taping of model examples for later demonstration, or for student practice and self-confrontation. (Heinich, Molenda and Russell, 1982.)*

Videoclip   If you require a series of examples of naturally occurring objects, phenomena or situations, to be used as 'vignettes', or 'videoclips' (moving snapshots) in an otherwise teacher-delivered lesson, then production of the necessary video material depends primariuly on locating the examples. As they occur naturally, just as you want to show them, the preparation and planning is minimal – selection of viewpoint and camera angle, type of shot (general wide angle, close-up, etc) and possibly some special lighting. The procedure is not that different from still photography, except that you are trying to capture the important aspects of motion as well as the essential visual content of your 'snapshot'. Provided that your programme does not require shots of the mating habits of rare spiders found only in the depths of the Amazon jungle, your production expenses are likely to be modest. Of course, some camera and lighting skills are required, but these are easily mastered. We shall not discuss them here as many excellent specialist books exist and in fact the best way to learn is to do it.

Full production   If, on the other hand, your lesson plan calls for dramatized case studies, composed of a number of scenes and involving several characters, then we are talking of a full-scale production. You will either require a studio set up with several cameras and a control room, competent and well rehearsed actors (not to mention the detailed scripting), a camera crew and bags of time, or you may follow the cinema tradition, taking multiple shots of each separate scene until you 'get it right' (only one camera is needed) and then produce the final product on the editing console (many long hours will be consumed here). Either way, the time, cost, variety of resources and people involved is much higher, as is the level of skill and experience, if anything approaching a professional production is required. Once more, we shall not go deeply into this area. Interested readers may refer to books such as Kirk (1975) or Combes and Tiffin (1978).

     Whether or not you have the resources, time or interest to get involved in full-blown video productions, it is, in this day and age, almost essential to be familiar with simple, single camera, video recording techniques, and have access to a portable single-camera-plus videocassette recording system. Not only is this useful for shooting videoclips to be used as illustrations in conventional teaching; a possibly more important and frequent use is to record student activity as a form of evaluation and feedback. This became popular in teacher education in the 1960s, as 'microteaching' – a method of developing specific classroom teaching skills, by watching a model performance (usually on film or tape), then practising the skill in a short, five-minute, 'micro lesson', which would be videotaped for feedback. This 'self-confrontation' proved to be a very powerful (if sometimes dangerous) feedback tool.

     In the 1970s, self-confrontation spread to most interpersonal skills training – interviewing, selling, negotiating, public speaking, supervision, you name it. More recently, a form of group-confrontation has been successfully employed, in which the class activities of a whole group are recorded during, say, a simulation-game, and the tape is replayed during de-briefing to evaluate more precisely the group dynamics that developed, the climate of the group, etc.

9.3.6 Delivering and evaluating instructional TV lessons

If you have gone through the paces of detailed lesson planning, as described earlier, then you are well prepared to deliver your lesson. Of course, a large part of the lesson delivery will be taken care of by the video programme, but you will still be responsible for the opening and closing activities, for discussion or exercise activities during any planned stops in the programme, for overall timekeeping and direction, and for final evaluation. When you are using repurposed material as video snapshots in your presentation, then your role is even closer to that of the conventional instructor. But however much your role is reduced during an instructional TV lesson, it is still very important and, indeed, has some unique characteristics that may require some special skills on your part.

Know your equipment
One very obvious set of special skills is concerned with the operation of the TV or video equipment that will be used. You should make sure that you are fully conversant with all operational aspects of your system, including basic troubleshooting and correction. Nothing disrupts a TV lesson more than a scrolling picture or distorted sound that the teacher tries, but fails, to correct.

Know your students
Another, less obvious, but even more important set of skills is concerned with being able to view and listen to the transmission from the students' and teacher's viewpoints at one and the same time. Particularly when you have not had the opportunity to preview the programme, your success in the de-briefing session will depend on how well you identify points that will be obscure or difficult for your students, examples that will require reinforcing or supplementing with other, more meaningful ones, key facts that students should remember and therefore be questioned on at the end of the lesson, etc. To some extent, this is a function of your knowledge of the topic and experience of teaching it to the specific type of students you now have. However, it is very easy to get lulled by the broadcast into only half paying attention (because you know the content already) or paying the wrong sort of attention – for example, attending to the programme as *you*, from the vantage point of your interest, experience and knowledge of the topic, rather than from the vantage point of the students, their knowledge and their learning skills and difficulties.

Know how to debrief
Yet another set of skills is involved in executing the de-briefing or closing activities. In this stage, it should be the students who do most of the talking, they who suggest new applications for the knowledge presented. The instructor acts more as a facilitator of the group's activities, yet must be ready to take on the role of tutor when required. The skills of the lecturer are, however, largely redundant.

Part of the instructor's role is to evaluate the lesson. In terms of learning, you should have developed, and will now apply, valid evaluation instruments, be they tests, observation checklists, or whatever. You should also evaluate the process adopted in the TV programme, in order to improve it if possible for the future. And don't forget to evaluate your own performance. In all these process aspects, it is a good idea to enlist the help of the students. One way to do this is by means of a student's evaluation questionnaire. An example of a possible questionnaire is shown in Figure 9.14.

Figure 9.14 *Model for a student questionnaire used to evaluate instructional TV lessons/courses.*

PART I: INSTRUCTORS

A. Instructor In The Classroom

1. Were the classroom instructor's objectives for the course made clear?

    1 Never stated
    5 Made quite clear

    1 □ 2 □ 3 □ 4 □ 5 □ NA □

2. Was the classroom instructor well prepared for each class?

    1 Never prepared
    5 Always prepared

    1 □ 2 □ 3 □ 4 □ 5 □ NA □

3. Did the classroom instructor summarize or emphasize major points of the televised lectures?

    1 Never
    5 Frequently

    1 □ 2 □ 3 □ 4 □ 5 □ NA □

4. To what extent did the classroom instructor work through sample problems, examples or illustrations to help clarify the material?

    1 Never
    5 Very frequently

    1 □ 2 □ 3 □ 4 □ 5 □ NA □

5. Was the classroom instructor available either in person or by telephone to help students who had difficulty?

    1 Never available
    5 Actively helpful

    1 □ 2 □ 3 □ 4 □ 5 □ NA □

6. What is your overall evaluation of the classroom instructor?

    1 Poor
    5 Excellent

    1 □ 2 □ 3 □ 4 □ 5 □ NA □

B. Instructor On Television

1. To what extent did the television instructor use appropriate examples or illustrations to help clarify the material?

    1 Never
    5 Very frequently

    1 □ 2 □ 3 □ 4 □ 5 □ NA □

2. Did the television instructor raise challenging questions or problems which encouraged you to think for yourself?

    1 Never
    5 Very frequently

    1 □ 2 □ 3 □ 4 □ 5 □ NA □

3. Does the television instructor have speaking or personal traits that interfere with your learning?

    1 Constantly exhibits distracting mannerisms
    5 No annoying mannerisms

    1 □ 2 □ 3 □ 4 □ 5 □ NA □

4. What is your overall evaluation of the television instructor?

    1 Poor
    5 Excellent

    1 □ 2 □ 3 □ 4 □ 5 □ NA □

PART II: MODES OF PRESENTATION

A. Television

1. Was the presentation of televised material organized?

	1	2	3	4	5	NA
1 Congested, disorganized	□	□	□	□	□	□
5 Clear, organized						

2. Were the televised visuals and/or demonstrations effective?

	1	2	3	4	5	NA
1 Not effective at all	□	□	□	□	□	□
5 Very effective						

3. Were there any sound or picture difficulties during the televised presentation that interfered with your learning?

	1	2	3	4	5	NA
1 Constantly exhibited distracting difficulties	□	□	□	□	□	□
5 No annoying difficulties						

4. Did instructional television make it easier for you to take courses or acquire information during this phase of your education?

	1	2	3	4	5	NA
1 Offered no particular advantage	□	□	□	□	□	□
5 Very convenient						

5. What is your overall evaluation of instructional television as it was applied in this course?

	1	2	3	4	5	NA
1 Poor	□	□	□	□	□	□
5 Excellent						

B. Printed Material

1. How would you rate the overall value of the textbook(s)?

	1	2	3	4	5	NA
1 Poor	□	□	□	□	□	□
5 Excellent						

2. How would you rate the overall value of the workbook?

	1	2	3	4	5	NA
1 Poor	□	□	□	□	□	□
5 Excellent						

3. How would you rate the overall value of the supplemental material (notes, handouts, *etc*)?

	1	2	3	4	5	NA
1 Poor	□	□	□	□	□	□
5 Excellent						

PART III: STUDENT/INSTRUCTOR DIALOGUE

1. Were you ever frustrated during the television presentations because you could not raise questions?

	1	2	3	4	5	NA
1 Never	□	□	□	□	□	□
5 Frequently						

2. If you had questions during the television presentations, did you note them so as to have them answered later?

	1	2	3	4	5	NA
1 Never	□	□	□	□	□	□
5 Frequently						

3. When tapes were replayed, did you generally review those tapes on which you had questions from the initial viewing?

	1	2	3	4	5	NA
1 Never	□	□	□	□	□	□
5 Frequently						

4. Do you consider the discussion sessions an essential part of the course?

	1	2	3	4	5	NA
1 I did not need them at all						
5 I could not have done without them						

9.4 Television and video equipment

9.4.1 Operating standards

An image (such as that formed on the tube of a TV camera by its lens) has to be split up into a very large number of discrete points and the information about those points (ie, brightness and colour) must be transmitted one point at a time. In current TV systems this is done by 'scanning' the image – looking at each point in a line, from left to right, and then line by line down the image, from top to bottom. The scanning process may vary in two ways: the number of lines into which the picture is divided, and the rate at which the scanning process is repeated (the number of pictures per second).

Line standards
In the USA, TV was introduced with a 525-line picture, a standard which persists today in the Americas, Japan and a few other countries (such as South Korea). In the UK, TV broadcasting started with a 405-line picture, but this 'standard' was completely replaced by the end of 1984 by the 625-line standard which was introduced with the arrival of BBC2 in 1964, and which is used for all colour broadcasting.

Field rate standards
Picture rate is governed by the need to portray motion smoothly and to eliminate flicker of the image. About 50 pictures per second are the minimum for the latter, and this proved a convenient rate for European TV set manufacturers, as it matched the frequency of the alternating-current mains supply (50 Hz, ie 50 cycles per second) which was used to 'lock' or synchronize the transmitted/received frame rates. In North America, the mains frequency is 60 Hz, so the field rate standard adopted there was 60 fields per second.

Colour systems
There are three major (and some minor) differences in the techniques adopted for carrying colour information within the TV signal. The 625-line/50 Hz system has two different colour signal 'standards' – PAL (most of Western Europe, Africa and Asia) and SECAM (France, much of Eastern Europe and those areas of Africa under French influence) – while the 525-line/60 Hz system (North and South America, Japan, South Korea, the Caribbean) has its own colour-encoding system, NTSC. Minor variations include the system used in Brazil – 525-line/60 HZ PAL – called PAL-M (M for modified).

If at the time of setting up a video system it is known that there will be a real need for playing recordings made on other standards (eg, an American videotape in the UK), then a point should be made of buying what are called 'triple-standard' recorders and monitors (*both* have to be triple-standard). The recording heads are mounted on a rotating drum around which the tape is wrapped in a full- or half-helical turn. The drum is spun at high speed (once for every pair of fields, ie, 25 times per second in the UK, and 30 times per second in the USA) while the tape is pulled past it at a modest 20–100 mm/s (it varies between systems). Tape consumption is thus reasonable, while writing speed is acceptably high.

Tape width
Broadcast recorders use 2 in- or 1 in-wide tape on reels (though 2 in tape is rapidly going out of use); 'industrial/educational' machines (generally) use ¾ in-wide tape in cassettes (the 'U-format', commonly referred to as 'U-matic'); and 'domestic' recorders use ½ in-wide tape, also in cassettes. The wider tape and faster writing speed of the broadcast machines give inherently better recordings than the narrower, slower tapes. The image produced is more stable, with better resolution (definition) and less 'noise' (superimposed spurious signals, such as patterning and 'busy' graininess). This becomes particularly important when tapes are copied. However, technical advances have occurred rapidly in video recording, with the result that what would formerly have been considered 'domestic' recorders are being increasingly used in institutional settings.

Recording standards
A tape recorded on one type of machine may not be playable on another type of machine, even though it uses the same width tape. In the domestic ½ in market there are three common systems: VHS, Beta and V2000, the former two of Japanese origin and the latter of European origin. All three use ½ in-wide tape in cassettes, but the cassettes are of different shapes and sizes so that a VHS recorder

will not play back a Beta tape, etc. Manufacturers often make ½ in tapecassettes for two or three formats, and so it is not enough to ask a supplier for, for example, 'a Fuji videocassette' or 'a 3M tape'; you must be precise about your adopted format and be constantly aware of the alternatives. This is important, too, when buying or hiring pre-recorded tapes or when planning to play back tapes brought along by visiting speakers. Incompatibility between the many video recording formats is one of the greatest irritations of educational and training video users.

9.4.2 Monitors and receivers

Receivers

The domestic television *receiver* conventionally has just one signal input connector; the aerial socket. This accepts the sound and picture through a single wire. The video and audio signals are combined on a 'carrier wave' at radio frequency (RF) for broadcasting by the transmitter. This combined RF signal must then be 'tuned in' at the television receiver. This signal must then be 'processed' to separate the video and the audio (and both from the carrier wave) before they can be presented to the viewer as picture and sound.'

Monitors

The television *monitor* accepts video and audio signals separately (sometimes video signals only). The video and audio are not combined on a carrier wave and the monitor is not equipped with electronic circuits for processing an RF signal. It is not possible to connect an aerial directly to a monitor to receive television broadcasts; a separate tuner is required to do that. Monitors are the display devices normally used in broadcast and the larger industrial/educational units.

Receiver/ monitors

A *receiver/monitor* combines all the facilites of the first two types of display units. It can accept separate audio and video inputs but has in addition a television tuner and circuitry for processing combined RF signals, so that it can receive and display television broadcasts. The better receiver/monitors commonly provide video and audio output, too, for linking to other display units. Receiver/monitors are becoming increasingly common in the home and in education, as 'television' rapidly evolves into 'video' (Whitaker *et al.*, 1985).

RGB monitor

Another type of monitor, an *RGB monitor*, accepts what is called an 'RGB' input: the colour video signal is fed in as separate red, green and blue components. RGB monitors are available for use as computer display units, giving very clear and sharp graphics displays. Most RGB monitors (unless specifically for computer use) are also provided with a 'video-in' socket for connection to a camera or recorder giving a composite video output.

The major argument in favour of video or RGB monitors is that they are capable of providing better quality. Going directly from an RGB source to an RGB monitor eliminates four electronic processing stages, while video-to-video eliminates two unnecessary stages. The fewer the stages of processing, the less degradation there will be of the picture. RGB to RGB should yield the best possible picture quality, video to video slightly less good, and RF to RF worst of all (all other things being equal).

9.4.3 Portable video recorders

Portable VCRs

Portable recorders are usually smaller and lighter than the mains-powered equivalents of their type and format. They are available for all tape sizes, from 1 in down to ¼ in, and for all formats (U, Beta, VHS, V2000, etc). Some use the standard tape package as used by their mains-powered equivalents, but others use smaller cassettes.

Portable recorders are almost invariably powered by rechargeable batteries – each battery pack has the capacity to run the recorder (and, in most cases, the mating camera as well) for at least one of its cassettes (normally with at least 100 per cent reserve energy) but then has to be recharged. Rechargeable batteries will give reasonable service if they are *correctly looked after*. They should not be stored in an exhausted state but should be fully charged after each use (though you must follow the manufacturer's instructions on this).

Portable recorders are designed for lightness and compactness and so have no tuners/timers built in. However, a tuner pack is often available either as part of the camera-recorder kit or as an optional extra. These are mains-powered and provide the same facilities as the units built into the mains machines. In some cases the tuner acts as the mains adapter for the portable recorder and as the recharger for the battery pack.

When choosing a portable recorder, check on the features and facilities it possesses and make sure that it can be fitted with all the options that you need. Check, too, that it has the connections you need.

Camcorders and 8mm video   Two recent innovations have made the portable VCRs even more portable. First came the '*Camcorder*' – a camera and recorder combined in one unit. This often uses a reduced size (and therefore playing time) videocassette (VHS and Beta models are available), but otherwise the equipment is not inferior to good quality domestic portable recorders. Then came the 8 mm video format, with a new, digital, recording technology, which promises to offer in this micro format a picture quality equal to today's 'institutional' equipment. By the time this book is published, there will no doubt be further developments and innovations.

Map 9.1 *Video recorder troubleshooting guide.*

Observation: Some of the suggested remedies and suggestions apply only to reel-to-reel VTRs

Problem	Possible Cause	Remedy	Explanation or Suggestion
Videotape system plays back audio but no video.	Tape recorded originally on a machine of a different format.	Find a compatible machine and use it, or duplicate tape on a usable format.	Always find out what format a borrowed tape was recorded on before scheduling it for use.
Snow in video.	Clogged video heads.	Clean heads with a cotton swab and generous quantities of cleaning fluid.	Sometimes caused by leaving function control in still for more than two minutes.
	White residue on all points of tape contact.	Discard tape and clean VTR thoroughly.	Bad tape in which binder adhesive has oxidized and rubbed off. Notify tape manufacturer of all numbers of tape reel. Usually, they will replace it at no charge.
Video, when played back, has a disruption in the image at evenly-spaced intervals.	Electrical interference.	Remove power cord and reinsert in wall outlet the opposite way.	Sometimes the electrical polarity is reversed and the only remedy is to change the direction of current flow from wall outlet to VTR.
	VTR out of adjustment. Drive motor probably does not maintain a constant speed.	Notify proper authorites of need for technical repair.	Tape speed through a video recorder must maintain a constant speed during recording and must be played back at exactly the same speed.
Tape doesn't move through videotape recorder.	Back side of tape adhered to guide posts.	Remove tape, clean tape path and guide posts. Allow to dry thoroughly.	Fresh tape is often secured with a gummed tape to keep the wrap tight until use. Always cut off the first two–three feet of tape prior to use. Do not secure end with gummed tape.
	VTR may be colder than room temperature.	Always allow VTR to warm gradually to room temperature.	A VTR that is colder than room temperature will collect moisture and cause videotape to adhere to guides and the drum on which video heads make contact with tape.

PART 3
Media as Instructional Systems:
The use of interactive media to promote individualization of instruction in both conventional and non-conventional settings

Introduction

As outlined in the foreword, there is a strong and growing trend in education and training, worldwide, towards greater use of, what might be termed, non-conventional formats or settings for the teaching/learning process. One particular trend of recent years has led to more extensive and more varied use of distance education methods. Another has been towards the individualization of instruction – this in itself has many forms, based on almost as many philosophies. Then there is the trend toward more student autonomy, both in terms of what is studied and by what methods, when, with whose help, etc. All these trends depend on the use of mediated instruction to a greater degree than does the conventional classroom-and-teacher setting that we all know so well. Many different non-conventional ways of offering what students, or their employers, request, in the way of education and training, have been tried out. Some have been more successful than others. One important factor in the success of independent study schemes of all sorts, has always been the amount and nature of the feedback information flowing between students and instructors, students and materials and, last but not least, students and other students. In other words, it is important to build in opportunities for interaction, of all sorts, into any instructional system.

The same years that have seen the emergence of these trends, have offered educators and trainers an array of new and complex media. Some, like the microcomputer on the student's desk, are (perhaps rather slowly) being incorporated into the conventional teaching setting. Others, notably, two-way videoconferencing systems, use the wonders of telecommunications technology to overcome most of the barriers to communication that distance has traditionally imposed. One thing that they all have in common, and which distinguishes them from the media discussed in the previous chapters, is an ability to promote high levels of interaction. They have been called the 'new interactive media' by some authors (eg Gayeski and Williams, 1985).

But some of these media are not all that new and the way they are being used in practice, often reminds one of methods and materials which have been around for a long time as part of the conventional forms of education and training. One may be excused for asking whether the new media are necessary innovations or just fads – whether they are solutions to existing problems or are in search of non-existent problems. In the chapters that follow, we shall be examining the interactive media in the context of a view of the trends in education that will help us not to lose sight of the *real* problems as we are bewitched by the possibilities offered us by new technologies of communication.

Chapters 10 and 11 examine two techniques that promote interactivity in the instructional process, without direct teacher-student contact, but which are not necessarily all that new. One could also argue that they are not, strictly speaking media, but rather methodologies. The first of these methodologies is *programmed instruction*, and similar techniques, which sought to build interactivity into print-based self-study materials. The techniques examined in this chapter are important, both in their own right (in spite of abuses made of them in earlier years) and in order to understand the structure and philosophy of much of the computer-based educational courseware currently flooding the market. The second methodology is *simulation and gaming*, also developed and used well before the appearance of the microcomputer, but now doubly important in its own right and as a methodology reflected in much computer and videodisc courseware.

Chapter 12 takes us into the field of new, computer-based media. This chapter is devoted to an analysis of the many ways in which computers are being used in education and training and identifying the specific contribution that computer-based materials play in the process of instruction. The several common modalities of computer-based instruction are analysed. It is here that we see how the earlier chapters on programmed instruction and simulation/games set the backdrop against which we can evaluate the real contribution of the computer to the instructional process. The extensive research on the use of computers in education and training is reviewed. The chapter closes with a job-aid designed to assist in the task of evaluating and selecting computer-based courseware.

In **Chapter 13**, we see the integration of yet other media already discussed earlier, into a new and more powerful combination. The chief way in which the videodisc is 'new' in comparison to other audiovisual media studied in earlier chapters, is that all the different modalities of full motion video, still visuals, audio on its own and print, may be conveniently stored in one easily accessed, near-indestructible and extremely capacious package. Add to this the interactive control possible over the content on the disc, offered by the microelectronic developments discussed in the last chapter, and we have an extremely powerful and versatile medium for almost any instructional task. That does not mean, however, that all instructional tasks need this power and versatility, nor that, just because we have it, we should use it for all and every bit of instruction. Some case studies serve to illustrate the appropriate and inappropriate use of this medium. The chapter closes with a look at recent technological developments which promise to extend the power of the medium yet further.

Finally, **Chapter 14** closes the book by examining the technological developments that are just becoming available – for example, new possibilities for distance education systems, computer conferencing, videotex and teleconferencing. This is followed by a rapid analysis of how computer technology is influencing the way in which people communicate and interact even though separated by both time and distance. The possible effects on education and training are noted and I speculate how all the technologies discussed integrate into one system – the all pervading learning network of the future.

10. Print-based interactive instruction

10.1 Programmed instruction and other forms of interactive structured communication in print

Perhaps the first, and certainly the most widely-used packaging format of individualized self-instruction, has been in printed handouts, modules, units, learning-activity-packs, etc. (There are almost as many names as there are authors.) Perhaps the advent of programmed instruction (PI), and its popularity in the early 1960s, brought the concept of an interactive text to the notice of most educators. Although early programmed instruction was often delivered by some form of 'teaching machine', the programmed *text* was the most widely-used format. There were, however, some earlier predecessors – self-study 'problem cards' have been used by mathematics teachers for at least 100 years. But the programmed instruction movement extended the use of printed self-instruction to all school subject areas and to adult and vocational education as well.

Much of the drive evaporated out of the mainstream programmed instruction movement towards the end of the 1970s, but many other forms of print-based interactive learning were developed and tried. Some of these were direct spin-offs from the PI activity, based in large part on the same instructional design principles. Others were developed to overcome some specific limitations of the early, small step linear and branching programmes. One methodology – structural communication – sought to overcome the apparent superficiality of the cognitive objectives that most programmes (based on behavioural learning theory principles) were restricted to. Another – information mapping – sought to give more control to the reader over what is to be read, how and in what sequence. I mention these two as examples of techniques which broke away from the basic 'demonstrate/explain, practice, test' instructional model of most PI and yet, if anything, created an even richer learning environment in terms of the amount and the type of interactivity between student and text.

The importance of interactive text has come back into prominence with the increased use of computer-assisted-learning in recent years. Much courseware is being produced in formats that could have been packaged just as well (or even better in relation to graphic design and layout) in programmed texts. One has to ask oneself what it is exactly, that computer-based instruction offers as a medium, that was not available to us before. For this reason, the study of the techniques of teaching interactively through print are of great current importance. I shall be devoting Chapter 12 to the computer as an instructional medium, but it is in this chapter that much of the analysis of the structure of interactive print-based materials will be dealt with. Much that I say here will be of relevance in the later context.

There are two reasons, therefore, for this chapter. One is that self-instructional modules, printed on paper and distributed to students are by no means uncommon, or so bad an idea, despite the 'bad press' that programmed instruction has received of late. The second is that many of the criteria that you might apply to the sensible selection and use of programmed self-instructional texts also apply to much of computer-based instruction.

10.2 'Traditional' programmed instruction

The first two chapters outlined some of the history and research behind programmed instruction. These discussed the main principles and showed how the 'self-correcting systems' approach to course-construction developed. We will now consider some of these principles in greater detail and examine some of the end products.

Basically a teaching programme is a course prepared as a result of an intensive analysis of the learning task. It is generally presented to the students one stage at a time. Each stage presents information and demands a response from the students. They may be required to answer a question, make a decision or practise a procedure. The response that the students make has two functions. Firstly it ensures that they are actively involved in the learning process and practise the tasks they are to master; secondly it provides a measure of their progress. This measure can be used by the students as knowledge of results, or by the course designer (programmer) to identify and remedy weaknesses in the teaching programme.

The pattern of responses demanded from the students should first and foremost be relevant to the terminal behaviour expected (performance on a job, skill at problem-solving, etc). Much of the work described in Chapter 1 is concerned with the types of responses most relevant to different types of learning tasks. Task analysis and the systems approach have as their cardinal aim the design of appropriate relevant training exercises.

However, the response must also be capable of evaluation. The students must be able to judge their responses for accuracy; to compare their own efforts with a master model. The programmer must be able to judge the responses in order to identify weaknesses in the programme. In the typical programme this may happen in two ways.

Linear prog-rammes

The student may be presented with the correct response immediately after he has made one himself. More often than not, he is obviously correct and proceeds to the next stage (or frame, to use the technical term). If there is a discrepancy, however, he must judge whether his own response is equivalent. If it is not, he must re-read the frame and attempt to resolve the difficulty before proceeding. In either case, he eventually proceeds to the next frame in the sequence – a linear sequence of frames. It is the task of the programmer to ensure that the difficulty of this linear sequence does not increase at a greater pace than the typical student can handle. Otherwise the student will find himself in a situation where he gives a wrong response, and cannot see why it is wrong. The programmer achieves his aim by testing sequences of his programme on sample students. If any response tends to cause difficulty, the reason is investigated and the sequence modified, by adding extra practice material, re-wording, supplying extra help in the form of prompts, etc. The result is the typical linear programme: a large number of relatively small frames, studied in sequence by all students (who rarely make wrong responses).

Branching prog-rammes

Another approach open to the programmer is to present the student with several alternatives. The student may make a response and then compare it with the selection, or he may simply be required to choose the correct response from a selection. If he chooses correctly, he proceeds to new materials. If he chooses incorrectly, he is branched to a remedial frame or sequence of frames. In the branching programme, it is not so important that every student can at every stage respond correctly or indeed judge the accuracy of his responses. Those who cannot are routed to extra material where they receive alternative explanations and further practice before re-joining the main stream of the lesson. The task of the programmer is to suggest a selection of possible responses which are plausible, which students do occasionally make, and which (if made) point to specific weaknesses or misconceptions on the part of the student. This is not an easy task. To do this he may draw on the logic of the subject, on past teaching experience and, as in the case of linear programmes, on the results of using his programme with sample students.

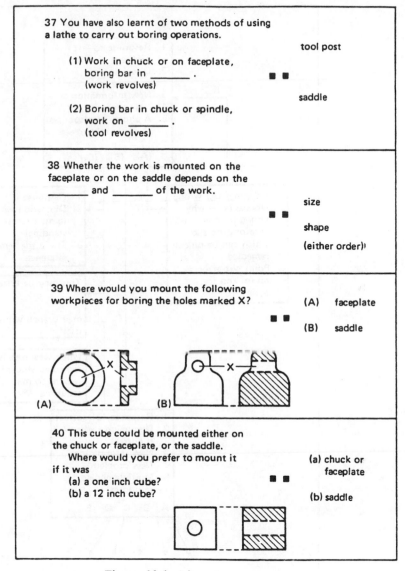

Figure 10.1 *A linear programme sequence.*

Mixed linear and branching techniques

Programme writers soon began to use both linear and branching techniques; it depended very much on the subject. When learning new words in a foreign language, for example, there are seldom any plausible wrong answers worth following up. Either the student can tell you the meaning of 'plafond' or he cannot. If a student selects a 'plausible' alternative such as 'walls, floor, door' instead of 'ceiling', it tells the programmer little about the student's trouble, except that he is confused. It does not help to produce remedial material. There is some reason to believe that presenting such a choice may in fact help to confuse the student. He may choose incorrectly, and thus practise and perhaps memorise an incorrect response. There are other subjects however, such as fault-finding on machinery, or some types of problem-solving, where specific incorrect approaches are well worth following up, and the student may learn much from his mistakes. These are ideal material for a branching programme.

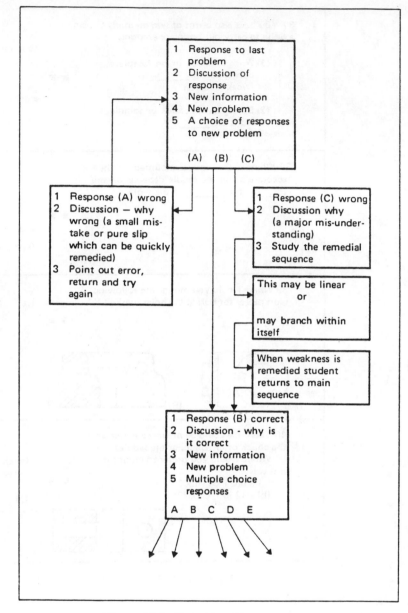

Figure 10.2 *Typical branching strategies.*

Whatever the technique used to produce the programme, what we end up with is a series of units or 'frames' to be presented to the student. The final structure is determined by the process of 'trying it out on the dog', ie, it is validated and revised until a sufficiently high level of learning is consistently achieved. Once this final version is produced, it can be used confidently with successive groups of students. It is the fact that the course and the end results can be reproduced which is one great attraction of programmed instruction. Also, it is the characteristic which limits its use to certain applications.

10.3 The changing concept of programmed instruction

Few of the characteristics of 'traditional' programmed learning, outlined above, have stood the test of time. Research over the last few years has cast doubt on the general validity of some. Practical experience has shown that others lead to the production of dull, unmotivating learning materials. Much of the valid research has been summarized by George Leith in a pamphlet entitled *Second Thoughts on Programmed Learning* (1969). Among the characteristics which he criticized are:

'Stamp out small steps!'

1. *Small steps.* Over-use of small steps leads, more often than not, to boredom on the part of the students. Current practice favours a step size as large as the student can manage. This is generally established by producing first drafts of programmes which are almost sure to be too difficult for the student, and then simplifying those sections which give students difficulty during validation.

Some errors are instructional

2. *Error-free learning.* Skinner suggested the maximum permissible error rate on the frames of a linear programme to be in the region of 5%. Subsequent studies have suggested that this figure is not very critical. Current programming practice pays much less attention to error rates within all the frames of a programme, and concentrates instead on analysis of student performance on post-tests and on key criterion frames within the programme.

Variations in mode of response

3. *Overt responding.* Again, studies have shown that in most instances, students who do not write down responses to a programme's frames, but simply think them out, do just as well on final post-tests and generally take less time in studying the programme. Leith carried out a series of experiments on this factor, which seem to indicate that less mature students benefit more from responding overtly, and that the benefit is related to the type of subject being studied – eg learning to spell is improved if students write their responses, learning concepts is not.

Variations in mode of pacing

4. *Self-paced learning.* This was held to be one of the main reasons for the success of early programmes – 'the learner can proceed at his own pace; he is not kept behind by the rest of the class'. Whereas this statement is often true, it has also been found that the learner's own pace – the pace he chooses – is often much slower than the pace he could proceed at if he were given some indication of what was expected of him. Today, programmes are sometimes designed with built-in pacing (a characteristic of some tape-slide programmes.)

Group-based programmed instruction

5. *Individual learning.* Allied to the above point, if self-paced learning is abandoned, one can also abandon individual presentations and revert to group-instruction (with a consequent saving of cost on hardware). Experiments have shown no loss of effectiveness for some programmes when used in the group situation, though this depends largely on the subject and the complexity of student responses demanded. However, even in complex, structured subjects such as mathematics, benefits have sometimes been gained from allowing students to work together in pairs or in small groups.

Alternative programming methodoologies

6. *Programming styles.* As already mentioned, programmers now tend to use both linear and branching sequences in the same programme, depending on the learning task they are tackling. There are also other programming styles in use. Some of these have developed their own jargon and sets of techniques. Examples of some notable current techniques (by no means an exclusive list) are:

   (a) *Mathetics* – the creation of Tom Gilbert (1962) and described in some detail in chapter 1 of this book.
   (b) *Information mapping* – the creation of Robert E. Horn (1969, 1974), this attempts to obey all the established principles of good communication, transforming them into a set of rules for the layout of information. Features include the titling, subtitling and cross-referencing of all

1a. Some electrical resistors have a colour band that tells how much they will resist electric current. On small resistors you can see colours better than numbers. Each colour stands for a number.

THE FIRST THREE COLOUR BANDS ARE READ AS THE NUMBER OF OHMS RESISTANCE

THE FOURTH COLOUR BAND IS READ AS THE PERCENT OF ERROR IN THE RATING

1b. Each of the **First Three Colour Bands** can have one of 10 colours. Read through this list twice. Learn the **Number** for which each **Colour** stands.

a **Five** dollar bill is **Green**	**Zero: Black** nothingness
One Brown penny	a **Red** heart has **Two** parts
a **White** cat has **Nine** lives	**Three Oranges**
Seven Purple seas	a **Four** legged **Yellow** dog
a **Blue** tail fly has **Six** legs	an **Eighty** year old man has **Gray** hair

2. List the number for which each **Colour** stands:

Red	White	Purple	Brown	Black
(heart)	(cat)	(seas)	(penny)	(nothingness)

Green	Gray	Blue	Orange	Yellow
(bill)	(hair)	(tail fly)	(oranges)	(dog)

3. List the **Number** for which each colour stands:

Black	Brown	Yellow	Gray	Green
White	Purple	Red	Orange	Blue

Figure 10.3 *An example of a training exercise for a discrimination task. This exercise uses associations already well established in the (American) student's experience, to help establish the new colour-number associations. Note that all the associations are taught at once. (This example is from a programmed course on Resistor Colour Code by TOR Laboratories Inc, 1961, and is written according to the principles of the Mathetics school of instructional programming (Gilbert 1962).)*

blocks of information in an attempt to make the purpose of the information clear and its retrieval easy. An example of information mapping, describing some of its techniques, is included later in this chapter.

(c) *Structural communication* – the creation of Anthony Hodgson (1968, 1972). This is a technique based on quite a different approach to learning than the previously described (mainly behaviourist) models. It does not pre-suppose a correct (or even a limited range of correct) answers. Rather, it is designed to enable the student to respond to a block of information presented to him, in as open-ended a manner as is

(a) The matrix method of guided questioning

This particular matrix is taken from a Discussion Guidance Unit on organizational styles. The 'items' are very carefully chosen and worded so that the reader is able to use them in various combinations, to express his ideas. If Manager 'A' wished to characterize a particular department of the Civil Service, for instance, he might do so by using the combination 3, 14, 17, 20. Note that he has not included 18, although he has chosen 3 and 20. By doing so, he has implied a weakness in organization that encourages people to take the initiative, yet prevents them, through established procedures, from using that initiative effectively. Manager 'B' might compare his own organization with this. In his case, the problem is that a paternalistic management robs the firm of opportunities at lower levels; thus, he might choose items 9, 12 and 13, and say that despite 20, his own firm does not practise 3.

Authority is concentrated at top level **1**	Staff management relations are formal **2**	Responsibility is delegated **3**	Top management are prepared to enforce change **4**
The firm is organised in levels, each of which has authority over all those beneath it **5**	Managers repeatedly emphasise objectives in meetings with subordinates **6**	Initiative comes from the top level **7**	Most information is written down and records kept **8**
Operations are controlled from the top level **9**	Standards of efficiency are set and maintained **10**	People are able to change their jobs within the firm **11**	Management attach great importance to staff welfare **12**
Staff feel dependent on the firm **13**	Adherence to established procedure is encouraged **14**	Formal systems are confirmed to essential operations **15**	Frequent contact occurs between top management and shop floor **16**
Departmental loyalty is strong **17**	Decisions tend to be made on the spot **18**	Jobs tend to be specialised **19**	Initiative is encouraged at all levels **20**

(b) The interactive discussion

Each individual response to the question posed, may be analysed in terms of the items included and excluded. Each significant combination of items is associated with a specific set of comments and feedback suggestions. There are literally hundreds of different routes through the Discussion Unit. (Adapted from Wilson 1970).

Figure 10.4 *The principle of structural communication.*

possible in a self-instructional exercise. The student composes a response from a set of 'building blocks' and the structure of this response is used to control the subsequent 'discussion' between author and student. Although textbook presentations in this format exist, it is better suited as a technique for computer-assisted instruction.

Audiovisual PI

7. *Presentation styles.* As already mentioned, 'traditional' programmed texts presenting only verbal information (plus occasional diagrams) are on the decline. However, audio-visual programming is on the increase, and one can also find examples of programmed film sequences. Group programmes are presented by some teachers, frame by frame on an overhead projector. Some of these are linked to feedback classrooms (devices allowing each student to respond to a question, the teacher receiving this information in some easily digestible form – eg percentage choosing each alternative answer).

The most significant development is the concept of the instructional 'package'. This is an assembly of instructional materials designed around clearly defined objectives, complete with tests and other necessary controls, teacher notes, etc, and utilizing the most appropriate instructional media.

Integration of PI into classroom instruction

8. *Implementation techniques.* The idea that programmed instruction might replace the teacher is as dead as the dodo. True, a good programme may be as effective as most teachers in achieving the limited objectives it sets out to achieve. However, there are whole classes of educational objectives which are not suitable for programmed instruction (at any rate, for 'traditional' programmed texts). In the next sections we give a method of assessing the suitability of a topic for programming. Other methods of instruction, such as group discussion, brain-storming, games, individual tutorials, case studies, sensitivity groups and even large-group lectures will always play their part in the total instructional package. Many of these require the presence and active involvement of the teacher. All of them require careful integration and systematic implementation and follow-up if they are to succeed.

Towards a more powerful technology

9. *From programmed learning to a technology of education.* Programmed learning has grown, but in its growth it has shed many of its earlier characteristics. The great revolution forecast by Pressey, Skinner, Crowder and others has not taken place. Or has it? The methods of instruction in the average school have changed appreciably. Scientific methods of educational management are gaining acceptance. A growing number of Education Authorities are taking an active interest.

The most notable changes have occurred in vocational, military, commercial and industrial training, where the 'instructional package' and 'training by objectives' are now fully established. We have therefore two extreme concepts of programmed instruction:

Pro- grammed instruction as product and as process

(a) 'Traditional' programmed instruction, defined in terms of its characteristics as a *presentation medium:* self-study, student paced, active responding, etc. As outlined above, more and more of these characteristics are absent from recently produced programmes.

(b) 'New' programmed instruction (otherwise called 'the systems approach' or 'training by objectives' or 'instructional technology'), defined in terms of a basic approach to problem-solving in education and training, involving the stages of *task analysis* leading to course objectives, further detailed *analysis of subject and student* leading to draft exercise design, *validation* leading to possible revision, and finally *controlled implementation* associated with *long-term evaluation*.

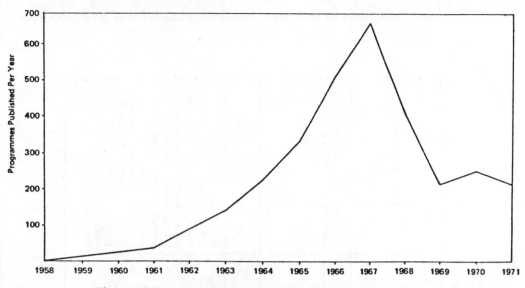

Figure 10.5 *Annual programme production: data from 1969 and 1972 yearbooks combined (from Hamer, Howe and Romiszowski, 1972, 'Changes in the pattern of programmed materials available commercially in Britain', in* Aspects of Educational Technology, *Vol VI, Pitman).*

The end product of the systems approach is not necessarily a 'traditional' teaching programme in text or machine. It may be some other teaching method, such as the use of case studies, or on-the-job training, or very often a combination of several methods.

Dr Len Biran has developed a detailed analysis of the factors one should consider before deciding to use 'traditional' programmed instruction. These are classified as characteristics in favour of, or against, the use of programmed self-instructional materials, in such a way as to be a useful job aid for the course designer. This analysis, first published in the 1972/3 *APLET Yearbook* is reproduced in Figures 10.6 to 10.10.

Multi-media prog- rammed instruction One further development has been the production and marketing of subject packages or kits. The instructional package may include programmed texts, models, complex training devices or apparatus, slides, films, and always full teacher's notes. This is the multi-media systems approach. Every component in the package is designed to perform a specific teaching purpose, and is evaluated for effectiveness. The package adopts several presentation media not so much to add variety to the lesson (though this is itself valuable) but because analysis of the subject and field testing has indicated that a particular method and medium ensures efficient learning of a particular concept or task. Do such packages warrant being called programmes? They certainly are designed on the same principles.

10.4 Selection of programmed instruction for a given course

Factor	Column 1 Characteristics in Favour of programmed self-instruction	Column 2 Characteristics Against programmed self-instruction	Reasons and Remarks
Subject matter	Symbolic Mathematical Tightly logical, but difficult to follow (eg derivation of formulae) Retention important	Descriptive Easy to follow Retention not essential	There may be no point in programming Column 2 material.
	Invariable, basic knowledge	Rapidly changing, advanced knowledge	
	Problems with unique answers (eg elementary physics)	Problems with variety of answers (eg human relations)	It is difficult to deal in a self-instructional programme with a variety of responses, unless one has a teacher, a computer or sophisticated students. The unexpected response clearly calls for evaluation by a human being.
	Sensory discrimination skills	Psychomotor skills (difficult but *not* impossible to programme)	It is easy to *present* the required variety of stimuli but difficult to *evaluate* a variety of responses. Simulators may help here.

Figure 10.6 *Analysis of 'subject matter'.*

Factor	Column 1 Characteristics in Favour	Column 2 Characteristics Against	Reasons and Remarks
Objectives: General	Short term Clear and distinct Easy to test	Long term Diffuse and interdependent Difficult to test	Attempts to 'programme' sections of academic syllabi at school or university level have often led to a general increase in the precision of definition and testing of objectives, and to supplementing long-term objectives by short-term ones.
Objectives: Cognitive (in terms of Bloom's taxonomy, see Chapter 1)	Knowledge and 'discrimination' skills (comprehension, analysis, evaluation) Algorithmic strategies of solving problems	'Production' skills (application, synthesis) Heuristic strategies of solving problems	In addition to this division, the higher levels of the taxonomy (analysis, synthesis, evaluation) are more difficult to treat in a programme than lower ones. Difficulties with evaluation of response in case of heuristic problem solving.
Objectives: Attitudes	Situations where change of attitude likely to result from achievement of cognitive objectives ('understanding' in everyday language)	Situations where change of attitude likely to require social interaction, making other methods more suitable (group discussion, games, role playing)	The neo-behaviourist theories of Skinner, on which linear programming is based, have also resulted in successful systems for changing attitudes and habits by means of conditioning, using positive and negative reinforcement, and punishment.

Figure 10.7 *Analysis of 'objectives'.*

Factor	Column 1 Characteristics in Favour	Column 2 Characteristics Against	Reasons and Remarks
Student population: Numbers and location	Numerous Dispersed The case of dispersed students is one where efficient and effective self-instruction may be especially helpful.	Scarce In a single group	A programme for a small group is relatively very expensive to produce, and may be difficult to revise, due to lack of 'human guinea pigs' on which to test it.
	Group of at least 30, easily available for testing materials during production.	Student population too small or too dispersed to provide a test population.	
Student population: Knowledge and academic sophistication.	Beginners in subject, general interest.	Advanced students, specialised interests.	In addition to 'subject matter variables', it may not be worthwhile to structure very closely the learning of advanced students, because their network of connecting ideas facilitates comprehension of any new communication in their field. Further, the advanced students' existing knowledge is likely to be very heterogeneous, making a uniform approach for everyone uneconomic.
Student population: Study skills	Students without well developed and currently used study skills (eg early school leavers, adults long out of school etc.)	Students undergoing 'academic' education, with recent practice of studying, abstracting, note taking etc.	The groups in Column 1 often particularly welcome a programmed approach. Groups in Column 2 may resent a closely structured programme, and do better with just guide lines and questions to check progress.

Figure 10.8 *Analysis of student population.*

Factor	Column 1 Characteristics in Favour	Column 2 Characteristics Against	Reasons and Remarks
Student population: **Age range, for students in schools, colleges, etc.**	Ages 13 onwards in secondary and technical education.	Advanced post-graduate work REPRESENTS A CONTINUUM OF IN-BETWEEN STAGES Beginning of primary school.	This is a rough summary which applies to conceptual subject matter and takes into account students' background knowledge and sophistication, the characteristics of the subject matter normally taught at different ages, as well as objectives which tend to be loaded on the affective side in early years. The summary does not apply to psychomotor or discrimination skills or to rote learning ('drill'). Here programmed self-instruction may be the best method at any stage.
Resources: **Teachers**	Not available, or not yet recruited.	Plentiful, in permanent posts.	In an educational system well endowed with entrenched teachers programmed self-instruction is expensive, since its adoption cannot lead to significant economies.
	'Converted' and interested	Hostile and apathetic	Hostility and apathy have killed many a promising innovation. Since the use of self-instruction changes the teacher's role, rejection is common.

Figure 10.9 *Analysis of students and teachers.*

Factor	Column 1 Characteristics in Favour	Column 2 Characteristics Against	Reasons and Remarks
Resources: Capital for development, and hence: Teachers' time for production of materials. Financing of an effective presentation of materials. Ability to use audio-visual presentation where appropriate. Re-training of teacher-users and establishing a system for revision and up-dating, with the help of teacher-users in rotation.	Available	Not available	Programmed instruction can be used in a way permitting useful economies (eg in staff/student ratio), but it requires a considerable initial investment, unless published materials happen to fit the needs of a particular project. Hence, re-allocation of resources may need to be the first step in adopting programmed instruction methods.

Figure 10.10 *Analysis of resources/constraints.*

10.5 Structured writing or 'mapping'

Theoretical basis of 'mapping'

The roots of this technique spread into every psychological 'camp'. It draws its principles from the work of such diverse workers as Gagné, Piaget, Lumsdaine, Skinner, Briggs, Ausubel and Glaser. It knits these principles into a set of rules and procedures for the preparation of written materials which may serve the purposes of instruction, of revision or of reference. It may also serve as the basis of organization of material for a computer-based information system.

If one was to attempt to classify these techniques into one of the major philosophical camps, defined earlier, we feel they would fit best in the 'student-directed learning' category.

What are maps?

A manual of structured pages, or 'maps', somewhat resembles an atlas of geography maps. Each map has a definite purpose, clearly defined. Each map attempts to present the 'shape' or 'structure' of the information it contains, and for this purpose it uses certain standardized conventions. Finally, just like in a geography atlas, one will find maps which give the 'global' view ('overview' maps, 'summary' maps, 'structure' maps) and other maps which give more detailed information on certain aspects of the whole topic (individual 'concept' maps, procedure maps, compare/contrast tables, etc.).

Cross-referencing

The whole manual is cross-indexed and cross-referenced to facilitate the student's choice of the material he needs to read. Thus the student can apply his own learning strategy to the material, going from the particular to the general, or vice versa, from the simple to the complex, or vice versa, from rules and principles to examples, or vice versa. The student may follow a holist or a serialist learning procedure. Furthermore, as all exercises (feedback questions) are to be found on separate, labelled pages, he may easily 'skip' them, to use the manual as a reference text, or select those he feels he needs to self-evaluate his learning, or read these pages first, to diagnose which sections he needs to review.

He may use the manual as a quick and general overview of the subject, reading only the review and summary maps, or he may look up detailed definitions and examples of specific concepts, or the steps of specific procedures, as and when he needs the information, thus using the manual as a job-aid. He may find what information he needs and at the level of detail he needs, just when he needs it.

As a rule, one item of content, for example a key concept, would have a page, or 'map', devoted to it. This eases reference and aids with the clear titling of the pages. There may, of course, be 'summary' or 'overview' or 'structure' maps, which illustrate the interrelationship between several concepts and how the manual's contents 'hang together'. This arrangement enables the reader to get a broad view of the subject, if he so wishes, or delve deeper into the parts of the subject which appear new, or particularly interesting, to him. The use of a manual which has been structured in this manner, is thus highly individualized, each reader selecting the content that meets his needs, at the level of detail that he requires in order to understand it. He may act as a first-time learner, or as a 'browser' wishing to gain a general idea.

In order to give a fuller account and a clearer idea of the techniques of structured writing, applied in advance, we shall continue this chapter using the very techniques we are describing. The 'maps' which follow are adapted from an early report (Horn, 1973), and have been adapted and updated by Robert Horn, especially for inclusion in this chapter.

Map 10.1 *Objectives of structured writing.*

Introduction	In the past 20 years, we have seen a significant increase in research projects concerned with the man–information interface. The reasons for this scarcely need repeating. We have more information to handle in almost every job and discipline. This information is increasingly complex. People switch jobs more often, thus requiring more and speedier retraining. Technology changes; people must learn to use the new. The information-generating capabilities of the computer have surpassed all predictions.
	Researchers are following many lines of inquiry in an attempt to augment the ability of human beings to interact with their new information environment. Hardware and software extend in many new and more flexible directions.
	Retrieval specialists are seeking new ways of indexing, abstracting, sorting, storing, and retrieving information. Computer-driven display units are becoming widely available. Time-sharing is enabling communities of workers to share the same database. Psychologists and training specialists have given much more attention in recent years to the practical problems of how human beings learn. Enormous efforts are under way to refine programmed instruction and computer-aided instruction in a larger attempt to produce an 'instructional technology'.
Basic aims	As one response to the burgeoning educational demands, structured writing has emerged as a system of organizing databases for self-instructional and reference purposes. Research and development have been concerned with these objectives: • To make learning and reference work easier and quicker. • To make the preparation of learning and reference materials easier and quicker. • To develop economical procedures for designing and maintaining (eg updating) training and reference materials.

Map 10.2 *Organization and integration of information important for learning.*

Introduction	Some important features of structured writing methods owe their origins to a topic of current theoretical interest among learning psychologists, namely, the logical and psychological structures of knowledge and their impact on learning and retention.
Theoretical discussions	Piaget had long ago speculated that 'learning . . . is facilitated by presenting materials in a fashion amenable to organization' (Flavell, 1963), but it is only in recent years that psychologists have actively taken up the problems of how cognitive structures develop and of the role of organization in learning and retention.
	The 'atomistic' approach of most programmed instruction materials has been criticized and a firm case made for the advantages of 'meaningful organization and holistic presentation of materials'.
	In a symposium on 'Education and the Structure of Knowledge', P H Phenix remarked: 'It is difficult to imagine how any effective learning could take place without regard for the inherent patterns of what is to be learned.'
	David Ausubel (1963; 1968) has developed a logical and psychological case for believing that learning and long-term retention are facilitated by 'organizers' which provide an 'ideational scaffolding'. He has now amassed considerable experimental support for his hypotheses.
	Studies with college students pointed up the importance of organization for learning and for retention.
	The relation of organization of materials to ease of learning also funds support in the area of verbal learning research (Underwood and Schulz, 1960).

Map 10.2 – *continued*

List of features	• Reviews and previews: to take stock of the ideas developed up to that point and to prepare the ground for relating them to new concepts about to be encountered. • Introductions to each map: to relate new ideas to previous concepts or to familiarize with nature and importance of new ideas. • Recaps or capsules: to summarize succinctly the essential ideas of rules or principles in nutshell form. • Tree diagrams: to sketch the ideas and procedures of a topic so as to show the role of each and its links to others. • Compare-and-contrast tables: to point up the similarities and differences between two concepts that are sometimes confused. • Summary tables: to chart in easy reference form the main concepts of an area. • Review tests after short sets of maps and at the end of units: to promote the integration of several concepts and to practise using them in problem solving. • Prerequisite charts: to show schematically the paths the learner can take through a subject matter in order to reach the learning objectives.

Map 10.3 *Map features for ease of reference.*

Introduction	In designing book-type materials for initial learning, we added features to facilitate the return to ideas previously encountered, an activity that is often frustrating with conventional texts where the contents of the paragraphs are unlabelled. Common sense, human factors research, and graphic technology were used in formulating aids for easy access to the learning materials. A list of these aids appears below. It is clear also that these same features would be important for reference manuals or job aids. If map materials were designed for those purposes alone, some of the introductions, explanations, and examples needed for initial learning would be omitted. Again we note that some of the features needed for easy reference purposes have already been mentioned as desirable on other grounds. For example, labels on information blocks aid in quick retrieval of ideas but they also serve to alert the learner to the nature of his learning task and prepare him to take in a specific kind of information.
List of features	• Tables of contents for learning books are organized and formatted to speed location of topics and special features. • A predictable format for each type of map (concept, procedure, etc) facilitates location of needed information. • Map headings in consistent typography help in scanning for page topic. • Marginal labels help not only in locating the kinds of information sought but also in skipping those not required. • Local indexes at foot of each map permit quick location of concepts relevant to the given map. • Decision tables display the choices appropriate for each possible situation. • Summary tables assemble main facts and relations for easy review and reference. • Capsules provide 'kernel' statements of key rules or concepts. • Flow charts show graphically the sequences of events in a process. • Indexes aid information retrieval.

Map 10.4   *Structured writing: its scope.*

Introduction	Structured writing is a system of principles for identifying, categorizing and interrelating the information required for learning-reference purposes. The system can be applied to production of books for self-instruction or to the specification of databases for computer-aided instruction. Most of the research and development work described in this report was concerned with information-mapped books.
Books	Structured books are learning and reference materials in which categories of information are consistently ordered on the page and are clearly identified by marginal labels. The arrangement of information blocks is dictated not only by logical analysis and classification of subject-matter content but also by analysis of the contingencies required for successful learning and reference use. Therefore, in addition to basic content material, structural writing books also have: • Introductory, overview and summary sequences • Diagrams, charts, trees • Feedback questions and answers in close proximity to material to be learned • Self-tests and review questions • Tables of contents, alphabetic indexes and local indexes with connections to related topics.

Computer database	Through our studies with structured books on various subjects, it has become clear that similar techniques could effectively organize a database for computer-assisted instruction.
	The database would be composed of separable labelled blocks of information together with their interconnections. This would afford a flexibility in using only those parts of the system that are required for a particular purpose.
	The flexible block-identified database could be rearranged for:
	
	• Initial learning
	    — for the naive student
	    — for the sophisticated student
	• Relearning or review
	• Reference use.

Map 10.4 – *continued*

In a book form maps are . . .

Stored this way . . .	. . . and displayed this way . . .
. . . on printed pages	. . . on the same pages

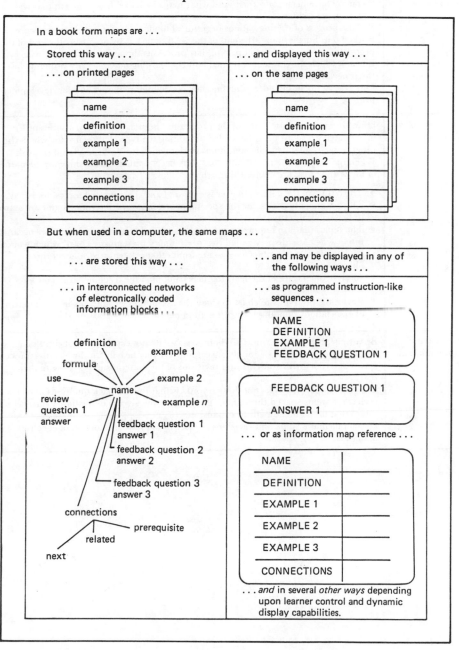

But when used in a computer, the same maps . . .

. . . are stored this way . . .	. . . and may be displayed in any of the following ways . . .
. . . in interconnected networks of electronically coded information blocks . . .	. . . as programmed instruction-like sequences . . .

. . . or as information map reference . . .

. . . *and* in several *other ways* depending upon learner control and dynamic display capabilities.

Map 10.5   *Other parts of the structured writing system*

Introduction	So far we have been concerned with what maps look like, how they got that way, and how they are written.
	But the process of writing cannot begin until fundamental curriculum plans are worked out. Furthermore, the end of the writing task is by no means the end of the production process: a crucial part of that process is the series of try-and-revise cycles through which the product is refined and the learning outcomes are brought closer to the programme objectives.
	Our system, then, includes guidelines for curriculum planning and for developmental testing.
Curriculum planning	Once the subject-matter area of the project has been agreed upon, a series of interrelated decisions must be settled, including the type of audience for which the programme is intended, the conditions under which it is to be used and so forth. When the scope of the programme has thus been defined, charts showing the nature of the writing task are evolved through the following steps:
	• The nature of the subject matter is explored and the potential topics are listed.
	• The learning objectives for the specific programme are determined and are stated in behavioural terms.
	• The topics that are required to meet the specified learning objectives are organized into a schematic display called the 'preliminary prerequisite chart' which works backwards from the objectives to the topics that are required to meet those objectives.
	• Analyse the nature of the learning tasks and plan the teaching strategies for achieving them.
	• Revise the prerequisite chart to show the assembling of concepts into the networks of associations building toward the final instructional goals.
Successive approximations	Because teaching and writing are both arts, we do not expect the first draft of a learning programme to be totally successful. We rely heavily on the iterative process – cycles of tryouts with students and revisions of the materials in response to their reactions.
	The most important aspect of these tryouts is that the feedback questions and sets of review questions spaced throughout the programme give us immediate evidence of the topics that need amendment or expansion.
	Developmental tryouts and revisions are key tools in the production of effective materials.

11. Simulators and games as interactive media

11.1 Basic concepts

The field of simulation and trainng games has expanded over the last few years to a point where it is often treated as a major training technique in its own right. Of course, simulation has for a long time been used in certain aspects of education. In primary schools in particular, the idea of learning through a game or dramatization (eg playing shop) is as old as education itself. Over the last fifty years or so, we have seen developments at the other extreme. Complex simulators are used to teach pilots to fly aircraft, starting from the wartime 'Link' trainers through to devices which simulate weightlessness or high gravity loadings, for the training of astronauts. We have also seen the birth of a variety of business games and simulations, ranging from role-playing in typical sales or interview situations to games which enable the players to take all the decisions necessary to run a complex business empire, in competition with other players (other companies) and under the control of a simulated 'economy' (often computer-based) which feeds in the elements of chance and change.

Fifty years of growth

But only recently have we seen the use of these techniques in secondary and further education. In technical training, special training exercises for psychomotor skills have been developed which often use simulated 'off the job' training situations. Much pioneering work in this field is due to Seymour's work on skills analysis training (Seymour, 1966). In secondary and further education, there has been a rash of simulation and training games exercises which aim at developing social skills or understanding of complex problems. Examples of the first type include simulations of job-interviews, classroom-discipline situations, boy-meets-girl situations, where the participants play out the roles which will actually be expected of them in later life. Examples of the second type include role-playing of others' roles to gain greater understanding of their problems (eg the Shelter simulation which investigates the problems of seven groups sharing an over-crowded house), or 'real' games (involving boards, cards or dice, etc) which, somewhat like the game of Monopoly, allow participants to make decisions within a system and 'see the system at work'. However, the game of Monopoly may be seen as a not-too-good example of simulation when we examine it more closely later in this chapter.

What is simulation?

Simulation has been defined as an attempt to 'give the appearance and/or to give the effect of something else' (Barton, 1970). This somewhat wide definition would seem to cover such things as play-acting, disguise, models, even photographs and paintings. Certainly a photograph gives the appearance of the real object and in some limited way it may also give the effect (otherwise how do we account for the sales of girlie magazines and posters). A computer-based model of the economy, on the other hand, certainly reproduces the effects of certain decisions, but the way it does this (paper print-out of data) has little resemblance to the appearance of these effects in a real economy (new jobs, rising prices, industrial action, etc).

There is one further aspect of simulation which our definition should include. All the examples we have so far mentioned have one thing in common: they actively involve the learners in making decisions, playing roles, adopting attitudes or operating the simulator. The learner learns by 'manipulating the model'. If we use the word 'model' here in the wide sense (ie a model of an object, or of a process, or of a complex system) then simulators are models which can be manipulated or operated in some way or other. We might therefore extend our definition of simulation as follows: an educational simulation

1. requires a model (something giving the appearance and/or the effect of something else)
2. requires that the learners operate or manipulate the model, in order to learn.

The model is usually a simplified version of the real object, process or system under study. However, the extent to which one can simplify the model depends very much on the learning objectives. Those aspects of reality under study must be reproduced as faithfully as possible in the model; aspects not under study may be omitted from it. Thus when learners operate the model the effects of certain actions or decisions are similar to the effects one would obtain in reality.

What is educational gaming?   Educational gaming is sometimes considered as a branch of educational simulation. However, there are some differences. Certainly the well-publicized 'war games' (in which army officers play out strategic moves against each other and a computer), or 'management games' (which pit executives against each other in similar battles concerned with production or sales) are examples of simulation. The participants make decisions and follow rules very similar to those in reality. The computer (or sometimes a human 'adjudicator') acts as a store of the sort of data which could normally be available in reality and sometimes also as a generator of the type of 'chance' events which again may occur in reality. The value of such games to the participant is in direct relation to how well the games simulate the decisions that have to be taken in real wars or in the real business world.

The main difference between these games and other simulations (such as computer simulations of a business structure or of an economy) is the element of competition which is introduced. Indeed this is perhaps the main discriminating factor between games and simulations. Some games may be simulations, others may not, but all games have an element of competition. This element of competition may be natural to the reality being studied, as in the two examples above, or it may be purposely introduced into the learning to make it into a game.

For example, during the period leading up to decimilization, or 'D' day in Britain, several organizations used a card game similar to 'Snap'. Some cards were labelled with various amounts in old currency, others with their equivalents in the new decimal currency. Players simply shouted 'snap' when two cards of equivalent value were turned up. The objective was to improve trainees' ability at identifying equivalent values in the two currencies. The game certainly worked. Trainees became quicker in their responses to such a degree that it was obvious that they were identifying the equivalents 'on sight' rather than by mental arithmetic. Similar games have been used for learning basic multiplication as an alternative to swotting up tables, or for learning foreign vocabularies. It is doubtful whether many readers would classify these games as simulations. However, they could conceivably be considered as partial simulations, based on very simplified models of reality. The decimal currency game, for example, deals with one skill that presumably was felt to be required for transition to the new currency. Whoever devised the game presumably had formed a model of how people would behave when the new currency was introduced. Rather than attempting a total simulation (such as playing 'shop') which would involve participants in practising a range of skills, he singled out one skill and devised a training exercise for it. Because his exercise contains an element of competition and scoring, we call it a game.

Five key points on the use of simulations and games   This digression into decimilization might serve to make several points:

1. Simulation and the design of special-purpose training exercises may be thought to lie upon a continuum. At one end we have reality, or a perfect simulation of reality. At the other end we have exercises designed to

develop specific skills or sub-skills which are required in order to perform in the real-life situation. In between we have exercises based on progressively more and more simplified models of the reality we are studying.

2. The benefit of a 'realistic' simulation is that the learner gets an overall impression of the object, process or system under study. He may come to an 'overall understanding of the problem' or he may practise 'the whole job'. However, the complexity of the whole may be such that he learns little about the component parts. In some circumstances this may not matter. In others, it would be beneficial to simplify the model and concentrate on simulating only those parts of reality which are relevant at this time. In still other circumstances, particularly where one component of the whole is particularly difficult to understand or to master, it may be beneficial to single out this component and design a training exercise for it.

3. There is no reason why a particular course of training should not include both special skill exercises and relatively realistic simulations of the whole job. A detailed analysis of the learning task is needed to decide on the best course structure.

4. If they contain an element of competitive fun, both training exercises and simulations tend to be called games. Sometimes the competitive element appears as a natural consequence of the reality we are studying. However, there is no harm in injecting an artificial competitive element, provided it does not destroy the 'realism' of the simulation.

5. Simulation requires an adequately realistic model of the reality under study (training exercises may be considered as dealing with only some part of this model). They will only be useful as training aids to the extent to which the model is correct.

A mini case study

At this point we might revert to considering the game of Monopoly. Is this a simulation? Is it an educational game? On face value it seems to give the appearance and some of the effects of property deals in the City. Also you can certainly become involved and 'operate' the model. You can, for example, take losses now in order to reap profits later, or you can make decisions to specialize in, say, 'commercial' property or to build up a 'balanced' portfolio. However, even the most superficial analysis reveals that the rules and possibilities in Monopoly are very different from reality. Monopoly is a very poor simulation of the real property game: poor not in the sense that it is simplified to concentrate on certain aspects, but in the sense that it diverges from reality in many respects. It is doubtful how much a building property speculator would increase his skills by the playing of Monopoly. However, you might possibly expect enthusiastic players of Monopoly to be more likely to develop a desire for real property speculation. There may be a motivational effect. One particular weakness of the game (considered as a simulator) is the disproportionate part that chance plays in the transactions.

The benefits of simulations and games

Among the usually quoted benefits of simulation and gaming exercises are:

1. They can provide the student with experiences and practice which are much closer to the real-life situations he will encounter than might otherwise be possible in a training course. In particular they can reproduce the pressures and stresses under which students will have to work.

2. They can therefore be useful as methods of measuring how well students are able to apply previously learnt facts, concepts, or principles to real-life situations.

3. They allow one to simplify reality, controlling which aspects of a real-life situation a student should attend and respond to.

4. They are often economically justified as a substitute for on-the-job practice when it would be difficult to arrange this, eg expensive, easily broken equipment (medical simulators), remote situations (space-travel simulators or school geography games), equipment used for production day and night (industrial process simulators), etc.

5. They are often justified on safety grounds, in that they enable students to practise dangerous or threatening jobs without any danger (pilot-training simulators, simulations of highly-stressed personal situations such as dealing with discipline problems in the classroom, war games, etc).

6. A well-designed simulation or game is generally found to involve students in the learning task more than other available techniques, both intellectually and emotionally.

7. As a result of 6 (and also of 3) they have been found to be an extremely effective way of measuring, changing and reinforcing student attitudes.

8. Finally, simulation can of course be used as a research technique. The model being used in the simulation should reflect reality. If we understand the real-life phenomenon under study sufficiently, we should be able to construct a valid model. If, however, we do not fully understand the real problem, we construct a 'tentative' model – a model which reflects our hypotheses about the problem. We then operate the model and observe the effects, comparing them with the effects we obtain in reality. Any discrepancies are analysed and the model is redesigned, and our hypotheses changed, if necessary. The study of complex systems such as political systems, nervous systems, sophisticated electronic systems (ie the science of cybernetics) relies heavily on simulation as a research technique.

11.2 A schema of simulation and gaming techniques

Several types of instructional techniques are commonly classified as simulation, gaming, or a combination of the two. They include case studies, role-playing, full simulations, educational games, instructional games and simulation games. In order better to define and distinguish these categories, we shall give a brief description of each. We may interrelate the categories as illustrated in Figure 11.1. The diagram attempts to show that all the techniques mentioned are based on the extraction of data or situations from the reality with which the learning is concerned.

Case study, role-play and simulation   Case studies are based on data extracted from a real case and adapted to illustrate better a specific phenomenon or to practise a particular decision-making process. Role-playing exercises may use some data about a real situation, but also include a specification of the characteristics, or roles, of the people involved, thus in some respects mirroring the reality more closely than a case study. A full

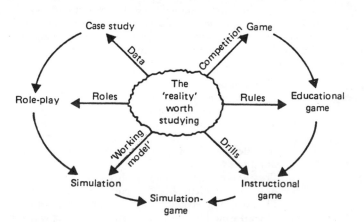

Figure 11.1 *Relationships between games and simulations used in education and training. This schema shows how the various types of simulation and game are related to each other and to 'reality'. (From Romiszowski, 1981, 1984.)*

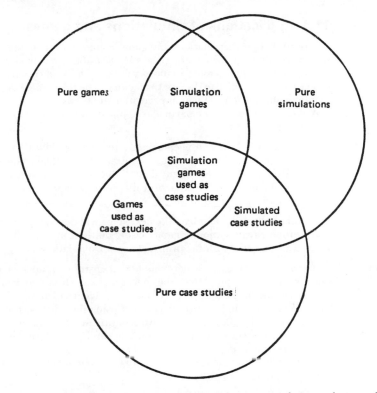

Figure 11.2 *Another view of the relationship between games simulations and case studies as 'overlapping sets'. (Percival and Ellington, 1980.)*

simulation is even closer to reality, being based on a model of certain aspects of the real situation under study that the learners may operate in an interactive manner.

Educational and instructional games

On the other side of the diagram there are games. First there are educational games, which aim at general educational objectives – basic skills, general knowledge. Then there are instructional games, based on specific objectives that the learners should achieve and are therefore more directly based on the analysis of a particular real situation. Games, whether instructional or educational, do not have to be full-scale simulations, as they may only practise isolated skills or specific steps of a much more complex real-life procedure. They do this in the context of *competition*, either between learners, or against some standard of performance.

Simulation games

At the bottom of the diagram is the simulation game. This is a learning exercise that combines elements of the full simulation exercise with the competitive element of games. This last category has become more generally used in recent years, at all levels of education and for all categories of objectives. We shall study several examples of simulation games later in the chapter.

A somewhat different view of the relationship between games, simulations and case studies is presented by Percival and Ellington, who conceptualize these three pure types of instructional techniques (Figure 11.2). This may be quite a useful way of classifying examples of the many types of games and simulations now used in education. However, it is important to emphasize the part that role-playing has as a technique in its own right and also as part of many simulations. It is also useful to draw a distinction between the 'educational' game, which has broad, general objectives, and the 'instructional' game, developed to lead students to the achievement of specific, often job-related objectives.

11.3 Applications of simulations and games

It is possible to use simulations and games across the whole spectrum of learning categories, although it may not always be desirable or particularly efficient to do so. We shall examine some specific examples of the application of simulations and games later. We will also discuss the factors to be taken into consideration when deciding whether to use them in particular situations.

Analyse the reality and the objectives

As in all other cases, the particular application must be analysed from two viewpoints:

1. Analysis of the real phenomena, situations or skills that are to be learnt, in order to be able to design an appropriately realistic model or exercise.
2. Analysis of the learning tasks and difficulties involved, in order to decide how much simplification of reality, or how much breakdown into simpler exercises, is appropriate.

Once this analysis is complete, the next steps will depend on the type and purpose of the proposed simulation or game. Using our four major skill categories as a basis, we can distinguish the principal uses of simulations and games.

Use for cognitive objectives

1. *Cognitive domain.* The learners should demonstrate an understanding of the phenomenon being simulated (the conceptual knowledge) and should use this understanding to explain the phenomenon, solve particular problems that involve the phenomenon, and invent new ways of using the phenomenon, etc. Most simulations and games may have two separate functions in this domain:
    (a) the transmission of new knowledge and/or the formation and restructuring of conceptual schemata;
    (b) the development of logical thinking, memorization, analytical, creative and other cognitive skills.

Use for psycho-motor objectives

2. *Psychomotor domain.* Any well-designed off-the-job training exercise is a form of simulation of the real job situation, or of a specific selected part (one sub-skill, for example). Occasionally, special exercises for the development of perception, or dexterity, or strength and stamina (which are of general use and not related to one specific job situation) may be organized in the form of games. The more complex 'total' simulations in this domain, such as driving simulators, the 'Link' trainer for pilots, or the simulated space capsule for astronauts, often involve the development of productive skills that require both the planning and the execution of actions. In such cases, the simulation exercise may also help the learner to acquire and organize relevant knowledge into effective planning strategies.

Use for attitudes and values

3. *Reactive domain.* In many simulations and games the main objectives are that the learners should emerge from the experience with a changed attitude, or with new values. Many so-called 'social' simulations fall into this category. Learning may involve the development of self-control skills, as in the case of a simulation of stress situations in business games, or the development of new attitudes as in the case of STARPOWER.

Use for interactive objectives

4. *Interactive domain.* In this domain, simulations are used to develop the learner's perceptions of other people's feelings and attitudes and their interpretation of other people's reactions and underlying motives. Some simulations in this category aim to develop the learner's skills in 'managing' others (leadership, selling, motivating, persuading), while other examples are more concerned with the knowledge structures that explain the behaviour of others.

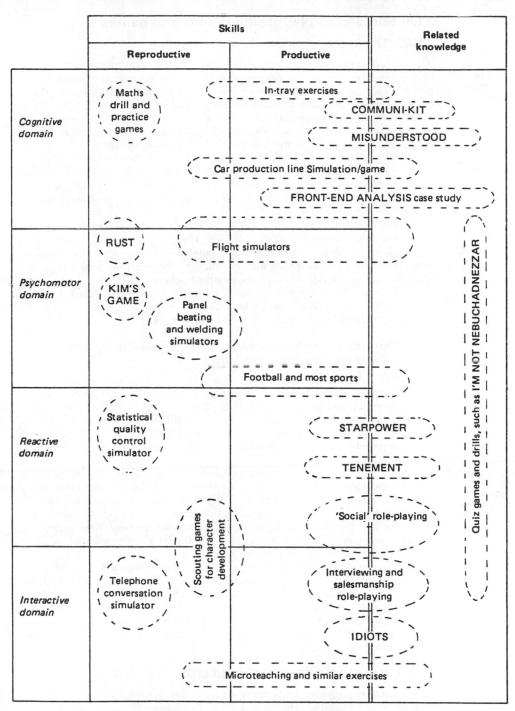

Note: The examples listed are those discussed in this section and in other parts of this chapter. The positions on the grid are only approximate. In certain cases, a particular form of exercise may step outside the bounds indicated here.

Figure 11.3 *A schema for the classification of games and simulations according to area of application/objectives achieved.*

11.4 Some examples of simulations and games

11.4.1 The in-tray exercise: a pure simulation

How the in-tray exercise works

The in-tray exercise is used very widely in the training of executives and decision-makers. The documents placed in the in-tray simulate the flow of data that normally occurs in the trainee's job environment. The trainee simply works through the pile and takes decisions on how to deal with the situations that present themselves. These decisions are fed back to the exercise co-ordinator, who analyses them and, on the basis of this analysis, feeds other data and documents to the trainee, thus simulating the dynamics of the real working situation.

When to use an in-tray exercise

Almost any bureaucratic decision-making process may be simulated in this manner. The realism and the instructional effectiveness of the exercise depend on the care and accuracy with which the real process is analysed and its essential elements identified and included in the model that governs the decisions of the exercise co-ordinator.

It is essential that the consequences of the trainee's decisions are as similar as possible to those that would occur in real life. However, the danger element which may exist in real life is eliminated. Time is compressed in the sense that, in a few hours of the exercise, the trainee may live through the stages of a problem situation that would take days or even months to develop in reality.

The in-tray exercise and its derivatives are examples of pure simulations. They do not include any gaming element, but to a high degree they do reproduce reality and the operational model that makes that reality work.

11.4.2 Group games and activities for communicating and analysing cognitive structures

Many exercises have been devised to promote introspection, analysis and the restructuring by an individual of his cognitive schemata. Perhaps the best known is brainstorming and its many derivatives. Brainstorming is not, however, a game or simulation; it is the organization of group activity for the analysis and solution of a given problem. Some practitioners, however, have injected a game element by organizing problem-solving competitions between groups engaged in brainstorming sessions.

The use of cards to picture cognitive structures

One very useful way of controlling and documenting a brainstorming session is to write down all the comments and contributions made by the participants on separate cards. These cards can later be displayed on a table or wall, and the participants invited to organize and reorganize them into groups or structures that reflect the way that the ideas are organized in their minds. New classification concepts may emerge and new ways of viewing the topic generated, and a visual record is left of the deliberations of the group.

The COMMUNI-KIT

Another interesting approach to the analysis and communication of cognitive schemata is the kit of hexagons, called COMMUNI-KIT, developed by Anthony Hodgson and his colleagues. This consists of a set of hexagon shapes made of plastic, on which it is possible to write with a fibre-tipped pen. These are used in a way similar to the cards, but have the advantage of having many edges and can therefore be organized into more complex shapes, which better communicate the structure of the ideas being discussed.

11.4.3 A management game based on a physical simulator

Most management games are paper shuffling exercises similar to the in-tray exercise described earlier. The players make decisions on the basis of data presented and the results of these decisions are then received by the exercise co-ordinator. The latter hands out further information or poses new problems, following a conceptual model of how the real management decision process being simulated actually works. More sophisticated games use a computer-based model of the organization, which may enhance the complexity and the speed of reaction of the model to the decisions being taken by the players.

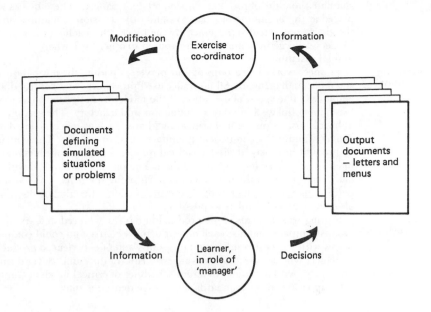

Figure 11.4 *The cycle of activities during an in-tray simulation exercise.*

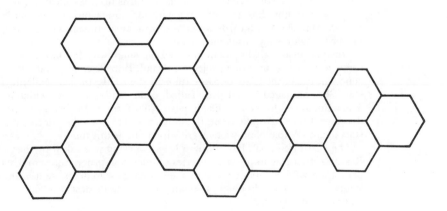

Figure 11.5 *A typical pattern of relations between ideas, obtained when using the communi-kit hexagons.*

A model as a simulation of the physical reality of a job

I was involved in the design of quite a complex situation of this type, as part of the design of a course for production line managers and supervisors in the motor industry. A large model of the real production shop floor was constructed on a trestle table. The production lines were represented by motorized moving belts, running the length of the table. The speed of these belts could be adjusted to simulate actual production rates for different car models and parts. Alongside the belts, the different production processes and machines were indicated in their correct positions, by labels or actual wooden models. Wooden blocks were used to simulate the units of production (say, 50 door panels). These blocks would be placed at the beginning of a belt to signify the decision to manufacture a batch of the given component represented by the block. On reaching the end of the line, the blocks would go into store or be re-routed to other lines where they would be used in final assembly.

Operating the model

Trainees worked in groups of four players, dividing the normal duties of shopfloor management. All normally used procedures and control documents were employed. The speed of operation of the model was adjusted so as to simulate, in two hours of play, a full day's production in the factory. The session controller had at his disposal a protocol of critical incidents, such as machine breakdowns, delivery failures by component manufacturers, strikes, etc. These incidents would be brought into play at predetermined moments, halting production on certain lines for predetermined periods of time. The players had to deal with all incidents and keep an eye on the movement of parts along the belts, while at the same time performing normal stock control and production scheduling tasks. The simulation of reality was as complete as possible.

Scoring the results

Scoring was in terms of the production figures achieved in a session. Various groups competed against each other during a course and could compare their scores with the best results of other groups and of experienced production managers who set the standards in early runs of the game. Several runs could be attempted, working under different schedules of critical incidents, until production rates approached the standards set by experienced managers.

11.4.4 Rust – or is it 'snap'?

The card game of 'snap' can be adapted to many instructional purposes, by the preparation of special packs of cards. One popular application is in the drilling of foreign language vocabularies. One player turns up a set of cards with English words and another has a set of cards with the same words in another language, say French. Whenever two cards which are equivalent appear on the table, the first player to shout 'snap' wins the cards.

The problem – rust

One practical teaching method based on 'snap' was developed by the author some years ago as part of a project in Brazil. Brazil's coffee production is concentrated in the State of São Paulo. In the 1970s, the coffee plantations in the state were damaged by a disease called, colloquially, *ferrugem*, which means 'rust'. The name refers to the rust-like deposits that form on the leaves as the disease develops. Once rust takes root, the only cure is to burn the infected plants and start again. Whole plantations were wiped out at this time.

The initial plan . . .

The Institute in São Paulo where I was working was asked by the Coffee Research Institute to produce a series of television programmes to teach coffee plantation workers about rust and show them how to diagnose it in the early stages, when only individual plants might have to be destroyed and hence the plantation itself saved.

. . . and its inadequacy

Why television? Well, we needed to show the coffee plants and the symptoms of rust. We could not use books, as most of the plantation workers were illiterate or, at any rate, not accustomed to learning by reading. The media experts and the instructional designers got to work, and it was soon obvious that the choice of media was not ideal. The photographers moaned that the quality of colour and picture on TV was not sufficient to show the fine differences between a healthy coffee leaf and one attacked by the early stages of rust. The media experts estimated that fewer than a third of the plantations in the state received television signals and that over half did not even have electricity. Complex plans were launched to produce slide/tape audiovisual programmes, which would tour the plantations in a truck with a generator. Costs were mounting and time was running out.

The game of Rust

It was at this point that suddenly 'snap!' – or rather, *rust*! – the light dawned. There was very little, in general, that the average plantation worker needed to know about rust that he did not already know (from news programmes and the gossip grapevine that existed). The only important thing to learn was to *recognize* the early symptoms of rust reliably and fast. We searched through the photographs already taken and selected a collection of photos of coffee plant leaves, some at various stages of the disease, others with defects that had nothing to do with rust, and healthy leaves. This collection of photos was printed to form a pack of cards. Instead of shouting 'snap', the players had to roar 'rust' whenever an infected leaf was turned up in the game. (They roar because you can only roar out a word like '*ferrugem*'!)

The packs of cards were circulated to the plantation owners, with instructions to put up the 'bank' money to get the first game started. From then on, the game took over. Everyone wanted to play, even after totally mastering the recognition skills involved. Months later, one would hear disembodied voices from amidst the coffee plants roar out, '*Ferrugem*, I've won!', indicating successful transfer of skills to the job.

11.4.5 Simulators for psychomotor skills

Simulators – complex and simple

The use of specially built simulators for the practice of practical skills is well known. These include driving simulators, flight simulators and the even more complex space flight simulators. However, not all simulators need to be very complex. As examples of the simplicity possible, there follow some simulation exercises developed for the training of sheet metal workers in the motor industry (Figures 11.6–11.10). Each of the diagrams is accompanied by a short description of the objectives of the exercise, the analysis that led to the design of the simulator and the method of self-evaluation that the trainee may use to monitor his own learning. The examples are taken from a longer sequence of such simulation exercises that were produced to develop the necessary skills one at a time, and then in combination, rather like microteaching in some respects. As the exercises are progressive and self-correcting, the approach also exhibits many features of programmed self-instruction. At the time of their development (1963–64) we called them 'programmed simulators'.

Application to sheet metalwork skills

The first exercise in the series (Figure 11.6) develops the skills of using a hammer to hit a given point accurately and squarely. Any error in the strikes on the real job may be identified by the fact that the dent in the sheet of metal, which should be vanishing, is instead getting bigger. However, the job only supplies delayed and intermittent feedback. The simulation exercise gives immediate and accurate feedback after every strike of the hammer.

Application to gas welding skills

The welding simulator (Figure 11.10) is rather more complex, in that several skills are being practised at once. The operator is controlling the distance of the welding torch from the work, the speed of motion of the torch along the seam being welded (which should be constant and slow) and the motion of the other hand, which is feeding in extra metal, in the form of a welding rod, in rapid and erratic movements. Once again, there is a considerable co-ordination skill to master here and the real job situation does not provide adequate feedback on whether the skill is being satisfactorily developed. The simulator provides such feedback by means of clocks and counters.

In the real job situation, the distance and speed of motion of the torch and the movements of the welding rod are all controlled by the operator's perception of the temperature of the work he is welding, the state of the molten metal below the torch, etc. If, at the time of trying to learn to interpret the real work and move the tools accordingly, the operator does not yet control the tools, no one can really say if his poor workmanship is the result of lack of co-ordination skills or lack of perceptual skills, or some combination of these. The simulator separates these two skills, providing practice in the co-ordination aspects of the task without the need for a high level of perceptual skills. Once a predetermined standard of performance is reached on the simulator, transfer to the real job gives practice in the perceptual aspects and makes the learner competent in his performance in a much shorter total learning time.

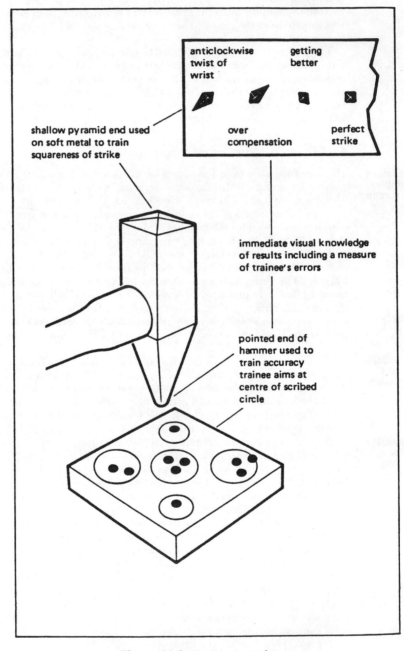

Figure 11.6 *Special training hammer.*

1. Use of the hammer

Objective: To strike accurately and squarely.

Analysis: Points of difficulty to learner – no obvious feedback either on accuracy or squareness, as hammer rebounds too quickly. Only difficult-to-interpret feedback such as sideways jump of hammer is present naturally.

Training design: (a) Accuracy: soft workpiece, pointed hammer. Mark circles of decreasing size as targets. Aim for centre.

(b) Squareness; soft workpiece; shallow pyramid point on hammer. Strike at a series of targets (eg along a line)

Evaulation: (a) Student self-judges progress by position of marks relative to centre of circle (knowledge of error).

(b) Square strike leaves a square indented pyramid. Any irregularities in indent point to specific errors in strike. Student refers to sample errors (knowledge of error) or instructor corrects strike (forced response).

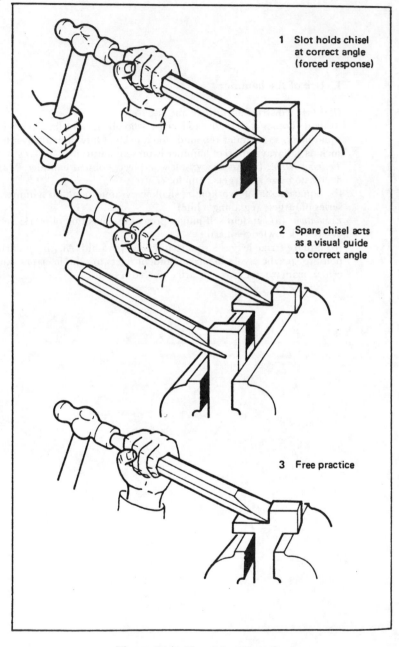

1 Slot holds chisel
   at correct angle
   (forced response)

2 Spare chisel acts
   as a visual guide
   to correct angle

3 Free practice

Figure 11.7 *Use of the cold chisel.*

2. Use of the chisel

Objective: To use chisel at the correct cutting angle.

Analysis: Points of difficulty – keeping angle constant and correct while hammering. Control of chisel angle is part visual and part kinaesthetic.

Training design: (a) First stage – guidance (by forced response). Chisel held in groove, fixed at correct angle. It cannot wander. Student concentrates on hammering.

(b) Second stage (visual guidance only). Correct angle is demonstrated by one chisel in slot while the student uses another freely alongside.

(c) Third stage – free practice.

Evaluation: First stage: No chance of error. Student learns 'feel'.

Second stage: Self-evaulation against a visual guide.

Third stage: Instructor must evaluate both method and resultant quality of work.

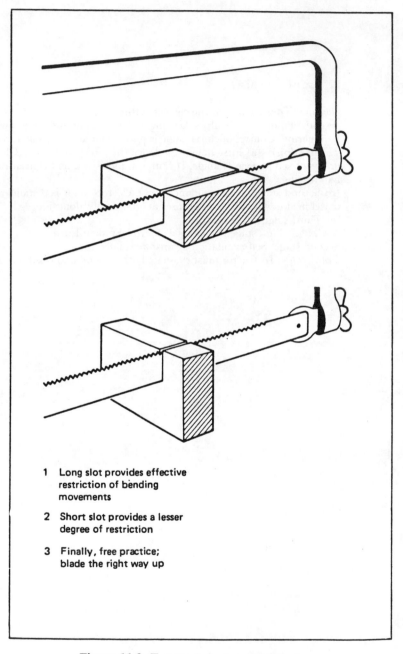

1 Long slot provides effective
   restriction of bending
   movements

2 Short slot provides a lesser
   degree of restriction

3 Finally, free practice;
   blade the right way up

Figure 11.8 *Training device for use of the hacksaw.*

3. Use of the hacksaw

Objective: To cut straight, vertical slots accurately.

Analysis: Student must learn new skill of moving hands in one plane. There is action feedback present in the job (eg the bending or bowing of the blade) but the strongest control comes from the kinaesthetic sense (ie student must learn the feel).

Training design: (a) First stage (physical restriction). Use a hacksaw with blade wrong way up, in an accurately pre-formed saw cut along the wide edge of workpiece.

(b) Repeat in another cut along narrow edge. (Less physical restriction.)

Evaluation: Bending of blade produces noise of teeth on sides. This artificial action feedback brings to student's attention his error and the less obvious 'natural' action feedback of the blade bending.

Progressive reduction of length of slot reduces guidance. Instructor must judge when to change slots. One weakness – device does not simulate the need to press harder on forward stroke than on back stroke.

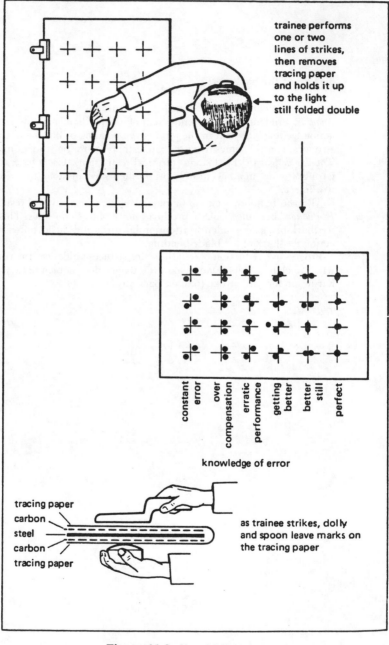

Figure 11.9 *Use of dolly and spoon.*

4. Use of dolly and spoon

Objective: To beat out small dents in metal sheet.

Analysis: Difficulty in learning to strike so that dolly and spoon are exactly at the right spot. Slight discrepancies can make the dent worse. This knowledge of error cannot be relied on in training as only several wrong strikes (ie practising errors) will make new dent appear obvious.

Training design: Sheet of steel for practice has carbon paper and tracing paper interleaved as shown. Target crosses marked on top sheet of tracing paper.

Student strikes with spoon at a series of crosses in turn, holding the dolly below.

Evaluation: After exercise (say 8 strikes) complete, tracing paper is removed. Student can see the relative positions of cross, upper impact and lower impact (knowledge of error). He can attempt to correct error on next exercise. Several characteristic types of error exist (eg dolly always to left, or lines of motion of dolly and spoon always at a fixed angle).

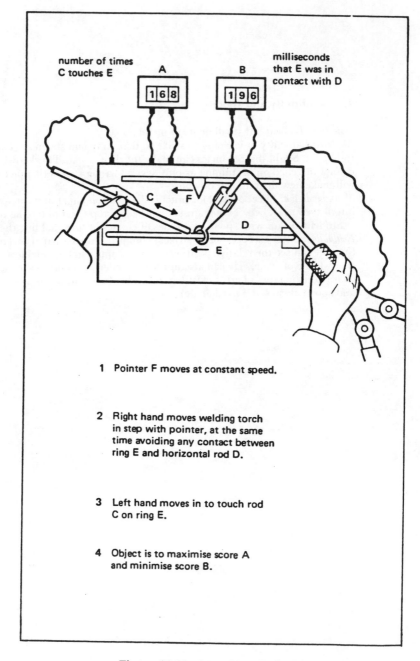

number of times
C touches E

milliseconds
that E was in
contact with D

1 Pointer F moves at constant speed.

2 Right hand moves welding torch
in step with pointer, at the same
time avoiding any contact between
ring E and horizontal rod D.

3 Left hand moves in to touch rod
C on ring E.

4 Object is to maximise score A
and minimise score B.

Figure 11.10 *Gas welding simulator.*

5. Use of welding torch

Objective: To move torch smoothly at constant speed along seam, while other hand is irregularly feeding in welding rod.

Analysis: Co-ordination of uniform movement of right hand and jerky movement of left hand difficult to learn. Both speed of progress and distance from metal of the welding flame are critical.

Training design: As in diagram. Welding torch is moved right to left in step with the clockwork pointer. Loop on torch nozzle must not touch horizontal wire. The other hand feeds in the rod to touch the loop as often as possible. Each touch of welding rod on loop registers 1 on counter A. Time of contact between loop and horizontal wire registers on counter B.

Evaluation: Object is to maximize score A and minimize score B. Scores act as terminal knowledge of results, and as a measure of progress against pre-set standards.

This device is more of a full simulator than the earlier examples, as several skills are practised in co-ordination. One can in training break this down and first practise the right hand alone, then add the left. The scores can be used with some degree of objectivity, as a measure of the skill. Although the lowest scores on counter B did not necessarily make the best welders, it was found in practice that scores above a certain maximum ceiling indicated the futility of attempting to train the individual as a welder. The device has been used to aid selection as well as training.

11.4.6 A simulator for changing attitudes

A problem often encountered in the training of adults might be called the 'doubting Thomas syndrome'. Trainees do not learn a given topic satisfactorily because they do not really believe that it has any relevance to their real-life situation, or that it is true at all. The proponents of andragogy – the science of adult learning – argue that it is much more important for an adult than for a child to see the relevance or the usefulness of what he is asked to learn. Otherwise, all manner of barriers to learning spring up.

The problem of negative attitude to learning

Some years ago, I was involved in planning and teaching courses on statistics for industry, with particular emphasis on statistical quality control. Here, there was a case of 'doubting Thomases' with a vengeance. I was teaching orientation courses about statistical quality control to supervisors and foremen and was confronted with disbelief that the performance of some 'mathematical magic' on a small sample of a batch of products could be as effective a means of quality control as the traditional inspection of the whole batch.

The solution – a realistic simulator

To overcome this resistance, a simulated production line was constructed. A special batch of defective washers, with the hole in the middle punched a little off-centre, was produced. The defect could be easily observed by the naked eye. The production line was simply a motorized belt. A hopper at one end fed the washers on to the belt, and they moved past an inspector stationed along the line. The inspector had to identify and remove the defective washers from the belt as they came past. The hopper was filled with a mixture of good and defective washers. The proportions of defective washers in the total batch could be varied as required. The instructor, who prepared the mix, was therefore the only person who knew the real proportion of defects in the batch. Then the simulator was set in motion, with the most forthright 'doubting Thomas' as inspector. Another person took a handful of washers out of the hopper, put them on a side table and analysed the sample. The inspector busily checked the washers in the batch as they travelled past him and removed all the defective washers identified. Witness the inspector's surprise when his effort proved no more accurate than the statistical estimate, performed in a fraction of the time. Inspectors always miss some defective products, and sometimes also accidentally remove good washers. The simulator could be operated at various speeds, and a graph may be drawn showing how this type of human error increases as the working pace increases. By contrast, the statistical method gave consistently accurate results.

Some of our 'Thomases' accused the instructor of feeding data to the statistical quality controller, so we built in a sophisticated element. We magnetized the defective washers and constructed a magnetically operated automatic separation device at the end of the production line. As the washers came to the end of the belt, they fell down a chute and were automatically guided to separate containers for the good and the defective products. Any defective washer missed by the inspector would be caught by the magnets. We could now mix up batches blindfolded, so that nobody knew the real proportion of defects. That did the trick.

11.4.7 Microteaching as an example of role-playing

Why 'micro'?

There are many variations of exercises for the development of teaching skills that go by the name of 'microteaching'. The original system, developed at Stanford University in the USA, could merit the label of 'micro' for two distinct reasons: first, the trainee teacher would practise only one or two of the skills normally used in a lesson during a session, and, second, the session itself was much shorter than the normal lesson. Thus, the microteaching session resembles a lesson, but is much less complex and very much shorter.

Other aspects of the session vary according to the application. Sometimes, the trainee teacher works with a small group of real students (the reduction in group size may be another reason for the label 'micro'), but often the other trainee teachers adopt the roles of the students; this mode of work is called peer teaching.

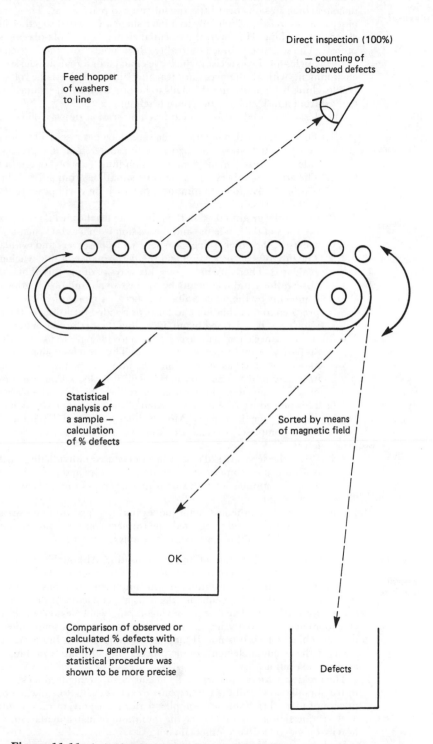

Figure 11.11 *A simulated production-line, designed to compare the effectiveness of 100% direct inspection with statistical quality control methods.*

**Why
role-
playing?**

Some aspects of the real classroom teaching situation are simulated, but the microteaching sessions bear little resemblance to real lessons. They are more a set of separate exercises, which only at a later stage are welded together into realistic classroom teaching. However, the essential elements of a role-playing situation are present. The scenario is based on reality. Real topics from the curriculum are used as the vehicles for the exercises which are enacted in a realistic classroom environment, with all the necessary teaching aids available. The roles are based on real teaching behaviour, and the skills to be practised by the trainee teachers are derived from a task analysis of typical teaching.

**The
micro-
teaching
procedure**

The classical procedure for a microteaching session runs as follows:

1. The instructor demonstrates the skill to be practised. This demonstration may be acted out by the instructor but more often, it is prerecorded on videotape (ready-made demonstration films may be bought or hired).
2. The group members select topics or situations from a list and prepare the session (of five to eight minutes), in which they will practise the particular skill that was demonstrated.
3. One of the group takes on the role of the teacher, while the others adopt the roles of the students, and the session is enacted. (When real students are used, the other trainee teachers act as observers and evaluators.)
4. The progress of the session and the performance of the 'teacher' are evaluated. There are many possible ways of doing this. These include observations and comments by the instructor and observations and comments by the other trainee teachers, supported by notes made on pre-prepared evaluation checklists or a video recording of the performance, which can be analysed by all, including the performer being evaluated.
5. If the trainee's performance is not up to the expected standard, he may prepare a second topic and try again. This 'teach-evaluate-reteach' cycle may be repeated as often, within the limits of the time available, as is necessary to reach mastery in the skill. Usually, all the other trainees will have a chance to perform once, before the reteach sessions are held.
6. This procedure is repeated for each of the separate basic skills considered important for the teacher. Models differ: the original Stanford University model comprised 16 separate skills; other models are restricted to 12 or fewer.
7. When the separate skills have been mastered individually, further practice is arranged on somewhat more complex topics and in sessions that may be about 15 minutes long, during which several of the skills are practised in combination.
8. Finally, when the instructor judges that the separate skills are sufficiently well mastered and integrated, the trainees continue their practice in supervised real-life classroom situations.

**Variations
on
the basic
procedure**

There are many variations on this basic routine. Although very commonly used, video feedback is not an essential element of microteaching. What is essential is the practice of real skills in simulated and simplified situations. Video feedback is most effective and tends to enhance the learning efficiency of the system but we can get by without it. The custom of videotaping whole lessons in the real classroom and later analysing the teacher's performance is sometimes passed off as microteaching, which it is not. It may be a useful exercise, but there is no effort to simulate the essential elements of the process, and absolutely nothing 'micro' about its execution.

The greatest variety appears in the means of supplying feedback. Some instructors like to get all the participants to act as evaluators of each other; others prefer not to do this. Some use complex performance inventories or interaction analysis questionnaires; others use the minimum of instrumentation. Some rely heavily on video feedback; others do not.

We have singled out microteaching because it is a representative example of a range of role-play exercises for the development of specific interactive skills. Other

Other applications of the principles

applications of basically the same methodology occur in the training of interviewers, bank managers, shop assistants, salesmen and many other types of professionals for whom interaction with the public is part of their job. In all such applications, the essential 'micro' elements of separating out the principal skills into separate exercises, thus reducing the complexity and duration of the exercises in the initial stages of training, are preserved.

Some applications may be more sophisticated than microteaching in terms of role-playing. For example, in one approach to training bank managers in the skills of interviewing clients seeking loans, the various clients were impersonated by professional actors, each with a well-defined character role.

11.4.8 I'm not Nebuchadnezzar – a versatile knowledge game

One knowledge-quiz game that is not well known but which is worth discussing is *I'm not Nebuchadnezzar*. It has the great advantage that it can be played anywhere, at any time, with any reasonable number of players (say two to twelve), and can provide practice for and reinforcement of any body of knowledge. It has sufficient appeal and simplicity to be adored by children and sufficient potential for complexity to be a don's delight.

Structure of the game

The game's structure is quite simple. One of the group of players is being interrogated by the others, who, in turn, ask questions of the type 'Did you use Jewish slaves to build the Tower of Babel?'. The central player must identify the person to whom the questioner is alluding and reply, in this case, with the phrase, 'I'm not Nebuchadnezzar'. The central player is, indeed, someone of his own 'choosing' (let us imagine he has chosen to be Moses), and if one of the questioners happens to guess who he is, by asking for example, 'Were you found in a basket floating on the Nile?', he must admit that he is found out and change places with the player who posed the question. The central player usually selects the subject on which the questions must be based. The topic in the example above may have been people in the Old Testament. The object of the game is to remain the central player for as long as possible. The other players may gain this position by correctly guessing the current central player's identity, or, more often, by posing a question that the central player fails to answer correctly. Had the player in the example above replied 'I'm not Goliath', he would be challenged by the questioner to give up his central position in the game. Sometimes arguments arise. For example, if the reply given to the question, 'Did you nearly conquer Europe but failed because your luck changed in Russia?' was 'I'm not Hitler', and the questioner had in mind Napoleon (the correct answer), a discussion might arise that would normally be put to a vote to decide whether the question was ambiguous or whether it was sufficiently precise to accept only the desired response. If the players are unsure, one resorts to encyclopaedias and other resources in order to resolve any differences of opinion.

The use of the game

The beauty of the game is that all players are constantly involved in recalling and reorganizing their knowledge on a given subject, and all players may learn new facts at any point in the game. The topics may be selected to suit any special interest and the complexity of the questions adapts to the intellectual capacities of the players. Though simple, the game is captivating.

The game has obvious educational value as a means of reinforcing areas of general knowledge. It can also be used in an instructional context, with the instructor defining the topic in the light of his teaching objectives. The topics are not limited to people, and the game can be used in the teaching of many different disciplines.

11.5 Using simulations and games effectively

We have seen that, depending on the category of objectives, different approaches may be necessary to the structure of simulation exercises.

Tansey (1972) suggests that there are three basic techniques used in simulation:

Three component techniques

1. the case study
2. role playing
3. gaming

He argues that although the plain case study would not be considered by some as an example of simulation, it does in fact present the learners with a model of a real-life situation. He also suggests that some form of case study is usually implied in the instructions for a role-play exercise.

Experience would seem to bear out that cognitive objectives of a simple nature do not necessarily need simulation exercises at all. Cognitive objectives at the concept, or principle level, and particularly at the problem-solving level, can be tackled effectively by case studies. Role-playing or gaming would not necessarily be essential, but may nevertheless be included to add interest and motivation to the exercise. Some cognitive objectives, such as learning to apply a particular interview procedure, may demand role-playing by their very nature.

Affective objectives, on the other hand, are most likely to be achieved by realistic role-play exercises, coupled to a detailed discussion at the end. How much value there would be in trying to inject an element of gaming (an artificial element) is debatable. In the author's opinion, anything interfering with the realism of the simulation might have an adverse effect on the attainment of affective objectives.

Finally, for psychomotor skills, some form of simulation is dictated, if learning 'on the job' is impractical or too difficult. Role-playing is used in the sense that the learner is playing his own future role (there is no point in learning a psychomotor skill if one is not going to use it). Gaming is rarely used, though 'against the clock' or 'against the target' exercises which simulate the piecework situation in industry have been found to be very effective (these, however, are examples of competitive elements that exist naturally in the real-life situation).

To complete this chapter let us look at some research results and at the way that some practitioners set about planning role-playing and gaming exercises, and finally conclude with a detailed consideration of psychomotor skill training.

11.5.1 Research on the use of simulations and games

There are well over 1200 different simulations and games on the educational market. There must be a similar number of unpublished products used for in-company training and development. Two directories of simulation games are: *Handbook of Simulation Gaming in Social Education* (Stadsklev, 1975) and R E Horn's *The Guide to Simulations/Games for Education and Training* (3rd ed) (Didactic Systems, Inc, 1977).

Most of the research is poorly designed

There has been considerable research, but a sizeable part of it has had such limited objectives as to be of little value. Can simulation gaming transfer factual information to the student? It turns out that the answer is, 'Yes, but not much better than if the facts are laid on the student by lecture or, even better, by dittoed handout'. But 'a lot of people have suspected for a long time that trying to pour facts into the student is not an especially appropriate use of simulation gaming' (Coombs, 1978).

Much of the well designed simulation gaming research that has been done has been conducted by the Academic Games Program at Johns Hopkins University. Before federal funding for that project ceased, almost 40 reports were issued. (The results of these reports are summarized in Stadsklev, 1975.)

The problem is that much of this research is validation of a particular game. What actually is being evaluated is the *play*, one or a few times, of the game. Fred Goodman has made that point and gone on to say he doesn't much care about gaming as gaming, 'but it's an extraordinary way to study learning'. In his words, 'We should stop concentrating on 'Does gaming work?' and concentrate instead on what gaming does and why it does it' (Coppard and Goodman, 1977).

Some of the conclusions

From the work that has been done, what do we know?

First, as already noted, simulation gaming does not seem to be a particular good way to teach cognitive skills. Coppard and Goodman (1977) sum up other aspects of simulation gaming as follows:

> 'Evidence in support of affective learning is also sparse, although somewhat more promising. Also, in spite of the wide use of simulation games, and the testimonies of teachers and trainers, there is little evidence to support claims that simulation gaming has any special utility in developing competencies. Simulation gaming may, of course, be useful in these areas but evaluative studies have yet to confirm it.
>
> More convincing evidence is available in other areas. There is a growing body of research that suggests that simulation games alter the character of the classroom in a positive manner. Convincing evidence is also being gathered which suggests that simulation gaming improves the motivation of students.'

One of the leading practitioners, Gary Shirts, in a highly significant article looked back on a decade of development:

> 'I am not suggesting that simulation games have been a disappointment. I believe that they create opportunities for learning which cannot be duplicated by any other pedagogical technique. For the user, they have high face validity. If there is one consistent finding in the research, it is that students and teachers rate them highly as interesting and worthwhile experiences.'
>
> (Shirts, 1976*a*)

But Shirts' overall assessment was properly cautious. There was still not a recognizable 'body of theory'.

> 'Many of the problems are caused by their uniqueness, by the fact that they do not fit easily into the time and space requirements of the school, the teaching styles of instructors or the marketing system of major publishers.'
>
> (Shirts 1976*b*)

Much research must yet be done

Shirts has also drawn up a list of nine major areas for research, which he termed 'An inventory of hunches about simulation as educational tools' (see Coombs, 1978).

There is much yet to be done. But as Taylor and Walford (1979) remark:

> '. . . it is important to remember that a great deal has been developed and achieved in a short space of time. Systematic review of the wealth of subjective comment from regular practitioners can be put alongside the comments of critical observers. This comparative alignment of assessment encourages perseverance and further work. We can expect more and varied experimentation with some of the simulation ideas and structures that have already proved their durability; what we need in the next ten years is not so much the introduction of new base models, but more a willingness to refine the good ones among those that already exist. We also need to look at these models in wider educational contexts, since it may be a change in the sequencing of work, or the use of the simulation in a different context which reveals the *full* potential of an exercise already popular and frequently misused.
>
> There is no doubt that simulation is often *mis*used, sometimes even by those who are its greatest champions. Its power is such that we should be wary of its indiscriminate use, precisely because its elegance and power can be seductive but unprofitable in the long run.

Much practical know-how has been built up

The key to future development may well lie in the full utilization of the knowledge that already exists within the system, but which is recognized by only a few – and even by some of them its importance may not be fully appreciated. Many more teachers and students, managers and workers, citizens and administrators need to be made more aware of the technology within their grasp. The expertise of the comparative few must be diffused to the grass roots of education, both adolescent and adult.'

The remainder of this chapter is devoted to presenting, in condensed form, some of this existing knowledge.

11.5.2 Using role-playing exercises

Peter McPhail (1972) suggests six factors which one should consider when planning a role-play exercise. A good role-play exercise should:

(a) have a clear purpose or purposes relevant to the needs of the participants;
(b) use a situation which is real to those participants;
(c) include only the number of people who can actively contribute;
(d) be conducted in physical conditions which make it easy for those role-playing to accept the reality of the situation and identify with it;
(e) have enough time allowed to let it run as long as the motivation lasts; and above all
(f) be non-authoritarian in organization and practice.

He then contrasts the procedures which one would use to build role-play exercises depending on whether one was attempting to establish a particular skill such as selling a car (cognitive objectives), or to help people to take into consideration others' needs, feelings or interests (affective objectives).

In brief the procedure he suggests for the *cognitive* domain runs as follows:

Considerations for role-play in the cognitive domain

1. The organizer states what the skill is which the role-play is designed to improve. He may expand his introduction by showing a film or video-tape to demonstrate skilled or unskilled performances.
2. The situation or situations to be role-played are selected for their relevance to acquiring the skill in question, preferably in consultation with the course members.
3. The course is divided up into role-play groups. For most situations small groups of 5 to 10 are best.
4. The amount of detailed information required by participants before they can respond to a situation will vary according to their experience and the particular situation. Nevertheless, classical role-play allows maximum freedom to those taking part and it reaps great motivational and learning benefit from doing so.
5. The participants play out their roles. Those who cannot have active parts are asked to observe the principal's solution, evaluate it and decide what they would do in his position.
6. As long as the participants are interested, and there is time, other members of the group can be asked to play out what they would do rather than just talk about others' performances.
7. The organizer of the role-play discusses in detail with the participants their approach to the problem posed and the role-play solutions to it. If he has a tape recorder or, better still, a video-tape recorder, a record of the proceedings will clarify exactly what individuals said and did.
8. When the role-play situations are simple dyadic (one to one) encounters – for example, where interview technique is practised by A interviewing B – a valuable feedback technique is to reverse the roles and try the whole exercise over again before further discussion.
9. Towards the conclusion of the course it is valuable to hold a plenary session where course members are encouraged to give their impressions of the course – to be uninhibited in their criticism.
10. After the plenary session some role-play organizers talk to the whole course about the insights which have been gained and learning which has taken place.

**Role-play
in the
affective
domain**

For *affective* objectives, particularly ones associated with teaching people to get on with others, he suggests:

1. A conflict situation is chosen for role-play, preferably by the game members themselves.
2. The situation described, with support from cartoon, straight drawing or photograph, is read and seen by the group. To make the impact even more vivid it can be acted.
3. Two participants naturally inclined towards the points of view in conflict are asked to play out what they would do, while the other group members watch and decide how they would react.
4. The conflict roles are reversed and the participants take the place of the other and play out what they would do.
5. Both participants then revert to their original roles and play out their 'final' responses. Wide experience suggests that the final responses are more considerate than the behaviour originally suggested and that this experience can, in many cases, affect people's life styles.
6. Other members of the group should be encouraged to criticise what they have seen and play out their solutions as long as they are interested.

11.5.3 Games

**Is a game
appropriate
for your
course?**

Rex Walford (1972) suggests that before deciding to use or design a game you should consider at least three points:

1. Is this the place in my classes where I really need a game? Is the game going to teach about a process or represent a decision-making situation more effectively than other teaching modes? Do I know why I am choosing to use a game?
2. Is the game that I choose to use, or adapt, or build from scratch, one that is a reasonable representation of reality? The game may be well-built, and good fun and exciting – but is it 'real'? (In this sense, an educational game may have different objectives from a commercial, entertainment game.) If the game is not founded on some kind of reality, it may be a pleasant interlude in class but a source of misconceptions at the same time.
3. Have I learnt enough about this game to run it properly? Do I understand the basic intentions of the game, and can I manage it reasonably in my own class situation? Games require a different kind of teaching technique, and the teacher who uses them needs a degree of managerial expertise.

He goes on to outline a procedure for the design of educational games as follows:

**Design
factors
to take into
consider-
ation**

1. What is the basic idea of the game?
2. What is the context of the game?
3. What style of game will be most suitable?
   Style can refer to the type of equipment needed (board? counters? or just talk?); the development of groups within the game (individuals? groups of five or six? larger groups?); the amount of competitiveness desired: games can be entirely co-operative if required.
4. Who will the players represent?
5. Are there to be defined objectives for the players?
   Sometimes such definition gives the game urgency and purpose. At other times, it is instructive to let groups work towards the definition of their own objectives – which may differ.
6. What do the players do to make the game work?
   What interaction is needed to move the game on? Talk? Or the throwing of a dice? Or a planned move on a board?
7. How does this become a game reality?
8. What limiting constraints are needed to make the game playable?

9. What are the operating instructions for the players?

   At this stage comes a self-testing device. Is it possible to set out rules in a 'How to play' framework, and make sense of them? The co-operation of someone so far uninvolved in the game is invaluable here. The rules, however, are not necessarily those which are given to players; better that their substance is explained in the classroom.

10. Does the game match up to reality?

   At this final stage, the model is held up to its source. It may be possible to have a playable, exciting game but one which is not a replica of the factors that actually exist. In the desire to motivate or to be 'fair to all', rules and interactions may have become detached from real-life sources. However good this game may be, it is not a simulation. Back to the drawing-board and start again . . .

Further readings

Games may again be sub-classified into those which aim mainly at cognitive objectives and those which are concerned with affective objectives.

Examples of available games in the *cognitive* domain include *Man in His Environment*, a game devised to help students understand some major ecological principles. This is produced by the Coca-Cola Export Corporation. The Sellotape *Airline Adventure Game* (produced by Sellotape) is a game about the operation of airlines along international air routes.

Examples of games which at least in part aim at *affective* objectives are *Streets Ahead*, a game designed to help children face and understand the problems of city life, by the Humanities Curriculum Project, and *Crisis in Lagia* – a simulation on aspects of war and society. Further examples may be found in Horn (1977), Taylor and Walford (1979), and Jaques and Tipper (1984).

11.5.4 Psychomotor skills – training simulators

In the remainder of this chapter we will be specially concerned with devices which communicate through the sense of touch and the kinaesthetic sense. Such concepts as hard and soft, hot and cold, rigid and flexible are established (at an early age) by confronting the learner with a series of objects, some hard, some soft, and identifying them as such. The child learns to discriminate first between very hard objects (like the floor he falls on) and very soft ones (like the porridge he spreads over the floor). In time he learns to classify objects as hard or soft with increasing precision.

Early perceptual learning

At a later stage of the learner's development, when he can understand a certain amount of verbal communications, you can cut corners. You might for example succeed in establishing the concepts flexible and rigid at that stage by simply saying: 'Flexible objects bend easily; rigid ones do not.' The intelligent student (or rather the one who is sufficiently prepared verbally) will probably straight away be able to classify the broomstick as rigid and the broom's bristles as flexible. He may still need quite a bit of practice, however, to classify different bristles according to flexibility.

Whereas he may even distinguish visually between the flexibility of a broom handle and the bristles, the fine discrimination between different bristle types may require a highly developed sense of touch, or a kinaesthetic sense, or both. Such precise discrimination skills often form part of industrial tasks. The training of such skills is often aided by special devices or simulators.

Another class of skills which rely on the kinaesthetic senses are skills of co-ordination – either the co-ordination of the position of the limbs (as in panel beating) or of movements as in many sports, driving or high-speed industrial operations. Again the learning of such skills is often aided by the use of specially designed devices.

We have seen the extent to which man relies on verbal communication. Visual and audio-visual methods tend to act as aids to the basic process of verbal communication. We did see, however, that certain information can only be effectively communicated by the use of non-verbal methods: characteristic noises or postures of mating birds, for example. We are now about to consider information which can only be communicated by the *feel* of the subject, or the feel of a certain action pattern.

Information used in learning a skill

Generally, one performs an action in order to achieve a specific result. A golfer's drive has the objective of getting the golf ball to move a precise distance in a precise direction. The novice soon learns this. He may then practise driving a golf ball down the fairway. Where the golf ball actually goes gives him an idea of his progress. Thus we have two forms of information in use: information on the purpose of an action (objectives, if you like) and information of the results (knowledge of results, or feedback).

This is still insufficient for efficient learning. The novice may note that one attempt was better than another, but will learn little unless he takes note of information about his actual movements. This may come either from some outside source, such as guidance from a trainer, or it can come from inside the learner. He may note the 'feel' of making a stroke which produces good results. A man may learn to drive a ball accurately without formal training. His technique may turn out to be unorthodox, but the results may nevertheless be quite good. Instruction and guidance by an expert may improve results or reduce learning time, but are not absolutely essential to the mastery of the skill. What is essential however, are the two forms of information feedback – knowledge of results (or *external feedback*)

Feedback

and knowledge of the 'feel' of the action (*internal feedback*). If either is removed or impaired, learning is inefficient. People who 'lack co-ordination' do not generally develop any high level of motor skill. If through illness they are completely lacking in the use of their kinaesthetic sense, they have difficulty in walking or in performing any controlled movement. They rely on visual information exclusively to control the position of their limbs. Similarly, learning to drive a golf ball in the dark, without knowledge of results, is not very effective. One might expect the learner to develop and practise a bad habit to perfection in these circumstances. The perfect slice!

There is strong evidence for the need for these two types of feedback. I mentioned earlier the experiments of Thorndike (1927) with groups of blindfolded people drawing lines on paper. Knowledge or results, in the form of saying 'right' or 'wrong' improved accuracy. Groups without knowledge of results lost accuracy. Further experiments on these lines indicated that the type of feedback supplied also affected accuracy. Feedback on the size of error was better than just 'right' or 'wrong'. Inconsistent feedback was worse than no information at all. Finally, persistent practice with no feedback resulted in progressively more consistent errors from the desired length. A 'bad habit' was being efficiently learned.

This illustrates an important change that occurs in the learning of a skill. In the early stages the learner relies heavily on external simuli. He must look down to find the gear lever. He must observe the ball in flight. As skill develops, internal, kinaesthetic stimuli increasingly take over control. He finds the gear lever 'instinctively' whatever gear he is in. He can tell whether his drive is successful almost before his swing is complete, just by the feel of it.

How to teach skills

Thorndike's experiments indicate one way of improving the conditions of learning a skill. If knowledge of results is not actually present in a particular task, some way of supplying it might be devised. For example, when tapping a screw thread in a hole, it is important not to put too much pressure on the tap. If you push too hard, the tap will break. The problem is to learn just how hard is too hard. One method is by trial and error which takes a long time and may be costly in replacement taps. If you can arrange for the tap to 'cry out' just before breaking point, then you might expect learning to be more efficient. You would certainly cut down on breakages.

Another method might be by guidance. The instructor may guide the student's hand while performing a job, or give him hints on what to watch for. In teaching a student to use a file, the instructor first imparts the correct stance and the correct way to hold the file. He may demonstrate the motions and then supervise, correct and even guide the student's motions. The golfer's swing is sometimes taught by strapping the novice in a harness, which controls the extent and direction of his motions.

When designing training tasks both the factors of feedback and guidance should be considered. They are not as simple as they appear at first sight. Any feedback won't do. Some guidance methods are better than others.

Action feedback

There are two types of feedback which may be present in a task. One tells the learner how well he has peformed – *knowledge of results*. The other tells him how he is performing right now – *knowledge of performance*. This second (termed *action feedback*)is of importance in continuous adjustment skills, like steering a car along a road. You are continuously using the visual feedback from the road to adjust your actions. However skilled the driver, he is technically out of control if all his lights ·fail on a dark night. Knowledge of results, on the other hand, only becomes apparent once the action is complete. Steering into a skid produces (generally) desirable results. Action feedback (in the form of visual and kinaesthetic information) tells us we are skidding. Previous learning tells us to steer into the skid. A comparison of the extent of our corrective action with the result it produces constitutes the basis for learning skid correction. Knowledge of results is therefore sometimes called *learning feedback*.

Learning feedback

Learning feedback is vital for efficient learning. Action feedback does not help much at all. This was demonstrated by an experiment performed by Annett and Kay (1957). Subjects were told to press down with a certain pressure on a spring balance. If they were allowed to see the scale while pressing (action feedback) they of course performed perfectly. If they were only allowed to see the scale after they had applied pressure (learning feedback) they initially made errors, but improved with practice. When, after an equal number of trials, all feedback was removed, the group that received learning feedback performed adequately for some time, but the group who had received continuuous action feedback immediately deterioriated. They had not learnt the 'feel' of the correct pressure. The learning feedback group's performance also tends to deteriorate in time if the feedback is withheld, but this happens more slowly. We might say that the group is 'forgetting' the feel of a two-pound pressure. This finding is important as well, as it indicates the limitations which some training devices may suffer from.

If the knowledge of results a training device supplies is quite different in form from that found 'on the job', the learning may not be permanent. Goldstein and Rittenhouse (1954) found that in training aeroplane gunners to aim on a simulator, performance could be vastly improved by supplying knowledge of results in the form of a buzzer whenever the gun was on target. When the aid was removed, however, performance rapidly deteriorated until it was much the same as people trained by normal direct methods. There seemed to be no long-term benefit whatever from using the extra artificial feedback.

Seymour (1954), on the other hand, used training devices successfully to teach the amount of pressure permissible in picking up fragile electrical insulators. He used dummy insulators which were spring loaded against micro switches and wired so that too much pressure gave a red light, the correct amount gave a white light and insufficient pressure gave no light at all. Other experiments have also given good results from the use of not normally available or 'artificial' knowledge of results during training. The evidence is conflicting and more research is needed, but it seems that success may depend on *what sort* of artificial feedback you use, and *how* you use it. How similar is the artificial feedback to that actually present in the task? How is the 'transfer of control' from the artificial feedback to the natural feedback effected?

For example, Annett's experiment with the spring balance gives better long-term learning if the subject is allowed to check his results only at alternative trials. Thus he follows each trial with artificial feedback by a trial in which he must rely on the natural feedback present in the task. Seymour's work shows similar results. Artificial feedback is supplied at progressively longer intervals till the learner does not need to rely on it at all.

The gun-aiming experiment described did not support this view. Intermittent supply of feedback was no better in achieving long-term learning. Perhaps the difference lies in the type of feedback and the information it gives. Gun aiming is a skill where there are degrees of error. You must recognize these degrees of error to apply appropriate degrees of correction. A buzzer is either on or off. It does not inform of the *degree* of error.

The scale reading in Annett's experiment does inform of the degree of error, and appropriate adjustments of pressure result in appropriate reductions of error. The artificial and natural feedback, although received through different senses, give the same sort of information.

Seymour's experiment is not so clear. The white light indicates a range of pressure which is safe. The learner may experiment for himself in adjusting pressure throughout the safe range. Perhaps, as in Annett's experiment, he can practise adjustments in pressure, and therefore the natural kinaesthetic feedback plays more of a part in the learning right from the start. It may on the other hand all boil down to the fact that most kinaesthetic skills are poorly developed and so show marked response to training, whereas the visual skill of gunners may be less prone to improvement.

These last observations are conjectures which could act as the subject for experimentation. However, we may make several practical suggestions on the basis of work so far completed:

How to train a psycho-motor skill

1. When training a skill, examine whether the normal method of training provides satisfactory knowledge of results.
2. When doing this, do not confuse action feedback with knowledge of results.
3. If the naturally present knowledge of results is not easily observable by the student (ie it uses undeveloped kinaesthetic or tactile senses), consider the possibilities of a training device which supplies more obvious feedback.
4. Try to arrange that the artificial feedback supplies information of a similar nature to that supplied by the natural feedback.
5. Try to arrange training so that the trainees occasionally rely on natural feedback alone, and progressively withdraw the artificial aids.

Types of guidance

We might guide the student in a learning task in a number of ways. We may give verbal guidance – 'Use your body weight!' We may demonstrate an action visually. We may actively guide the physical responses of the student.

The first two types of guidance are really supplying pre-knowledge; what to do and how to do it. The techniques are those discussed in the earlier sections. For example, when demonstrating ana ction it is best to demonstrate it as seen from the learner's viewpoint; hence one value of film or television in training skills. The decisions on what verbal knowledge is required to perform a task and how it should be taught spring from the task analysis.

It is the third type of guidance, actual physical control that can be built into training devices or simulators, that is our concern here. This can be achieved in two ways. You can physically 'force' the correct movements out of the learner (forced response), or you can allow the learner to make his own motions, but restrict the direction or extent of these motions (physical restriction). Both methods are used in training devices. We have already mentioned the harness used for training a golfer's swing. This is an example of physical restriction of the learner's movements. The learner makes his swing but he cannot deviate from the correct path. Of course, he may still produce a poor swing. He may not follow through as far as he should. His movements may be even more restricted than the harness allows. Many golfing coaches therefore employ the forced response techniques, by standing immediately behind the learner, holding the learner's wrists or club, and physically guiding the stroke every inch of the way. Such methods are of application to motor responses, where the extent of a movement or its exact path are critical. Physical restriction is often employed in training devices and simulators, by the use of stops at the end of a machine bed, for example. Forced response techniques are more often employed by instructors. They are rarely employed in training devices as it is difficult to construct a mechanism that would adequately simulate the required complexity of movement.

How effec- tive is guidance in skills training?
Both methods of guidance do produce training results. They have been employed for simple tasks such as the pencil tracing of mazes, and have been found to reduce training time appreciably. Holding (1965) describes an interesting series of experiments on the use of physical guidance. These are an adaptation of Thorndike's earlier line-drawing exercises. In this case a knob had to be moved a distance of four inches along a rod. One group acted as control, receiving no guidance or feedback. Another received forced guidance by means of a spring that towed the learner's hand through the appropriate distance. A third received a mixture of forced guidance and free practice. The fourth group practised in a physically restricted set-up – a stop was fixed at the 4-inch point. The last two groups received no guidance, but did receive knowledge of results 'à la Thorndike'. Group 5 had 'yes–no' feedback, and group 6 had feedback on the magnitude and direction of their errors. The restricted response method using a stop gave most effective learning. Then came: full knowledge of results, yes–no feedback, and finally forced response and the mixed method about equal last (but still producing an appreciable amount of learning). Holding argues that the relatively poor results of the forced response in this case were because the simulation was inappropriate. Instead of pushing the knob, the learner's hand was being pulled by the spring. A modified experiment where the final task involved the pulling of a handle, produced much better results for the forced response technique – superior in fact to the restricted guidance method.

The lessons for the training officer or instructor therefore are:

1. Restricting the possibilities for motion or forcing the correct movement can produce effective learning.
2. Restricting the extent or direction of motion (eg by stops or grooves) is easier to apply appropriately and can be expected to train as effectively as methods based on the supply of knowledge of results.
3. Forcing the response is more difficult to arrange (except by direct human effort) due to difficulties in simulating the exact condition. It can be as effective as restriction or feedback if applied well, but inappropriate forcing (eg pulling instead of pushing) reduces effectiveness drastically.

Simple training devices and simulators
Training devices need not be complex electronically controlled simulators, such as flight trainers. The complexity of a training device will naturally be a reflection of the complexity of the task being trained. The object of a flight simulator is to give the pilot every possible experience of flying without risking valuable lives and equipment. You therefore arrange for every possible relevant stimulus to be fed to the pilot. The ideal flight simulator would react to the pilot's responses in every detail – instrument reading, noise, vision through cockpit and the feeling of gravity changes through the seat of his pants. Simulators of such complexity are used in the training of astronauts, but the cost precludes their more general use. For many purposes a partial simulation suffices.

When a full task analysis is carried out, certain skill elements are often found to be particularly difficult to master. Such elements should be isolated and trained separately, irrespective of whether a progressive-parts training technique is being used for the whole task, or whether it is being practised all at once. Very often, simulation can help in training these elements.

The learning problems associated with the difficult element must be identified. This may involve detailed observation and questioning of skilled performers *and learners*. The questions to consider are:

1. How is the element learnt? What sort of a task is it? What senses are involved and how?
2. What is making the learning difficult? Lack of aptitude? Underdeveloped motor skills? Conflict with previous learning? Fear of equipment?

If the difficulty is due to certain defects of perception or muscular co-ordination, then the possibility of a special training exercise should be considered. This may take the form of eye-focusing exercises for inspection skills, or a special bit of equipment for sensory-motor skills. As an example of the design of training devices, let us consider once more the sheet metal and welding simulators presented earlier in this chapter (Figures 11.9 and 11.10). These are extremely simple devices, yet they have very significant effects on the rate of learning of the skills by novice trainees. This is the result of appropriate design which applies basic principles of learning through guidance and feedback, as described above.

12. Interactive computer-based learning

12.1 The field of study: computers in education

12.1.1 The impact of computers

Before we get down to the detailed study of computers as instructional media, let us get a clear overall view of the impact that computers have had on education and on training. This is, in fact, much more than the computer's potential to deliver instruction. The major impact of the proliferation of computers in just about all walks of life, has been on the *content* of education and training, rather than on the methods. As more and more people use computers in their work (and also their play), it has become necessary to include instruction *about* computers and computing in more and more courses.

The three waves of information technology

Seigel and Davis (1986) refer to three 'waves' of the technology and the related know-how. The first wave was related to the new technology itself – the design and programming of computers and computer applications. This involved a relatively small proportion of the population, who required highly technical, job-specific training in the sciences of computing and programming. The second wave came with the advent of the cheap microcomputer and its use by a much greater section of the population (including many teachers). This led to a 'hobbyist' approach to computing, everyone 'having a go' at programming and the growth of a movement in education towards 'computer literacy' for everyone (although what this means is different for just about every writer on the topic). Finally, the 'third wave' (which is just engulfing us) is characterized by the permeation of all sectors of social and professional activity by computer systems. This wave brings with it the need for a variety of new skills and attitudes, which will enable us to use these tools and systems efficiently, without necessarily being expert in the skills of programming, or having any specialist knowledge of computer science. In this 'third wave' people will use computers as today they use cars or television sets or telephones. They have to acquire the specialist knowledge and skills to control the equipment and get the best possible performance out of it, but they do not expect to have to fix it when it malfunctions, or devise new applications for it. They just acquire the equipment that is designed for the task they wish to perform, learn to use it efficiently and if it breaks down, or their requirements expand beyond the equipment's present capabilities, they call in a specialist. This image of three consecutive 'waves' (borrowed from Alvin Toffler, 1980) is useful in the educational computing context, as it illustrates the different, and changing, requirements for education and training *about* computers. We might refer to this as 'computers as content' in contrast to our main interest in this book in 'computers as instruments' in the education or training process. We shall not pursue very deeply this discussion of computers as something to learn about, other than to indicate that probably this part of the overall field will have a greater influence on change in education than the use of computers as something to learn *with*.

Computers as content of education

Computers as tools in education

We might also add that the two are to some extent inseparable. A good example is the effect on teaching methods that the mere existence of word processing, spreadsheets and database management software is already having. In most universities it is quite rare for students to type out their work on conventional typewriters. Soon, word processors will be as common in the secondary schools. As students become more skilled in the use of this tool, the way they think about written assignments is changing. Once written, a page or a paragraph is a block of information that has an entity of its own. It may be shifted about and pasted in at will. Experimental composition and rewriting become painless. What is written once, for one assignment, becomes easily usable as a component of a future paper. And why not? The student wrote it once and it has become part of his or her store of knowledge – the difference is that now a part of that store is not in the student's head, but in an external knowledge base on a diskette.

12.1.2 Describing the field

Figure 12.1 presents our view of the 'field' of discussion in respect of computers and education. Our field is divided into two main sectors, which we may call 'informatics as content of education' and 'informatics as an instrument of education'. This distinction separates the problems of designing curricula for computer specialists or for general computer literacy, from the problems of utilizing computers in the educational process. Interesting and important as the first of these two sectors is, we shall not be able to devote time and space to it in this book. Our aims here are concerned with the use of computers as an instrument of education. However, this is still an enormous field, as the right-hand half of Figure 12.1 attempts to show. We have divided this sector of the field into three sub-sectors, dealing respectively with the use of computers as an *administrative tool*,

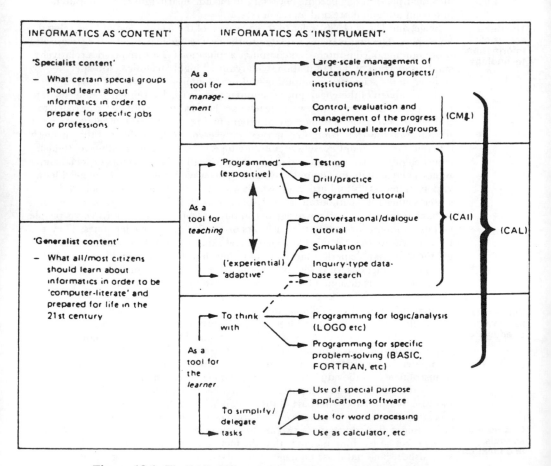

Figure 12.1 *The 'field' of 'Computers in education' divided into 'sectors' (as an aid to the analysis and discussion of the topic) (Romiszowski, 1986).*

as a tool to assist (or substitute) the teacher (a *teaching tool*) and as a tool to assist the learner – we prefer to call it a *learner's tool* (rather than a learning tool) for, as the diagram illustrates, the learner may use the computer to help him learn or to take over routine tasks and thus reduce the drudgery of the learning process.

CAI or CAL?   Alongside the specific examples of applications of computers in education (which we shall discuss more deeply later on), we have placed some brackets to indicate how we are using the three principal technical terms CAL, CAI and CML. Our usage does not necessarily agree with that of all other authors. Indeed every author seems to have his own definitions and classifications for the same technical terms. One marked difference is in the use of the terms 'Instruction' and 'Learning' on either side of the Atlantic. In the USA particularly, the term 'Instruction' tends to be used in a more global sense, for any type of teacher/learner interchange, whereas in Britain the term CAI has of late become restricted to 'programmed instruction' types of exercises, the preferred generic term being 'computer-assisted learning' (CAL). It seems that Canada, caught between the two influences, cannot make up its mind, although recent publications, such as *The Elements of CAL* (Godfrey and Sterling 1982) suggest that perhaps the British view – that *learning* may be assisted in many diverse ways but only some of them have the characteristics of true *instruction* – seems to be gaining ground.

However, detailed differences exist between the usage of CAL/CML/CAI in the works of British authors, even though they do agree that CAI is a subset of CAL. Some consider CMI (computer-managed instruction) as a variety of CAL. After all, the continuous formative evaluation of a student's progress and the feedback of the results, either to improve course materials, select different options or merely to inform the student of his progress/errors/weaknesses is one very effective way of assisting the learning process. Others exclude CML/CMI as a separate category, not a part of CAL in the strict sense. For Godfrey and Sterling, the development of a CML element is part and parcel of the development of *any* CAL materials (they refer to this as the 'tracking layer' in their model for CAL materials design). Nicholas Rushby, on the other hand, in his book *An Introduction to Educational Computing*, seems to separate these two modes, dealing with them in quite distinct chapters (Rushby, 1979). He also differs from us slightly in other aspects of terminology, using a four-paradigm classification of CAL:

1. The *instructional* paradigm (including our programmed tutorial, drill-and-practice and, *perhaps*, the conversational or diagnostic tutorial modes).
2. The *revelatory* paradigm (including, principally, the simulation mode, but perhaps as well the objectives-directed research of a complex informational database).
3. The *conjectural* paradigm (including model building and problem solving through programming – roughly equivalent to our category of 'learner's tool, to think with').
4. The *emancipatory* paradigm (including principally the use of the computer as a calculator/problem-solver (to take over the routine tasks) and also its use for 'serendipity' learning, or the 'browsing' through databases without clearly defined specific objectives.

The 'tutor, tool, tutee' model   Various authors have presented somewhat different schemata for organizing the different ways in which computers are being used in education and training. A simple but very useful classification was used by Taylor (1980) in his book *The Computer in the School: TUTOR, TOOL, TUTEE*. Taylor's TUTOR category includes most of the applications listed in our 'tool for TEACHING' sub-section. His TOOL category is equivalent to our 'tool for the LEARNER to SIMPLIFY or DELEGATE tasks'. His TUTEE category incudes most of the applications we would include in 'tools for the LEARNER to THINK WITH', especially the programming of computers in order to gain a deeper understanding of a given problem solving strategy or knowledge domain (as in the use of LOGO to gain insights into mathematics). In the remainder of this book, we shall occasionally use the 'tutor, tool, tutee' classification schemata as a quicker way of saying what the right-hand part of Figure 12.1 illustrates schematically. Note, however, that Taylor's classification does not include the upper sub-section of our schema; the use of the computer to manage the instructional process. This is because Taylor's schema is set up from the viewpoint of the learner – for example, the 'tutee' category contains applications in which the learner 'teaches' (programs) the computer and in this sense the computer becomes the learner's 'tutee'. Our schema is set up from multiple viewpoints – learner's, instructor's and manager's.

Yet another model

To close, we might mention Kearsley's (1983) classification. When discussing computer-based training (CBT), he divides the field into CMI, CAI and CAL as follows:

- CMI – Computer-Managed Instruction, which includes all the routine data processing tasks that an instructor might wish to have performed to assess students, revise materials.
- CAI – Computer-Assisted Instruction, which includes drill-and-practice, tutorial and Socratic (our dialogue) categories, but not testing (which is considered as a totally separate category) and
- CAL – Computer-Assisted Learning, which is taken to include simulations and games, database search/inquiry methods and programming of computers. Note that this classification uses similar terminology with quite different meanings from our own. Kearsley's use of 'CAL', is quite different. Whereas, in Figure 12.1 CAI is seen as a sub-set of a much broader category termed CAL; he uses these two terms as mutually exclusive sub-categories of computer-based training (CBT), or, presumably, education (CBE).

The other difference concerns the breadth of the concept of 'instruction'. Kearsley's categories imply that simulations and games and database-search exercises are not examples of 'instructional' materials. We defined the term 'instruction' somewhat more broadly in Chapter 1. Whereas some existing examples of these types of computer applications would not qualify to be considered instructional systems or system components, there are many that do qualify to be thus classified.

Let us come back to earth, however, from these rather philosophical comments, to stress that the reader might come across a variety of classification systems in the literature, but the example applications being classified are in all cases the same. Let us proceed, therefore, to an analysis of the most common types of applications.

12.2 The computer as instrument for learning

12.2.1 Computer-managed instruction (CMI)

Computer-managed instruction (CMI) can best he defined as the use of computer programs for the on-line management of the instructional process. This may include the planning, organizing, controlling and evaluation functions as they occur *during* the instructional process. I stress the word *during*, to exclude the planning and organizing that occurs in the early stages of the instructional design/development process and the controlling and evaluation that occurs at the macro level *after* a particular course of instruction has been given. We are restricting CMI to the management of the teaching/learning process.

Built-in or stand-alone CMI

CMI is not a recent concept. Indeed, the useof the computer to store, analyse and interpret data about a process is a very typical type of application. No wonder that CMI was one of the first applications of computing to the instructional process. Note that CMI can be an integral feature of a computer-assisted or administered (CAI) instructional system, or it can be a 'stand-alone' application of computer-based management of more or less conventional classroom instruction. As such, it may use an existing computer, installed for other data processing purposes, to assist the classroom teachers in the management of their courses.

Built-in   Almost all serious CAI systems do have a built-in CMI component. However, in many microcomputer-based systems of recent years this is quite rudimentary, restricted perhaps to the scoring of a student's success on the questions in a given lesson and summarizing this in a final report. As soon as the student switches the computer off, these data may be lost. Other micro-based systems are a little more sophisticated, in that they store these student records on the diskette, allowing more sophisticated analyses of results by the instructor/author.

Computer-based CAI systems, designed for use by large numbers of students at distributed terminals, are much stronger on CMI. A good example is the PLATO Learning Management (PLM) system built into Control Data's PLATO computer-based-instruction system. We shall discuss the PLATO system in more detail later, when we analyse tutorial CAI. For the time being, Figure 12.2 serves to show the wealth of data storage, organization and analysis options open to the

---

See or Change Someone's Record
  Change password
  Change spelling of name
  Curriculum status
    Student progress in the curriculum, course, module, and objective.
  Leave a message
  See or change data collection options
  Special options
    See student variables, see router variables, change current lesson, change current unit

Roster Operations
  See or change someone's record
  See the roster of people
  Add someone to the roster
  Delete someone from the roster
  Leave a message for someone
  See who is now running

Statistics on Records
  Statistics on sign-on and lesson usage
  PLM summary statistics
    Name lists
      Course record data, course progress summary, module progress summary, last module mastery dates.
    Average progress data
      Tables and graphs for summary statistics for each course in the curriculum.
    Scheduling reports
      Deviations from schedule, projected student progress, projected course completion dates, print student schedules.

Special Options
  Set up a template record
    Select a user record to serve as a template for all new records or for existing records.
  Change group-wide data collection options
  Copy a record from another group
  Delete all records
  Print group records data
    Print the total amount of time signed on for each record in the group.

Curriculum Design
  Edit or inspect curriculum
  PLM group controls
    Scheduling
      Determines whether scheduling will be based on course or module durations; or on instructor-specified course completion dates.
    Student gradebook access
    Response recording
      Activates the data collection features of the PLM system.
    Test access controls
      Controls student access to tests.
    Test lockout controls
      Specifies the conditions under which students are allowed to take module tests.
    Test interruption controls
      Determines which options are offered to students when they press SHIFT-STOP during a test.
    Testing and printing controls
      Specifies if students can select testing mode, students must take on-line tests, or students must take off-line tests; allow test question feedback on printed test; allow student to print study assignments; printer type.

Space Usage Information
  Total parts used in the group, total 64-word records, and total names available.

Group Description
  Group information
    Group director information, group information.
  Associated files
    Student notes, data collection, TERM-ask group, routers, curriculum file.
  Security codewords

People Currently Running

Figure 12.2 *PLM instructor options available on PLATO.*

instructor using the PLATO system. Apart from such obvious facilities as the recording and monitoring of student progress, the system offers very extensive formative evaluation possibilities geared to both the diagnosis and correction of weaknesses in the instructional materials design, as well as individual weaknesses and difficulties of each student. Other facilities include: control over 'who has access to what', allowing one to vary the extent of learner control over the learning process, as well as access to progress statistics; an electronic mail facility allowing individual communication between instructor and student or between students.

– Stand-alone dedicated systems

A large-scale example of the second type of application was PROJECT PLAN, which was developed in the late 1960s in the USA. This project used computer-marked objective tests, to accompany all the primary and some of the secondary school curriculum in American schools. The schools subscribing to the system were equipped with special 'post office' terminals, one to a classroom. After covering a particular unit, of, say, three or four objectives, the learners, either individually or as groups, would take a pre-printed objective test, in multiple-choice format. They would respond on special cards, marking the choices by scoring the appropriate letters (A, B, C, or D) alongside the question's number, already pre-printed on the cards. They would also mark their individual code numbers. Then they would 'post' the cards into a slot of the terminal, to update their individual file, kept in a computer at a distance. The individual student received feedback of results and suggestions for further study. The teacher could compare the individual student's progress with that of his group and of other students and groups in other schools, right across the country. The computer was programmed to follow a highly complex control algorithm, that could use this extremely large bank of data to generate individual student profiles, individual guidance, suggestions of the best methods and materials of study for particular students or particular course objectives, predictions of success in particular types of career and so on. The system involved several thousand American schoolchildren and used an even larger database on long-term success in life, related to school performance, which had been collected in an earlier project – PROJECT TALENT – that had involved five million children. (Flanagan, 1968.)

Project PLAN used a large mainframe computer dedicated to the instructional management functions. During the life of the project, which was sponsored by the Westinghouse Corporation, schools on both sides of the USA were effectively in communication, linked through the one computer at Westinghouse in California. There were even some American schools as far away as Saudi Arabia, receiving on-line management services from the one computer. This may be one of the principal reasons why the project lasted only a few years. At that time – late 1960s and early 1970s – the costs of running such a service were very high, and the long distance data communication links were not all that reliable. Neither of these limitations are true today and, although project PLAN is no longer with us, many similar large-scale CMI systems are currently operating in various countries. Perhaps one of the biggest is the system operated by the US Navy. However, the British Open University operates a somewhat more limited sort of CMI capability (the data are not so detailed nor are they collected as frequently, but there is a higher number of students involved). Other Open learning systems are following suit, the Open University of China for example, with over one million students, would have difficulty in achieving effective instructional management without extensive computer assistance.

Stand-alone time-sharing systems

However, stand-alone CMI systems do not have to be so big, nor do they need a dedicated computer system. Some of the earliest systematic research and development on computers in education used a little bit of spare time in an existing multi-purpose computer to manage classroom-based or print-based programmed instructional systems. At the University of Aston in Birmingham, UK, Croxton and Martin (1970) added a simple computer-based management system to an existing engineering structures course, using printed modules, and in so doing more than doubled the frequency of distinction passes (equivalent to A grades) on final national examinations. At the Middlesex Polytechnic in London,

I developed a CMI system to accompany a remedial mathematics course offered to freshman undergraduates in social sciences as a totally individualized programmed instruction unit of 20 modules. The roles of student, computer and tutor are shown in Figure 12.3. The tutor would only be involved in the teaching role with those students and on those modules where the self-instructional materials had proved to be inadequate. The CMI system enabled the course to run successfully on a full mastery-learning model of control (all students must pass on all relevant modules) with an intake of over 600 students and a tutor/student ratio of 1/300 (Romiszowski, 1969).

The traditional 'system-control' model of CMI

A diagram similar to Figure 12.3 was suggested by Leiblum (1982 based on Rushby, 1979) as a general model of the CMI process. This model is seen to assume three general characteristics for the course that is being managed. These are:

1. *Individualization.* The instruction is assumed to be individualized to a greater or lesser extent, in terms of learning rate, methods, media, even content and objectives in some cases.
2. *Behavioural objectives.* The instruction is assumed to be designed on the basis of a task analysis that established a set of specific behavioural objectives (and sometimes a learning sequence).
3. *Educational technology principles.* The instruction is assumed to be designed/developed in accordance with general educational technology principles, including some model for the selection of methods and media, some model for the measurement and control of mastery of the pre-specified objectives, and so on.

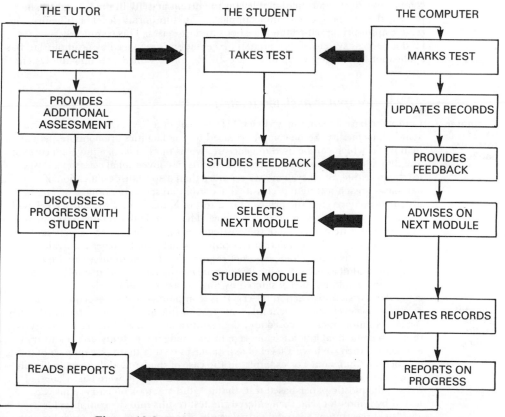

Figure 12.3 *Function of CMI in the Enfield remedial mathematics system.*
(Romiszowski, 1969)

A 'learner-control' model of CMI

These three assumptions are generally apparent in the majority of CMI systems developed to date. However, in recent years, with the development of database management technology, there is a new trend that may prove very important. This is the trend towards the structuring of bodies of knowledge (both specific subject matter and specialist expert problem-solving know-how) in the form of so called 'knowledge bases'. Such knowledge bases are essential components of the new 'AI' generation of problem-solving software (the so-called 'expert systems'), but they may also be used as resources by learners to identify the knowledge required for a purpose of the learner's own choosing. The management system of such a knowledge base is not centred on specific behavioural objectives, but must identify and present the knowledge content relevant to some personal objective that the learner brings to the exercise, which may not be fully predictable in advance. Such knowledge-base management systems may be important elements in CMI systems of the future. An example of such a system is embedded in a digital electronics course I helped to develop for the rapid and flexible retraining/updating of electronics technicians (Arce and Romiszowski, 1985, Romiszowski, 1986). This is basically a laboratory/workshop-based course, organized in a series of two-week modules. The instructor spends most of his or her time on the practical laboratory/workshop exercises. The underlying electronics, mathematics and logic theory is available in a large number of reference sheets (information 'maps') which are organized in the form of a knowledge base. This is intended to include all the knowledge (both basic theory and specific technical/practical know-how) that an electronics technician working with digital logic circuits may require, whatever the specific industry/application/state of sophistication of the technology, etc. Anyone entering the course (whatever the module, whatever his or her current state of knowledge and learning skills) should be able to locate, quickly and completely, all the information relevant to current activity in the laboratory, be presented with specific relevant examples, at an appropriate level of difficulty, and receive appropriate self-testing questions and exercises. This completely random-access system of information presentation is managed by a simple database applications package (set up in D-base 2). Figure 12.4 illustrates how the system operates.

12.2.2 Computer-assisted testing

Computer-based test-item banks

Computer-based testing may (like CMI) be part of a CAI system, or may be a stand-alone facility. Some computer-based testing facilities are no more than an item bank, which can be used to generate two or more tests of equivalent content and difficulty, to be used at different moments in conventional classroom teaching/testing. Such systems are no more than a specialist application of databases – each test item is classified according to several parameters. The instructor may request the print-out of a test of X items, of Y difficulty level, with Z content-type on a given set of objectives. The item bank contains a sufficient number of test items in each of these categories to enable random selection of items to generate several quite different test-papers which are, however, equivalent. Such an application is stand-alone, does not require the student to interact with the computer and does not score the test or analyse the results. As it stands, such an application would not be considered by anyone as an example of computer-assisted-instruction (CAI). It is 'computer-assisted-test construction'.

Computer-based on-line testing

When, however, the student takes the test on-line at a computer terminal, when the test is automatically scored and the results analysed, and when that analysis results in some final guidance message to the student (eg 'study unit 5 and try the test again') then we have a level of assistance in testing that takes on part of the instructional function. For example, in the case of the 20-module remedial maths course mentioned earlier, early versions of the CMI system were based on a 20-part diagnostic paper-based test, that all students took on entry. This was scored by a monitor who then entered the test results into the computer for analysis, prescription of an individual study plan (which of the 20 modules each

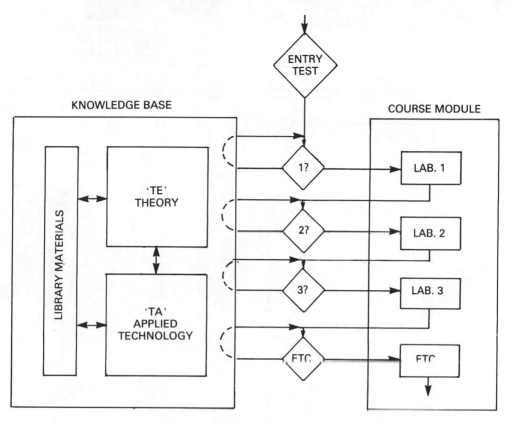

Figure 12.4 *Flow chart showing the way that a modular laboratory course interfaces with a knowledge base, which can be accessed by microcomputer searching for keywords (Arce and Romiszowski, 1985).*

student should study) and control of student progress. In later versions, however, the students would take the diagnostic test on-line. This offered one immediate benefit. In the earlier system, a weak student would spend a lot of time getting all the items of the massive diagnostic test wrong (and would get discouraged in the process). When taken on-line, the computer keeps track of student performance as he or she takes the test, and, as soon as error rates on a given section of the test exceed acceptable limits, the testing stops, a partial prescription (to study the relevant programmed instruction module) is given and the student goes off to pick up the module in the resource centre. After studying, the student returns to the computer terminal, automatically picks up the test at the point where he or she had difficulties, gets post-tested on the skills just studied (but with items that are selected to be new) hopefully succeeds this time and proceeds further into the diagnostic system until another weakness is identified and the appropriate study module is prescribed. In this set-up, the diagnostic pre-testing and post-testing are completely administered and managed by the computer. These are, of course, essential components of the instructional system, so we can look on this computer-assisted testing procedure as a form of partial CAI. It would only require the study material to be converted into computer-based information screens, to transform the whole system into a CAI tutorial. Figure 12.5 illustrates the computer-based testing procedure used in this example. Note how the same diagram could represent a CAI tutorial if we but change the presentation media.

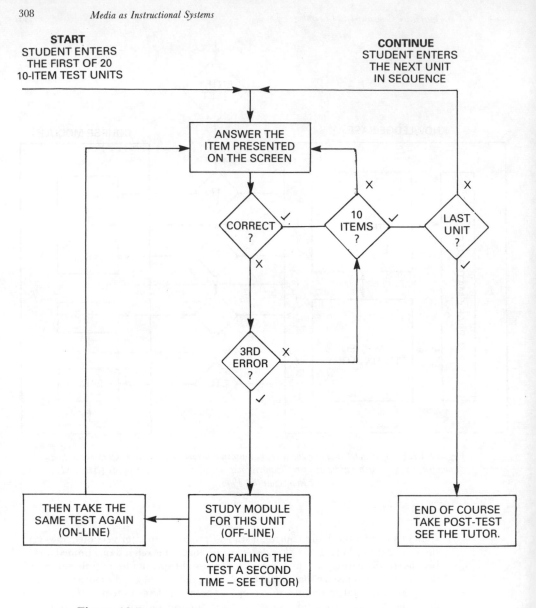

Figure 12.5 *An adaptive, on-line, pre-testing procedure used in a remedial mathematics course (studied off-line by printed modules (Romiszowski, 1969)).*

12.2.3 Drill and practice

Early re-search at Stanford University

Some of the earliest research and development related to drill and practice exercises on computers was performed by Patrick Suppes and his collaborators at Stanford University in the 1960s (Suppes *et al.*, 1968). The major findings of these studies supported the thesis that, at least in the area of mathematical skills, well designed drill and practice routines could develop higher levels of competence, in less time than was normally the case when other means of organizing the practice sessions were tried.

Since those early days, the number of different drill applications has increased and, of course, the costs of computers and software development have fallen, turning Suppes' effective, but exceedingly expensive, techniques into everyday reality. The type of sophisticated, matrix-based, model of complexity and difficulty in a given set of problems, may be quite easily accommodated in even quite a modest computer. As a guide, the memory needed to run the type of complex drill and practice routines designed by Suppes is much less than that required to run a reasonably sophisticated version of VISICALC, SUPERCALC or one of the other spreadsheet programs now available for most home computers in the 32K RAM or upwards range of memory.

Figure 12.6 shows the basic organization of a set of practice maths problems in a given skill domain (say the division of fractions). The practice items are classified according to complexity (how many and how many different operations must be carried out) and difficulty (how difficult do students typically find this example, within a set of similar examples of equivalent complexity). Depending on success in correct solution of examples at a given point of complexity and difficulty, students will progress to more challenging examples, or get more practice at lower levels.

The real importance of drill-and-practice

This mode is unduly criticized by some people, as being a 'lesser form' of CAI. We would not agree. There are, of course, whole areas of the curriculum and whole classes of objectives, for which this mode of practice is not appropriate. However, there are also whole areas where some form of drilling is necessary in order to develop basic skills or to reinforce essential knowledge. No one learns a foreign vocabulary without the need to practise and repeat the words. This may occur in the natural context of using the language. But if one is in a hurry, some artificial drilling exercise is needed. If the computer can offer entertaining and efficient drill exercises at an economic cost, there is nothing 'second class' about it. If a clerk has to develop a high level of skill in the performance of a routine task,

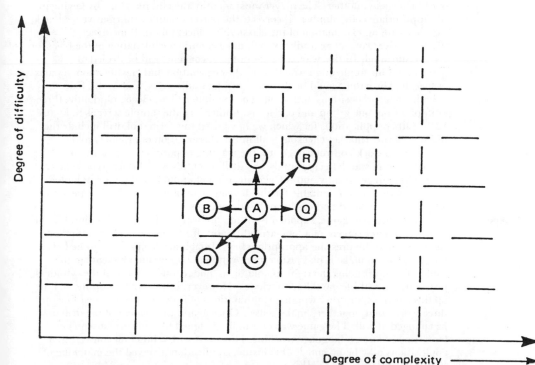

Figure 12.6 *A matrix for the classifying of problems according to complexity (number of different operations to be carried out) and difficulty (probability of error).*

such as the error-free calculation of pay-as-you-earn tax deductions from employees' wage packets and a computer-based drill proves to be the most effective and efficient means of developing this skill, why should we frown on this form of application?

We are rather of the opinion that drill and practice, though not very spectacular, is destined to be one of the main uses of CAI, as long as people have to learn routine and repetitive tasks of any nature.

Drill and practice 'shells' – prepare your own exercises

A number of versatile packages, rather like the test packages described earlier, are now available, that allow the teacher to change the content of the exercise while maintaining the general format of the exercise. The difference between these drill exercises and the test packages mentioned earlier, is in the form of feedback supplied to the student and in the conscious effort to develop the mastery of specific objectives. Once again, many of these exercises are disguised as games and are often, indeed, based on well known games, adapted to the computer-based format. Some of these, marketed by Wida Software, are specifically designed to develop associations, as in the learning of a new vocabulary. One version is an adaptation of the card game of SNAP. Two words or phrases appear on the screen at any one time, one in each language. The words change in a random fashion, first one then the other. At times, the two words which are visible are equivalent – in that case, the player must register that he/she observed the association, by depressing a key. If the key is not depressed within a certain time limit, the computer gains a point. If the player responds within the time limit, he/she gains a point. There are nine different speeds of play that can be pre-set at the beginning of the exercise. The game can be used for any association-learning, where rapid identification and response is an asset; eg in understanding a foreign spoken conversation, in learning map codes and conventions, in identifying traffic signs and in many other association and discrimination learning situations.

Odd man out

Another exercise, named ODD MAN OUT, presents four words or short phrases on the screen, three of which belong to one class and one (the 'odd man out') belongs to another. The player must identify the odd man out, by keying in the appropriate code number. If correct, the player obtains confirmative feedback, together with an explanation of the classifying concept used. If incorrect, the player receives corrective feedback and, once again, an explanation of the basis for the classification. In this way, a whole range of concepts can be drilled to perfection. One application would be in the recognition and classification of parts of speech. The game would be 'loaded' with four adjectives, four verbs, four adverbs, four prepositions and so on. The computer then selects, randomly, three examples from one group and one from another (see the sample screens in Figure 12.7). Other applications for which we have used this format of drill include the training of supermarket checkout staff in the classification of products sold according to stock-control categories, the training of postmen to classify streets according to postal delivery rounds, the drilling of 'town and river' type of factual information in geography and the classification of animals and plants in biology. It is a drill format that is suitable for the development of most concepts, especially groups of interrelated and easily confused concepts.

Jackpot

Yet another drill game, supplied by Wida Software, is based on the simulation, on the computer screen, of a 'one-armed bandit' fruit machine. Three cylinders can be rotated, by pressing appropriate keys. Imaginary 'coins' have to be fed to the computer to make it play. At certain, randomly occurring moments in the game, the player gains the right to hold or to 'nudge' one or more of the cylinders, just as in the real-life gambling machines. However, instead of attempting to line up three lemons, or other winning combinations of fruit, the player must line up three words that, together, 'make sense'. Once again, the content of the drill may be changed at will. The game was originally designed to drill correct sentence formation in foreign language teaching. However, with a bit of ingenuity, other applications may be invented. One history application involved the matching of WHO did WHAT and WHEN.

This last example, although a simulation of a sort, is not the type of CAI mode

(a) ODD MAN OUT

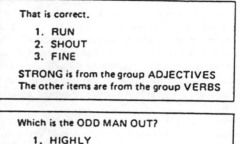

Which is the ODD MAN OUT?

1. RUN
2. SHOUT
3. FINE
4. STRONG

(Student types in — 4)

That is correct.

1. RUN
2. SHOUT
3. FINE

STRONG is from the group ADJECTIVES
The other items are from the group VERBS

Which is the ODD MAN OUT?

1. HIGHLY
2. VERY
3. HIGH
4. ALMOST

(b) JACKPOT

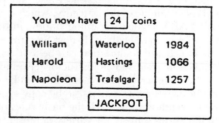

You now have 24 coins

William	Waterloo	1984
Harold	Hastings	1066
Napoleon	Trafalgar	1257

JACKPOT

Figure 12.7 *Sample screens from the games 'ODD MAN OUT' and 'JACKPOT'.*

referred to as 'simulation'. The type of instructional process is very much a drill of a specific skill or body of knowledge, that has previously been learnt. An essential aspect of the 'simulation' mode, is that the student learns experientially how a particular system behaves under certain conditions, by 'playing' with the model of the system, which is the basis of the simulation. In the fruit machine example, the player 'plays' the machine, but does not play with the model on which the fruit machine operates and learns nothing of a general nature about the probabilities of winning and losing, how they are controlled and how they are stacked in favour of the machine (at least, there is no intention on the part of the instructional designer to promote any such learning).

Drill and practice of manual skills on simulators

However, simulators, based on computers, have many applications in the drill and practice mode. A classic and very illuminating example is Gordon Pask's SAKI (Self Adaptive Keyboard Instructor), developed in the early 1960s, but only recently generally available, due to the fall of computer prices. The SAKI machine was initially devised to train the skills of punching a numerical keypad of ten digits. A later, more sophisticated version was developed to train and drill typing skills. The trainee is presented with a keyboard that has no markings on the keys and two screens. One screen presents information to be typed and the other shows a picture of the keyboard layout on which the keys light up to indicate the position of the key to be pressed at a given moment. The trainee approaches the simulator after some initial instruction on correct technique, typing rhythm and related essential knowledge.

Randomly selected letters appear on screen 1 and the position of each appropriate key is 'cued' by the lights that appear on the simulated keyboard on screen 2. As practice progresses, the general speed of presentation of data to be typed increases, and the intensity of the lights on the simulated keyboard decreases. However, all this happens in function of the error pattern and response rate of the trainee. He/she gets longer to respond to the letters which give difficulty, gets more intense cues and over a longer period of time for these letters and, furthermore, these letters begin to occur at a frequency proportional to their level of difficulty. All this occurs in response to a particular trainee's individual pattern of errors. He/she gets more practice, more time to respond and more help, adjusted on a continuous, 'on-line' basis b y the control algorithm built into the trainer. This highly adaptive learning environment is extremely efficient, leading typical learners to achieve first-rate typing speeds in only a few hours of drill and practice.

Similar adaptive, computer-based, training devices now are fairly common for developing psychomotor and perceptual skills, such as radar tracking, missile firing and aircraft gunnery. Many arcade and home video games also develop, perhaps not all that intentionally, certain basic coordination or manipulation skills. It is more difficult to classify such devices as the full-scale flight simulators, or Moore's (1962) 'talking typewriter' used for the automated teaching of writing and reading skills. Basically, they too are simulated environments that provide the opportunity for intensive practice of some basic skills. However, a lot of initial learning (including basic principles) may also take place during the experience.

An illustrative example of this category, which contrasts with the SAKI system, is the EASYLEARN keyboard training station, initially developed for the British Post Office and now marketed by Hi-Port Systems in the United Kingdom. This is a full-function keyboard trainer, that can be used as a stand-alone individual trainer, or linked in groups to an instructor terminal, for use as a form of learning laboratory. Only one screen is used and this can be used to present a variety of displays, including stimulus material to be copy-typed by the trainee and explanatory presentations, to teach the basic rules of efficient keyboard technique. Figure 12.8 illustrates some of the variety of presentations that the trainee receives at different stages of the program. The system may be used in the 'conditional' mode (akin to a tutorial) in which trainees only progress to new material after a correct response and correction of any errors, or in the 'unconditional' mode (pure drill and practice) which allows progress irrespective of errors.

12.2.4 *The 'programmed' tutorial mode of CAI*

The programmed tutorial mode of CAI is indeed akin to 'computer-based programmed instruction'. All the most commonly used techniques of the early days of programmed instruction are now being revived and applied in the design of CAI programmed tutorial sequences. Both linear and branching structures are used, though many people argue that the use of a computer to present a linear instructional sequence is rather like using a steam-hammer to crack a nut. This may, in general, be true, though there are some instances in which computer-generated effects or the computer control of ancillary media or equipment, may justify the application.

The possibilities for creative use of branching

In relation to branching, the computer opens up a range of possibilities that would have been difficult to arrange in the scrambled text, or primitive teaching machine, days of the 1960s. Theoretically, the computer can be programmed to branch to any number of alternatives, not to a limit of four or five at most,

(a) Here, the student is to type 'E', having the 'home' keys as a guide. Note that the 'D' is underlined, to show the finger to be used.

Lesson material . . . . . .

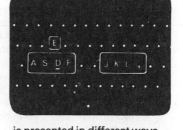

. . . . . . is presented in different ways

(b) Later, the 'E' has to be hit with much lower levels of visual help. Only the general layout of the keyboard is indicated by the dots.

. . . increasing the level of difficulty

(c) Later still, combinations of letters are typed at a rate controlled by the movement of the dot, which is currently under 'C'. The rate responds to student error-rate.

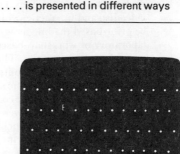

until the trainee responds unaided

(d) Finally, full copy-typing exercises are performed still under control of the moving dot. The rate progressively increases as student develops skill.

(*Hi-Port Systems, Lee on Solent, U.K.*)

. . . with confidence.

Figure 12.8 *The 'Easylearn' keyboard trainer.*

restricted by the number of plausible choices that the instructional designer can invent for one given multiple choice question, and also by the difficulty of organizing the pages in a scrambled text when there are very many different routes through the book.

In theory, a large library of computer-based instructional materials could be cross-referenced and indexed in a way that permitted students to back-track to any prerequisite learning that has become necessary in a new context but has unfortunately been forgotten through lack of use. Branching decisions, to faster or slower streams of instructional presentation, can be taken on the basis of a cumulative analysis of several responses over time and not just on the last, possibly atypical, response made. A variety of other non-computer-based materials may be incorporated into the system, their use being prescribed by the diagnoses of individual student progress and needs, that are constantly being prepared and updated by the computer. These alternative materials may be visual, as in videodisc and interactive videocassette systems already on the market. They may be print-based reading assignments, annotated bibliographies for free study, laboratory or workshop-based experiments and practical exercises, or specific group-learning activities. They may be all of these, knitted into a complex, multi-media, computer-controlled, truly individualized instructional system.

The reality is not always that creative

Unfortunately, in practice, few real CAI systems exploit these possibilities to the full. Too many are totally computer-based when they could be more effective and more economical if they were partly based on other media. Too many are a mixture of linear and branching sequences, not very different from programs that actually existed in print and paper form some 20 years ago. Too many are not even good examples of the instructional programming art. We have seen examples of ostensibly CAI systems that did not really differ much from a standard textbook – presented electronically. They did not even follow the three basic principles of instructional programming:

- Active participation, by learners, in the learning process.
- Immediate knowledge of results and corrective feedback.
- Avoidance of excessive errors on the part of the learners.

Still less did they show creativity and perspicacity in the analysis of typical students' errors and difficulties, and the design of appropriate instructional solutions.

For want of a better starting point, the basic principles and techniques of programmed instruction, which have stood the test of time, should be systematically and creatively applied in the design of programmed tutorial CAI.

An example

However, if one merely applies the basic techniques of programmed instruction, it is often difficult to justify the use of a computer to present the material. Figures 12.9 and 12.10 illustrate this. Figure 12.9 presents the original version of a step in a CAI sequence on set theory. This step introduces the concept of 'UNION'. It is reasonably well designed in that it supplements the formal definition by an example (albeit a generalized example presented in abstract Venn-diagram notation – a practical example might enhance the basic presentation). Then the exercise that follows tests comprehension of the concept, by application to a specific case. It would have been better, though, to ask students to generate a response rather than merely selecting one from a set of suggestions. This is the difference between construction and recognition of an appropriate response. However, the author seems to have been so conditioned by the multiple-choice single-letter response format that was required by early teaching machines and most 'scrambled text' branching programs, that he/she has overlooked that in a computer-based application we can ask the student to construct a response and then write a routine to analyse and classify any response in relation to its source of error, thus matching it to an appropriate feedback comment.

The modification in the method of asking for a response, introduced in Figure 12.10, is the least that could be done in order to make use of the capabilities that computers offer over and above those present in textual presentation. But we can

Union of two sets

The union of two sets is the set that contains all the elements of one set and all the elements of the other. The Venn diagram illustrates this.

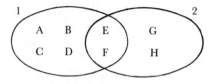

The union of sets 1 (A, B, C, D, E, F) and 2 (E, F, G, H) is a set with the elements (A, B, C, D, E, F, G, H)

Rank No.	Name	Score
1	Mary	95
2	John	88
3	Peter	76
3	Maggie	70
5	Joan	66
6	Paul	58
7	Annie	45
8	Mark	35

In the test results presented here, what elements are included in the union of the set 'girls' and the set 'passing grade' given that the pass mark is 50.

.... rank nos. (12345678) .... PRESS A
(145) .... PRESS B
(1457) .... PRESS C
(1234567)... PRESS D
(123456) .... PRESS E

Your response: B
You seem to have misunderstood the question, or you have not understood the definition given above. Your response is the INTERSECTION of 'girls' and 'passing grade'. Reread the definition of UNION and select another response.

Figure 12.9 *One step from a tutorial CAI sequence on set theory. Why use a computer to present this?*

Union of two sets
The union of two sets is the set that contain all the elements of one set and all the elements of the other. The Venn diagram illustrates this.

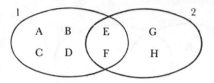

The union of sets 1 (A, B, C, D, E, F) and set 2 (E, F, G, H) is a set with the elements (A, B, C, D, E, F, G, H)

Rank No.	Name	Test score
1	Mary	95
2	John	88
3	Peter	76
4	Maggie	70
5	Joan	66
6	Paul	58
7	Annie	45
8	Mark	35

In the test results presented here, what elements are included in the union of the set 'girls' and the set 'passing grade', given that one must score at least 50 to pass? (RESPOND BY KEYING IN THE RANK NUMBERS OF THE STUDENTS YOU WOULD INCLUDE AS ELEMENTS OF THIS NEW SET)

YOUR RESPONSE 1 4 5
You seem to be confusing UNION and INTERSECTION, (which you studied earlier). You have listed the GIRLS WHO GOT A PASSING GRADE (ie the elements that are common to both 'girls' and 'passing grade'). Read the definition of UNION given above once more
Then

If you want to attempt the same question again,   PRESS 1
If you want another example of UNION of two sets,   PRESS 2
If you wish to backtrack to review INTERSECTION,   PRESS 3

Figure 12.10 *A somewhat improved version of the CAI step originally presented in Figure 13.9.*

do more. The feedback comments in the two versions illustrate another point. In the original version, the feedback is very categorical and the corrective strategy is to suggest re-reading the present screen of information and try to answer again. This is a further legacy of print-based self instruction. Any more complex branching would lead to excessive page turning and any benefit from enrichment of the branching might be outweighed by lost time looking for the correct page and the possibility of losing one's place altogether. When presented by computer, however, any amount of to and fro branching can be handled quickly and smoothly. As the error illustrated may be a mere slip on the part of the student, or may have deeper causes, why not plan for alternative forms of corrective feedback. We can allow for the student who immediately sees his error when presented with the feedback message and for the student who found the bare formal definition insufficiently clear and would like more and more practical examples to improve his understanding of the new concept. We can allow for the very unsure student, who would like to back track to the earlier concept that he has confused with the new one. In Figure 12.10, we have left these options under student control (applying the principle of learner control), but we could bring these alternatives under program control, by asking subsidiary questions which would help to diagnose the seriousness and source of the individual student's misconception.

Another possible enhancement that would be easy to introduce would be the substitution of a different practice example of equivalent difficulty for each subsequent wrong answer, so that students do not have the chance to zero in on the correct answer by a process of trial and error. One could, of course, use many other computer-based tricks, like animating the Venn diagrams and showing the union of two sets forming a new set with all the elements included in one circle. Whether this would enhance learning, or would just be a gimmicky application of the 'bells and whistles', is a moot point. Finally, of course, we could abandon the basic original tutorial design and opt for a discovery-learning conversational strategy, or a simulation perhaps – if we can justify it.

12.2.5. Conversational or dialogue tutorial CAI

'Intelligent' CAI   There are many different approaches that may be classified in this category of CAI. Some are referred to as 'Socratic' dialogue and are based on a mixed-initiative strategy, where both computer and student may either ask or respond to questions. Such tutorials are based on 'artificial intelligence' (AI) models of the teaching learning process and require very complicated and time consuming programming in little used and difficult to learn programming languages, such as Lisp or Prolog. It is not surprising, therefore that, at the time of writing most of these systems are research laboratory playthings, rather than widely used and practically cost-effective instructional systems. They include such early systems as SCHOLAR (Carbonnell, 1970), and CASTE (Pask and Scott, 1973) and more recent ones such as SOPHIE (Brown, Burton and deKleer, 1982). They differ very much from each other in terms of the specific models for interaction and learning/teaching upon which they operate. But they have the common element of adaptiveness to the individual learner by some means of 'learning about the learner'. This is where they attempt to model the expert human tutor more closely than other forms of CAI and, therefore, they have gained the popular name of 'intelligent tutoring systems' (Sleeman and Brown, 1982) or more colloquially 'Intelligent Computer Assisted Instruction' (ICAI).

However, not all conversational, in-depth dialogue, CAI methodologies are based on the concept of the computer learning about the learner and thus improving and further individualizing the instructional strategy being used. It is possible to build some very complex interactive dialogues purely on the basis of deep questioning techniques and multi-faceted analyses of the responses given by the student. After all, this is what happens in many university courses as the general rule, especially when student/staff ratios are high. The professor teaching a large group seldom gets to know all the students.

However, by setting suitably deep and multi-faceted 'essay' or 'seminar' type assignments, the professor can get a very accurate picture of the individual student's present conceptual schema (or knowledge structure) on a given topic. In his or her reply to the essay or the seminar presentation, the professor can be very perceptive and helpful to the individual, although the only data available to the professor is the content of a complex written or spoken argument on the topic, prepared by the specific student in question, together with accumulated experience of how students in general react to the topic, what difficulties or misconceptions they have, etc. One very successful approach to the simulation of such professor–student interchanges on specific complex problems on a computer is the technique called Structural Communication, developed by Hodgson and his associates in the United Kingdom at the end of the 1960s (Hodgson, 1968, 1971, 1974; Romiszowski, 1986). This method is based on the analysis of a multi-faceted multiple choice response which the student constructs by selection of a combination of response components from a 20 to 40 item 'response matrix' (see Figure 12.11). The construction of such in-depth, interactive tutorial dialogues is quite complex from the viewpoint of subject matter expertise and knowledge structure analysis, but relatively simple in terms of the computer hardware and software required.

12.2.6 Computer-based simulation

Whereas the conversational, or dialogue, modes of CAI are perhaps among the least practised on a large scale, SIMULATION is probably the most used and fastest growing mode. This is probably due to a series of factors:

Why use simula-tions?

- Computer-based simulations are sometimes the only way of developing certain types of learning experiences.
- They use the particular advantage of the computer as an ultra-rapid calculating and data processing machine, to the best advantage.
- The computer may often play a part in a more elaborate, not entirely computer-based simulation-game.
- Unlike the conversation mode, simulations (although possibly difficult, or at least, time consuming to program for the computer) are often quite simple to plan from the instructional viewpoint. Thus, the instructional designer may delegate a major part of the production task to specialist computer staff.
- The use of simulations is usually an adjunct to normal teaching procedures – it does not disrupt traditional organizational practices, upset conventional teachers by threatening the jobs of anyone, or tie up the computer on a nearly permanent basis for instruction.
- Many computer-based simulations are in the science area, where staff are most receptive to the new technology.
- There are, however, ample valid applications for this mode in almost any educational or training context.

The applications abound. One area in which dozens, perhaps hundreds of successful simulations have been developed, is medical education. Trainee doctors learn how patients with diabetes react to the intake of sugar in various quantities. Other simulations teach about the reactions of the body to different drugs or medicines. Yet others deal with environmental factors that promote epidemics, the control of a common disease by the vaccination of different proportions of the population. In all such simulations, the student may vary some of the critical variables and observe how other variables are affected.

Another popular area for process simulations is in the sciences. Ellington, Addinall and Percival (1981) list dozens of examples, including a simulation of process – of discharge of a capacitor, the flow of fluids through nozzles, gaseous diffusion, gravitation, interference and diffraction patterns of light waves, motion of satellites in orbits, and many others.

This particular matrix is taken from a Structural Communication Unit on organizational styles. The 'items' are very carefully chosen and worded so that the reader is able to use them in various combinations, to express his ideas. If Manager 'A' wished to characterize a particular department of the Civil Service, for instance, he might do so by using the combination 3, 14, 17, 20. Note that he has not included 18, although he has chosen 3 and 20. By doing so, he has implied a weakness in organization that encourages people to take the initiative, yet prevents them, through established procedures, from using that initiative effectively. This particular set of items (or any other) can generate a unique, personal, feedback comment. The computer selects comments on the basis of which items were included or omitted (Wilson, 1970).

Authority is concentrated at top level **1**	Staff-management relations are formal **2**	Responsibility is delegated **3**	Top management are prepared to enforce change **4**
The firm is organized in levels, each of which has authority over all those beneath it **5**	Managers repeatedly emphasize objectives in meetings with subordinates **6**	Initiative comes from the top level **7**	Most information is written down and records kept **8**
Operations are controlled from the top level **9**	Standards of efficiency are set and maintained **10**	People are able to change their jobs within the firm **11**	Management attach great importance to staff welfare **12**
Staff feel dependent on the firm **13**	Adherence to established procedure is encouraged **14**	Formal systems are confirmed to essential operations **15**	Frequent contact occurs between top management and shop floor **16**
Departmental loyalty is strong **17**	Decisions tend to be made on the spot **18**	Jobs tend to be specialized **19**	Initiative is encouraged at all levels **20**

Figure 12.11 *The matrix method of conversational CAI.*

Yet another interesting area of application is economics and finance, where effects of interacting market forces, tax laws or inflation rates may combine to surprising effects under certain conditions.

Complex multi-faceted simulations

There is one other application to be mentioned here – the flight simulator. Simple navigational simulators (you can buy one down the road, for operation on most makes of home computer) are a form of *decision-making exercise*. They teach more or less accurately, the factors that must be taken into account when flying and navigating a plane. In playing with these simulators, one learns when to drop the undercarriage, in relation to airspeed, when and how much to trim the flaps, how to allow for a crosswind when approaching an airfield, and so on. Such a software package, sold as a game for recreational purposes, does therefore give practice in the decision-making aspects of flying. As it presents the player with up to three visual displays – the instrument panel, the view in front of the cockpit and a map of the area in which the plane is situated – it is a simulation of the navigational and instrument-flying tasks in the pilot's job. When this same decision-making package is incorporated in a model of a real plane, that also supplies the correct physical feel, guidance and feedback for the manual skills of control, we have introduced the element of *apparatus operation*.

12.2.7 Database inquiry

The final classification in our schema of CAI only just qualifies to be included as a category of 'instruction'; it is really a mode of *information retrieval* from some form of organized bank of information, or *database*. However, if the database is organized to supply all the information necessary to achieve certain groups of educational objectives and if the learner is given (or formulates for himself) a set of specific objectives to be achieved, then we have a form of instructional system indeed, a very flexible self-instructional system.

The instructional and the 'serendipity' use of a database

There is, on the other hand, the unstructured, 'browsing' use of a computerized database, analogous to browsing in a public library, which is not aimed towards specific learning objectives and is therefore not 'instruction' in the sense that we are using the term. This is what Nicholas Rushby (1979) termed 'serendipity learning'. The planning of a bank of information for unstructured, serendipity learning, is not unlike the planning of the purchasing policy of a public library. We do not know exactly who will turn up to use the resources, or what they will be looking for. We do, however, have some information concerning the demand, by analysis of the requests we receive, through study of the bestseller lists, by careful analysis of the reports on new publications (from publishers or independent critics), and so on. How well we satisfy demand can be assessed through the study of user reactions, rather than the measurement of specific objectives achieved.

The 'global library'

One potential growth area for the application of the computer in education is, no doubt, the creation of computer-based libraries, computer-based information banks on specific subjects, etc. One such application already in use in the UK is Prestel. Other videotext systems, available to the public in general and devoted to educational and cultural purposes, as opposed to advertising and newcasting, will no doubt appear in increasing numbers, throughout the world. Pundits already draw mental images of immense national or even international networks linking dozens of specialist libraries into one huge system which, to use the words of Roy Jenkins (1983), 'can allow the contents of all the world's great libraries to flow through every living room in the land'.

The organization of information for retrieval

This vision, to become a functioning reality, will need a lot of work on the organization of the information of these 'great libraries' in such a manner that the not-too-skilled potential user can find his way about, locate what he wants, or what he might want if he only knew that it existed. The task of organizing such immense databases is not all that well understood. Many people are now interested in the topic and much research is under way. In relation to educational, scientific and other specialist use of such systems, the need is felt for a technology of subject matter analysis and organization that can produce a database on a given subject that is as helpful to the learner/researcher, as a human expert on the subject would be, if available for a personal interview. This has led to the concept

Expert systems

of EXPERT SYSTEMS – computer-based information banks which emulate a human expert in a given subject area.

A database on a specialist subject is, however, little more than a well organized and cross-referenced library. It is an important and useful tool in the hands of an expert. However, it does not take over the role of the expert. The important aspect of a true expert system is that it takes on at least part of the problem-organization and problem-solving roles of the human expert. It is capable not only of furnishing the information solicited, but should be able to interrogate the user for relevant input information, prompt the user in the steps to be followed in solving a problem, or even take over the problem-solving process as a whole.

The special-purpose scientific software that solves a set of pre-determined equations has been with us for a long time – any computer program is a 'problem solver' in this sense. But the solution of complex problems that require one to weigh various factors in relation to each other and make a decision on incomplete data – that is, *heuristic* problem solving – has only recently been successfully computerized. The 'expert system' is one form of a computerized heuristic problem solver.

12.2.8 Learning through programming

Taylor's (1980) classification of the computer in education as 'Tutor, Tool and Tutee' emphasizes that one major way in which computers are used by learners is to learn how to program them. The computer is Tutee, in the sense that it is the LEARNER who takes on the role of 'tutor' or rather, programmer. There are two justifications for such an approach, one related to the development of specific programming skills, the other related to the development of general problem-solving skills and 'powerful ideas' (Papert, 1980).

Vocational and non-vocational reasons for learning to program

The argument that learning to program the computer is best achieved through practice in programming the computer is unassailable (except to add that mere unstructured practice does NOT make perfect – it is necessary to build the practice into an overall well-designed instructional plan, that will include much more than just practice at the terminal). However, who needs computer programming skills? Well, those who earn their livelihood by programming computers. But the idea, born with the appearance of cheap microcomputers, that all computer users would engage in some programming, is fast dying. The 'vocational training' argument for teaching computing to everyone is not strong, and we can see how recently the concept of 'computer literacy' has been changing – whereas in the early 1980s just about all such programs included instruction in one or more computer languages (usually BASIC), the late 1980s tendency is towards much less emphasis on programming languages and much more on the efficient use of special purpose applications software (word processors, spreadsheets and database managers, etc.)

This trend is spurred on by expediency – by the need to concentrate on what is immediately useful. But there are many educators and computer scientists who argue that a knowledge of computing has general value as a discipline in logical thinking, problem formulation and solution, etc. They argue that experience in programming is time well spent in any student's general education, whatever their future vocational needs might turn out to be. Not all educators agree. Some remember that for centuries (right up to the late 1950s in England) the inclusion of Latin as an obligatory subject in the general school curriculum was defended largely on the grounds that 'Latin is a logical language and therefore, through learning Latin, students would learn to think logically'. There was no shred of evidence to suggest that this was in fact so, but the pressure group for Latin was so strong that many generations of argument were needed in order to introduce a change in the curriculum. Are we witnessing a similar 'pressure group' situation developing in respect of computer studies in the general curriculum? Or is there some real evidence that learning to program has some more general educational effects?

The answer from the 'pressure group' is that of course it depends on what language you learn and on how it is taught. The majority of computer scientists criticize the inclusion of BASIC as an introductory computing experience, arguing that the structure of this language is not conducive to the learning of good programming strategies. The educators, on the other hand, argue that the programming experience should be planned to include concepts of more general utility. The juxtaposition of these two opinions largely explains the popularity of LOGO, since its appearance in microcomputer versions in the early 1980s. Before we look at the evidence, let us examine just what LOGO is and how it is being used in schools.

LOGO – its origins

LOGO was developed at Massachussetts Institute of Technology (MIT), by a team of educators and computer scientists interested in logic programming and Piagetian concepts of child development. This, at first sight, rather strange combination of interests came about when Seymour Papert, a student of Piaget and interested in implementing his ideas in education, joined the faculty of MIT, at that time one of the leading research centres on artificial intelligence. The current 'AI' programming language was LISP (LISt-Processing), a powerful but not too easy to learn tool. The MIT team was working on the development of a simpler version. Papert saw, in this development, the opportunity to introduce young children to logic programming at a very early age and, through this, to create a computer-based 'learning environment' in which children could discover for themselves most of the concepts and relationships of mathematics (Papert, 1972; Papert and Solomon, 1972).

Papert's ideas stimulated a lot of excitement in the 'AI' fraternity and led to a number of projects in the mid 1970s. Notable among these was the Brookline LOGO project (Papert, 1977; Papert *et al.*, 1979; Watt, 1979) and the Edinburgh LOGO project (duBoulay and O'Shea, 1976; Howe and O'Shea, 1978; Howe *et al.*, 1979). Projects like these were exploratory 'let's see what can be done' studies, rather than strict research. The Edinburgh project was perhaps the more rigorous, in that standard mathematics tests were administered to students participating in the project. However, these projects served more to illustrate the potential for creative use of computers with young children, rather than any spectacular learning improvement towards the accepted school mathematics objectives. The experience gained in these projects, was synthesized in Papert's classic book *Mindstorms* (Papert, 1980) which appeared at the same time that microcomputer versions of LOGO were released on the market. Thus the LOGO movement was launched.

Turtle geometry and recursion

One aspect that Papert built into LOGO was the 'Turtle', triangular cursor that can be moved and rotated by the user, to create a geometrical drawing. Figures 12.12 and 12.13 show how a child can build a simple shape by writing a short program and the use that shape as a component to build much more complex figures. The capacity of LOGO to allow the user to define his own commands (eg SQUARE) and thus extend the power of the language, is one of its main attractions and strengths. The programmer uses the idea of 'recursion' to simplify the structure of the program. Recursion means 'repeat what you already know (but with a slight difference)', well illustrated in the 'SPINSQUARE' program illustrated in Figure 12.14. The complex figure is drawn by using one previously defined command (SQUARE) and repeating several times with small changes in size and rotation. By experimenting with such programming, Papert argues, children gain insights into how complex ideas are structured from simpler ones. This insight, gained in the context of 'turtle geometry', is claimed to transfer to other domains of learning as well.

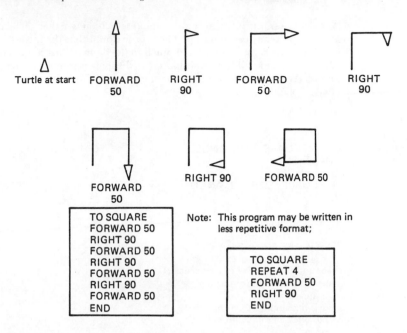

Figure 12.12 *Building a square. With the turtle at the starting point, this sequence of commands will produce a square. These commands can also be turned into a LOGO procedure.*

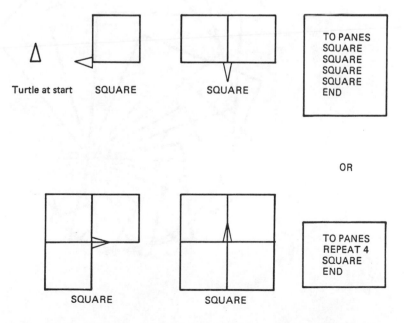

Figure 12.13 *PANES as evolved from SQUARE. The figure is made by repeating the SQUARE procedure four times (Adapted from Solomon, 1982).*

We shall examine later on some of the research on whether the claims made for using LOGO really do stand up. There is no doubt that the introduction of LOGO in schools has contributed much to the de-mystification of computers (for both teachers and children) and has created some very entertaining educational activities. What is not so clear is whether any world-shaking change in learning has taken place.

```
TO SPINSQUARE: SIZE: ANGLE
SQUARE: SIZE
RIGHT: ANGLE
SPINSQUARE: SIZE + 3: ANGLE
END
```

The result of running

SPINSQUARE 1 10

as shown in Figure 12.14 is a sequence of squares of increasing size starting with a square of one-step size. Each square is three units larger than the previous one and rotated from it by 10 degrees.

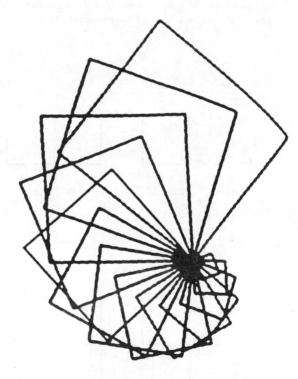

Figure 12.14 *A pattern formed by using recursion (Adapted from Abelson, 1982).*

12.3 Research on the use of computers for learning

12.3.1 Comparative studies: computers vs. teachers

Meta-analyses of studies on CAL

In earlier chapters we reviewed the studies comparing the use of a given medium with so-called 'conventional instruction'. In all cases, we found that very many such studies have been carried out, but the results are, to say the least, inconclusive. With some notable exceptions, well designed comparative research has shown, at best, a slight improvement in learning for the mediated version of the lessons compared. More often, analysis has shown 'no significant difference'. We have seen that a more sophisticated approach to the analysis of the data from many similar studies has been tried by Kulik and his collaborators. Not surprisingly, Kulik has performed a series of such 'meta analysis' studies on the very large number of comparative studies on CAL – one analysis of comparison studies in higher education (Kulik *et al.*, 1980), one in secondary education (Kulik and Kulik, 1982) and one in elementary education (Kulik *et al.*, 1984). All three of these 'meta-analyses' involving the combination of hundreds of separate comparative research studies, showed significant, if not spectacularly large, advantages for the computer-based materials, over the teacher-administered lessons.

Possible limitations of comparative research

These meta analyses have come under fire from several writers. Some (eg Heinich, 1984) have argued that many comparative studies may induce the teachers involved to take extra pains over their lesson planning and delivery as they find themselves 'on trial' and thus the CAL benefits normally attainable would be reduced or masked. Others (eg Clark, 1984) argue that the opposite effect may be present – the extra effort, time and instructional design skill that has gone into the development of the computer-based materials results in superior lesson designs and exaggerates the effect of the computer. Clark indeed reanalysed the results of the Kulik studies, discarding the poorly designed studies and separating those in which the same teacher was responsible for the development of the CAL material and for the conventional class teaching, from those where different teachers taught the control classes (Clark, 1985). He found that when the same teacher was both author of the CAL materials and instructor of the classroom-based control group, the advantage for the computer-based instruction was much reduced. He argues that, probably, this is because in those studies there is more similarity in the basic instructional design of the two alternatives being compared and, if this similarity were to be controlled rigorously in all studies, there would probably be no significant advantage of the computer-administered lessons over the teacher-delivered instruction. He concludes by arguing that, as was the case with his findings in the case of video and other mediated instruction, computers '. . . make no more contribution to learning than the truck which delivers groceries to the market contributes to improved nutrition in a community. Purchasing a truck will not improve nutrition just as purchasing a computer will not improve student achievement. Nutrition gains come from getting the correct groceries to the people who need them. Similarly, achievement gains result from matching the correct teaching method to the student who needs it.' (Clark, 1985.)

Clark's position on effect of media on instruction

Implications for CAL research

Now, this apparent criticism of CAL is really no more than a criticism of comparative studies that form such a large percentage of the research. When all possible variables (other than the presentation medium) have been controlled and balanced, it is not at all surprising to find no difference between any two presentation media. However, this implies that the content of learning selected for a comparative study must be such that it is equally capable of being presented by the various media being compared. It also implies that the teaching methods implemented in a study must be capable of being implemented equally well in all the media being compared. And there is ample evidence to suggest that the really effective way of using computers in teaching is to implement instructional designs which could not be implemented by the unaided classroom teacher. One use of

CAL which is so defended is the computer-based simulation/game, in that it presents real life-like experiences to all students within realistic time-frames, in a way that was hitherto impossible. Another argument is that many instructional designs that could, in theory, be implemented by the unaided teacher do not generally get to be implemented because they are too time consuming or difficult to use on a day-to-day basis. But the high speed of data processing offered by the computer makes these designs practically viable (examples include sophisticated drill and practice designs which require the detailed tracking of the performance of each student in order to select the most appropriate practice examples – see the examples of maths drills and typing drills discussed above).

So, to find the real benefits of the use of computers as instruments of instruction, we should look for real problems that have been solved, or real improvements that have been gained by the use of CAL. These 'case studies' may turn out to be more informative than formal research studies. They are capable of showing the effect of a number of the medium's characteristics over a significant period of time. They may also suggest benefits which are not measured (nor measurable) by the standard testing procedures of formal research.

12.3.2 Case-studies: benefits gained through CMI

Such case studies abound in just about all the categories of CAL that were described in the previous section. To start with computer-managed instruction (CMI), one should note the many reported success stories that document the benefits actually achieved when previously existing non-CAI courses were enhanced with an element of computer-based management. The case of the Engineering Structures course at the University of Aston in the UK, mentioned

CMI in formal education

earlier (Croxton and Martin, 1970), is a notable example in this category. By adding a computer-managed diagnosis system to an existing, self-study module-based, university level course, the authors succeeded in raising the success rates of their students on nationally administered examinations to such an extent that ALL their students' results fell in the top 10 per cent of the national score distribution. This result was so outstanding, in relation to that particular university's previous record and in terms of the students' outstanding results in structures but not necessarily in any of the other engineering examinations, that the examining body initially refused to believe that some form of 'cheating' was not involved. Only after the students took a second 'cheatproofed' structures exam and achieved similar outstanding results, did the new teaching method get the credit that was due to it.

Why CMI makes a difference

The main reason for the spectacular improvement was in fact nothing more than the increased level of diagnostic control that could be exerted when the computer was used to process the results of the week-by-week study assignments. With 300 or more students registered on a lecture-and-modules based course, there was no way for faculty to keep track of individual progress until it was too late to do anything about individual learning problems. With rapid computer-based diagnosis of learning progress, it was possible to use all existing teaching resources to give the maximum of individual coaching (not much, with the staff–student ratio available, but the little possible made all the difference).

12.3.3 Case studies: the benefits of computer-based testing

The use of computer-assisted testing also has its share of success stories. One, already described earlier, was the added smoothness and practicality that on-line diagnostic testing introduced into a remedial mathematics 'learning-by-appointment' system that had been running previously on the basis of

Efficiency of on-line testing

paper tests (Romiszowski, 1979). Other benefits of the on-line 'adaptive' testing approach are documented by Weiss (1979) who shows that to achieve similar levels of precision in diagnosis, computer-based adaptive tests use 30–50 per cent fewer test questions than a similar paper-and-pencil test. This saves testing time, cuts down on student effort and reduces the frustration of the weaker student faced with many over-difficult questions to tackle and knowing that he/she will almost certainly answer incorrectly.

Utility of test-item banks

A further form of benefit that has often been gained in practice is increased facility in the construction of appropriate levels of tests and, therefore, increased use of systematic diagnostic testing procedures. This benefit comes about through the mere existence of a test item bank on a given subject matter, organized according to objective, difficulty level, etc. Such an item bank maybe constructed by small contributions from many teachers and is then available to all teachers as a service. Lippey (1974) describes how such computer-assisted testing may be used and gives examples of the benefits achieved.

12.3.4 The benefits of drill and practice

Uses and mis-uses of drill and practice

The drill and practice mode of CAI has often been attacked as an uncreative and anti-educational use of the computer. But, relaly, this criticism should be levelled not at the medium but at the method, WHEN USED INAPPROPRIATELY. To be sure, kids are often drilled into memorizing useless information or into executing useful procedures (eg arithmetic) without real understanding of what they are learning. But there are also quite valid uses for drills in both education and training. The learning of foreign language vocabularies is one example where repeated use is essential and some form of drill exercises, whether computer based or not, are appropriate. High-speed reflex skills, like typing and computer keyboard operation, are another outstanding example of a type of learning which is heavily dependent on drill and practice and where computer-based drills have

Case studies of keyboard skills drill and practice

shown themselves to be vastly superior to any previous training method. We mentioned in previous sections of this chapter, the early SAKI keyboard trainer and the later EASYLEARN system developed for the British Post Office. These systems (and others like them) have shown themselves to be most effective, achieving results that were unknown under conventional classroom instruction. 'Twice the typing speed in half the learning time, or your money back', are slogans that can safely be used in marketing these systems, as practical experience has shown that such results are nearly always achieved by motivated learners.

12.3.5 The benefits of 'programmed tutorial' CAI

Coming now to TUTORIAL CAI, we should remember that all the previously mentioned modes are often, and indeed should almost always, be present in a tutorial. Individual student progress is monitored and managed by the changing of

Limitations of computers as presentation media

the path through the material in response to individual needs. This necessarily involves computer-based testing which is adaptive in nature. When drills are appropriate, they may be built in and may also be made more palatable by the use of game-like contexts for practice. The extra characteristic of the tutorial is the presentation of new information to be learnt. This may be more or less effective than it would have been by means of other media. Until recently, for example, there were serious limitations on the degree of resolution of the graphic materials that could be presented on most school-use microcomputers. This aspect has improved significantly as more powerful (and cheaper) graphics packages have become available. Also, the current trend towards the linking of CAI tutorials with video material from laser discs (see Chapter 13) has effectively overcome the problem of visual resolution for most purposes. But this does not make the computer screen the ideal presentation medium for all the types of information that the learner may require. The very size of the screen is sometimes a severe limitation, leading one to break down a complex network or a map, into separate screens, or to use an inconvenient 'windowing' technique in order to allow the learner to see the 'big picture'. However, for most typical instructional content, the modern computer system, enhanced with interactive video, is a pretty adequate presentation system, but not necessarily superior to other presentation media. The benefits, if any, should be looked for in the speed and precision of storing, accessing, presenting, revising and individualizing of the information. When these are of importance, and are not achievable in the conventional teaching situation, then we can expect benefits to accure for CAI.

Benefits due to the consistency of complete CAI courses

It is for reasons such as these that there is such a discrepancy between the not-so-spectacular findings of formal comparative research studies and the reported successes of individual case studies, Kulik's meta analyses typically showed advantages to CAI over classroom instruction of the order of 15 percentage points. This is not to be 'sneezed at', if it represents a gain that can truly be expected over a long-term period, in real life instructional conditions. Clark seems to argue that the bulk of this difference is due to superior instructional design of the lesson structures given by computer and that there is no reason why similarly efficient lesson structures could not have been given in classroom instruction. But the tendency in real life classroom instruction is to have varied success with different teachers and even with different classes, taught by the same teacher. It is difficult to always maintain the same standard of teaching that was achieved during a relatively short comparative study when 'everyone was watching'. It is not surprising, therefore, that many case studies of large-scale CAI use report instructional improvements well in excess of those 15 percentage points found by Kulik.

Another benefit, reported over and over, especially in case studies of computer-based job skills training, is a significant reduction of the time required to complete a given program of instruction. Trainees reach the required job-performance standards in an average of two thirds or sometimes less than half the time previously required in the conventional instructional situation (Kearsley, 1983; Orlansky and String, 1979).

CAI segments built into classroom instruction

Of course, not all tutorial CAI is the large-scale substitution of classroom instruction by machine instruction. Much the more common situation, especially in schools, is the integration of short CAI tutorials on specific topics, into an overall course design, planned, implemented and partly delivered by the classroom teacher. In such a case, it is very difficult to separate out any benefits of CAI over alternative instructional designs. What can be measured is the overall effect of the teacher/computer media combination, as opposed to the teacher alone (or indeed the computer alone). There seems to be much less formal research along these lines (the number of possible uncontrolled variables probably scare off the would-be researcher). But informally, it is this sort of situation that impresses the enthusiast teacher most. The bulk of the more popular literature on the use of computers in the classroom abounds with examples of the creative integration of the computer as one of the media at the teacher's disposal. There is insufficient space in this book to explore the richness of possibilities for the integration of computer-based courseware into the conventional classroom teaching situation. Many books especially devoted to the classroom use of the computer have been written and interested reader should study some of the practical suggestions reported (try '*Classroom activities for Computer Education*', Flake *et al.*, 1987).

12.3.6 *Research on conversational and intelligent CAI*

Much promise . . .

The trend towards the development of 'conversational' CAI was in part spurred by the limitations of the 'programmed instruction' model as a basis for the effective use of the computer as a medium of instruction. Already in the late 1960s there were several alternative models proposed. We have already mentioned the conversational approach built into the CASTE system (Pask and Scott, 1972; Pask, 1976) and the 'structural communication' approach (Hodgson, 1968, 1971, 1974). Both of these methods were successfully tested in paper-based tutorial versions, but the computer technology of the time was inadequate to support their use as models for the development of large-scale CAI applications. Now that the technology has caught up, we find these techniques are little used because of the great skill and effort needed to design effective materials that exploit the systems' capabilities of interaction. There are a few examples of successful implementations of conversational tutorials, but hardly any large-scale regular use.

... but little progress

A similar situation exists with respect to the 'intelligent' tutorial systems (ICAI) that we read so much about (eg Sleeman and Brown, 1982). There is a history of research and development that spans over 30 years. Experimental systems have been operational for at least 20 years (Carbonnell, 1970) but no real impact on everyday instruction, whether in the school classroom or in job training situations, has as yet been felt. As Frank Roberts of Control Data remarked at the 1986 conference of the Association for the Development of Computer-assisted Instructional Systems (ADCIS): 'to my knowledge, some 15 or so intelligent tutorial systems have so far been developed beyond the conceptual design stage . . . of these, only five or six have been used at all extensively in real life instructional situations . . . and none have been systematically evaluated'. As far as research on ICAI is concerned, we are still in the laboratory stage.

12.3.7 Benefits of computer-based simulation

Use of simulations as components in discovery learning

The situation is very different with respect to the 'simulation' mode of CAL. This has been the fastest growing area in recent years and has the largest number of enthusiastic adherents among teachers and trainers alike. By its nature, a computer-based simulation is usually a component in a lesson. The computer is used to dynamically illustrate the cause–effect relationships that hold true in some real-life phenomenon. An example is the famous simulation of Mendel's laws in action in a computer-based fruit-fly mating experiment. In an hour or so on the computer, it is possible to simulate many generations of fruit-fly offspring for many different mating patterns. This allows students to deduce the Mendelian laws for themselves – to discover in one school session what took Mendel many years of detailed and painstaking observations (Bitzer, 1976). Similar discovery experiences can now be conveniently arranged in just about every area of science education, as well as economics, management, etc. The educational success of such simulations is, however, much dependent on how well they are introduced and followed up by the teacher. As with all experiential, or discovery, learning, it is important to reflect on the specific cases and identify the general principles at play. This is best achieved by careful initial orientation (briefing) of the students and, even more importantly, deep final analysis and evaluation of what was learned (de-briefing). Most simulation packages do not perform these functions. The way the teacher plans and executes the briefing and debriefing is the key factor in the overall instructional effectiveness of computer-based simulations, used in the classroom for conceptual learning.

Use of simulations for learning procedures

The use of computer-based simulation to teach machine operation is somewhat different. In this case, the instructional objectives are to learn a specific procedure. A well-designed simulator may present more varied practice, more concentrated experience of rarely occurring situations and enhanced feedback and guidance, all in a safer and possibly less expensive environemnt than 'real life'.

The reports on the use of computer-based simulations tend to be generally positive. Business games, using the computer as an interactive data bank, have been used and praised for nearly 30 years now (eg Sprowls, 1962; Graham and Gray, 1969; Frazer, 1977). Computer-based simulations for procedural learning have a similarly long history, especially as embedded training for computer-related procedures but also in all branches of military training (Kearsley, 1983). There is a respectable body of research showing that computer-based operations training can be as effective as using the real-life (more expensive, dangerous, inconvenient, etc.) equipment (eg Adams, 1979; Crawford and Crawford, 1978; Dean and Whitlock, 1983).

Use of simulations for higher-order learning objectives

In the cognitive learning field, the research is less conclusive. This is partly due to the points made earlier, with respect to the simulation often forming only part of the teacher's overall lesson plan. This makes it difficult to sort out whether improved learning was due to something inherent in the simulation exercise or to the skill with which the teacher exploited the experience in subsequent activities. There is a certain body of research that suggests that simulations used on their own are sometimes less effective than they appear to be. Licht (1985) reports studies which show rather poor learning of factual information from business simulations that were, on the face of it, excellent and absorbing exercises. Nor were concepts or principles sufficiently well generalized. There seemed to be some learning of a general 'feel' for management decision making, which was difficult to measure by normal testing methods. Oakey (1986) reported studies with situational simulation-games in which students worked in groups to solve complex problems (eg escaping from a computer-simulated flood). The objectives of the simulation-games studied included general problem-solving skills and working effectively as a group, as well as content-related objectives. He found that very little real learning had occurred, especially as relates to the general problem-solving and interpersonal skills.

12.3.8 The benefits of 'inquiry' CAL

We are now stepping beyond what may be strictly called 'computer-assisted instruction'. A database located in a computer is an information resource. As such it may be no different in content from some other resource, say a filing cabinet or a section of a library. It is different, however, in terms of the ease and speed with which specific items of information may be located. Improving the efficiency of access to information has obvious effects on the efficiency of learning. This 'tool' use of the computer thus brings automatic benefits to the instructional process, whether that process itself changes or not.

Databases used for student-directed learning

What interests us specifically in this chapter, however, is the effect of the existence of databases on the process of instruction itself. When information was difficult to access, there was a strong tendency to pre-prepare all the materials that students would use in a course of instruction. These would be written up in a 'set book' or collected together as a set of 'required readings'. Students would seldom branch out beyond this prepared material. With easy access to a much wider range of resources, it is possible to design course activities around problem-statements, leaving the students responsible for the identification and selection of appropriate learning resources. This seems a natural approach at the higher levels of education, as it accustoms students to do their own library research. But there is increasing evidence that it is both possible and desirable to structure instruction this way at all levels of education. Given an appropriately structured database, even elementary school children can discover for themselves, not only the facts about a subject, but also its structure and integral relationships. A database of geography facts has been used for children to learn about the animals and plants that can be found in different regions. But in searching the database for this factual information, they are led to discover the relationships that exist between climate, feeding habits, physical attributes such as colour, size, speed, living habits such as migration and hibernation, etc. A few hours of guided searching of the database develops an understanding of a body of geography as a related whole, rather than as a set of individual facts.

Databases with expert guidance systems

It is only a small step further to develop computer-based guidance in the searching of the database, in order to create a different form of computer-assisted instruction. This approach has not received the attention that it deserves. Its potential for the promotion of student autonomy in learning is obvious. Perhaps not so obvious are the benefits of developing one package on a given subject area in such a way that many different levels of student may find it useful for many different objectives. After all, the content of the subject is comprehensively covered, if the database is to be at all useful. But the 'level of discourse' about the subject may not suit all users, unless some form of adapting this to the needs of the user were to be devised. Some may need more and simpler examples in order to understand basic concepts. Others may wish to go much deeper into practical applications of the content. Yet others may wish to engage in a philosophical analysis of the importance/implications of a given topic. A database can be structured to deal with any number of such aspects of a subject at several different levels of difficulty, so that, in theory, any user might find the information required, presented in understandable language. Of course, in order *to* find the appropriate content and level of discourse, the user will need help. This help function can be performed by a computer-based form of 'expert guide' that is capable of interacting with any user in order to diagnose individual needs in relation to the specific database in question. With the advent of large databases accessible from anywhere by telecommunications links, such 'intelligent' databases are beginning to generate a lot of research interest. They have even earned their own jargon name – HYPERTEXT. Like intelligent CAI, they are as yet at the stage of laboratory research, but are showing much promise.

12.3.9 The benefits of LOGO

Coming now to the 'computer as tutee' we shall restrict ourselves to examining the research on the use of LOGO in education. The topic of how useful, in general educational terms, it is to learn to program a computer is a fascinating question, but one which is not directly related to our interest here in the use of computers as instructional media. It is worth devoting a little space to the use of LOGO particularly, as so many claims have been made for its value in developing 'powerful ideas' which are generalizable to situations and content other than that used in the LOGO exercises themselves.

Lack of formal research

It should be stressed here, that LOGO is a general programming language, based on LISP and capable of being used for a variety of programming tasks. I have seen excellent examples of databases, and CAI courseware set up in LOGO. But its use in schools has generally been limited to the 'turtle geometry' aspects which are unique to this language and which were popularized so effectively by Papert (1980) and his followers (see the August 1982 edition of *BYTE*). We illustrated earlier in this chapter how LOGO uses recursion, by a very simple turtle graphics programming exercise. The arguments of LOGO's supporters is that such generalizable concepts, once grasped in the context of playing with the turtle, are generalized to other branches of mathematics and indeed beyond. Paradoxically, however, there has been very little scientifically controlled research on such a theoretically interesting topic. The enthusiasts say that classical research is not appropriate, as we are witnessing highly personal learning experiences which can only be adequately described by detailed case studies. The doubters argue that little research has been published because the claims made for LOGO have generally not been substantiated when research was attempted. These two viewpoints are well illustrated by one of the earliest and most intensive and controlled studies of the use of LOGO – the Edinburgh project.

Edinburgh project findings

This project involved a small group of some 11 students who attended the LOGO laboratory at Edinburgh University, regularly over a period of two years. When compared with their colleagues who had followed the same school maths studies but had not attended the LOGO experiences in the laboratory, the experimental group scored somewhat better on tests that measured comprehension of mathematical concepts, but worse on tests of mathematical procedures. The major finding reported was not measured by standardized tests, but was the observation that the experimental group were 'more willing to argue sensibly about mathematical issues' and were able to 'explain their mathematical difficulties more clearly' (Howe *et al.*, 1979). Other writers (eg Watt, 1982) suggest that the benefits in mathematical reasoning reported in this and some other experiments may be due more to the attitudes and teaching methods adopted by the teachers involved than to anything intrinsic in LOGO itself.

Is LOGO Piagetian?

The picture is therefore far from clear. Some teachers have, as Thornburg (1986) put it, accepted LOGO as a religion: they accepted its benefits on faith and felt that criticizing LOGO bordered on sacrilege'. Yet the widest reviews of the research literature (eg Michayluk, 1986) have failed to show any very significant or systematic benefits to learning accuring from experience with LOGO. Perhaps the 'religion' syndrome is due to the Piagetian roots of Papert's philosophy. Those who believe in Piaget's view of the way that learners mature through a series of stages and progress from being 'concrete operational' learners to higher and more abstract ways of thinking, have tended to accept the LOGO approach on faith. But they forget that Piaget argues that the process is one of personal development which cannot be hurried on by instruction (this is one of the points where Piaget and Papert diverge). Perhaps the theoretical underpinnings of the LOGO approach are not as sound as they appeared at first sight. But perhaps the approach suffers from the incapacity of untrained teachers to get the best out of it, as Michalyuk (1986) suggests.

12.4 Deciding whether to use computer-assisted learning

12.4.1 'Macro' decisions: is a course suitable for CAL?

Computer-assisted learning, like other self-instructional media, can be selected as the basis of a complete, automated instructional system. Alternatively, teachers may select specific CAL exercises as components in their overall course or lesson designs, just as they select a set of slides or film. In the first case, the CAL system becomes the principal medium of instruction, replacing classroom teaching entirely or at least in a large part. It implies investment in a complex system of computer-based delivery of instruction and an infrastructure of courseware development/modification/updating, hardware maintenance and repair, etc. In the second case, the computer becomes just another instructional aid, which supplements the teacher at certain points in a course, but the teacher still remains the principal planner of each lesson and delivery medium of most parts of the lesson.

The levels of decision making   The decision of *whether* and the planning of *how* to use CAL is different in these two cases. In the first case, it is a mixture of 'level I' and 'level II' considerations (to use the four-level classification described in Chapter 2). One combines an analysis of overall course objectives, content, resources and constraints (level II) with overall organizational, economic and political considerations which affect the viability of the project (level I). In the second case, when CAL is used as a component in a lesson, its selection becomes part and parcel of the lesson design process (what we have called 'level III' of instructional development). In this case, the teacher selects an existing CAL package that fits into the overall lesson design and that can be used effectively with existing hardware.

There is, of course, yet another (level IV) possibility: the teacher may decide to develop the courseware that he needs for his lesson. However, we shall not discuss this level of detail here. Another whole book would be needed.

To deal with the 'macro' decision levels first, we shall consider the course for which CAL is being considered, as a SYSTEM. We can then organize our decision making process in terms of:

- SYSTEM OUTPUTS – what we hope to gain from the use of CAL that we cannot gain by presently available course methods/materials or other viable (and possibly cheaper or simpler) innovations;
- PROCESS FACTORS – how the use of CAL will change the course in terms of the degree of individualization which will be possible/desirable, the interaction between student and course materials, the form and degree of control and automated management of the course that will be possible, other effects on student motivation, learning skills, satisfaction, etc;
- INPUT FACTORS – what resources will be required in order to implement CAL as desired – what computer hardware and communication systems will be necessary, what courseware must be obtained or developed and what human resources will be required in order to get the whole idea implemented;
- CONTEXTUAL FACTORS – what economic and organizational factors should be taken into account in order to judge the probable chances of success or failure of the proposed innovation.

The specific questions that should be considered under each of these four headings are presented in the four reference maps that follow (Maps 12.1 to 12.4). These maps are designed to be used as job-aids to assist the decision-making process when faced with the possible selection of CAL as a principal medium of instruction for a given course.

Map 12.1 *Output factors: what do we hope to gain through CAL?*

Effectiveness	• Are the course objectives difficult to achieve by conventional methods? • Is there reason to believe that CAL will facilitate the achievement of the objectives? • Are there any secondary objectives that are particularly likely to be promoted by the use of CAL?
Efficiency	• Would reduction in the time required for instruction be beneficial? • Would the use of CAL lead to better integration of theory and practice? • Would the use of CAL reduce the need for other costly instructional resources? • Would CAL reduce other costs associated with the course – travel, hotels, etc?
Control/consistency	• Are existing courses or materials badly used or administered? • Is the standardization of the content of instruction important? • Is control over the methods of instruction important? • Is testing and record keeping difficult under present methods?
Diffusion/dissemination	• Would it be beneficial if the course were to be available at all times? • Is student demand very variable or seasonal? • Is frequent re-cycling required due to lack of regular practice? • Can the course be disseminated through an existing computer system? • Is the demand for the course large, growing and likely to be longlived? • Will the materials need to be updated or revised frequently?

Map 12.2 *Process factors: how will CAL change the course?*

Individualization	
	• Are there special reasons why self-instruction is desirable?
	• Are students likely to vary greatly in learning rate or learning style?
	• Do students vary considerably in terms of ability or pre-requisites?
	• Are students likely to have different end-of-course objectives?

Interactivity	
	• Is it difficult to give sufficient individual attention by current methods?
	• Will CAL permit more frequent or more precise feedback to students?
	• Will CAL permit feedback of a nature that is impossible by other methods?
	• Would it be beneficial to give feedback on the basis of a pattern of responses?
	• Would it be useful to measure and control the time of presentation and response?
	• Should it be necessary to accept and respond to student-generated queries/responses?
	• Would it be necessary to automatically control other presentation media?

Management	
	• Is there a need for close tracking of individual student's paths of study?
	• Is a competency-based or 'mastery' model of learning management desired?
	• Are detailed reports of individual or group progress required frequently?

Motivation	
	• Is motivation a problem and is it likely to be improved by use of CAL?
	• Is it possible to profit from CAL by embedding learning in a game format?
	• Is attrition/dropout a problem and will CAL reduce this?

Map 12.3 *Input factors: have we got what it takes?*

Hardware/system requirements	
	• Adequate output display characteristics for the course/content requirements
	• Adequate input capabilities for the types of student responses envisaged
	• Adequate memory/processing capability for the courseware to be used
	• Adequate memory/processing capability for the CMI system to be used
	• All necessary communications and interfacing capabilities available
	• Networking/timesharing systems up to handling peak student capacity
	• Reliability and maintenance can be guaranteed for life of the course
	• Will system behave adequately under peak demand conditions?

Map 12.3 – *continued*

Courseware requirements

- Is suitable courseware already available?
- Will it operate on the hardware installed?
- Do suppliers guarantee the maintenance and updating of courseware?
- If courseware is to be developed, is there sufficient lead-in time?
- Is courseware development software already available/adequate?
- Are all necessary support materials and documentation available/in production?

Human resource requirements

- Are teachers trained in the use of the hardware and systems to be used?
- Are teachers trained in the effective use of the courseware in instruction?
- Do we have instructional designers who can plan the CAL lessons to be developed?
- Do we have developers skilled in the use of the authoring systems/languages?
- Are all necessary support/maintenance personnel available and trained?

Map 12.4 *Contextual factors: should we go ahead?*

Cost/benefit considerations

- Has a cost study of the proposed CAL project been carried out?
- Have costs of all other feasible alternatives been estimated as well?
- Do annual operation costs of CAL compare favourably with other alternatives?
- Do initial development costs appear to be recoverable in reasonable time?
- Can part of development costs be offset against future similar projects?
- Are there any quantifiable benefits to be gained through CAL over other methods?
- What are the final cost/benefits and break-even points of viable alternatives?

Organizational considerations

- Is there sufficient top management support to ensure full implementation?
- Is the organizational climate open to an innovation like CAL?
- Are there any foci of opposition or apathy that may disrupt the project?
- Is the CAL project likely to enter in conflict with other projects/activities?
- Is the general attitude of instructors favourable to the use of CAL?
- Is the organization likely to approve the necessary up-front expenditures?
- Is the budgeting system flexible enough to permit the project to keep to schedule?
- Is the project management/control system appropriate for a CAL innovation?
- Does the project manager have any experience of CAL development projects?

12.4.2 'Micro' decisions: is this CAL package suitable?

We now come to the second case – the selection of suitable courseware for a given course or lesson, from the plethora of materials available on the market. The quantity of CAL materials has grown so fast that all attempts at documenting and evaluating all packages have proved to be inadequate. Several bodies have attempted this task and have offered some help to the teacher faced with selecting courseware from some supplier's catalogue.

Courseware evaluation services/ clearing- houses

One of the oldest and largest courseware evaluation services is offered by the Educational Products Information Exchange (EPIE), which has existed since the late 1960s specifically to provide objective evaluations of educational hardware and software. EPIE covers all types of instructional media and materials, publishing regular quarterly and monthly reports. In the area of computer courseware, EPIE publishes, since 1982, a special monthly newsletter of reports — *EPIE MICROgram newsletter*. Other similar evaluation services have sprung up. Some have died and others still continue. Notable examples are the CONDUIT project and the MicroSIFT clearinghouse (1982). These were responsible for the development of a complex form to be used for the evaluation of courseware by teachers. Many courseware evaluations were prepared and circulated to the interested (and initiated) few. Similar projects have been set up, by the Council for Education Technology in the UK, by the National Council of Teachers of Mathematics, in the USA (Heck *et al.*, 1981) by UNESCO and other international bodies and by some for-profit organizations.

Have a go yourself

All these services have their uses. If nothing else, they serve as pointers to what is available and may act as a 'first line of defence' to eliminate from your consideration those packages that obviously do not fill your requirements. But there is no substitute, in the final analysis, for 'having a look at the package yourself'. This can be done in two ways. Some courseware suppliers will let you have a copy for a limited time, on approval. This is the ideal situation, as it may enable you to try it out on a sample of your own students as well as analysing it yourself in as much detail as you see fit. If a loan copy cannot be obtained, then you should be able to preview a copy at a local software distribution shop. In this case, your time, and therefore the detail of analysis you will be able to perform, will be limited. In both cases, however, the very detailed and descriptive evaluation forms developed by EPIE, CONDUIT, MicroSIFT (there are some dozen or so others (eg Bitter and Camuse, 1984)) are unnecessary and inconvenient. You are not going to write a general evaluation report for an unknown readership, but simply prepare a specific judgement of the suitability of the package for your specific lesson application.

In order to help you do this, a much simpler, more direct methodology is adequate. Many short, half-page checklists can be found in the media selection/use literature (eg Heinich, Molenda and Russell, 1985; Locatis and Atkinson, 1984). These touch on only the most important or obvious factors. Maps 12.5 and 12.6 which follow, adopt a middle course – not too detailed but not too condensed.

Map 12.5 *A: courseware selection guide: questions to ask of any type of courseware.*

A. QUESTIONS TO ASK OF ANY TYPE OF COURSEWARE
A.1. OBJECTIVES AND CONTENT ● Are the stated objectives congruent with the objectives of the course/lesson planned? ● Are the objectives as perceived on inspection congruent with those planned for the course? ● Is there any evidence available of the effectiveness of the courseware? ● Are the final tests/evaluation instruments congruent with the objectives? ● Is it possible to perform an independent field test of the package? ● Is the content appropriate in terms of subject, examples, context, language, etc?
A.2. ALTERNATIVE MATERIALS ● Is the courseware under consideration as appropriate (in terms of A.1) as other alternatives? ● Is any cost differential between it and viable alternatives acceptable? ● Is the convenience of using this courseware acceptable, as compared to viable alternatives?
A.3. USEFUL LIFE/PROBABLE RETURN ● Is the content sufficiently stable to justify investment in the package? ● Will the number of students using the package justify the investment? ● If repeated use is expected, will the package hold student interest sufficiently? ● Is the package copy protected – if so, will it stand up to projected frequency of use?
A.4. HARDWARE REQUIREMENTS ● Will the package run correctly on the available computer system?
A.5 DESIGN CHARACTERISTICS ● Does the package have a teacher's guide with full specifications of objectives, target population, pre-requisites, etc? ● Does the teacher's guide also contain hints on how to integrate the package into a course lesson, extra activities, support materials, etc? ● Is the content and its treatment sufficiently complete and clear (judgement of 'SME')? ● Is the use of examples, repetition, feedback, illustration appropriate (judgement of 'ID')? ● Is the language difficulty appropriate for the target population? ● Is the treatment given to the topic likely to be motivational for the target population? ● Is the rate of progress/size of step well chosen for the target population?

Map 12.5 – *continued*

- Is there sufficient variety of stimulus to maintain interest and attention throughout?
- Is the form of questioning/student activity appropriate to the objectives being pursued?
- Is the form and content of feedback given to students appropriate/adequate?
- Is the guidance/orientation on how to use the package sufficiently clear to students?
- Are the step-by-step instructions such that all students follow them correctly/easily?
- Is all assessment data treated so that students may see their own progress, but not others?
- Are non-utilized keys rendered inoperative by the software to make the package 'foolproof'?
- Can students record their place and pick up from where they left off last session?
- Can students back-track to review earlier material if they feel the need?
- Can students access an overview or menu, to see what they have done and what is left?

Map 12.6 *B: questions to ask with respect to specific CAI modes.*

B. QUESTIONS TO ASK WITH RESPECT TO SPECIFIC CAI MODES

B.1. DRILL AND PRACTICE EXERCISE/GAMES

If the package has a fixed content:

- Are the practice items appropriate to the target population and objectives?
- Are the items graded in appropriate steps of difficulty/complexity/speed/etc?
- Is the logic by which students progress to more difficult items appropriate?
- Can students go back if their performance deteriorates, as well as going forward?
- Can students be given more than one chance to respond correctly, before changing difficulty?
- Can the control logic be varied by the teacher or student (choose difficulty level)?

If the package can be loaded by the teacher, with different sets of items, then in addition:

- Is the item authoring system easy to learn and use, without programming skills?
- Is it easy to save copies of all teacher-made drills for repeated future use?
- Is the format allowed for the drill items sufficiently flexible to accept useful items in the subject area of interest?

Map 12.6 – *continued*

If the drill exercises are embedded in a game:
- Is the game appropriate to the age and itnerests of the target population?
- Are the game aspects likely to distract the student's attention from the learning aspects?
- Are the screen effects likely to encourage intentional wrong answers 'to see what happens'?
- Is the scoring system used in the game congruent with the instructional objectives?
- Does the game context involve violence or other irrelevant/socially undesirable aspects?

B.2. PROGRAMMED TUTORIAL CAI

General instructional design aspects:
- The tutorial is sequenced in a series of 'lessons' which interlink in a pedagogically planned manner (eg known-to-unknown/overview-to-specifics)?
- Each lesson starts by defining its objectives and place in the whole package?
- Each lesson attempts to maintain/improve the students' interest in the topic?
- Each lesson employs instructional strategies and sutdents' itnerest in the topic?
- ach lesson employs instructional strategies and tactics appropriate to the objectives?
- Appropriate, well chosen examples are used with sufficient frequency for all new concepts?
- Appropriate practice examples and questions are used to promote student learning?
- Appropriate feedback is included and remedial sequences are provided where necessary?
- Sufficient repetition and redundancy is included to ensure successful learning?
- Each lesson is summarized and linked to following lessons and activities?
- Each lesson has its own embedded post-test, as well as any final overall evaluation?

Specific CAI/screen design aspects:
- The use of graphics is appropriate and effective, without needless 'special effects'?
- The use of colour, motion and animation is likewise appropriate and restrained?
- The screen layout design is clear, uncluttered and not overloaded with content?
- The student input instructions are clear and appropriate to the content and clientele?
- All CMI data necessary for student assessment and guidance, package revision, etc. are stored?
- The CMI system ensures mastery of key objectives?

Map 12.6 – *continued*

B.3. COMPUTER-BASED SIMULATIONS

Simulation of systems and equipment to teach operation:

- Is there any advantage in using the simulation over the real system or equipment?
- Is the simulation sufficiently realistic for students to see the relationship to reality?
- Are all the system/equipment characteristics, that relate to the learning objectives, reproduced with sufficient fidelity?
- Is it possible to reproduce all normal operating states, common faults/problems etc?
- Does the simulation react to student inputs in a way analogous to the real system/equipment?
- Are performance measures used for student assessment congruent with real life criteria?

Use of computer databases in decision-making sim/games:

- If the computer is a mere data source, is it a realistic representation of reality?
- If a series of decisions are taken, does the database react realistically to the decisions?
- If the students play against the computer, are the computer's decisions based on reality?
- Is the decision-making model capable of being discovered and formalized by the student?

Use of simulations to model processes/phenomena:

- Is the simulation based on a mathematical model of cause–effect that approximates reality?
- Can students interact with the simulations by inputing specific data and observing the effects?
- Is it possible to identify the cause–effect relationships from a number of specific cases?
- Is the simulation so constructed that students are likely to discover the general principles that govern the relationships observed?

In all the above cases:

- Is the simulation package accompanied by teachers notes, explaining the objectives, content, underlying model and principles and suggestions on how to make the link from simulation to reality?

13 Interactive video systems

13.1 What is interactive video?

The term 'interactive video' may be understood in a general or a highly specific way. In the general sense, interactive video simply means visual (or rather, audiovisual) communication which has the characteristic of interacting with the viewer/listener. Is not resource-based learning, which uses audiovisual instructional packages, and is controlled by an algorithm of criteria and test items to be mastered in any order, a close cousin of interactive video? Is the Postlethwaite Audio-tutorial System not an early forerunner of today's systems? How about the use of your home TV set to access a Teletext or Prestel system that permits you to choose from an extensive menu of information options? Or what about a two-way video link used for a teleconference linkup between two distant classrooms? All these examples involve the use of the video medium in an interactive manner.

Interactive videodisc   In the specific sense, however, the term 'interactive video' has recently come to be used to describe the latest and (to date) most sophisticated audiovisual communication system for individual use; the laser videodisc linked to a microcomputer with graphics and text generation capabilities, through a special interface, which allows the computer to be used to control the videodisc, transforming it into a random-access store of moving images, stills and text. This is the ultimate of current technology. There are of course simpler systems, such as user-controlled random-access videocassette players, which are also referred to by many as 'interactive video'. And why not indeed? It is video and it does interact with the audience. But it is the interactively controlled videodisc that seems to have grabbed the imagination of many media experts in the educational and training fields.

The reasons for this are not hard to identify. The videodisc, as a storage and playback medium, offers a number of distinct advantages over its rivals. Some of these are:

- a very high storage capacity for its size (a single laser videodisc about the size of a gramophone record, may store over 100,000 still images or pages of text, or about 500 hours of audio recording, or about two hours of full audiovisual, twin soundtrack, stereo video programming);
- flexibility of storage (the same disc may be used to store any combination of stills, moving images, text, or indeed any information that can be digitized – computer programs for example);
- easy and rapid access to specific items of information (as in the case of a gramophone record, the reading head may move instantly to any given track on the disc – in contrast to magnetic tape, which must be laboriously wound forward and back to locate specific sections);
- robustness and long life (the disc is pressed from strong plastic, surface scratches do not necessarily influence the quality of reproduction, there is no contact between the disc surface and the reading head so wear is negligible, etc);
- cheapness when mass produced (pressed in large quantities, from a master, rather like a gramophone record) – however, the costs of the master are

high, so the medium is not very attractive economically for short-run production;

- security of copyright (due to the high cost of the master and the special equipment used for pressing copies, the problem of copyright infringement is much smaller than is the case with videotape, audiotape and magnetic discs).

13.3 Modern systems of interactive video: the hardware

A modern interactive video system has four principal components:

1. a video player (despite the tendencies to 'think disc', we shall consider both videodisc and videocassette players as possible candidates – the cassette machines do also have some advantages in certain circumstances, as we shall see);
2. a computer (usually a microcomputer, as portability is desired and no very great computing power is required – nevertheless, any size of computer could be used);
3. an interface unit, or card, designed to link the player and computer;
4. a video monitor, or adapted television receiver (which will present video from the player, audio, computer-generated graphics or text and the computer programs during the programming or debugging of the system).

These are the basic hardware requirements, but of course there are many variations in system characteristics and complexity.

Instructional systems incorporating videodisc are usually categorized in levels, according to their capabilities for interaction.

Four 'levels' of Interactivity

Level 1 systems are the simplest, comprised of a video player and a monitor. As the material is to proceed linearly, the player may be a videocassette player. Player has little memory capability and no processing power. Level 1 systems are essentially playback machines.

Level 2 systems consist of a videodisc player and a controller, either internal or external. Control data can be decoded from a videodisc with a limited command set to handle most of the requirements. Combines a simple program with branching. Best limited to simple dedicated applications.

Level 3 systems combine all the capabilities of the videoplayer and the microcomputer, providing increased memory and data processing capabilities. Sophisticated branching is possible.

Level 4 systems usually imply two videodisc players and advanced capabilities (multichannel audio, windowing, etc). These allow almost instantaneous feedback and more complex branching. Level 4 systems are constantly developing and evolving to include more advanced capabilities.

Figures 13.1, 13.2 and 13.3 illustrate three levels of sophistication, as envisaged by Richard Currier (1983). Figure 13.1 shows a typical 'Level 1' system – little more than a simple video playback system. There may be a special keypad to facilitate random access, but the accessing is done by the learner, possibly with the help of instructions in a printed study guide.

Figure 13.2 shows a Level 2 system with an internal dedicated microprocessor, which allows it to branch automatically to certain segments. This branching may be activated in a variety of ways – by means of a keypad, a bar-code reader that picks up coded instructions from the printed study guide, a light pen that selects from a menu that appears on the screen (or alternatively a touch-sensitive screen activated directly by the learner's finger). Normally, a system of this nature would be equipped with but one or two of these options.

Figure 13.3 shows a fully fledged interactive videodisc system. It has all the four principal components mentioned at the beginning of this section – player, micro, interface and one or more monitors. Depending on the number of monitors, the complexity of the control program and the other control options available, this system would classify as a Level 3 or Level 4 interactive video system.

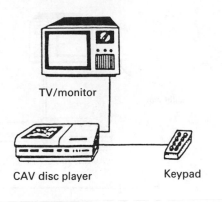

CAV disc with audio
and video only

TV/monitor

CAV disc player

Keypad

Study guide

Figure 13.1 *A typical Level I interactive videodisc system.*

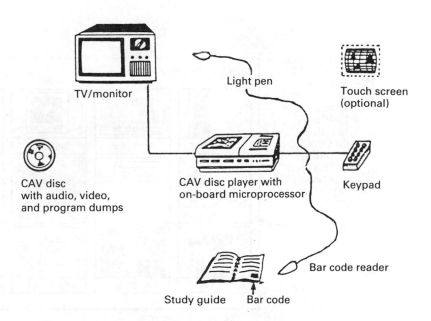

TV/monitor

Light pen

Touch screen
(optional)

CAV disc
with audio, video,
and program dumps

CAV disc player with
on-board microprocessor

Keypad

Bar code reader

Study guide   Bar code

Figure 13.2 *A Level II interactive videodisc system with some of the different available means of interaction.*

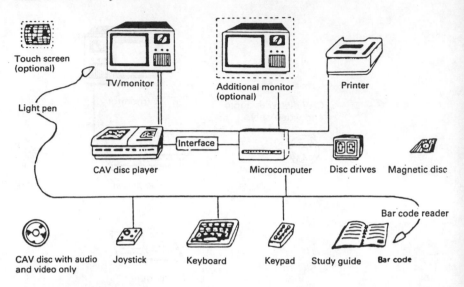

Figure 13.3 *A full (Level 3 or 4) interactive videodisc system.*

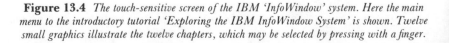

Figure 13.4 *The touch-sensitive screen of the IBM 'InfoWindow' system. Here the main menu to the introductory tutorial 'Exploring the IBM InfoWindow System' is shown. Twelve small graphics illustrate the twelve chapters, which may be selected by pressing with a finger.*

Note the difference between the discs specified for the different versions illustrated. The Level 2 system uses a disc that, in addition to the audio and video material, also stores the control program for the disc. When loaded in the player, this program loads into internal storage built into the player and via the built-in microprocessor, controls the videodisc's branching. The more sophisticated system shown in Figure 13.3, uses the microcomputer's disc drives and magnetic disc storage for the control programs.

The difference between 'Level 3' and 'Level 4' systems is not uniformly defined; essentially it is a scale of complexity (Iuppa, 1984). A Level 3 system is a videodisc player controlled 'by an external computer' whereas a Level 4 system is 'a larger system of information retrieval, eg banks of videodisc and tape players that are connected on-line to a central computer'. Schwartz (1987) on the other hand feels that 'many look at Level 4 for its use of overlayed text, graphics, other visual information and digital data from the external computer . . . The Level 4 system is the highest level of interactivity that is currently available on the market.'

New and fast developments in the technology

This is obviously a fast developing field and what was just last year considered the 'highest level' is today commonplace and next year may well be obsolete. For example, the Interactive Videodisc Information System (IVIS), manufactured by DEC was the 'top of the line' professional system in 1985, pioneering extensive use of touch-screen and overlay graphics of high quality. By 1987, over half a dozen IBM-PC based systems, on both sides of the Atlantic, have similar capabilities. Even IBM has entered into the fray with the INFOWINDOW Interactive Videodisc System (see Figure 13.4). This, some say, will (as usual) impose a sort of industry standard on the disparate and incompatible systems currently being sold. But what about the new alternative technologies already being announced, it would seem, at the rate of one or two a year? Can the CD-ROM CD I and DVI technologies merge amicably with existing systems, or are we on the brink of an outright war? More on this later on in the chapter.

13.3 Some examples of interactive video

13.3.1 A simple classification of applications

'When a new technology is introduced, there is a tendency to use it in the same manner as the technology it has replaced' (Tennyson and L'Allier, 1980). These authors made this remark in relation to computer-assisted instruction and we have seen, in the previous part of this book, that most CAI methodology up to quite recently bore out the truth of this statement. One of the same authors (L'Allier, 1983) has felt it necessary to repeat the same observation in relation to current approaches to the utilization of interactive video.

In an article published in November of 1983 Samuel Howe (1983) mentions four 'current ways of using interactive video in the classroom'.

The four 'most popular' interactive video modes

1. *As a FILE*. This is no more than the rapid access of specific 'clips' from a file of video segments. These would then be incorporated as 'audiovisual aids' in a normal classroom teaching situation, or alternatively, students may individually access the segments, following some study guide (as in 'conventional' resource-based learning systems) or without a systematic study guide (as in 'conventional' use of a library). The access may be computer-controlled, but really a booklet listing the titles of the segments and their location is all that is necessary, together with a Level 1 video set-up, to make the system work.

2. *As an INSERT*. This involves the insertion of text or questions into an existing video presentation. Howe suggests: the insertion of textual frames explaining or describing an upcoming segment of the video; a few key questions at the end of the segment, to test overall comprehension; extra information to 'enhance' the video message or adapt it to the needs of a given target population; the inclusion of a glossary of terms which may be used by viewers who do not understand some of the terminology employed in the video; and so on. Some other authors (eg

Lawrence, 1981) call this approach the 'repurposing' of an existing videotape. It has the advantages of cheapness, as existing materials are utilized, ease of production and the possibility of non-professional, teacher-made productions. Generally, such repurposed materials would gain little by transfer to videodisc, as they are essentially a linear sequence of segments (the original tape was planned for linear, continuous presentation) interspersed by some reading assignments and exercises.

3. As PROGRAMMED LEARNING. This is essentially the preparation of branching sequences, as used in Crowder-type branching texts or in the programmed-tutorial CAI mode, except that some, or even all, of the information is presented in video form. These 'video information frames' are interspersed by computer-generated 'practice' and 'test' frames.

4. As SIMULATION. This is essentially the CAI simulation mode, with enhancement of video segments to present the case material and also the debriefing commentaries. This has been especially well applied in simulations of human interaction situations. Howe quotes the example of first aid training in which video segments show the accident and victims, CAI segments teach and test how to deal with the situations illustrated and video is also used for demonstration of proper techniques, etc. This is an example of a simulation exercise based largely on expositive instructional strategies. There are however many examples of experiential simulation exercises presented in videodisc. In medical diagnosis and treatment (a favourite field of application at present) there are many videodiscs which allow the viewer to make decisions which then affect the outcome of the treatment being given. The viewer may 'cure or kill' the patient (and in many different ways) depending on the pattern, and even the speed, of the decisions taken.

The file

If Howe is correct in his analysis of the current 'state of the art' as regards the chief trends in the practical use of interactive video, then we may observe that L'Allier's comments quoted at the beginning of this section are, in the main, correct. The FILE mode is no more than the automation of access to a collection of non-print media. For convenience, they are stored on one videotape or disc and when the size of the collection warrants it, are better accessed by means of a computer than the alternative booklet index or card file. The rapid access times and relatively cheaper per-slide storage costs offered by videodiscs are very important administrative considerations in large non-print media collections. They may offer significant benefits in terms of large-scale duplication and dissemination, but hardly make the headlines from an instructional design or development viewpoint. The simple cataloguing and organizing of existing media does not, of itself, lead to improved instruction.

INSERT

The INSERT mode, or 'repurposing' of existing video material, may be a useful method of getting more 'mileage' out of earlier investments in video production. If the earlier materials are instructionally sound, but a bit out of step with current needs, this may be a most cost-effective approach. If the existing materials are not 'instructional', but merely 'informational', then the repurposing required may be quite extensive. It is possibly better to think of this case as the generation of new instructional designs (usually CAL designs in the present context) which utilize excerpts of existing video as part of the informational content. The instructional materials developed on the computer are not then 'inserts' in an existing video programme, but segments of the existing video programme become 'inserts' in the newly designed instructional programme.

Pro-grammed learning

This brings us to Howe's third mode. We are, however, alarmed at the rather indiscriminate way that some of the early methodologies are currently being revived and applied in the production of CAL courseware. We have already shown, in Chapter 12 of this book, how the majority of CAL courseware authoring modes (especially those most employed in commerically distributed packages) are closely based on programmed instruction methodology of the 1960s. An anlysis of CAL packages currently on the market, in qualitative terms, shows that a significant proportion suffer from the same ills that contributed to the rapid demise of programmed texts in the late 1960s. A quantitative analysis, if performed, may well reveal that 1987 or thereabouts will be the turning point in the growth graph for 'generic' CAL packages publication, just as 1967 was the turning point for the 'generic' programmed text. We hope this will not be the case, but fear it might be, if the principal growth area continues to be in the use of computers to do what can equally well be done by texts.

It is doubly worrying, therefore, to see that one of the principal growth areas for the new interactive videodisc technology is seen to be in programmed-instruction-type designs with the added 'bells and whistles' of video. This does not bode well for the long-term health and survival of interactive video.

Simulation   Fortunately, the fourth mode quoted by Howe – SIMULATION – holds out hope for a better future. Without a doubt, the use of CAL in the simulation mode has, so far, made the greatest general impact as an instructional innovation.

The incorporation of video segments, large collections of still shots filmed in high resolution, audio and all the other media options offered by the videodisc, into computer-based simulations, opens up a vast new field of possibilities. Many machine-operation simulations which would not be cost-effective if attempted by the construction of special simulation equipment, may be attempted through video-based simulations. Many diagnostic skills that require colour or shape perception to a high degree of perfection may now be developed (eg the spate of interactive vide-based medical diagnosis simulation exercises). But perhaps most significantly, simulations which involve the interpretation of the behaviour of other human beings (which up to now would require role-play or other real-life interaction sessions) are now open to the development of self-study, individual, computer-based simulation exercises.

13.3.2 Interactive-video-files and databases

Any collection of visuals or audiovisual footage can, of course, be called a 'video library'. It probably has to be organized along some system of topic classification to warrant the name of 'video database'. As any other form of database, a single-topic section of the collection would be called a 'file'. Because of its impressive storage capacity, especially for still visuals, the laser videodisc has from its inception been seen as an ideal medium for storing databases that are not subject to constant updating or modification. The addition of interactivity, whether it be simple Level 1' random access by means of a keypad, or sophisticated 'Level 3' computer control, opens up possibilities of new, creative, uses of such a 'video database'.

'Generic' videodiscs as 'databases'   An example of such a database is the 'Bio Sci' generic videodisc, which contains over 6,000 full colour images, mostly stills, but also some short filmed video and animation sequences, covering some dozen or more areas of biology (eg Plant taxonomy, Ecology, Cell biology). The visuals are carefully organized according to main topics and are cross referenced as necessary. An image directory allows one to quickly locate any visuals that might be of relevance to a given lesson or objective. This directory may be used in its printed version, with a 'Level 1' system, but is also available on a floppy disc, to facilitate quicker search and access when using a computer-controlled, 'Level 3' system. The teacher can use the disc as a source of visuals to illustrate a live lecture, or can plan an individual project in which students use the videodisc as a resource.

Not all video libraries are equally easy to use in this way. Perhaps the largest, and certainly the best known, videodisc-based collection is the 'Video Encyclopaedia of the 20th Century' produced by CEL Educational Resources and Time-Life. Over the past twenty or so years, CEL has built up an enormous collection of original film and videotape documentary material. The video encyclopaedia has made the most significant footage available on 38 double-sided videodiscs – a total of 75 hours of video. This collection is accompanied by 'a comprehensive alphabetical and chronological index system' which 'allows the user easy access to the 2,217 units.' However, in practice, access is not all that easy. If you want to research a topic, you are lucky if you find it in the index. Despite its four large volumes, the index lists only a fraction of the ways in which a teacher or a student might wish to access the database. For example, one of my students wished to research the topic of civil rights. He tried a number of obvious key words, like, civil disobedience, women's rights, racial inequality, minorities, but did not find one of them in the index. However, searching under, Ghandi, Martin Luther King, or Little Rock, revealed more material than he could use. A subject matter expert might find the indexing system adequate, but a student is unlikely to unearth what would be of interest without some expert help. Such inadequate cross-referencing makes it difficult to use these discs as interactive resources for student-directed learning. There are other problems with a collection this big. If, for example, you wished to use the material as part of a course in some sport, say American football. You wish to select good examples of particular strategies. The trouble is that the very extensive footage is spread chronologically, across all 72 sides of the 38 discs. You may end up spending more class time changing discs and locating the shots you want than actually viewing. Such fragmentation precludes the use of automatic search-and-screen programs, generally available with 'Level 2' and higher interactive video systems.

Our comments here are not intended to detract from the immense documentary value of the 'video encyclopaedia', nor its educational utility as a non-print library resource. They illustrate, however, that if a database-type videodisc is to be used on an interactive system, then some thought must be given to how it will be used.

The Domesday Project

A very good example of a database planned for interactivity is the DOMESDAY PROJECT developed by the British Broadcasting Corporation (BBC) in the UK. The original Domesday Book was a database compiled in 1086, by the laborious, handwritten, listing of all properties, landowners and other information about the England of William the Conqueror. In 1986, the 900th anniversary, the BBC launched the Domesday Project, with the intention of providing a similar detailed database on life in the very much more complex England of the 1980s. The database structure was carefully designed to be of use to a number of specific user groups (education principally, but also tourism organizations, estate agents, courier and distribution services, local government and so on). It was also designed to make special use of the search facilities that are possible with 'Level 3' interactive video.

The information was selected, collected and packaged by many organizations and institutions. Information of a general and statistical nature is organized as a hierarchical structure of four major subject areas – culture, economy, society, environment – each subdivided into several levels of topics and sub-topics. There is ample built-in cross referencing, which ensures that the user will find all information pertinent to a particular inquiry. This information is stored on a so-called 'national' disc (see Figures 13.5 and 13.6).

A second, 'community', disc stores local information on specific towns, villages, local history or customs, tourist attractions and so on. This information was compiled by groups of children from some 14,000 local schools, as well as numerous community groups and institutions. Over one million people were involved in compiling the database. The information can be accessed in a number of interesting and original ways. The BBC's promotional literature describes the two discs as follows:

'The *National Disc* contains information on the *economy, culture, society* and *the environment*. You can locate the inforamtion you want by starting at one of these and specifying progressively more precise keywords – using the trackerball – as you home in to the subject. For example, at each stage the system will tell you what it has available as text, data or pictures on the subject of your choice (see example). Alternatively, if you can already specify the keyword you want, you can type this in immediately. At whatever level you start to explore the subject you can find your way to what you need to know.

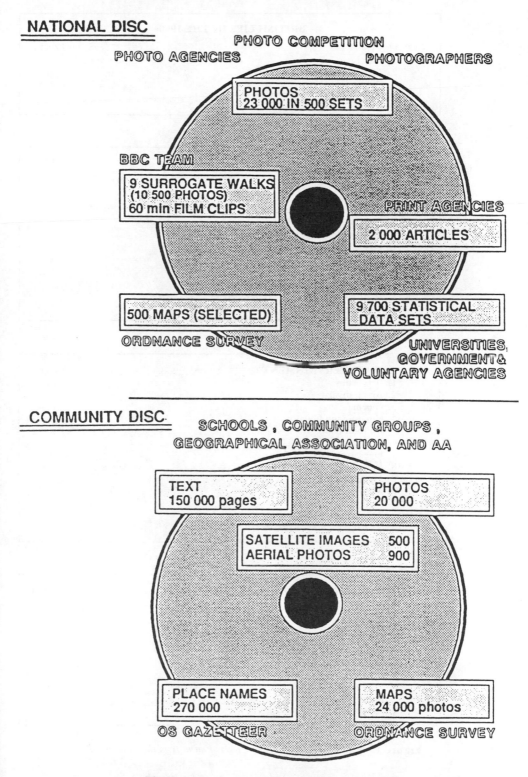

Figure 13.5 *Structure of the two Domesday Project discs.*

BRITISH LIFE IN THE 1980s

CONTENTS   Level 1
 1. Society
 2. The economy
 3. Culture
 4. Environment

CULTURE   Level 2
 1. Arts and entertainment
 2. Beliefs and attitudes
 3. Consumption
 4. Customs and heritage
 5. Home and community
 6. Life style
 7. Leisure and recreation
 8. Language
 9. Mass communications
 10. Religion and philosophy
 11. Sport and games
 12. Tourism

ARTS AND ENTERTAINMENT   Level 3
 1. Arts centres
 2. Arts festivals
 3. Cinema
 4. Circuses and funfairs
 5. Cultural policy
 6. Dancing and nightclubs
 7. Fetes, carnivals and shows
 8. Literature
 9. Museums, galleries and libraries
 10. Music
 11. Performing arts
 12. Theatre
 13. Visual arts and design

VISUAL ARTS AND DESIGN   Level 4
 1. Architecture
 2. Design
 3. Illustration
 4. Printing
 5. Contemporary photography
 6. Sculpture
 7. Crafts
 8. Video
 9. Interior design
 10. Fashion design

Figure 13.6 *Domesday Project: four levels of menu from the 'National disc'.*

'This "discovery learning" aspect is illustrated in an informative and entertaining way by the Domesday Gallery, a visual index for the user, and by what are known as "surrogate walks". Some of the 20 000 photographs on the national disc are used to present a series of contemporary environments: typical houses, a market town, a farm, and a nature reserve. Using the trackerball you can explore these environments as if you were walking into them, going through doors, round corners and discovering what is going on there in precise photographic detail.

'In all there are some 9000 sets of data on the National Disc, all organized for rapid access through a simple system of keywords, which allows you to range widely over the subject matter of the disc, and to home in on the subjects that interest you.

The Community Disc
The Community Disc contains some 150 000 screen pages of text and 20 000 photographs, yet in spite of this massive amount of data it is probably the easiest part of the system to use.

'The organization of the disc is based on some 24 000 Ordnance Survey maps arranged in six levels with text and photographs available at each level.
Level 0 – The United Kingdom, including the Channel Islands, Orkneys and Shetlands: satellite photograph, text
Level 1 – Countries and island groups: satellite photograph, text
Level 2 – 40 × 30 km regions: satellite and aerial photograph, text, maps
Level 3 – 4 × 3 km local blocks: community photographs, text, maps
Level 4 – Street maps: special feature photographs, text
Level 5 – Floor plans of special sites: special feature photographs, text

'The enquirer can enter the system at any level, by typing in a place name, a regional description, a grid reference, or by using the trackerball to move a pointer on the screen. At any level it is simple to move across the map, to access photographs, descriptions and data, or to move to levels above and below.

'Using the Community Disc in this way is like a journey of exploration. At any point you can move along a road, check where you are generally by "zooming out" to a larger scale map, or find out more about places of interest by "zooming in" and requesting photographs and text information. As a desk research tool for anyone who wants to know where places are, what they look like, and what goes on there, the Community Disc is an unrivalled resource.

'It is even possible to use the system to measure accurately and automatically the distance between two points on the map, either directly or by road, or the area covered within any boundaries you set.'

13.3.3 Creating inserts, or repurposing existing videodiscs

In Chapter 9 we already dealt with the topic of 'repurposing' an existing film or videotape, by re-editing it in order to select just those scenes that are relevant to the objectives of a new course. During this process, it is, of course possible to shoot a small amount of new material necessary to link the scenes or to complete the desired message. It is also possible to build in some pauses for other learning activities. This is done, typically, when a lengthy demonstration film of an industrial operation is to be used for on-the-job training. The film is divided into step-by-step segments, with pauses between each step, so that trainees may practice one step to perfection (repeating the video demonstration if necessary), before they progress to the next step.

This form of repurposing may turn an old group-demonstration film into an effective individualized instructional system. However, if the procedures being taught are not always sequenced in the same linear sequence, or if some steps may require the use of prior learning (which some will remember and others not), then a fair amount of rewinding back and forth to locate scenes out of sequence may be required. This becomes difficult and time consuming on normal video equipment. Interactive video systems can overcome these difficulties and can offer yet further advantages.

Repurposing for 'Level 1' interactivity

The simplest form of repurposing is to use a 'Level 1' system and a printed study guide. Instead of performing all the operations of winding back the tape to a previous scene manually and checking that it is at exactly the desired starting point, the student uses a keypad to punch in the starting and stopping frame numbers and the system finds and plays the requested scene. This type of repurposing may be done on both videodisc and videotape systems with equal ease. In the case of home-produced videotape, this is a particularly useful technique, as the required shots can be selected from the original tape and played back in the required sequence, without the need to first edit the tape. Tape has, of course, the disadvantage of taking a considerable time to wind back if the two consecutive scenes are far apart on the original. This is a problem when the two shots are to be viewed end-on without a pause. But in the individualized system, with pauses for practice between shots, it is not such a great disadvantage.

Repurposing for 'Level 3' interactivity

When a full 'Level 3' interactive videodisc system is used, the insert technique can be much more sophisticated. Using an existing videodisc, it is possible to select and play scenes from any part of the disc with almost imperceptible search pauses. Furthermore, a variety of computer-generated materials and special effects may be developed by means of the authoring systems normally available on such systems. A linking title page may be computer generated and presented to mask the search time. Questions may be asked on screen. Overlays or 'windows' can be superimposed on the video image to concentrate attention on a particular part of the original picture, to add captions, arrows, colour, etc. This, of course, demands mastery of the authoring software package, but many of these are now very user-friendly, menu-driven or iconic systems that are very quickly mastered. In this way the 'Bio Sci' generic disc, mentioned earlier, can be used to build any number of tailor-made presentations.

13.3.4 The PROGRAMMED INSTRUCTION of CAI mode

As you get more ambitious with your repurposing, you will eventually start developing sequences of practice exercises between video segments, complex remedial branches and all the other characteristics of a programmed tutorial. If the authoring system can handle it (and most can) you may also develop a CMI element to keep track of individual student progress, allow two or three attempts at a task with graded remedial hints, build in automatic assessment and report generation and all the other characteristics of tutorial CAI. The danger with this progression, as outlined earlier, is that the instructional design quality may, in some cases, be rather poor and the return for all this investment of time and repurposing effort may not be spectacular. If, on the other hand, a very thorough instructional design exercise is undertaken, it will almost certainly lead to the specification of much video material which is not available in already existing material. Rather than repurposing old video, one will be shooting new footage. This is going somewhat beyond the selection and slight adaptation of media, which is the primary focus of this book. We are entering the specialist realm of interactive video courseware design.

Selecting good interactive video materials

It is much more likely that most of us will be faced with the selection or rejection of ready-made interactive video courseware. The approach should be essentially similar to the one outlined for CAL in the previous chapter, with the addition of some questions specifically directed towards the use made, and the quality of the video component. It is important to distinguish the effective use of video from the embellishment of an otherwise mediocre bit of courseware with some flashy video sequences. It is not unknown for CAL courseware development houses to take a package that has not been at all exceptional in terms of evaluation results or market success, and try to wring some more mileage out of it by adding some video material. This is the opposite of the INSERT approach. One can only sort out the wheat from the chaff by some form of systematic analysis/evaluation process similar to the one described for CAL earlier on. In so doing, one evaluates the package as regards its probable (or proven) instructional effectiveness and analyses the exact function of the video content in the total package.

Example of good use of interactive video capability

An analysis of a couple of real examples may help. The first is an interactive videodisc program developed for the US Army which goes by the fancy name of STARS (Space Time Army Reconnaissance System) (C.I.D.E., 1985). This is not the name of any real Army system, but a fictitious setting in which to embed instruction on the reading and use of army equipment maintenance manuals. The reason for this fictitious context was mainly motivational – the setting of the manual reading and maintenance tasks in a real war situation which would help to keep trainees interested and alert, as well as vividly portraying the need for speed and accuracy in battlefield equipment maintenance. Another general reason for the use of audiovisual media was the relatively low literacy levels often encountered in the target population – it was hard work enough to read the maintenance manuals, without extra reading on their interpretation and use. The use of video for the explanations should help to overcome any initial reading difficulties. These reasons may, in themselves, have been enough to suggest that interactive video might be more appropriate than straight tutorial CAI. However, the instructional design process reveals yet other, more pertinent reasons. The reading of the drawings in the manuals and their correct interpretation is one essential skill that must be developed. The learning of the correct procedures to put things right accounts for another handful of the objectives. The first of these involves the perceptual identification and matching of an engineering drawing with the real component or assembly – this requires both drawn AND 'real' (or photographic) visual stimuli for comparison during training. The second involves manipulative activities that require a moving-image presentation.

These instructional design requirements are even more compelling reasons to incorporate video sequences for specific instructional objectives (see our media selection approach in Chapter 3). However, once it is decided that visual media should be used, there remains the question of *how* they may best be used. Here, the special characteristics of 'Level 3 or 4' interactive video offer opportunities to do things that would not be possible in other AV media. The reading of drawings, for example, is trained through the presentation of a still photo of an assembly and then superimposing on top of the slide an engineering drawing of exactly the same size, generated by the computer software. This superposition is performed by means of a fade-in/fade-out technique, so that the real photo transforms itself into the drawing before the eyes of the trainee. The process is under trainee control and is reversible – photo to drawing and back to photo, as often as the trainee desires. In this way, the relationships between all drawing conventions and real-life equipment are naturally established, without the need for an intermediate stage of learning the jargon terms. Such special video effects, together with the dramatized, motivational context and real 'soldier-talk', combine to create a product that teaches in a way no other alternative media could emulate. The authors refer to this part-scientific/part-artistic ID approach as 'imagineering'.

A not-so-good example

As a contrast example, one might cite the interactive video program 'Introduction to the IBM-PC' produced by Comsell Inc. This is one of very many IV packages available on aspects of computers and computer science, from this and several other companies. This particular package teaches the fundamentals of operation of the IBM-PC and PC compatibles – key operations, function keys, formatting and copying diskettes, operating system commands, etc. The objectives are all basic concepts and standard procedures. Many packages exist that have proven themselves to be effective in teaching all these objectives to most categories of trainees that may wish to use a PC. These effective packages range from self-instructional manuals to 'embedded' CAI lessons. This particular lesson uses two interesting and rather uncommon embellishments. One of these is an interactive videodisc. The other is the control, by means of appropriate software, of the functions of the PC during the training sessions, so that for example inappropriate keys are 'blocked' and audio 'beeps' inform the trainee that an incorrect key has been depressed. Furthermore, the trainee cannot 'get lost' as the PC will not respond to inappropriate commands in unexpected and mysterious ways. This control, through software, effectively transforms the PC into a sort of 'teaching machine'. Like many equipment simulators, the PC prevents the practice of errors through enhancing the guidance and the feedback received by the trainee during practice.

And what is the contribution of the interactive videodisc? This is totally integrated with the practice routines, providing some motivational explanations from a genial 'talking head' instructor, demonstrations on video of appropriate sequences of key depressions and resultant changes on the computer's monitor and, finally, the talking head again enhancing the computer-generated feedback with encouraging comments like 'that's right – well done' or 'not quite – let's try it again'. The whole package is most professionally put together. Video quality is high. The changes from video simulation of a live tutorial to computer-based practice, and back, are so smooth that a very realistic impression of a 'live, face-to-face tutorial' is created. The overall instructional design is not bad, as regards the appropriateness of content, practice and feedback for each of the objectives.

But is the undoubtedly effective use of the video medium COST-EFFECTIVE? Costs for hardware are substantially more than double the price of a PC alone (the system needs something like the IBM InfoWindow system than the cost of a PC. With many users, we might be able to spread these up-front additional costs, but what do we get in return? The system teaches the concepts and procedures effectively – perhaps very effectively. But so do many other simpler packages. The video presents moving demonstrations of key-pressing, but no one is learning the skill of pressing a key; just the knowledge of *which* key to press. Print (for example, on the computer screen, if you don't want to use a manual) can do this 100 per cent effectively. The video shows the result of user input as data on a video image of a video monitor. Does that add anything over just showing it directly on the monitor? The PC itself can be programmed to do that. The video appears fun and is no doubt a motivating factor. But does anyone who has just spent a thousand or two on a new computer, or whose job security depends on using a PC efficiently, *need* the extrinsic motivation of a genial 'talking head'? Finally, the use of video cuts down on the amount of reading required of the trainee, as a portion of the explanations are delivered in audio. But would-be users of a PC are not likely to be illiterate – indeed their typical capacity to absorb print messages is probably several times faster than the speed of delivery of audio. If we add to this the greater learner control that a reader can exert over what he or she needs to read (given a clearly structured format of presentation) as opposed to the lack of learner control over a spoken message, this aspect could possibly detract from instructional effectiveness and certainly would increase average study time for the same content.

Well, there's a bunch of questions. Are there any answers? Perhaps some reader may like to take this up as a research project. But I know where I would place my bets. Hopefully, these two examples have illustrated the types of questions that should be asked in evaluating the probable benefits of interactive video CAI. They are a combination of CAI specific questions and media-selection questions, similar to those already outlined in earlier chapters.

13.3.5 The simulation mode

Simulation is almost always part of good interactive video

As mentioned earlier, the use of interactive video in the presentation of computer-controlled simulations is perhaps the most promising innovation. The video medium can present the realism of people's verbal and non-verbal communication, the detail of complex processes and procedures, the real life setting in which a problem is embedded, and so on. We saw that many of the better applications of IV discussed so far have included an element of simulation, even when the principal instructional mode was a programmed tutorial, or a drill and practice exercise. The video medium was used to 'paint' a context which would help to make the required learning more relevant, more intersting or more important. The upshot is increased motivation for learning. However, some learning tasks are set in a simulated real-life environment because that is an essential part of the conditions for learning. A good example is any objective that deals with the development of inter-personal skills (interviewing, supervising, teaching). Another group of learning tasks uses simulated environments in the attempt to employ a case-study based on experiential learning methodology. Good examples include case studies that seek to develop management decision making skills.

Medical diagnosis simulation

A popular application of interactive video has been in the field of medical diagnosis and treatment. Typically, the patient appears in the hospital or consultation room with a particular complaint or set of symptoms. The trainee has to delve deeper into the patient's condition, by specifying tests to be carried out, observing more closely any parts of the patient's body that are considered relevant and, finally, has to reach a diagnosis. Only that information which the trainee seeks is given. This may be through patients' replies to questions, or through visual information observed either directly or by special tests (eg microscope slides). Some of these medical simulations are fairly like a simulation/tutorial, leading the student by means of prompting and correction of individual responses as they are made. A more complete and indeed more ambitious style of simulation is open-ended in structure. Whatever decision a student takes is followed up, just as it may be in real life. If a wrong diagnosis is made and inappropriate treatment is prescribed, the story goes on as if that really had happened. As, with time, the patient does not respond to treatment, the student is eventually made aware that *possibly* some earlier decisions were not correct. However, which decisions to review, and how to back-track and change treatments, is entirely up to the individual. There may even be some element of chance built into the simulation's model – after all, not all patients get better, even if correctly diagnosed and treated – so students really have to make sure what level of confidence they are prepared to place on a given course of action. They may end up by killing or curing their patient, and in several different ways. Several 'plays' are generally needed to discover all the heuristics used by a skilled doctor in similar cases.

Classroom behaviour simulation

A very similar design, but in a subject area more up our own street, is the interactive videodisc '*Classroom Discipline: A Simulation Approach*' produced by the University of Alberta. This is a Level 2 videodisc, with its control software already built into the disc. Trainees respond to the simulated situations in one of several ways. Each response leads to a new situation and a new set of alternatives. Several scenarios are enacted separately. Examples are student lateness, insubordination, etc. After each scenario, there is a de-briefing session, which analyses the path followed and compares it with other alternatives. Similar approaches have been used on videotape-based simulations designed to develop client/consultant relationships in instructional development projects (CID, Syracuse Univesity) and in various aspects of teaching instructional design and, notably, the effective use of interactive video (University of Twente, Holland).

Decision point – a living case-study

A somewhat different design structure is illustrated by some management decision-making case-study type simulations. One which I have been using quite extensively of late is '*Decision Point: A Living Case Study*' (Digital Equipment Corporation, 1985). Ten decisions have to be taken by the student in the role of vice president for sales, in a fictitious company. The problem (of poor sales performance) is a result of a complex of ten interrelated sub-problems. Each of these have to be addressed and resolved satisfactorily if projected sales figures are to be achieved or surpassed. To help with each of the ten decision points, several types of information may be called for – typically these are data about present policies and procedures and their impact on the sales record (often these are computer-based mini-simulations embedded within the overall situational simulation) and the opinions of various other key employees, whom the trainee may interview; naturally, they often give conflicting opinions on what's wrong and what should be done about it.

The ten areas of decision are: commission policy, credit policy, discount approval policy, difficult promotion decisions, distribution of sales reports, technical support systems, size of the sales staff, sales support workflow, quota system and general management style and effectiveness. Naturally the decisions taken on one point interact with some others, giving a complex and realistic situation to handle. The assessment of student performance takes into account all ten decisions points, both individually and their interaction, giving a figure for the overall annual sales achieved by each student.

This always proves to be a fascinating experience for the participants. But trainees learn with very variable efficiency, largely dependent to the extent to which they take note and reflect on their decision pattern. Sometimes, many plays (some two hours each time) are required in order to finally achieve the sales projections.

Research on how to use 'decision point'
We have found that learning can be enhanced by strengthening the end of game debriefing. In the simulation, as distributed by DEC, the final feedback to the student is restricted largely to which decision points contributed to increasing the sales and which points were unsatisfactorily dealt with. But there is no real discussion of where the individual student went wrong. By strengthening this aspect (either by the inclusion of a teacher-led debriefing session, or by means of a further, 'conversational tutorial' on-line) it is expected that learning from one play of the game would be considerably improved. These questions are the subject of an ongoing research project. In reality, we are doing no more than has been found beneficial in the case of non-computer-based simulation games (see Chapter 12). There is no reason to suppose that the importance of reflective debriefing sessions should be any less in the case of complex experiential computer-based simulation games, than in similar non computer-based strategies. The chief drive of our research is to identify the most effective techniques for development of such refelctive self-analysis situations in a computer-based learning package (Romiszowski and Grabowski, 1987). The chief reason for mentioning this case here is to remind us that although simulation games can be so absorbing and so much fun, they do not necessarily constitute all the learning activities that a student has to engage in, in order to develop higher order cognitive strategies and heuristic problem-solving skills. It still rests with the teacher to analyse the IV package under consideration, identify the instructional functions that it performs well, but also those which perhaps need to be developed by the teacher or incorporated into other, more appropriate learning exercises.

13.4 Some research results and some further questions

Due to the relative novelty of the medium there is as yet sparse, research evidence on the use of interactive video in education and training. One such study, described by Laurillard (1984), illustrates the importance that the type of control strategy used has on the effectiveness of interactive video as a medium of instruction. Laurillard describes experiments performed with students of the British Open University, to investigate three key questions: what should be the balance of student control versus program control with respect to –

Student control versus program control

(a) the sequence of presentation of content in the video part of the package (Laurillard refers to this as the 'receptive' mode of learning);
(b) the choice of how many practice exercises to do and at what level of difficulty (this is called the 'active' mode of learning);
(c) the strategy for alternating between these two modes of 'receptive' and 'active' learning.

For the purposes of the study, an existing, well tried and successful Open University course segment was chosen and the existing video lesson was converted into interactive video form. This was done by isolating concepts covered by the original lesson as separate self-contained video sequences and then developing, for each of these sequences, a CAL program to provide practice exercises with tutorial guidance where necessary. The teaching built into these CAL units did not go beyond that contained in the original texts which formed part of the OU course, used as a basis for the experiment. This structure enabled the researcher to verify that, in general, the interactive version of the lesson was at least as effective as the previously used lesson package. However, the principal findings are related to the three questions mentioned above.

Methods and results of student control of sequence

As regards the sequence of presentation of the video component, student choice was built-in in two ways. At the end of each segment of the video presentation, students could opt to do an exercise or to continue with another video segment. Similarly, they could choose more exercises or more video at the end of each CAL exercise. The choices were presented as menus of all the video segments and CAL exercises available, facilitating free choice of sequence to each student. Some groups received advice on the most 'appropriate' (in the author's view) choice and other groups did not receive such advice. The second way of allowing student choice of sequence was within a given video segment – students could interrupt the presentation and choose to repeat it, review the last 30 seconds, skip forward 30 seconds, or just leave it and move to another learning activity. In summary, the results were as follows:

- between segments, students expressed the desire for some advice on appropriate choices of study activity (those who did not receive such advice complained of feeling 'lost');
- however, when such advice was given in respect of the next 'appropriate' video segment to view, it was followed in only 48 per cent of cases;
- the option to stop/rewind/skip parts of a given segment of video was hardly used at all by the students (they would tend to view-on 'passively' until the video stopped automatically).

Student control of practice exercises

As regards the freedom to choose practice exercises and do as many as were felt necessary, the students tended to exhibit yet more variety of individual choice. Once more, author's advice was given, in some cases, as to the most 'appropriate' moment for attempting a given set of exercises. Also, the number of exercises attempted in a given set, was under complete student control. The results were as follows:

- when advice on 'appropriate' moments for taking a given exercise set was given, it was followed in only 28 per cent of cases;
- students varied considerably in the number of exercises attempted in a given set (from one to 12 exercises) and these variations were highly complex, the same student attempting many exercises of one set and only one or two of another (this being clearly related to individual difficulties with individual concepts of the lesson).

As regards the overall strategy of alternating between the 'receptive' and 'active' modes of study, students showed a similar degree of individual preferences and styles. All in all, based on these experimental results and on interviews with the participating students, Laurillard concluded that

'students can make full use of most aspects of control and moreover make use of them in such a variety of ways that it becomes clear that program control must seriously constrain the individual preferences of students. To justify the use of program control, the designers must demonstrate that they 'know best' what the student needs at each stage, ie that program control gives improved learning outcomes. Given the continual failure of educational research to ever find an evaluation instrument sensitive enough to produce

significant differences of this kind, it must be preferable to give students the
benefit of the doubt. We should acknowledge that the unpredictability and
variation in their learning behaviour could be derived from perfectly
legitimate and effective learning strategies, and that these should be
considered in the design.'

Laurillard was, of course, working with a fairly sophisticated group of adult
learners and with certain specific types of objectives. It may be that with other
types of students, on other types of learning tasks, the conclusions would not be as
overwhelmingly in favour of the use of student-directed control strategies.
However, it is clear that there are whole areas of education and training where the
above-mentioned findings could be expected to hold good and it is perhaps in
these areas that the special advantages of interactive video might be best exploited.
The students in this experiment learned as well as or better than previous groups
using non-interactive materials, *irrespective of the learning strategies adopted.*

The usual   This research study is worth reporting in full, as it breaks somewhat new
inconclusive   ground, in studying how to get the best out of the medium, rather than performing
comparative   yet another futile comparative study (although some overall comparisons were also
studies   reported). This sort of approach, characterized also by our own research reported
earlier, may prove more useful in practice, avoiding the barren overall
comparisons of alternative media so criticized by Clark and others. Reeves (1986)
reports, however, that 'interactive video has already been subjected to the
ill-favoured comparative research paradigm.' Although the field is so relatively
young, Reeves reports the research by Kellock (1981) comparing straight videodisc
to lecture, Holmgren and others (1980) on videodisc versus Super-8 film,
Schroeder (1982) on videodisc versus role-play and programmed instruction,
Ketner (1982) on videodisc versus hands-on training, Giunti and Kimberlin
(1982) on interactive video tutorials versus CAI and Reeves and King (1986) on
interactive video simulations versus real military field exercises. We should not be
surprised, that none of these studies found any significant differences in
instructional effectiveness between any of the media alternatives compared.
Nevertheless, Reeves argues that interactive video may offer significant
instructional advantages over other media alternatives, but that comparative
studies are not the way to go about measuring them. He suggests five alternative
research methodologies, all geared to the measuring of micro-level differences in
the effects of the different instructional design models that may be implemented,
with greater or lesser success, by means of interactive video technology. His
suggestion is equivalent to Clark's position, that what makes the difference in
instructional effectiveness are significant improvements in instructional design,
with the added belief that the creative use of interactive video capabilities will in
fact yield some forms of significant ID advances that are at least difficult to
implement in other media. Whether Reeves' position will prove defensible,
whether the term he helped to coin – IMAGINEERING – has anything really
new and different to offer the ID process, has yet to be fully investigated.

A somewhat different, perhaps more 'traditional', research agenda on interactive
video effectiveness is proposed by Hannafin (1985). He suggests a research agenda
structured around twelve basic propositions to be investigated:

1. IV instruction is generally more effective than non-interactive video
   instruction and effectiveness increases with degree of interactivity.
2. Type and nature of interactivity affects the type and quality of learning.
3. Interactivity reduces the passivity of learners towards the instruction they
   get.
4. Learning is likely to be most effective when criterion questions are
   embedded throughout the lesson.
5. Comprehension and attention are increased by questioning and feedback
   procedures in interactive video.
6. Learner control is not effective unless coaching or advisement procedures
   are utilized.

7. Speed of learning is negatively correlated with the amount of interactivity.
8. IV is not appropriate for all learners, content and task types.
9. The more rapidly program segments are accessed, the more effective the instruction.
10. Positive attitudes to IV are more a function of novelty than any intrinsic aspects of the technology.
11. The form of interactivity that works in IV is not necessarily what works in other forms of lessons.
12. Pre-designed interactivity does not capitalize on the unique mental processing capabilities of individual learners.

Many of these propositions are derived from research findings already available in other areas of instructional research – examples include item 4 (from early programmed instruction research and oft repeated), item 5 (generally true), item 6 (already shown in CAI research). Other items are 'popular beliefs' about IV which nevertheless require verification – examples are items 7, 9, 10 and 11. Yet others are fundamental beliefs in the basic tenet that 'interactivity is good for you'.

Whatever one's views on the state of knowledge concerning the real instructional benefits of interactive video, or one's general opinions on the value of media-related research, one thing is for sure – there will be an increasing level of production (in terms of quantity) and variety of products (in terms of quality) as the new information technologies which make slick interactive programming possible, expand in power and scope, whilst diminishing in costs to a fraction of original prices. There are so many 'breakthrough innovations' every year that it is difficult to foresee just where the development of already existing IV technologies and the blending of yet other technology combinations will lead us. We shall examine some of the possible new directions of development of information technologies for education in the next chapter. Before we go on, however, it may be useful to take stock of where the technologies are at present and the short-term impact this will have on the costs and the power of interactive video, whether used for education, for commercial purposes (as in point-of-sale displays) or in the leisure industries.

13.5 Advances in the technology

13.5.1 Optical recording capabilities

One aspect of videodiscs has made the technology seem irrelevant to many instructors working in small organizations, or teachers on a tight budget. This has been the high cost of 'mastering' a videodisc, which, until recently, ran at $2,000 (£1,250) or more (not counting any costs incurred in producing the master videotape). At that kind of price for the master disc, it makes no sense to produce a cheap, home video production, or simply record hours of group dynamics observation for later analysis and feedback. No: the videodisc was reserved for high quality productions, which would justify the cost by being produced in large numbers. The teacher wishing one copy only of a video segment, to be used in his or her teaching, was effectively obliged to stick to videotape recording.

But, in a case of several hours' worth of short clips of, for example, trainee teachers' classroom behaviour, collected painstakingly over yeas of observation and used as a database of good and bad examples, the rapid search and location capabilities of videodiscs would offer great advantages over the laborious winding back and forth of videotape cassettes. Well, the recordable videodisc, so long announced, has at last arrived and is in a price bracket which competes with videotape. Investing in your own videodisc recording equipment is still very expensive as compared to half inch videocassette recorders, but the price of the cheapest models is coming down to something like the price of mastering just one disc a few years ago. No doubt, as has become customary, we shall all be surprised by the way that, in time, prices will tumble even further.

The currently available technology permits you to record once only on the disc.

It has, therefore, gained the name of 'Write Once, Read Many' (times), or WORM. Whereas this is not as convenient as record-and-erase videotape, for many purposes, it makes the transfer of any existing video material to disc format much more accessible. The cost of the discs is so low that for large amounts of data, optical storage systems are often competitive with paper filing systems. It is rather pointless to quote prices when these change, in a generally downward direction, every month.

Use the 'Worm' for archives or for low-cost interactive video

For the storage of video or plain visual material, to be used in a random manner to support teaching, the methodology should be unrivalled. With space for 54,000 still images, many teachers could store their lifetime's collection of slides and transparencies on just one disc. Of course, that is what causes some problems. One does not usually have a lifetime's collection of anything at one time. Collections build up and, at the moment, it is not possible to add or change the information on the disc once it has been written on. However, this may soon change as current developments in high storage digital videodiscs will, no doubt, percolate down to the semi-professional one-off market in due course.

In the meantime, apart from the storage of large collections of visual material that is to be preserved, but easily accessed, the other great benefit of the WORM disc is that it enables just about any school media centre or training unit to experiment with the production of interactive video programmes on a reasonable budget. Also, many professional production companies are turning to the WORM for pilot test copies of a disc, to enable any instructional weaknesses in the programme to be corrected on the master videotape before pressing the final optical disc.

13.5.2 CD-ROM and CD-I

CD-ROM: digital storage of data

The compact disc (CD) has been with us just a few years, it seems, and has already become almost a standard item of equipment in any music lover's stereo system. What is perhaps less well known outside the computer fraternity is CD-ROM, which stands for the same Compact Disc used as a Read Only Memory (ROM) of immense proportions, as compared to the storage capacity of the well known 'floppy discs' or even the Winchester hard discs that were considered the last word in memory storage for microcomputers. As computer memory, the compact disc can store 550 megabytes, or about 20 times the information you can pack into one of the larger Winchesters that are normally fitted to IBM PCs. To get an idea of what this means, the Grolier Encyclopaedia, a 20-volume work when printed, is packed into one compact disc, together with a cross-referencing index system of such detail that it takes up another 20 volumes' worth of space – and the disc is not even one quarter full.

CD-I: optical storage of data and images

CD-ROM only hit the market in about 1985. It caused so much interest that the first international conference devoted specifically to this technology, organized by the computer software company Microsoft, attracted more than 1,000 delegates. However, the show was stolen by another newcomer – CD-I, or 'Compact Disc-INTERACTIVE'. Basically, this is a compact *optical* disc, like the 12-inch, but improvements in processing have made it possible to pack in a lot more information. This enables the little disc to run quite a reasonably long and very high quality video presentation, as well as doubling up as an audio disc player and, probably, a high capacity disc drive for external memory for your computer. This is intended to be marketed as a domestic product with an initial price tag of not much more than $1,000 (£650). This system immediately was seen as yet another step along the road to cheaper and more accessible interactive video. The interactive capacity is to be built into the player, so that it will be directly usable with commercially produced interactive games, etc. But it will also open the door to various educational and training applications. Of course, the optical storage system, similar to the 12-inch videodiscs, does not allow recording and erasure and so, initially, educators will rely on commercially mass produced programmes. But, no doubt, the WORM technology for low-cost low-quantity special productions will also become available, if the system becomes any sort of commercial success (Rosen, 1986).

And that's the proverbial $64,000 question! For no sooner was the CD-I technology announced, than other rival systems reared their heads. A year after the demonstration of CD-I as a technical possibility, and before it even made the market in production versions, we saw the announcement of a new challenger to the interactive video crown.

13.5.3 DVI: Digital Video Interactive

DV-I: digital storage of data and images

For as long as the interactive video movement has been around, researchers were talking of the potential benefits of digital storage for video. Progress was steady, giving us, for example the 8-millimetre, digitally recorded videotape system. But the capacity to compress digital information to such an extent as to store a reasonable amount of video on a compact disc seemed to be more difficult than first imagined.

The problem was not one of the hardware technology, but rather the treatment given to the digitized data to compress it and so store it in less space. Compression of data in this manner has been used for many applications in the past, such as in compressed audio transmission of telephone conversations. But the degree of compression that was necessary for the storage of video on a compact disc in digital form was much greater. At the first Microsoft conference, where the optically recorded CD-I was first demonstrationed 'up and working', experts estimated that digitally recorded compact discs were about ten years into the future. Then, at the *second* Microsoft conference on CD-ROM technology, held in March 1987, a fully working digitally recorded compact disc, with excellent video quality and storage capacity, was shown. The necessary software breakthrough in data compression had occurred. As Hurst (1987) put it – 'a delegation from GE/RCA Laboratories in Princeton, NJ, stunned the 1,100-person gathering by actually demonstrating precisely what the experts said was a decade away: 72 minutes of full-motion video on a normal one-sided CD-ROM.' *DVI*, or *Digital Video Interactive*, was born. What is more, the disc was played on a standard CD-ROM player built to feed data to a computer. The major breakthrough that enabled this 10-year 'compression' of the expected development process was *software* – a more efficient algorithm to perform the compression and decompression operations on the data.

Implications of the DV-I breakthrough

The reason why this development is of much more than passing interest is that, at one swoop, it throws open so many intriguing possibilities for advancement in cheap interactive communications. On the one hand, it means that we are well on the way to having high quality record/playback/erase/dub compact videodisc players. Coupled to this, we can expect higher and more reproducible quality standards in video, less deterioration of quality in successive copies of copies and many other practical advantages. In addition, we have the chief one – *Many inexpensive video recorders/players will have built-in capabilities for interaction.*

As if that was not enough, there is one further potential spinoff – *the same compression algorithms used in DV-I may be used to compress video for transmission through telephone lines. The video-phone may soon become economically viable.*

14 Interactive distance education systems

14.1 The networked society: a vision of the future

In this chapter, we shall examine some of the trends in telecommunications and the ways in which they can be utilized in distance education. In particular, we shall see how these developments enable us to achieve the goals of utilizing more education-at-a distance, while maintaining, or indeed increasing, the degree of individualization and student autonomy in the instructional process. We will see ways of overcoming the apparent limitations of distance education as an impersonal, inflexible and centralized system of teaching. We shall see that distance-teaching can be interactive, can involve groups as well as individuals, can be totally private and one-to-one when required and can be learner controlled in all senses of that term.

Will new means of telecommunication cause a revolution?
But at what cost? Will the new telecommunications media be accepted generally and implemented in education? Or will they tend to be restricted to certain privileged sections of military and industrial training? Will they really make a difference for all of us and our children? This chapter argues that big changes are on the way. There are so many converging trends in society as a whole and so many other pressures for the installation of the telecommunication links and systems we shall be analysing, that educational (and specifically instructional) applications will be able to, as it were, 'piggyback' on investments that will be made anyway. My thesis is that we are indeed on the road to vast changes in the form of education, brought about by advances in technology. But haven't we heard this before? What makes this phase of technological development so different? So many good ideas and grand predictions of change have come and gone, but educational systems have been little affected. Why should this time be any different? Let us proceed by analysing some of the emergent 'new technologies'.

14.2 Teleconferencing

14.2.1 The telephone

The telephone was the first real advance in two-way, interactive, communication over distances that improved on written correspondence. The earlier telegraph system reduced time-lag between message and feedback, but imposed severe restrictions on the form of message and its complexity and length. The telephone combined the instant feedback of the telegraph with the versatility of the spoken word and even the nuances of expression and tone that often communicate as much as the words themselves.

Basic telephone conferencing
It is not surprising that the telephone quickly became an indispensable tool of modern life. Its main use was (and is) for one-to-one communication, but from the earliest days it was also used for a limited form of 'teleconferencing'. Early films show Al Capone and his henchmen using several extensions on one phone line as a means of group participation in planning a bank robbery. The phone line only linked two localities, but several people, in different rooms of 'headquarters' would interact with the man in the phone box in front of the bank (and with each other as well). The step to amplification of the telephone message at the two ends of the

line, so that a group at each end could listen to one loudspeaker, was a logical and relatively simple extension of this idea.

Telephone conferencing between two localities has been used in the business world quite extensively and for a long time. Only more recently, with advances in telephone 'bridging' technology, did it become possible to link up more than two different localities to the same conversation, but now this too has become commonplace. Most telephone companies offer such multi-user link-ups as a standard service to their subscribers. Anyone can have a teleconference with a few individuals by just dialling the exchange. To set up a teleconference between several groups, each party must rent or buy a proprietary telephone amplification system. Telephone conferencing, with real-time two way audio communication is a 'utility' as readily available as tapwater.

The tele-phone as a 'utility'

If telephone conferencing is not used as much as water, it is because the need is not as universal. But it is also true that the potential has not been perceived by all. This is noticeable if we compare different companies in the same general line of business. I have, for example, worked in two management consultancy organizations. One operated on 'conventional' lines, with an imposing head office building, office space and secretaries for all the consultants and most communications in writing. The other organized as much of its communications as possible around the telephone. One-to-one reporting and group discussions were never face-to-face or immortalized in print, unless this was essential for some specific secondary reason. The telephone bill was almost higher than the payroll. But the bottom line was that, for every ten secretaries in the conventional organization, the teleconferencing firm had one, for every twelve office rooms, there was only one, and consultants spent much more time consulting and less time authoring reports, reading, travelling to meetings, etc. The investment in the telephone as a 'utility' certainly paid off.

The tele-phone as a medium of instruction

In education and training, particularly, there has been little general perception of the telephone as an important medium of instruction. Even correspondence education was slow to adopt it. This may have been because of the relatively high early costs of telephone communication. Even if the student was willing to pay this, the correspondence school had to invest in a switchboard and a permanent staff of tutors available to deal with student queries. The incentives to do this were small for the private, profit-motivated correspndence schools. But when public education became involved seriously with distance education, and systematic research and course development was done, the rapid-feedback qualities of the telephone were at last generally perceived. The Open University in the UK has used telephone tuition, on a one-to-one basis since the early 1970s (George, 1979). In the USA, the University of Wisconsin educational extension programmes have, for some decades, made extensive use of telephone tutoring and group conferencing (Baird, 1984). The commercial sector was not able to ignore this trend. As the telephone permeated society and call charges became more reasonable, student demand led some private correspondence schools to offer telephone tutoring. The Italian-based Radio Escola Elettrica, which offers a variety of technician training courses by correspondence, installed a permanent telephone tutoring back-up service for its students, early in the 1970s. The response was beyond all expectations. It is significant that this school grew considerably during the 1970s, expanding into most of the Western European countries and beyond, at a time when many correspondence schools, including such traditional 'giants' in the field as Sweden's Hermod, were suffering severe cuts in demand, forcing them out of business. It is not clear to what extent the telephone tutoring innovation contributed to the Italian school's success, as it was a part of a general modernization of operations, but there is reason to believe that it was a significant factor.

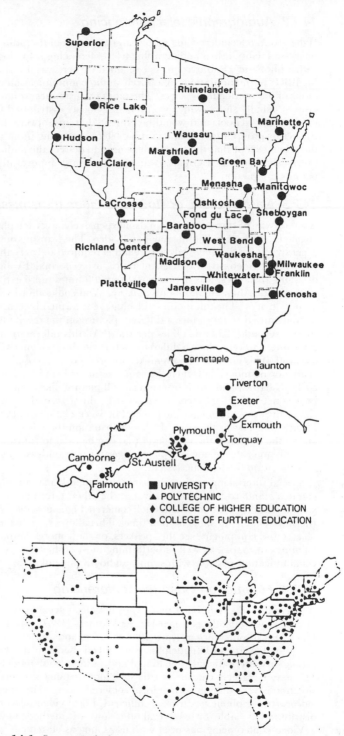

Figure 14.1 *Some typical education and training teleconference networks (a) University of Wisconsin – Extension. Operational for over 20 years. (Baird, 1984). (b) Experimental system in South-West England. (Winders and Watts, 1984). (c) AT&T's 'Teletraining' network for sales training. Installed 1983: 203 sites by 1985. (Chute et al, 1986).*

14.2.2 Audiographic teleconferencing

If the group teleconferencing mode can be compared to 'radio broadcasting with a phone-in facility', then audiographic teleconferencing is analogous to 'radiovision with a phone-in'. Radiovision, as explained earlier, was a response (pioneered by the BBC) to the limitations of a purely audio communication channel for some forms of instructional messages. The radio programmes would refer to a series of visuals, usually slides, which would be previously distributed by post to the participating schools and would be presented at appropriate moments by the local teacher or group leader. Audiographic teleconferencing in its simplest form, is just the same, except that the telephone is used to deliver the audio commentary on the previously distributed visuals. And, of course most importantly, the telephone also permits interaction.

14.2.3 Narrow band, or slow scan video transmission

What is slow-scan video?

Another way of transmitting visuals inexpensively, over telephone transmission channels, is the so-called narrow band video. The transmission of a video image is expensive as a relatively wide waveband is required to carry the signal. At 1986 costs, a full video two-way teleconference, using normal TV broadcast methods over long distances, was between 100 and 200 times more expensive per hour of transmission, than an audio-only link-up. Who could afford video teleconferencing at those prices? The full motion video image is formed by scanning the picture to be transmitted to reproduce a different picture on the receiving screen 50 or 60 times a second (525 or 625 lines per scan). All this information has to be transmitted to reproduce a different picture on the receiving screen 50 or 60 times a second. This ensures smooth flicker-free reproduction of movements. But if there is little or no movement, then the same picture is being repeated over and over again. Narrow band video transmits a still picture, like a photo by scanning the image once only every second, ten seconds, thirty seconds, or whatever. The slower the scan, the longer the interval between changes in the transmitted picture. The slower the scan, the less information there is to transmit per second and so the narrower the waveband that can be used to transmit it. In practice, transmission rates of one still picture every two seconds can be readily transmitted over the normal telephone system.

Its use in teleconferencing

Special interfacing equipment is required to link a standard video camera at one end to a standard television receiver at the other. Given cameras and receivers at several stations, fully interactive teleconferencing is possible with two-way transmission of still shots in 'real time'. This allows remote locations to examine objects and equipment, see the speakers, or show more complex visuals (such as paintings or maps), as well as performing most of the types of message communication possible with simple audiographic link-ups.

14.2.4 Full-motion video-teleconferencing

We have already mentioned that two-way video teleconferencing, over normal broadcast wavebands, is expensive. As Winders (1987) put it '. . . at an INTELSAT conference in April 1984 speakers and audiences in London, Sydney, Toronto, Tokyo and Philadelphia were linked. Because of the costs involved, only prestigious international educational and training conferences are held at present'. This may be largely true as regards such long distance satellite link-ups, but the situation is very different when local conferences are concerned, or when one-way video with telephone feedback is sufficient. Local video-teleconferences may be distributed by cable, or by several other low-cost methods now available.

Two-way cable video systems

Video-conferencing has been with us as long as closed circuit television. Two way cable link-ups have been technically possible since the 1960s, if somewhat expensive. Goldmark (1972, 1973) defended the feasibility of linking all households and institutions in a community by two-way video cable – not cheap, but quite an easy achievement from a technical standpoint. A few communities

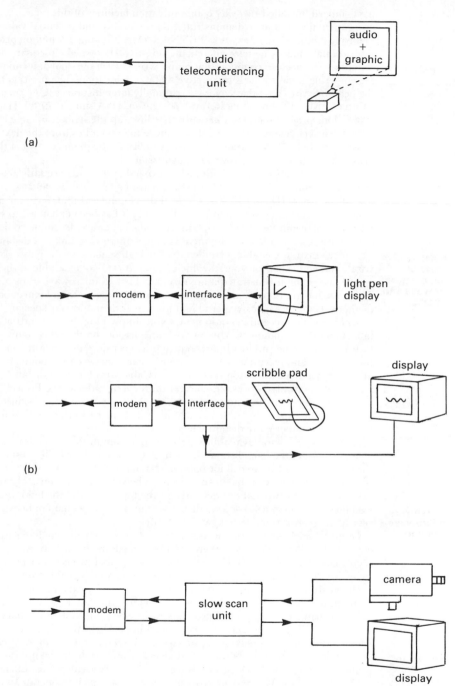

(a)

(b)

(c)

Figure 14.2 *Some forms of audiographic teleconferencing. (a) Two-way audio bridge, with pre-circulated graphics (slides, transparencies, charts, etc). (b) Interactive graphics, using light pens of digitizing pads. Another, slower technique uses commercially available facsimile document transmission equipment. (c) Narrow-band, slow-scan or freeze-frame video transmission. Transmits one still 'shot' every few seconds.*

have, indeed, installed two-way communication facilities of this type experimentally, and have demonstrated their viability and potential value (eg the Pennsylvania Learning Network 'PENNARAMA', linking 1½ million people). Educational small-scale teleconferencing on privately-owned closed circuit systems has, however, been so common that many writers even overlook it as one aspect of the emerging trend towards interactive distance education. The projects that make the headlines are those that cover exceptionally large distances. One such is Project CIRCUIT, operating in rural Wisconsin, USA since 1979/80 (Hagon) 1986). This project operates a network that links up the schools in eight rural school districts. Some of the schools are more than 50 miles from the next one. Most of the links are by means of two-way cable although one or two of the longer distances are linked by microwave transmission.

Usage of the network has continued to expand and results are satisfactory in terms of acceptance by staff and students, learning effectiveness and cost-effectiveness (Hagon 1986). A typical development is that, once the network is in existence, new uses are found for it. Recently it has been enhanced to send and receive data, computer programs, educational courseware, facsimile copies of documents, etc. Another development is a new microwave link to a distant
Relative costs of cable, microwave and satellite
Technical Institute, enabling students at the high schools on the network to take vocational and extension courses which were hitherto not available in the region.

The last example illustrated a mixture of cable and microwave transmission. This was due to the economic implications of the different interconnection methods. Cable is expensive per mile, but costs little in terms of special transmission and reception equipment – you simply plug the two ends of the cable into cameras and monitors. Microwave transmission, on the other hand, costs very little extra per mile (up to a limit), but requires considerable investment in transmission and reception towers. As the distance between the points to be linked increases, the economical solution changes. Cable wins for short distances of a few miles, but microwave works out cheaper on the longer distances. Project CIRCUIT illustrates the most economical solution in many cases – clusters of local sites, interlinked by cable to each other and the cluster as a whole linked by microwave to other more distant clusters.

As I write, costs and availability patterns of communication satellites are changing. Soon, the long distance links may be cheaper by satellite, especially if the distance is such as to call for booster stations in a microwave link. Microwave transmission is only possible in straight lines between two stations. The maximum distance between two stations depends on the topography of the land, but usually
A two-way microwave system
averages some 30 miles. For long distance transmission, a chain of booster, or repeated, receiver transmitters must be built.

Despite the gloomy economic assessment of two-way video conferencing, expressed by Winders (1987), there are many medium distance projects which report cost-effective results. One of these, as yet a pilot project, started by linking two fairly distant rural schools in Northern Michigan – by cable from the schools to the nearest towns (a mile or two distant) and then by existing microwave links between the two towns. To obtain two-way video, the system occupies (and pays for) two channels during scheduled classes. In effect, the system is composed of two normal TV transmission channels, used in parallel. Although the project is so small and incurred quite large set-up costs, it is seen as potentially cost-effective
The argument for one-way video and two-way audio
over a relatively short operating period (Keck, 1987). Indeed, the project's name promises this – PACE, which stands for Providing Academics Cost Effectively.

Of course, the PACE project costs nearly twice as much to operate as a one-way only video link with telephone feedback. PACE rents two channels whenever it transmits. As this is a local TV link, the cost may not be as high as the '100 to 200 times a phone link' estimates quoted earlier. Nevertheless, full motion video must be considered a luxury (as far as feedback links are concerned) in many cases. Users often report that courses which are not basically visual in their content seem to be just as effective and acceptable to students when video is restricted to the basic one-way presentation and audio teleconferencing is used for interaction. This is, indeed, the most popular modality, after the basic two-way audio teleconferencing mode. Large-scale distance education projects are designed around the use of the mass media in this modality. The Open University model of the 1970s, (using one-way radio and TV broadcasting) is evolving into a model which uses the mass media principally for interactive instruction. Gone are the pre-recorded lessons. Back come the gifted teachers and in comes the 'phone-in' habit. The University of Athabasca in Canada and several projects in Alaska have set up systems along these lines.

Such developments, of course, are not limited to the North American continent. There are several universities in Australia which use long distance interactive instruction, with one-way television and return telephone. The British Open University also seems to be tending in that direction. Many business organizations all over the world make extensive use of this modality. As Winders (1987) observes, '. . . several hotel chains now have satellite receivers linked to their conference suites' and these are available as a standard service to the organizers of any form of meetings.

Finally, we should not forget the developing nations. Distance education often plays an exceptionally important role. The step from one-way TV transmission to TV plus telephone interaction is not that great, yet it can offer great improvements in overall course effectiveness. One of the earliest national teleconference systems of this type was indeed installed in Brazil in the early 1970s.

> Long-distance communications in Brazil are operated by a national company, EMBRATEL, that operates both international (satellite) communications and national (microwave) communications. The microwave system consists of a network of booster stations linking all large towns, which transmits both telephone, radio and television signals from one region to another. As EMBRATEL already had the capacity to transmit television signals between all large towns, it was relatively simple to install television studios in several of the chief centres of population and reception/study centres in all the other large towns, all these facilities being installed on EMBRATEL property. The system operates by renting time to any user organization that is interested in communicating with groups in various cities. It offers live video transmission from the studio centres to all other centres and live audio communication between all centres. It is therefore possible to hold a seminar employing real-time live presenters and/or sophisticated audiovisual presentations, to a geographically scattered audience, who may participate with questions, or comments, and may engage in cross-talk conversations and small group discussions as part of the experience. Apart from its most popular usage – to transmit the messages of head office to outlying branches (this usage alone paying for the investment in the system in little over one year), the TV-EXECUTIVO is used by many non-commercial groups, such as universities, research groups, special interest groups and also for the training of all universities, research groups, special interest groups and also for the training of all categories of personnel. Many of the applications are indeed experiential in nature, encouraging discussion, arguments, the use of dramatizations, case studies and so on.
>   (Romiszowski, 1986)

The promise of video compression

Yet another recent technological advance that has drastically reduced the cost of video transmission, is the COMPRESSION of the digitized video information – a process which allows the transmission of full motion video by means of standard telephone lines, etc. This is the really important breakthrough. I mentioned the compression and decompression of digitized information at the end of the last chapter, when discussing recent advances in the field of interactive video. We saw how one advance in the ability to compress data cut ten years off the projected development time for DVI (Digital Video Interactive). I also mentioned how this advance and further expected progress completely transform the economic viability of such innovations as the videophone. I have come back to the same topic. After all, the videophone *is* two-way interactive teleconferencing at its most sophisticated.

The digitization and compression of video has already reduced transmission costs. As Phillips (1987) says, '. . . point-to-point transmission costs are of the order of one cent on the dollar, compared with broadcast television . . .' Of course, there are other costs, not least the rather expensive video compression equipment (codecs) which can cost $100,000 or £70,000 each (and one is required at every communicating site). However, these costs are expected to tumble and the compression capabilities of successive generations of equipment will increase. As in all recent microelectronic developments, the pace of progress is surprising even the scientists. By the time this book is printed, the last paragraph will be hopelessly out of date.

Even at present costs, compressed video systems are being used with beneficial results by many large organizations that make extensive use of teleconferencing. At least one University – Pennsylvania State – is experimenting with its use in education. These are exciting times!

14.3 Computer conferencing and networking

14.3.1 What's special about computer conferencing?

Why computer conferencing?

In the previous sections, we have seen how the various electronic transmission methods are tending to merge into one integrated system of digitized information. Whereas a short while ago, we had separate transmission systems for telephone communications, special broadcast channels for radio, other quite different channels for TV and so on, we now have the potential to transform all of these very different forms of analogue signals into digital form. Then, by appropriately compressing the digitized information, all these different types of information can be transmitted along similar transmission channels – standard telephone lines, or narrow-band broadcasts. As businesses came to rely on the rapid transfer of data from local to central computers and back, the data transmission quality of the standard telecommunications networks had to be improved and guaranteed. At first, special data-transmission links between key cities were installed, but in the long run it makes sense to replace old networks with new mutli-purpose ones, rather than duplicating the transmission systems.

Now, computers talk to computers along the same transmission lines that people talk to people. So it was no great surprise when people started talking to distant computers and computers to people and that computers have become go-betweens in people-to-people communications. But why should this be so? What do we gain by using a computer as an interface in long distance communications with other people. As the other forms of teleconferencing, that we have just examined, are becoming so accessible, why call someone by typing a message, if you can just pick up the telephone, or soon the videophone, and speak directly?

One reason for typing a message concerns its permanence. There is a written copy of what you communicated, which can be kept for as long as may be necessary. Of course, that would also be true if you sent a telex. However, placing a call yourself and knowing that the message you are typing is instantly available at its destination, is reassuring as well as efficient. If your respondent is available, you may get an almost instantaneous reply, like on a telephone. Of course it is slower because of the need to type in the message, but this in itself has some advantages, as it helps one to organize and compose a better response.

Electronic mail

If the person you call is not available, then a further benefit of computer conferencing appears. The message is stored until such time as the person comes back, or has time to deal with it. Though other means of long distance communication share this capacity to store messages, the flexibility and informality of a personal computer or terminal is far superior to a telegram or tape recording. This basic, one-to-one, message transmission and storage has become generally known as ELECTRONIC MAIL. There are several communication networks that facilitate electronic mail communications. One of the most popular is Bit-Net, which links subscribers in most parts of the world. As a subscriber, you have a calling code, just like a telephone number and anyone who wishes to send

1. *The notice board* This is the bulletin board application described above. It can be used to set tasks or assignments, provide a general study guide and so on. It is, of course, interactive, in that each student may query the message, ask for further information or reply to the question posed by the instructor. All this feedback will be available to the instructor on his or her own computer terminal.

2. *The 'public tutorial'* If a particular student has a given problem or query which requires the instructor to draft a detailed explanation and the instructor suspects that other students may be having similar problems, then the student's query and the instructor's explanation can be put on-line, available for all to read. The effect is similar to the individual student's question in class, answered in such a manner that all the group benefits from the discussion.

3. *The individual project* By directing a message to only one student, or to a small group, the instructor may keep up a conversation on a topic or problem that is not of general interest. This one-to-one contact may be more, or less, effective than a telephone call, depending on the type of interchange and its objectives. Communication is usually clearer, more concise and better thought out than in spoken contacts. Of course, it lacks the personal warmth and encouragement of a human voice. It is also much cheaper than telephones.

4. *Free-flow discussion* McCreary and Van Duren see this as different in style and content from the tutorial. It is a general interchange of ideas on a topic, for example a brainstorming session on a novel, open-ended problem.

5. *Structured seminar* This application uses the computer network as a medium for discussion of a common task, or of an individual student's prepared contribution. The comments made may be well prepared, with reference to the original reading materials, etc. This is what makes the computer-based seminar quite different from the live classroom or teleconference experience.

6. *Peer counselling* The network may, of course, be used freely for interchanges between distant students. More advanced students may assist those who are experiencing some difficulty with course material or assignments. A form of systematic peer-tutoring, under instructor guidance, may also be tried. Rather like the Keller plan, this can provide a level of individual assessment and corrective feedback that is otherwise difficult to achieve on courses with large enrolments. The peer tutors share the tasks of the instructor and by so doing, gain valuable reinforcement of their own mastery of the course content.

7. *Collective database* Students' library research may be pooled, in that all students enter their findings into a common database accessible by all. Experimental results may also be pooled. Imagine that each student carries out a small social survey in the locality where they live. Pooling the results will produce a regional or national picture. Further tasks of analysis and interpretation may then use all the data.

8. *Group project* Smaller sub-groups can use a computer conferencing system to cooperate on a project or to prepare a seminar topic for later presentation to other groups.

9. *Community decision making* This is not really an instructional use, at least not directly. The network is used to vote on issues that affect all the students or to express opinions/rally support for a new policy, etc.

10. *Inter-community networking* Local groups, who are studying a subject may exchange ideas with similar groups at another campus or school. The communication is between the groups, rather than between specific individuals. The local groups may meet face-to-face to plan their long distance messages, or they may communicate between themselves on a local network, before sending a joint communication to other groups.

Figure 14.3 *Educational uses of computer conferencing and networking. (Adapted from McCreary and Jan Duren, 1987, and Beckwith, 1987.)*

you a message can reach your computer with no more difficulty than placing a long distance call. Of course, you can also set up your own private communication network, using the normal phone system and connecting the computers that are to communicate to the phone system by means of modems.

Bulletin board

Yet another advantage of communicating by computer is the ease with which you can send a message to several, or indeed to all the subscribers to the network. Having as 'backup' the computing and data processing power of the computer, it is possible to set up automatic classifications of subscribers and direct a message to one or other of these classes. For example, a computer conferencing network linking up all the schools in a particular district could be used to transmit a general message of interest to all, using the BULLETIN BOARD modality. You type the message in once only, indicate that it is to be available on the 'bulletin board' and all users will see it whenever they access the computer messages.

On the other hand, you may wish to direct a note on a delicate matter to all principals. You would type it in, and would establish a special access code, so that only those who know the code can read what you have to say. Furthermore, you can make sure they read it, by putting a note in their normal electronic mail to call their attention to it. You can also set up a tracking program to record automatically when the special message is accessed, so you know which members of your target group have read it and which have not. Gone are the days of fabricated excuses: 'I didn't get your message – it's that new switchboard operator again! Too bad I missed the meeting.'

Educational uses

Now, all that is very well for the administrator, but what are the educational uses of computer networks and computer conferencing? Are there any real advantages or benefits to be gained from using such link-ups for instructional purposes? McCreary and Van Duren (1987) list ten types of educational applications that have been tried with some success. Some of these are very open, information-sharing modes, but many have distinct instructional use. The ten modes of use are shown in Figure 14.3.

14.3.2 Some case studies

In case this litany of ten possible uses of computer conferencing networks in education looks a bit like a 'solution looking for a problem to solve', let us look at one or two practical examples where the use of computer conferencing networks paid specific dividends.

Distance teaching of writing skills

The first example turns one of the greatest basic disadvantages of computer-mediated communication into an advantage. I am referring to the restriction to a text-only mode of communication. In this respect, computer conferencing compares unfavourably with other forms of teleconferencing and, even more so, with face-to-face instruction. But in the teaching of writing skills, this basic limitation of the computer terminal may be turned into an advantage. After all, students should be practising what they are to learn – and that means writing. Several projects have been implemented to develop basic communication-through-writing competencies. One of these, described by Thompson (1987), uses a special, split-screen display. One half of the screen is used to communicate through the network with the instructor and other students. The other half is a 'private' screen, on which the student can compose messages and revise them before sending them out. Typical exercises involve the rewriting of a paragraph that the instructor distributes to all the screens. Each student composes a new version on one half-screen, having the original alongside to compare. The instructor may view any student's attempt and may distribute it to all others for comment, or to just one of the other students as a compare/contrast example. Many other modes of interaction are possible, including group cooperation in composition of a story, interchange of points of view on the interpretation of an assigned reading, and so on.

Cultural interchange and attitude formation

Another, quite different use of computer conferencing, is reported by Hart (1987). This involves an international link-up of about 75 schools from several different countries – Canada, England, France, Italy – in an electronic network for cultural interchange and group discussion of current events. This project, called RAPPI, simply coordinated the networking of existing computers at the various participating schools, by means of the simplest possible modem connections to the telephone system, a sort of 'open house' for message interchange. There was no attempt at strict structuring of the network's use. It was simply a channel for international group discussion on a variety of topics that ranged from geographical and cultural comparison studies, through analyses of current events such as the US bombing of Libya, to debates on 'hot' issues like abortion or AIDS. It proved, however, to be a catalyst for local research and fact/idea organization activities, necessary to put together a clear communication. Many of the social science teachers involved were able to pursue specific instructional objectives with their students in a more creative and motivating atmosphere, due to the stimulus of group interchange of reports between the cooperating schools from the various countries (Williams, 1986).

A learning network in a telephone company

Another example, from a different part of the world and a different sector of education, is the CIRANDA PROJECT, operated by the Brazilian long distance telephone company EMBRATEL. Earlier in this chapter, we considered the microwave network of booster stations that EMBRATEL installed in the early 1970s for the long distance transmission of telephone and TV communications between all major cities in Brazil. We also saw how the existence of this network allowed the relatively simple implementation of a nationwide one-way video/two-way audio teleconferencing service, that has been operating profitably since about 1978. EMBRATEL, of couse, tended to use this 'executive TV' teleconferencing service for its own internal communication and training needs. In the early 1980s, as microcomputers began to be manufactured locally, it was a natural step to extend to computer conferencing facilities. The first development was, however, for exclusively internal communication and education of its own 20,000 strong workforce, spread all over Brazil. The concept of a 'global village' style of wired community was born. Employees were encouraged and subsidized to buy personal microcomputers and modems that would allow them to link into the nationwide network. The system was used for information dissemination, cooperative decision making, voting on important company issues, computer teleconferencing to support the video and audio sessions used for management development and stand-alone CAI lessons which would be downloaded to a given micro, on request, from a central mainframe computer. Many other types of application software could also be accessed in this manner by anyone linked into the system.

An interesting aspect of project CIRANDA is that, although it was conceived as a private network to be used by company employees, it was soon almost forced, by popular demand, to open its doors to other institutions. In particular, at that point in time, schools had very little access to micros, and still less to appropriate CAI courseware. Given that CIRANDA was the first large-scale network to be set up, and only the most basic of locally produced hardware was needed to link in, the easiest route for interested schools to experiment with computer-based education was to 'twist the arm' of EMBRATEL. Soon, project CIRANDA found itself not only the communications network supporting the major part of CAL experimentation in the country, but also supporting several educational courseware authoring projects and even subsidizing schools by loaning or financing the hardware required to use the system. At one point, some 5,000 individual micros were linked into the network, less than half of them owned by EMBRATEL employees (*see* Romiszowski 1987).

14.4 Videotex and information utilities

14.4.1 The concept of an information utility

The word 'utility' is perhaps a peculiarly North American term, when used in relation to services that are paid for in proportion to the amount used – water, gas, electricity, telephone services, and so on. In the United Kingdom and some other English speaking countries, it is more common to refer to these as 'services', and distinguish between such 'public' services as electricity and water provision and other, 'specialist' services like haircutting or TV repair. The words used are different but the basic concepts are in fact very similar in one respect. There is a tendency to distinguish between the services which are available 'at the press of a button' or 'turn of a tap' and are expected as part of the normal organizational structure of society, and those which are of interest and use to only certain sub-groups of society, or which it is normal to seek out and buy in the 'marketplace' as and when they are required. Water supply is a 'utility' or 'public service'. Meat supply is a business – true at least in the capitalist world.

What is an information utility?
This brings us to the concept of 'information utilities' (or services). The term implies that information should be treated as an 'on tap' commodity, available to everyone, wherever they are, in any quantity they may reasonably require. Furthermore, the cost of this information to the citizen should be proportional to the amount of use made of it. Now, a little reflection will suffice to make clear that, traditionally, information has tended to be treated as a specialist service or commodity, not as a public 'utility'. There seem to be exceptions, such as lending libraries, which, if they charge at all, charge on a more or less pro-rata usage basis. This is not really true, because all the local taxpayers contribute to the purchase of the books quite independently of whether they use them a lot or at all. Even the book borrower, if charged a fee, pays for the book borrowed and perhaps the time kept out, and not for the amount of information he extracted out of it, or the hours spent reading it. There is little difference, in reality, between the public library user and private buyer of books in a bookshop, in relation to how they are charged. Powerful computer networks, may however turn information into a real 'utility' – you get what you want and you pay only for what you use.

14.4.2 Videotex or Viewdata

Viewdata was pioneered in the United Kingdom. Indeed, British Telecom's Prestel service was the first, and continues to be the most developed, public service of its type. It has had a chequered history, having been hailed in its early days as a 'revolution' (eg Fedida and Malik, 1979) and assessed as not having lived up to its early promise by some later observers (eg Kearsley, 1984). Other recent authors enthusiastically stress the potential for new and more efficient ways of using information to transform the way we buy, sell, communicate, work and play (eg Gayeski and Williams, 1985), while more cautious analysts remind us of the all-pervading synergetic changes in lifestyle, family or social structure, personal freedom and dignity, that global access to all forms of information may imply and recommend caution and care in the large-scale implementation of mass information utilities, as are made possible by systems such as Videotex (Tydeman *et al*, 1982).

The difference between teletext and videotex
We discussed Teletext in an earlier chapter, and mentioned at that time the critical difference between it and Videotex/Viewdata. *Teletext is a one-way means of transmitting text* and graphic information, at no real transmission cost, as it piggybacks on unused capacity in the normal TV broadcasting channel. *Videotex is a two-way, interactive medium.* To get a clear idea of the significance of this difference, you need only think of the experience of accessing the programme guide channel on a typical Cable-TV system. Usually, some two hours' worth of programme details are presented and then recycled. In a system of some thirty user channels, you need three to five 'pages' or screens of information to show just what is on at a particular moment. So two hours' worth, at typically 30 minute programme changes, would imply some 12 to 20 full screens of text cycling through. How long to read a screen full? How long to wait till the right screen of information comes up? The trade-off is a totally unsatisfactory situation, where programme details have to be so cryptic and stay on screen for so short a time that unless you are a speed-reading expert in deciphering acronyms, you never get a clear idea of

'what's on'. But if they were to put a really full description of the programmes up on screen for a comfortable reading period, the programme would be over before we find out what channel it's on. With Videotex, you could select what interests you from one 'menu' page (say 'newsreel programmes showing now') and at once get a full description of just what interests you, in just one screen. If you chose to copy it down in full, no problem – YOU decide how long the page stays on the screen.

Educational uses of videotex

A recent television documentary on new technological developments showed children in English schools using Prestel as a resource in cookery classes. By combining database information on the basic nutritional value of different foods, with on-line up-to-the-minute information on local food prices and availability, these youngsters could plan well-balanced and within budget menus in a totally realistic classroom-based simulation of the family cook's planning tasks. Some educational materials have been made available on Prestel and other proprietary systems. Many of these are in the form of interactive games, involving drill and practice of basic skills. These may be aimed at adults, schoolchildren or even pre-school age groups. They have not become very prevalent, probably because really good and entertaining educational games, which can be effectively presented by means of the typical static 'text plus very simple graphic' Videotex page format, are hard to come by. Also, you pay by the time you use the information, so game playing on the telephone/TV may not be viewed too kindly by all heads of household.

Some of the more successful projects in educational applications for home use, have been in the adult/further education field. An example is the experiment run by Bell Canada with an interactive health education series. This was used on a trial basis by 500 households who were linked into the Canadian Telidon system and so had a variety of other types of information to choose from. The health education material turned out to be the most used and the most highly praised. Interestingly, this material, since the pilot project, is only available on a local area network of some fifty hospital and clinic waiting rooms in Montreal, a network which, in addition to providing this educational material, fulfils its major function of making available to doctors a database of medical information for diagnostic and other purposes.

On the whole, to date, Videotex services have not been very significant additions to the range of interactive media used for education or training. They are limited by the type of information that the providers choose to make available. Also, the move towards home study rather than attendance at some outside locale has not gone as far as some predicted. There are obvious reasons for this, social ones concerned with the need of parents to send their children to school, sociological ones concerned with the needs of both young children and adults to interact with others, and also instructional ones, based on data which shows that distance education is much more effective when students gather in local study groups.

14.5 Conclusion: towards the educational utility?

14.5.1 The concept of an education utility

Earlier in this chapter, we explored the concept of information distribution as a 'utility' or public service industry, supplying information to all who require it and charging a pro-rata cost. Videotex systems and most large publicly available database search services can be thought of as such utilities. Note that the networks which enable access to the databases are the utilities (the databases themselves are the information). Among the best known US services of this type are the 'Source' (a subsidiary of Readers Digest) and 'CompuServe' (owned by H and R Block). These, and other similar 'information utilities' offer an integrated service of electronic mail and conferencing, advertising and news information, access to a range of key databases, and so on.

The Education utility's origins

A man who was much involved with the initial conceptualization and development of these utilities, Jack Taub, from about 1985 has been promoting the concept of an EDUCATION utility, a distribution system that would be able to provide 'education' where and when required, 'on tap' as it were. Perhaps the term 'education utility' is a bit misleading. In reality, the utility would deliver well-organized INFORMATION for EDUCATIONAL PURPOSES, on tap. He is promoting this concept, through his multi-million dollar company the National Information Utilities Corporation and, at the time of writing, is poised, with some of the giants of the US telephone and telecommunications industry as potential partners, to launch the education utility as a reality in North American (and eventually world) education.

Its Goals

What are the goals of the education utility? No less than to link every school in the nation, every public library, every university campus, and every other educational or cultural institution to one massive communications network, that would meet all the communication and information dissemination needs of all the member institutions. In short, the aim is to integrate all the emergent communications technologies we have discussed in the last three chapters, to weld them into a more powerful and more versatile totally interactive system of communications than the world has ever seen and to put this system at the service of US education as a utility corporation.

Its potential benefits

The education utility will meter the use made of a given product and pay to the information provider a royalty proportional to the real use. Software piracy will be a thing of the past. Also, packaging, marketing and distribution costs will be almost completely eliminated, as the information will travel everywhere as digitized data. So everyone should come out on the winning side – except existing sales and distribution 'middlemen', who more than double the price between producer and consumer. It all sounds too good to be true. Maybe it is. But the concept has certainly caught the imagination of some very astute businessmen.

What about the educational considerations? Space does not allow us to go deeply into all the possibilities and potential pitfalls. We would need a book devoted exclusively to the topic. Indeed, a book on this topic has already been written by Dennis Gooler, Dean of Education at Northern Illinois University, and former chairman of the instructional technology graduate program at Syracuse University. He has analysed both the potential benefits and dangers in a total of nearly 200 pages (Gooler, 1986). His description of the potential of the education utility concept is, on the whole, extremely positive, as the book's sub-title indicates (*The Power to Revitalize Education and Society*).

My own arguments, in the last few chapters, have been tending in a similar direction, as regards the power of the new information and communication technologies and how their integration opens up immense possibilities for the improvement of education and training systems. I tend to share Gooler's enthusiasm about the exciting new scenarios that we could build into education.

If nothing else, the next few years up to the end of the century should be interesting – hopefully *not* in the sense of the old Chinese curse '. . . I wish you an *interesting* old age'. Despite all the futurologists' predictions, it is not clear whether the Tofflerian decentralized society will arrive, whether we shall be deschooling society, for reasons other than those proposed by Ivan Illich, or whether we have already sealed our fate as a viable human race on this super-populated and super-polluted planet. One thing is for sure – if we don't kill each other off, either slowly or overnight, then we shall live through some vast changes in the next decade or two – changes triggered and fuelled largely by the incredible rate of development of information and communication technologies. Schools, universities and training systems in industry and commerce will see their fair share of these changes.

Bibliography

Abelson, H (1982) A beginner's guide to LOGO: LOGO is not just for kids. *BYTE*, August.

Adams, J A (1979) On the Evaluation of Teaching Devices. *Human Factors*, **21**.

Agar, A (1962) Instruction of Industrial Workers by Tape-Recorder (original in Swedish). *Affarsekonomi* No 10, Stockholm, Sweden.

Allen, W J (1967, 1974) Media Stimulus and Types of Learning. *Audiovisual Instruction*, January. Reprinted (1974) in Selecting Media for Learning: Readings from Audiovisual Instruction, *Association for Educational Communications and Technology*, Washington DC.

Amswych, R J (1967) An Investigation into the Use of Tape-Recorded Programmes for Craft Training. *Programmed Learning and Educational Technology*, July 1967.

Anderson, J S A (1987) Exploring teletext as a resource. In Rushby, N (ed), *Technology Based Learning: selected readings*. Kogan Page, London.

Anderson, R II (1976) *Selecting and Developing Media for Instruction*. Van Nostrand Rheinhold, New York.

Annette, J and Kay, H (1957) Knowledge of Results and Skilled Performance. *Occupational Psychology* **31**.

Arce, J F and Romiszowski, A J (1985) Using a Relational Database as a Means of Integrating Instructional and Library Materials in a Computer-managed Course. *Proceedings of the 20th ADCIS International Conference*. Association for the Development of Computer-based Instructional Systems, Washington, DC.

Ausubel, D P (1968) *Educational Psychology: A Cognitive View*. Holt Reinhart and Winston, New York.

Baird, M A (1984) Teleconferencing in Wisconsin: adding freeze-frame – highlights, 18th year. In Parker, L A and Olgren, C H (eds), *The Teleconferencing Resource Book: A Guide to Applications and Planning*. North-Holland, Amsterdam.

Beckwith, D (1987) Group Problem-Solving via Computer Conferencing: the realizable potential. *Canadial Journal of Educational Communication*, **16** (2).

Belson, W A (1952) *An Inquiry into the Comprehensibility of 'Topic for Tonight'*. BBC Audience Research Department, BBC, London.

Belson, W A (1956) Learning and Attitude Changing Resulting from Viewing a Television Series 'Bon Voyage'. *British Journal of Educational Psychology*, **24**.

Bertran, S (1962) *Research into the Use of Closed-Circuit Television for the Training of Teachers*. Centre Audiovisuel, Saint-Cloud, France.

Biran, L (1972) The Limitations of Programmed Instruction. In Romiszowski, A J (ed) *1972/3 APLET Yearbook of Educational Technology*, Kogan Page, London.

Bitter, G and Camuse, R A (1984) *Using a Microcomputer in the Classroom*. Reston Publishing Company, Reston, VA.

Bitzer, D B (1976) PLATO: An Adventure in Learning with Computer-based Education. Paper presented at the *LACFEP Latin American and Caribbean Meeting on New Forms of Post-Secondary Education*. Caracas. (Published in the proceedings 'New Forms of Learning.')

Blackaby, L, Georgakas, D and Margolis, B (1980) *In Focus: A guide to using films*. Zeotrope Publishers, New York.

Bloom, B S, Engelhart, M D, Hill, W H, Furst, E J and Krathwohl, D R (1956) *Taxonomy of Educational Objectives, Handbook I: The Cognitive Domain*. David

McKay Inc., New York. (Reprinted (1972) in paperback by Longman, New York and London.)

Bluhm, H P (1986) Local Area Networks in the School Setting. *Educational Technology*, May.

Bork, A (1987) Computer Networks for Learning. *Technological Horizons in Education (the) Journal*, **14**(9), May.

Branson, R K, Rayner, G T, Cox, J L, Furman, J P, King, F J and Hannum, W H (1975) *Interservice Procedure for Instructional System Development* (5 vols). US Army Training and Doctrine Command, Fort Monroe, Virginia, August, 1975.

Brethers, R (1956) What I Know about Making Drawings for Young Children. *Visual Education*, October.

Bretz, R (1971) *The Seleciton of Appropriate Communication Media for Instruction: A Guide for Designers of Air Force Technical Training Programs*. Rand, Santa Monica, CA.

Bretz, R G (1984) Satellite Teleconferencing in Continuing Education: what lies ahead? In Parker, L A and Olgre, C H (eds), *The Teleconferencing Resource Book: A guide to applications and planning*. North-Holland, Amsterdam.

Briggs, L J (1970) Handbook of Procedures for the Design of Instruction. American Institute for Research, *Monograph No. 4*, Pittsburgh.

Briggs, L J, Campeau, P L, Gagne, R M and May, M A (1967). Instructional Media: a procedure for the design of multi-media instruction: a critical review of research and suggestions for future research. American Institute for Research, *Monograph No. 2*, Pittsburgh.

Brooker, F E (1946) Training Films in Industry. US Office of Education, *Bulletin No. 13*.

Brown, J S, Burton, R P and de Kleer, J. Pedagogical network language and knowledge engineering techniques in *SOPHIE*, I, II and III. In D Sleeman and J S Brown (eds), *Intelligent Tutoring Systems*. Academic Press, New York.

Bruner, J S (1966) *Towards a Theory of Instruction*. Norton, New York.

Campeau, P L (1972) Selective Review of the Results of Research on the Use of Audiovisual Media to Teach Adults. Council of Europe *Publication No. CCC/TE* (**72**) 5, Council of Europe, Strasbourg.

Carbonell, J R (1970) AI in CAI: An artificial intelligence approach to computer-assisted instruction. *IEEE Transactions on Man-Machine Systems*, Vol. II.

Cartwright, S R (1986) *Training with Video*. Knowledge Publications, White Plains, NY.

CENDRO/CEPED (1976) O Datilografo do Governo do Estado. An audiovisual presentation developed by A J Romiszowski as an introduction to a self-paced, typing training program, for the State Government of Bahia, Brazil.

Chu, G C and Schramm, W (1967) *Learning from Television: what the research says*. Stanford University Institute for Communication Research, Stanford University.

Chute, A, Bruning, and Hulick, M (1985) *AT&T Communications National Teletraining Network: Applications, Benefits and Costs*. Paper presented at Fourth Annual Conference on Teletraining and Electronic Communications, Madison, WI.

Chute, A, Hulick, M, Messmer, C and Hancock, B (1986) *Teletraining in the Corporate Environment*. Paper presented at Fifth Annual Conference on Teleconferencing and Electronic Communications, Madison, WI.

CIDE (1985) *Computer-based Instruction Project: final evaluation report*. Report on the STARS videodisc-based courses, prepared for ACES, by the Center for Instructional Development and Evaluation, University of Maryland, University College, Maryland, USA.

Clark, R E (1983) Reconsidering Research on Learning from Media. *Review of Educational Research*, **53**(4).

Clark, R E (1984) *Learning from computers: theoretical problems*. Paper presented at AERA conference, New Orleans, LA.

Clark, R E (1985) Evidence of Confounding in Computer-Based Instruction Studies: Analyzing the Meta-Analyses. *Educational Communications and Technology Journal*, **33** (4).

Cohen, P A, Ebling, B J and Kulik, J A (1981) A Meta-Analysis of Outcome Studies of Visual-Based Instruction. *Educational Communications and Technology Journal*, **29** (1).

Combes, P and Tiffin, J (1978) *TV Production for Education: A Systems Approach*. Focal Press, London, UK.

Crawford, A M and Crawford, K S (1978) Simulation of Operational Equipment with a Computer-based Instructional System: a low cost training technology. *Human Factors* (20).

Croxton, P C L and Martin, L M (1970) The application of programmed learning in higher education. In A J Bajpai and J Leedham (eds), *Aspects of Educational Technology IV*. Pitman, London.

Currier, R L (1983) Interactive Videodisc Learning System. *High Technology*, **3** No. 11, Nov.

Davison, M C, Davison J A G and Apter, M J (1966). A Comparison of the Effectiveness of Book and Audiovisual Presentation of Two Linear Programmes. In J F Leedham and D Unwin (eds), *Aspects of Educational Technology*, Vol. 1, Methuen, London, UK.

Dean, C and Whitlock, Q (1983) *A handbook of Computer-based Training*. Kogan Page, London.

DeBlois, M J (1982) *Videodisc/microcomputer Courseware Design*. Educational Technology Publications, Englewood Cliffs, NJ.

Diamond, R (1980) The Syracuse University Model for Course Design, Implementation and Evaluation. *Journal of Instructional Development*, **4** (?)

Dick, W and Carey, L (1979, 1985) *The Systematic Design of Instruction*. Scott Foreseman, Glenview, Ill. (The second, 1985, edition is extensively revised and enlarged.)

Dienes, Z P (1960) *Building Up Mathematics*. Hutchinson, London.

Dienes, Z P (1964) *The Power of Mathematics*. Hutchinson, London.

Digital Educational Services (1985) *Decision Point: a living case study*. Manual to accompany the interactive videodisc program. Digital Equipment Corporation (DEC), Bedford, Mass.

Dubin, R and Hedley, R A (1969) *The Medium May Be Related to the Message: college instruction by TV*. University of Oregon, Center for the Advanced Study of Educational Administration.

du Boulay, B and O'Shea, T (1976) How to work the LOGO machine: a primer for ELOGO. *DAI Occasional Paper No. 4*. Edinburgh University, Edinburgh, Scotland.

Duncan, C and Hartley, J (1969) The Effect of the Mode of Presentation of Result on a Simple Learning Task. *Programmed Learning and Educational Technology*, July.

Durham, N H, Gearhart, R G and Austin, J H (1974) *Selecting Instructional Media and Instructional Systems*. Charles County Community College, La Plata, Maryland.

Ellington, H, Addinall, E and Percival, F (1981) *Games and Simulations in Science Education*. Kogan Page, London.

Ely, D (1980) *Guidelines for Media Production*. US Environmental Protection Agency, Office of Water Program Operations. National Training and Operational Technology Center, Cincinnati, Ohio.

Evans, J L (1964) A Potpourri of Programming Technology. In G D Ofeish and W C Meierhenry (eds). *Trends in Programmed Instruction*. National Education Association and National Scoiety for Programmed Instruction, Washington, DC.

Fedida, S and Malik, R (1979) *The Viewdata Revolution*. John Wiley and Sons, New York.

Flake, J L, McClintock, C E, Edson, L, Ellington, K, Mack, F, Sandon, M L and

Urrutia, J (1987) *Classroom Activities for Computer Education*. Wadsworth, Belmont, CA.

Flanagan, J C (1968) Project PLAN. In *Technology and Innovation in Education*. Praeger, New York.

Flawell, J H (1963) *The Developmental Psychology of Jean Piaget*. Van Nostrand, Princeton.

Foxall, A (1972) Television and Radiovision in the Teaching of Modern Mathematics: a comparative study. *British Journal of Educational Technology*, **3**, No. 3, Oct.

Frazer, J R (1977) *Introduction to Business Simulation*. Reston Publishing Co., Reston, VA.

Freeman, F N (ed) (1924) *Visual Education*. University of Chicago Press, Chicago, Illinois.

Furhammer, L (1963) *Film Influence on Attitudes*. University of Illinois Press.

Gagné, R M (1965) *The Conditions of Learning*. Holt, Rinehart and Winston (1st edn) New York.

Gagné, R M (1975) *Essentials of Learning for Instruction*. The Drysden Press, Illinois.

Gagné, R M and Briggs, L J (1974) *Principles of Instructional Design*. Holt, Rinehart and Winston, New York (2nd edn, 1979).

Gallaher, J J (1964) Productive Thinking. In Hoffman, M L and Hoffman, L W (eds) *Review of Child Development Research*. Russell Sage Foundation, USA.

Gane, C P, Horabin, I S and Lewis, B N (1966) The Simplification and Avoidance of Instruction. *Industrial Training International*, July.

Gayeski, D and Williams, D (1985) *Interactive Media*. Prentice Hall, NJ.

Gerlach, V S and Ely, D P (1971) *Teaching and Media: a systematic approach*. Prentice Hall, Englewood Cliffs, NJ.

George, J (1979) *Tutorials at Home: a growing trend*. Open University, Milton Keynes.

Gilbert, T F (1961) Mathetics: the technology of education. *Journal of Mathematics*, Vols. 1–2. Reprinted (1969) as supplement No. 1 of the *Review of Educational Cyperbetics and Applied Linguistics*, Longman, London.

Giunti, F E and Kimberlin, D A (1982) *Distributed instructional system*. Paper presented at the Annual Conference of the Association for the Development of Computer-based Instructional Systems (ADCIS). Vancouver, BC. June.

Godfrey, D and Sterling, S (1982) *The Elements of CAL*. Press Porcepic, Toronto.

Goldmark, P C (1972, 1973) Cable TV, Videophones, Satellites, Data Networks Will Soon Change the Way You Live, Work and Play. Originally in *Popular Science Monthly*. Reprinted in Glessing, R J and White, W P (eds), *Mass Media: the invisible environment*. Science Research Associates, Chicago.

Gooler, D D (1986) *The Educational Utility: the power to revitalize education and society*. Educational Technology Publications, Englewood Cliffs, NJ.

Graham, R G and Gray, C F (1969) *Business Games Handbook*. American Management Association (AMA), New York.

Greenhill, L P and Tyo, J (1949) *Instructional Film Production, Utilization and Research in Great Britain, Canada and Australia*. Pennsylvania State College, PA.

Greenhill, L P (1956). The Evaluation of Instructional Film by a Trained Panel Using a Film Analysis Form. *Instructional Film Research Reports*, **2**, US Instructional Device Center.

Gropper, G L (1983) A Methodology of Instruction. A Framework for analysing and evaluating instructional theories and models. In Reigeluth, C M (ed) *Instructional Design Theories and Models: an Overview of their Current Status*. Lawrence Erlbaum, Hillsdale, New Jersey.

Hagon, R (1986) Serving the Undeserved: two-way cable TV links rural schools. *Tech Trends Journal*, January.

Hames, J W, Romiszowski, A J and Howe, A (1972) Changes in the Pattern of Programmed Materials Available in Britain. PIC Occasional Publication No. 9. Middlesex Polytechnic, London.

Hannafin, M J (1985). Empirical Issues in the Study of Computer-Assisted Interactive Video. *Educational Communications and Technology Journal*. Winter.

Hart, R (1987) Towards a Third Generation Distributed Conferring System. *Canadian Journal of Educational Communication*, **16**(2).

Hartley, J (1971) Using Slides in Lectures. *Visual Education*, August/September 1971.

Hartley, J (1978/1985) *Designing Instructional Text* Kogan Page, London (2nd edn, 1985).

Hartley, J (1980) *The Psychology of Written Communication*. Kogan Page, London.

Heck, W P, Johnson, J and Kansky, R J (1981). *Guidelines for Evaluating Computerized Instructional Materials*. National Council of Teachers of Mathematics. Reston, VA.

Heinich, R (1984) The Proper Study of Instructional Technology. *Educational Communication and Technology Journal*, **32**(2).

Heinich, R, Molenda, M and Russell, J D (1982, 1985) *Instructional Media and the New Technologies of Instruction*. John Wiley, New York.

HEUS (1985) Video and Audio Technologies in Higher Education. A review of research findings from the 1985 Higher Education Utilization Study. *The Chronicle of Higher Education, Special Report*.

Hodgson, A M (1968) A Communication Technique for the Future. *Ideas*, No. 7. Curriculum Laboratory, Goldsmiths College, University of London.

Hodgson, A M (1971) An Experiment in Computer-guided Correspondence Seminars for Management. *Aspects of Educational Technology* **V**. Pitman, London.

Hodgson, A M (1974) Structural Communication in Practice. In A J Romiszowski (ed.), *APLET Yearbook of Educational and Instructional Technology 1974–75*. Kogan Page, London.

Holding (1965) *Principles of Training*. Pergammon Press, Oxford.

Holmgren, J E, Dyer, B N, Hilligron, R E and Heller, F M (1980) The Effectiveness of Army Training Extension Course Lessons on Videodisc. *Journal of Educational Technology Systems*, **8**.

Hopkins, G W (1983) The New ITFS System in South Carolina. *Educational and Industrial Television*, **15**.

Horn, R E (1973) *Introduction to Information Mapping*. Information Resources Inc., Lexington, Mass.

Horn, R E (1974) *Course Notes for Information Mapping Workshop*. Information Resources Inc., Lexington, Mass.

Horn, R E *et al.* (1969) *Information Mapping for Learning and Reference*. Information Resources Inc., Lexington, Mass.

Howe, A (1986) *Information Maps: an outline of aspects of information technology of particular significance to trainers*. Manpower Services Commission, Training Technology Section. Moorfoot, Sheffield, UK.

Howe, A and McConnell, D (1984) The use of the Cyclops Telewriting System for Teaching Electronics. *International Journal of Electrical Engineering Education*, **21**, Summer.

Howe, J A M, O'Shea, T and Plane, F (1979) Teaching Mathematics through LOGO Programming: an evaluation study. *DAI Research Paper No. 115*. September.

Howe, J A M and O'Shea, T (1978) Learning Mathematics Through LOGO. *ACM-SIGCUE Bulletin*, **12** (1), January.

Howe, S F (1983) Interactive Video. *Media and Methods*, November.

Hughes, W H, Collard, P and Cardew, P N (1953) The 'How To Do It' Teaching Film: an experiment in its use. *The Lancet*, October.

Hurst, R (1987) Putting Motion and Graphics on Compact Disc. *Educational and Instructional Television* (EITV), **19**, No. 8.

Industrial Training International (editorial) (1966) Swedish Training System Breaks the Language barrier. *Industrial Training International*, September.

Iuppa, N V (1984) *A Practical Guide to Interactive Video Design*. Knowledge Industry Publications, White Plains, NY.

Jaques, D and Tipper, E (1984) *Perspectives on Gaming and Simulation: learning for the future with games and simulations.* Society for the Advancement of Games and Simulations in Education and Training (SAGSET), UK.

Jonassen, D H (ed) (1982) *The Technology of Text*, Educational Technology Publication Englewood Cliffs, NJ.

Jenkins, R (1983) Preface to Megarry, J *et al* (eds) *The World Yearbook of Education 1982/3: Computers in Education.* Kogan Page, London.

Kearsley, G (1983) *Computer-based Training: a guide to selection and implementation.* Addison Wesley, Menlo Park, CA.

Kearsley, G (1984) *Training and Technology: A handbook for HRD professionals.* Addison Wesley, Reading, MA.

Kearsley, G (1985) *Training for Tomorrow: distributed learning through computer and communications technology.* Addison Wesley, Reading, MA.

Keck, J (1987) *Distance Education with Interactive Television in Northern Michigan.* Paper presented at 1987 AECT Conference, Atlanta, GA.

Kelly, M and Haag S (1985) *Teaching at a Distance: ideas for instructors.* University of Waterloo, Teaching Resources and Continuing Education, Canada.

Kemp, J E (1971, 1975) Which Medium. *Audiovisual Instruction*, December 1971. Reprinted (1974) in *Selecting Media for Learning: Readings from Audiovisual Instruction*, AECT, Washington DC.

Kemp, J E (1980) *Planning and Producing Audiovisual Materials* (4th edn). Harper and Row, New York.

Ketner, W D (1982) Video Interactive Two Dimensional Equipment Training. *Proceedings of Fourth Annual Conference on Video Learning Systems.* Society for Applied Learning Technology (SALT), Washington, DC.

Krathwohl, D R, Bloom, B S and Masia, B B (1964) *Taxonomy of Educational Objectives: Handbook II – The Affective Domain.* McKay, New York. Reprinted (1972) in paperback by Longman, New York and London.

Krevitt, E, Baal-Schem, J, Saslove, B and Fenichel, H (1986) *A Decision Maker's Guide to Videotex and Teletex.* General Information Programme and UNISIST, UNESCO, Paris.

Kulik, J, Kulik, C and Shwalb (1986) Effectiveness of Computer-based Adult Education. *Journal of Educational Computing Research*, **2**.

Kulik, C, Kulik, J and Bangert-Downs, R (1984) Effects of Computer-based Education on Secondary School Pupils. *Proceedings of the AERA Conference.*

Kulik, J, Kulik, C and Bangert, R (1985) Effectiveness of Computer-based Education in Elementary Schools. *Computers and Human Behavior*, **1**.

Kulik, J, Bangert, R and Williams, G (1983) Effects of Computer-based Teaching on Secondary School Students. *Journal of Educational Psychology*, **75** (1).

Kulik, J, Kulik, C and Cohen, P (1979) Research on Audio-tutorial Instruction: a meta-analysis of comparative studies. *Research in Higher Education*, **11** (4).

Kulik, J, Kulik C and Cohen, P (1980) Effectiveness of Computer-based College Teaching: a meta-analysis of findings. *Review of Educational Research*, **50**.

L'Allier, J J (1983) An Opportunity to Shape a New Technology. *Performance and Instructional Journal*, November.

Landa, L N (1976) *Instructional Regulation and Control: cybernetics, algorithmization and heuristics in education.* Educational Technology Publications, Englewood Cliffs,

Laner, S (1954) The Impact of Visual Aid Displays Showing a Manipulative Task. *Quarterly Journal of Experimental Psychology.* **4** (3).

Laner, S and Sell, R E (1960) Pictorial Methods. *Occupational Psychology*, **24.**

Langdon, D G (1978) *The Audio Workbook* (The Instructional Design Library, Vol. 5). Educational Technology Publications, Englewood Cliffs, NJ.

Laurilard, D M (1984) Interactive Video and the Control of Learning. *Educational Technology*, June.

Lawrence, J S (1981) Videodisc: here at last. *Electronic Learning*, April.

Leiblum, M D (1982) Computer-managed Instruction: an explanation and overview. *AEDS Journal*, Spring.

Leith, G (1969) *Second Thoughts on Programmed Learning.*

Levie, W H and Lentz, R (1982) Effects of Text Illustrations: a review of research. *Educational Communications and Technology Journal*, **30** (4).

Lewis, B N and Woolfenden, P J (1969) *Algorithms and Logical Trees: a self-instructional course.* Algorithms Press, Cambridge, UK.

Lewis, R and Paine, N (1986) How to Find and Adapt Materials and Select Media. *Open Learning Guide No. 8.* Council for Educational Technology, London, UK.

Licht, N C (1985) *What Makes Microcomputer Simulations Really Work.* Paper presented at the First Annual Conference on Microcomputers in Education. Clarkson University, October.

Liddell, D C and Pinches, C A (1978) *Cyclops: an audiovisual cassette television system.* Paper presented to the Institution of Electronics and Radio Engineers, London, UK, September.

Lippey, G (1974) *Computer-assisted Test Construction.* Educational Technology Publications, Englewood Cliffs, NJ.

Locatis, C N and Atkinson, F D (1984) Media and Technology for Education and Training. Bell and Howell Publication, Charles E Merrill, Columbus, Ohio.

Lundin, C H, Grant, M M and Ehnborg, A (1968) *RITT Audio Instruction Programming Manual.* Ericsson Instruktionsteknik, Stockholm, Sweden.

Macintosh, D M (1947) *A Comparison of the Efficiency of Sound and Silent Films as Teaching Aids.* Scottish Educational Film Association, Publication No. 3. Edinburgh, Scotland.

Magel, M (1987) Optical Recording Systems. *AV Video*, **9** (9), September.

Mager, R F (1968) *Developing Attitude Toward Learning.* Fearon, Belmont, CA.

Mager, R F and Beach, K H (1967) *Developing Vocational Instruction.* Fearon, Belmont, CA.

Mager, R F (1962) *Preparing Instructional Objectives.* Fearon, Belmont, CA.

Marlow, E (1981) *Managing the Corporate Media Center.* Knowledge Industries Publications, White Plains, NY.

McLuhon, M (1964) *Understanding Media: the extensions of Man.* McGraw-Hill, New York.

McConnell, D (1986) The Impact of Cyclops Shared-screen Teleconferencing in Distance Tutoring. *British Journal of Educational Technology*, **17** (1), January.

McConnell, D and Sharples, K (1983). Distance Teaching by Cyclops: an educational evaluation of the Open University's telewriting system. *British Journal of Educational Technology*, **14**.

McConnell, J T (1974) If the Media Fits, Use It! In *Selecting Media for Learning: reading from audiovisual instruction.* AECT, Washington DC.

McCord, B (1976) Job Instruction. In Craig, R L (ed), *Training and Development Handbook.* Publication of ASTD (2nd edn), McGraw-Hill, New York.

McCreary, E and Van Duren, J (1987) Educational Applications of Computer Conferencing. *Canadian Journal of Educational Communication*, **16** (2).

McIntosh, D K (1984). Interactive Distance Learning Technologies. *E-ITV Magazine*, **51** (16), No. 8, August.

McPhail, P (1974) Building a role-play exercise. In Stadsker, R (ed.) *Handbook of Simulation Gaming in Social Education.* University of Alabama. Mech F (1965) Science Education and Behavioural Technology. In Glaser, R (ed.) *Teaching Machines and Programmed Learning II: Data and Directions.* National Education Assocation of the USA (DAVI), Washington, DC.

Merrill, M D (1971) Necessary Psychological Conditions for Defining Instructional Outcomes. *Educational Technology*, August.

Merrill, M D (1983) Component Display Theory. In C M Reigeluth (ed.), *Instructional Design Theories and Models: An overview of their current status.* Erlbaum, Hillsdale, NJ.

Merrill, M D and Wood, N D (1974) *Instructional Strategies: a preliminary taxonomy* ERIC Information Analysis Center for Science, Mathematics and Environmental Education, Columbus, Ohio.

Mickayluk, J V (1986) LOGO: more than a decade later. *British Journal of Educational Technology*, **17** (1), January.

MicroSIFT (1982) *Evaluator's Guide to Microcomputer-based Instructional Packages.* Northwest Regional Educational Laboratory, Portland, Oregon.

Miles, J R and Spain, C R (1947) *Audio-Visual Aids in the Armed Services.* American Council for Education, Washington DC.

Miller, G A (1968) *The Psychology of Communication.* Penguin Books, London and New York.

Miller, R B (1962) Task Description and Analysis. In Gagne, R M (ed), *Psychological Principles in Educational System Development.* Holt, Rinehart and Winston, New York.

Mitchell, D (1987) The Concept of Individualized Instruction in the Microelectronics Era. In N Rushby (ed), *Technology Based Learning: selected readings.* Kogan Page, London.

Moore, O K (1962) *The Automated Responsive Environment.* Yale University Press, New York.

Munday, P G (1962) *A Comparison of the Use of Television (BBC) Programmes for Schools and Sound Films as Teaching Aids.* MA Thesis, University of London.

Naisbitt, J (1982) *Megatrends: ten new directions transforming our lives.* Warner Books, New York.

Nugent, G C (1987) Innovations in Telecommunication. In Gagne, R M (ed), *Instructional Technology: foundations.* Lawrence Erlbaum, Hillsdale, NJ.

Orlansky, J and String, J (1979) *Cost-effectiveness of Computer-based Instruction in Military Training.* Institute for Defense Analysis, Arlington, VA.

Papert, S (1972) Teaching Children Thinking. *Programmed Learning and Educational Technology*, **9**.

Papert, S (1977) Assessment and Documentation of a Children's Computer Laboratory. *LOGO Memo 48.* MIT LOGO Group. MIT, Cambridge, MA.

Papert, S (1980) *Mindstorms: children, computers and powerful ideas* Basic Books, New York.

Papert, S, diSessa, A, Watt, D and Weir, S (1979) Final Report of the Brookline LOGO project: project summary and data analysis. *LOGO Memo 53.* MIT LOGO Group, Massachusetts Institute of Technology, Cambridge, MA.

Papert, S and Solomon, C (1972) Twenty Things to Do With a Computer. *Educational Technology.*

Parker, L A (1987a) Teleconferencing: meeting the $5 billion challenge. *EITV Journal*, January.

Parker, L A (1987b) Key Ingredients for Successful Teleconferencing. *E-ITV Journal*, February.

Parker, L A and Olgren, C H (1984) (eds), *The Teleconferencing Resource Book: a guide to applications and planning.* North-Holland, Amsterdam.

Pask, G (1976) Conversational Techniques in the Study and Practice of Education. *British Journal of Educational Psychology*, **46**. Reprinted in J Hartley and I K Davies (eds) (1978). *Contributions to an Educational Technology – Volume 2.* Kogan Page, London.

Pask, G and Scott, B C E (1973) CASTE: a system of exhibiting learning strategies and regulating uncertainties. *Journal of Man-Machine Studies*, No. 5.

Phillips, D L (1987) Videoconferencing at Penn State. *Technological Horizons in Education (the) Journal*, **14** (8).

Piaget, J (1965) *The Child's Conception of Number.* W W Norton and Company Inc., New York.

Piaget, J (1957) *Logic and Psychology.* Basic Books, New York.

Polya, G (1945) *How to Solve It: a new aspect of mathematical method.* Princeton University Press, Princeton, NJ.

Polya, G (1963) On Learning, Teaching and Learning Teaching. *American Mathematical Monthly*, **70**.

Postlethwaite, N S, Novak, J and Murray, H T Jr (1972) *The Audio-tutorial Approach to Learning.* Burgess, New York.

Pressed Steel Co (1964) *Industrial Safety*. An audiovisual version of a linear self-instructional program, developed by the present author and used by him for experimental comparison of printed and audiovisual programmed instruction.

PSSC (1981) *TeleGuide: a handbook for video-teleconference planners*. Public Service Satellite Consortium (PSCC), Washington, DC.

Radio Shack (1985). New Opportunity in Education with Radio Shack's Network 4 Shared Learning System. *Technological Horizons in Education (the) Journal*, **13** (3).

Reeves, T C (1986) Research and Evaluation Models for the Study of Interactive Video. *Journal of Computer based Instruction*, **13** (4).

Reeves, T C and King, J M (1986) *Evaluation of a Group-based Interactive Videodisc System for Military Training*. Paper presented at the annual conference of the Association for Educational Communications and Technology (AECT), Las Vegas, Nevada.

Reid, G M (1984) Videoconferencing and British Telecom: From Confravision to the Visual Services Terminal. In Parker, L A and Olgren, C H (eds), *The Teleconferencing Resource Book: a guide to applications and planning*. North-Holland, Amsterdam.

Reigeluth, C M (ed) (1983) *Instructional Design Theories and Models*. Lawrence Erlbaum, Hillsdale, NJ.

Reiser, R A and Gagne, R M (1983) *Selecting Media for Instruction*. Educational Technology Publications, Englewood Cliffs, NJ.

Romiszowski, A J (1968) *The Selection and Use of Teaching Aids*. Kogan Page, London.

Romiszowski, A J (1969) Report on the Use of a Computer-managed Remedial Mathematics Course at Undergraduate Level. *PIC Occasional Publication*, Middlesex Polytechnic, Enfield.

Romiszowski, A J (1970) Classifications, Algorithms and Checklists as Aids to the Selection of Instructional Methods and Media. In Bajpai, A C and Leedham, J (eds.), *Aspects of Educational Technology*, Vol. 4, Pitman, London.

Romiszowski, A J (1974) *Selection and Use of Instructional Media: a systems approach*. Kogan Page, London.

Romiszowski, A J (1975) Media Selection. An audiovisual presentation developed under UNESCO auspices for the Hungaria National Educational Technology Centre (OO), Budapest, Hungary.

Romiszowski, A J (1976) Computer Generated Examinations and Tests. In Howe, A and Romiszowski, A J (eds.), *International Yearbook of Educational and Instructional Technology – 1976–77*. Kogan Page, London.

Romiszowski, A J (1981) *Designing Instructional Systems: decision making in course planning and curriculum design*. Kogan Page, London.

Romiszowski, A J (1984) *Producing Instructional Systems: planning for individualized and group learning activities*. Kogan Page, London.

Romiszowski, A J (1986) *Developing Auto-instructional Materials: from programmed texts to CAL and Interactive Video*. Kogan Page, London.

Romiszowski, A J and Grabowski, B (1987) Some Neglected CAI Methodologies and their potential for new Interactive Systems of Instruction. *Proceedings of the Third Annual Conference on Development of Effective Interactive Instruction Materials*, Stamford, Connecticut, June. Society for Applied Learning Technology (SALT), Warrenton, Virginia.

Romiszowski, A J (1987) Information Technology in Brazil: a challenge for vocational education in developing countries. In Twining, J (ed), *World Yearbook of Education, 1987*. Kogan Page, London.

Rosen, D (1986) History in the Making: a report from Microsoft's first International Conference on CD–ROM. *Educational Technology*, July.

Rowntree, D (1974) *Educational Technology in Curriculum Development*. Harper and Row, London.

Rumble, G and Harry, K The Distance Teaching Universities. Croom Helm, London.

Rushby, N J (1979) *An Introduction to Educational Computing*. Croom Helm, London

Saettler, P (1968) Design of Selection Factors in Instructional Materials: educated media and technology, *Review of Educational Research*, April.

Salomon, G (1979) *Interaction of Media, Cognition and Learning*. Jossey Bass, San Francisco.

Scandura, J M (1983) Instructional Strategies based on the Structural Learning Theory. In Reigeluth, C M (ed) *Instructional Design Theories and Models*. Lawrence Erblaum, Hillsdale, NJ.

Schramm, W (1967) *Big Media – Little Media*. Sage Publications, Beverly Hills, CA.

Schroeder, J E (1982) US Army VISTA Evaluation Results. *Proceedings of Fourth Annual Conference on Video Learning Systems*. Society for Applied Learning Technology (SALT), Washington, DC.

Schwartz, E (1987) *The Educator's Handbook to Interactive Videodisc*. (2nd edn). Association for Educational Communications and Technology (AECT), Washington, DC.

Scupham, J (1970) Broadcasting and the Open University, *British Journal of Educational Technology*, **1**(1).

SEDL (1987) *A Model for Linking Statewide and Regional Telecommunications Networks*. Paper presented at the annual conference of the Association for Educational Communications and Technology (AECT), Atlanta, February. Southwest Educational Development Laboratory (SEDL), Austin, Texas.

Seigel, M A and Davis, D M (1986) *Understanding Computer-Based Education*. Random House, New York.

Sewart, D, Keegan, D and Holmberg, B (1983) *Distance Education: International Perspective*. Croom Helm, London.

Seymour, W D (1966) *Industrial Skills*. Pitman, London.

Seymour, W D (1968) *Skills Analysis Training*. Pitman, London.

Shannon, C E and Weaver, W (1949) *The Mathematical Theory of Communication*. University of Illinois Press, Chicago.

Shulman, L S and Keisler, E R (eds.) (1966) *Learning by Discovery: a critical appraisal*. Rand McNally, Chicago.

Skinner, B F (1961) *Cumulative Record*. Methuen, New York.

Sleeman, D and Brown, J S (1982) *Intelligent Tutoring Systems*. Academic Press, New York.

Smith, I M (1968) Experimental Study of the Effect of Television Broadcasts on the G courses in Engineering Science – parts 1 and 2, *The Vocational Aspect*, **20** (45 and 46).

Solomon, C (1982) Introducing LOGO to Children. *BYTE*, August.

Sprowls, R C (1962) Business Simulation. In Borko, H (ed), *Computer Applications in the Behavioral Sciences*. Systems Development Corporation, Santa Monica, CA.

Stadskler, R (1974) (ed) *Handbook of Simulation Gaming in Social Education*. Institute of Higher Education Research and Services, University of Alabama.

Suppes, P et al (1968) *Computer Assisted Instruction: Stanford's 1965/66 Arithmetic Program*. Stanford University, California.

Tardy, M (1963) *Live Television and Its Pedagogical Implications*, Ecole Normale Superieure de Saint-Cloud, France.

Taylor, J L and Walford, R (1974) *Learning and the Simulation Game*. Open University Press, Milton Keynes.

Taylor, R P (ed.) (1980) *The Computer in the School: tutor, tool and tutee*. Teachers College Press, New York.

Tenner, E (1986) *Tech Speak*. Crown Publishers, New York.

Tennyson, R D and L'Allier, J J (1980) Breaking out of the Skinner Box. *NSPI Journal*, **19**(2).

Tennyson, R D and Merrill, M D (1971) Hierarchical Models in the Development of a Theory of Instruction, *Educational Technology*, September.

Thompson, D P (1987) Teaching Writing on a Local Area Network. *Technological Horizons in Education (The) Journal*, **15** (2), May.

Thornburg, D D (1986) LOGO. *A+ Magazine*, March.

Thorndike, E L (1927) The Law of Effect. *American Journal of Psychology* No **39**.

Tiffin, J W (1980) ETV: A Phoenix in Latin America? In Romiszowski, A J and Chadwick, C (eds.), special issue on Educational Technology in Latin America of *Programmed Learning and Educational Technology*, **17** (4).

Tiffin, J W and Combes, P (1980) Processo de Selecao de Meios. Portuguese language version of paper prepared for the Organization of American States, Multinational Project in Educational Technology. Ministry of Education and Culture (FUNTEVE), Rio de Janeiro, Brazil.

Toffler, A (1980) *The Third Wave*. William Morrow, New York.

Townsend, I (1973) Tape, Film and Slide Teaching Manipulative Skills in Science, *Visual Education*, March.

Tydeman, J, Lipinski, H, Adler, R P, Nyhan, M and Zwimpfer, L (1982) *Teletext and Videotext in the United States*. Institute for the Future, Menlo Park, CA McGraw-Hill, New York.

Tyler, M (1979) Videotex, Prestel and Teletext: the economics and politics of some electronic publishing media. *Telecommunications Policy*, **3**(1).

Underwood, B J and Schulz, R W (1960) *Meaningfulness and Verbal Learning*. Lippincott, Chicago.

VanderMeer, A W (1949) *Report on a 16mm Motion Picture Production Conference*. Pennsylvania State College, PA.

Vernon, M D (1952) The use and value of graphical methods of presenting qualitative data. *Occupational Psychology*, **26**.

Vernon, M D (1953) The Value of Pictorial Illustrations. *British Journal of Educational Psychology*, **23**.

Wadsworth, R M (11983) *Basics of Audio and Visual Systems Design*. Howard Sams, Indianapolis, Indiana.

Watt, D. (1979). A Comparison of the Problem-solving Styles of the Students Learning LOGO. *Proceedings of the National Educational Computing Conference*. Reprinted in *Creative Computing*, December.

Watt, D (1982) LOGO in the Schools. *BYTE*, August.

Weber, J J (1930) *Visual Aids in Education*. Valparaiso University Press (reported in Saettler, P, 1968).

Weiss, D J (1979) Computerized Adaptive Achievement Testing. In O'Neill, H F (ed.), *Procedures for Instructional Systems Development*. Academic Press, New York.

Whitaker, P D and Roach, D K (1985) *Video Systems: a guide to the application and selection of suitable equipment*. Council for Educational Technology, London.

Williams, C (1986) *The RAPPI Experience at Bishop Pinkham Junior High School* (Report to the Federal Minister of Communications). Department of Communications, Calgary, Alberta.

Wilson, J C (1970) *Structural Communication in Management*. Structural Communication Systems, Ltd, London.

Winders, R (1987) Teleconferencing: student interaction by telephone – The PACNET experience. In Rushby, N (ed), *Technology Based Learning: selected readings*. Kogan Page, London.

Winders, R and Watts, J (1984) Teleconferencing: a case study for a major project in the UK. In Parker, L A and Olgren, C H (eds), *The Teleconferencing Resource Book: A guide to applications and planning*. North-Holland, Amsterdam.

Wiener, N (1948) *Cybernetics*. Wiley, New York.

Winer, L and de la Mothe, J (1987) Computer Education and the 'Dead Shark Syndrome'. In Rushby, N (ed), *Technology Based Learning: selected readings*. Kogan Page, London.

Woolfe, R (1980) *Videotex: the new television/telephone information services*. Heyden and Sons, London.

Woolfe, R (1987) Videotex and Teletext: similarities, differences and prospects. In Rushby, N (ed), *Technology Based Learning: Selected Readings*. Kogan Page, London.

Young, H W A (1906) *The Teaching of Mathematics in the Elementary and Secondary School*. Longman Green, London.

Zuber-Skerritt, O (1984) *Video in Higher Education*. Kogan Page, London.

Author Index

Subject Index